Spirituality and Mental Health

Spirituality and Mental Health

Indian Psychiatric Society Publication

Editors

BN Gangadhar
MD DSc
Professor Emeritus, Department of Integrative Medicine
Former Senior Professor of Psychiatry and Director
National Institute of Mental Health and Neurosciences (NIMHANS)
Bengaluru, Karnataka, India
Chairman, National Medical Commission, India
National Distinguished Scientist
Chair, Under the Ministry of Ayush, Government of India

Rajashree Ray
MD FRCPsych (UK) CCT (General Adult and Addiction Psychiatry, UK)
PGDMLE (NLSIU, Bangalore) PGMHSC (De Montfort Univ, UK)
Professor and Head
Department of Psychiatry
Gouri Devi Institute of Medical Sciences and Hospital (GIMSH)
Durgapur, West Bengal, India
Former Clinical Director and Consultant
Birmingham and Solihull Mental Health NHS Foundation Trust, UK
Honorary Member, World Psychiatric Association
Secretary, Section on Religion, Spirituality and Psychiatry, World Psychiatric Association

Anju Dhawan
MBBS MD (Psychiatry)
Professor and Chief (Addiction Psychiatry)
National Drug Dependence Treatment Center
All India Institute of Medical Sciences
New Delhi, India

Foreword

Matcheri Keshavan

JAYPEE

JAYPEE BROTHERS MEDICAL PUBLISHERS

The Health Sciences Publisher

New Delhi | London

JAYPEE **Jaypee Brothers Medical Publishers (P) Ltd**

Headquarters
EMCA House
23/23-B, Ansari Road, Daryaganj
New Delhi - 110 002, India
Landline: +91-11-23272143, +91-11-23272703
+91-11-23282021, +91-11-23245672
E-mail: jaypee@jaypeebrothers.com

Corporate Office
4838/24, Ansari Road, Daryaganj
New Delhi - 110 002, India
Phone: +91-11-43574357
Fax: +91-11-43574314
E-mail: jaypee@jaypeebrothers.com

Overseas Office
J.P. Medical Ltd
83 Victoria Street, London
SW1H 0HW (UK)
Phone: +44 20 3170 8910
E-mail: info@jpmedpub.com

EU GPSR Authorised Representative
Logos Europe, 9 rue Nicolas Poussin
17000, La Rochelle, France
Phone: +33 (0) 6 67 93 73 78
E-mail: contact@logoseurope.eu

Website: www.jaypeebrothers.com
Website: www.jaypeedigital.com

Inquiries for bulk sales may be solicited at: jaypee@jaypeebrothers.com

Spirituality and Mental Health

First Edition: 2025, Reprint: **2026**

ISBN: 978-93-6616-868-5

Printed at: Samrat Offset Pvt. Ltd.

Dedication

A Life Well Lived

Dedicated to Late Dr Avdesh Sharma (1956–2022)

Dr Sharma was born on November 19, 1956, in Lucknow to middle-class Punjabi parents. The younger of two siblings, he completed his schooling at Ramjas School, New Delhi, and graduated from Maulana Azad Medical College, New Delhi, in 1979. Inspired by psychiatry during his internship, he pursued postgraduate training at NIMHANS, earning a Diploma in Psychological Medicine (DPM) and an MD in Psychiatry. In 1984, he received the Gold Medal for MD and the prestigious DLN Murthy Rao Award as the best outgoing student of his batch.

During his time at NIMHANS, he met his future wife, Dr Sujatha, who was pursuing her MPhil and PhD in Clinical Psychology. The two married in 1983, forming a lifelong partnership built on shared professional and personal values.

Their daughter Manasi, a Doctorate in Public Health from Harvard University, is pursuing her career as a Research Epidemiologist.

Upon returning to Delhi, he began his career as a Senior Resident before transitioning to private practice. Alongside his wife, he established the Parivartan Center and Delhi's first private Deaddiction Clinic, Thalanjali, in 1986. He was the Founder of Mind Vision Enterprises and the Managing Trustee of RAHAT Charitable Medical Research Trust, which worked tirelessly to reduce stigma around mental health issues.

Dr Sharma's pioneering efforts in mental health education extended to the media. He directed and produced numerous shows, documentaries, and radio programs, including Mann Ki Baat, Mind Watch, and Mind Your Mind. Mind Your Mind was India's first television series on mental health. As a Creative Director with the National Film Development Corporation (NFDC), he also anchored over 300 programs on Doordarshan and served as an Expert on several international and national TV channels.

He authored five books, including *Distress to De-Stress* and *Couples in Harmony*, and contributed over 20 chapters and 1,000 articles in peer-reviewed journals and lay publications. His co-authorship of *Spirituality and Mental Health* reflected his deep interest in the integration of spiritual practices with psychiatric care.

Dr Sharma was actively involved in numerous professional organizations. He served as the International Lead on Public Education for the World Psychiatric Association (WPA) and chaired the WPA's Section on Spirituality, Religion, and Mental Health. He also held leadership roles in the Indian Psychiatric Society and was an International Distinguished Fellow of the American Psychiatric Association. Additionally, he was the Secretary General and Director of Communications for the World Academy of Spiritual Sciences (WASS).

His efforts earned him several prestigious awards, including:

- Health Care Oscar (2017)
- IGPI Outstanding Contribution to Psychiatry Award (2016)
- National Medical Excellence Award by the Jhunjhunwala Foundation (2013)
- Rashtriya Gaurav Award (1998)
- Gem of India (1997)
- Lifetime Achievement Award at the Indian Brand Story Conclave (2022, posthumous)

A spiritual seeker for over three decades, he was deeply associated with the *Brahma Kumaris*, following the Rajyoga meditative lifestyle. He was an eminent faculty member at their spiritual workshops, conferences, and retreats. He co-authored the chapter, *Meditation: The Future of Medication?"* with his wife, detailing their shared belief in the transformative power of meditation.

He was a creative soul with a passion for Sufi music and guitar playing. He had a profound curiosity about world cultures, loved traveling, and enjoyed reading nonfiction, especially works on philosophy and spirituality.

Professor Dinesh Bhugra described him as "a true guru, an ascetic who found joy in teaching, charity work, and looking after patients. Each message from him was inspirational." As the WPA Public Education Lead in 2014, his creativity and commitment shone through his innovative strategies. He initiated mental health ambassador programs and authored articles across various media platforms, raising awareness about mental health, the organization's mission, and the profound effects of mental illness. This legacy of service and education has likely left a lasting impact on the mental health community.

Dr Nikhil Patel fondly recalls a remarkable milestone in Dr Sharma's life—his miraculous and complete remission from advanced grade IV Hodgkin's lymphoma during 2018–2019, publicly shared by Dr Sharma at the World Congress on Spirituality in Jerusalem in December 2019. Dr Sharma and his wife collaborated to author a thought-provoking chapter titled *Meditation: The Future of Medication?* reflecting their deep belief in the transformative power of meditation. Their incredible spiritual journey as a couple was celebrated in a feature by The Times of India, published in the *Speaking Tree* column, showcasing their inspiring story of healing, spirituality, and togetherness.

Dr Vinay Kumar remembered him as one of the most sought-after speakers at national and international conferences. His sweet, mesmerizing voice had a spellbinding effect on audiences, and his talks were always enlightening. While he was widely respected across various professional associations in India, his commitment to the Indian Psychiatric Society remained steadfast. He was a pioneer in introducing the interface between spirituality and psychiatry, establishing its scientific foundation by conceptualizing and editing the groundbreaking book *Spirituality and Mental Health.*

Professor Alan Fung acknowledged Dr Sharma's contributions to global psychiatry, particularly through the WPA's Spirituality and Religion Section, which he joined as an Executive Committee Member in 2014, becoming the Section Co-Chair in 2017, and the Chair in 2020. Notably, in 2016, Dr Sharma and his wife organized a landmark roundtable discussion with faith leaders from 12 organizations and mental health professionals in

Cape Town, South Africa, fostering principles of interprofessional collaboration. In 2019, WPA International Congress in Spirituality and Psychiatry (and 4th Global Meeting in Spirituality and Mental Health) in Jerusalem, he delivered a keynote speech on *Integrating Spirituality and Mental Health.*

Dr Sharma worked tirelessly until the very end, bearing his terminal illness with dignity and without complaints. His life—rooted in compassion, wisdom, and service—continues to inspire all who knew him. He will be remembered as a pioneer in his field and a beacon of light for those seeking harmony between mental health and spirituality.

He was the Editor of the Book *Spirituality and Mental Health, Reflections of the Past, Applications in the Present, Projections for the Future,* published by Indian Psychiatric Society, in association with Medical Wing, Rajyoga Education and Research Foundation, Mount Abu in 2019. This book is an Enhanced Version and is dedicated to his memory.

With grateful thanks for their contribution:

- Dr Sujatha Sharma [Wife of (Late) Dr Avdesh Sharma]
- Professor Dinesh Bhugra, Former President, WPA 2014-2017
- Dr Nikhil Patel, Chairperson, Yoga and Mental Health Specialty Section of IPS
- Dr Vinay Kumar, Past President, Indian Psychiatric Society
- Professor Alan Fung (Chair of Religion, Spirituality and Psychiatry Section of WPA)
- Dr Manasi Sharma [Daughter of (Late) Dr Avdesh Sharma] Tribute to Dr Avdesh Sharma

Contributors

Abhay Dey MBBS DTCD MD (Psychiatry)
Consultant Psychiatrist
Psychiatry Unit, Department of Medicine
Ramakrishna Mission Seva Pratishthan
Howrah, West Bengal, India

Afzal Javed MCPS DPsych (Lond) Board Cert.Psych (UK) MPhil (Edin) FRC Psych (UK) FRCP (Ireland)
Honorary Clinical Associate Professor
Department of Psychiatry
Warwick Medical School
University of Warwick, UK

Alan Fung MD ScDMD ScD FRCPC DFAPA
Chair, World Psychiatric Association Section on Religion, Spirituality and Psychiatry
Research Professor, Tyndale University
Professorial Fellow, Wycliffe College, University of Toronto
Medical Director
Department of Psychiatry
Mount Sinai Hospital Seniors Wellness Centre
Temerty Faculty of Medicine, University of Toronto, Canada

Anju Dhawan MBBS MD (Psychiatry)
Professor and Chief (Addiction Psychiatry)
National Drug Dependence Treatment Center
All India Institute of Medical Sciences
New Delhi, India

Aratrika Sen MBBS MD (Psychiatry)
Project Officer (Medical), Asian Bipolar Genetic Network
Department of Psychiatry
Institute of Psychiatry, Centre of Excellence
Institute of Postgraduate Medical Education and Research (IPGMER)
Kolkata, West Bengal, India

Astha MBBS MD
Specialty Doctor AMH
Psychiatry Adult Mental Health
Tees, Esk and Wear Valleys (TEWV) NHS Foundation Trust
Darlington, UK

Avinash De Sousa MD DPM
Consultant Psychiatrist
Department of Psychiatry
De Sousa Foundation
Mumbai, Maharashtra, India

BN Gangadhar MD DSc
Professor Emeritus
Department of Integrative Medicine
Former Senior Professor of Psychiatry and Director
National Institute of Mental Health and Neurosciences (NIMHANS)
Bengaluru, Karnataka, India
Chairman, National Medical Commission
National Distinguished Scientist
Chair, Under the Ministry of Ayush
Government of India

Bharath Holla MBBS MD (Psychiatry) PhD
Associate Professor of Psychiatry
Department of Integrative Medicine
National Institute of Mental Health and Neurosciences
Bengaluru, Karnataka, India

Bruno Paz Mosqueiro PhD
Professor of Psychiatry
Department of Medicine
Universidade Federal do Rio Grande do Sul
Brazil

Debanjan Banerjee
MBBS MD DM (Geriatric)
Consultant Psychiatrist
Department of Psychiatry
Apollo Gleneagles Hospital
Kolkata, West Bengal, India

Diane G Tillman MS
Educational Psychologist (Rtd)
Brahma Kumaris Rajyoga Meditation Center
California, USA

Dinesh Bhugra CBE MA MSc MBBS DSc (Hon) PhD FRCP FRCPE FRCPsych FFPHM FRCPsych (Hon) FHKCPsych (Hon) FACPsych (Hon) FAMS (Singapore) FKCL MPhil LMSSA FAcadME FRSA DIFAPA
Professor Emeritus
Mental Health and Cultural Diversity
Institute of Psychiatry, Psychology and Neuroscience
King's College, UK

E Mohan Das MD
Consultant Psychiatrist
Department of Psychiatry
Sun Medical and Research Centre
Thissur, Kerala, India

Gautam Saha MD FRCP (Edin)
Founder Director
Department of Psychiatry
Clinic Brain Neuropsychiatric Institute and Research Centre
Kolkata, West Bengal, India

Hiya Dey MBBS
Intern
Kalinga Institute of Medical Sciences
Howrah, West Bengal, India

Kaustav Chakraborty
MBBS MD DNB (Gold Medalist)
Professor and Head
Department of Psychiatry
College of Medicine and Jawaharlal Nehru Memorial Hospital
West Bengal University of Health Sciences
Nadia, West Bengal, India

Kishan Porandla MBBS MD (Psychiatry)
Professor and Head
Department of Psychiatry
Prathima Institute of Medical Sciences
Karimnagar, Telangana, India

Manasi Sharma PhD MSc
Public Mental Health
Research Associate (Epidemiology)
Harvard School of Public Health
USA

Mrugesh Vaishnav MBBS MD (Psychiatry) DPM
Director
Samvedana Happiness Hospital, Ahmedabad
Department of Psychiatry
Institute of Psychology and Sexual Research
Samvedana Foundation
Ahmedabad, Gujarat, India

Natália Macedo Cavagnoli MD
Specialist in Psychiatry and Psychoanalysis
Hospital Nossa Senhora da Conceição
Rua Miguel Tostes, 679, 801, Brazil

Nikhil G Patel MBBS DPM MD FIPS MAPA (USA)
Head and Senior Consultant Neuropsychiatrist
Neuropsychiatry and De-addiction
Global Hospital and Research Centre
Mount Abu, Rajasthan, India

Parth Vaishnav MBBS MD (Psychiatry)
Consultant Psychiatrist
Department of Psychiatry
Samvedana Happiness Hospital
Ahmedabad, Gujarat, India

Pooja Vora MSc (Clinical Psychology)
Clinical Psychologist and Research Associate
Department of Psychiatry
De Sousa Foundation
Mumbai, Maharashtra, India

Prasad Rao Gundugurthi MD DPM FRCP
Director
Schizophrenia and Psychopharmacology
Asha Hospital
Hyderabad, Telangana, India

R Srinivasa Murthy MBBS MD
Professor of Psychiatry (Retd)
Department of Psychiatry
National Institute of Mental Health
and Neurosciences
Bengaluru, Karnataka, India

Rajashree Ray
MD FRCPsych (UK) CCT (General Adult and
Addiction Psychiatry, UK)
PGDMLE (NLSIU, Bangalore) PGMHSC
(De Montfort Univ, UK)
Professor and Head
Department of Psychiatry
Gouri Devi Institute of Medical Sciences
and Hospital (GIMSH)
Durgapur, West Bengal, India
Former Clinical Director and Consultant
Birmingham and Solihull Mental Health NHS
Foundation Trust, UK
Honorary Member, World Psychiatric Association
Secretary, Section on Religion, Spirituality and
Psychiatry, World Psychiatric Association

Ranjan Bhattacharyya MBBS MD DNB
(Psychiatry) MNAMS IDFAPA
Professor and Visiting Psychiatrist
General Adult Psychiatry, Substance Use
Disorder, Child and Adolescent Psychiatry,
Sexual Dysfunction
Department of Psychiatry
Bankura Sammilani Medical College, Ruby
General Hospital
Medica Superspecialty Hospital
Kolkata, West Bengal, India

Russell D'Souza MD DPM
Consultant Psychiatrist
Department of Psychiatry
International Centre for Bioethics
Mumbai, Maharashtra, India

Saikrishna Puli MBBS MD
Professor
Department of Psychiatry
Prathima Institute of Medical Sciences
Karimnagar, Telangana, India

Sathyanarayana Rao TS DPM MD PG Diploma in
Hospital Administration
Professor Emeritus in Psychiatry
Department of Psychiatry
JSS Academy of Higher Education and Research
Mysuru, Karnataka, India

Shubhangi R Parkar
DPM MD MSc PGDHR PhD (Pursuing)
Professor and Dean
Administration and Psychiatry
Vedantaa Institute of Medical Sciences
Palghar, Maharashtra, India

Simhachalam Gurugabelli MD
Consultant Physician
Visiting Physician and Professor of Medicine
Department of Medicine
Madison General Hospital, USA

Soumitro Ghosh MBBS MD (Psychiatry)
Professor and Head
Department of Psychiatry
Assam Medical College
Dibrugarh, Assam, India

Sphurti Pusukuri MBBS MD (Psychiatry)
Assistant Professor
Department of Psychiatry
Dr Patnam Mahender Reddy Institute of
Medical Sciences
Ranga Reddy, Telangana, India

Srividya Bellapukonda MD PDF (Child and
Adolescent Psychiatry)
Consultant Psychiatrist
Department of Psychiatry
Santhi Hospital
West Godavari District, Andhra Pradesh, India

Sujatha D Sharma MPhil (Medical & Social
Psychology) PhD (Clinical Psychology)
Consultant Clinical Psychologist Managing
Trustee
Department of Psychology
Parivartan Center for Mental Health
RAHAT Charitable and Medical Trust
New Delhi, India

Sumegha Mittal MBBS MD (Psychiatry)
Senior Resident
Department of Psychiatry
All India Institute of Medical Sciences
New Delhi, India

Sunil Kuyare MBBS MD DHA FME DBE
Lab Director
Academics and Diagnostic Healthcare
Apoorva Academics and Apoorva diagnostic and Healthcare
Mumbai, Maharashtra, India

Suresh Sathe MBBS MD (Psychiatry)
Consultant Psychiatrist
Department of Psychiatry
Ahmedabad, Gujarat, India

Susham Gupta FRCPsych
Consultant Psychiatrist
Department of Psychiatry
East London NHS Foundation Trust
London, UK

Swati Banerjee MBBS (Hons) MD (Psychiatry) DNB
Senior Resident
Department of Psychiatry
Calcutta National Medical College and Hospital
Kolkata, West Bengal, India

Uday Chaudhuri MBBS DPM MD (Psychiatry) DNB
Professor and Visiting Psychiatrist
Psychiatry Unit
Department of Medicine
RK Mission Seva Prathisthan Hospital
Kolkata, West Bengal, India

Umadevi Avasarala
Intern, Undergraduate
Department of Psychiatry
Asha Hospital
Hyderabad, Telangana, India

Vijay Gogoi MBBS MD PGDHI
Associate Professor
Department of Psychiatry
Lokopriya Gopinath Bordoloi
Regional Institute of Mental Health
Tezpur, Assam, India

Vinay Kumar MBBS MD
Consultant Psychiatrist
Department of Psychiatry
Manoved Mind Hospital & Research Centre Pvt Limited
Patna, Bihar, India

Vishal Indla MD DNB (Psychiatry)
Chief Psychiatrist
Department of Psychiatry
INDLAS Hospitals
Vijayawada, Andhra Pradesh, India

Vishnu Vardhan M MBBS MD
Assistant Professor
Department of Psychiatry
Dr Patnam Mahender Reddy Institute of Medical Sciences
Ranga Reddy, Telangana, India

Foreword

The relation of well-being to spirituality is a key frontier in our understanding of health and healing. This remarkable volume which spotlights foundational concepts, clinical, and societal implications of spirituality, is a timely and essential contribution to this evolving dialogue. As someone deeply engaged in exploring Eastern psychological insights, including the teachings of the Bhagavad Gita and the transformative potential of yoga, I am honored to write this foreword.

Spirituality is intrinsically tied to the exploration of consciousness—a journey that involves not only the mind but also the brain. Advances in neuroscience have begun to illuminate the biological correlates of spiritual experiences, shedding light on the intricate interplay between brain regions such as the prefrontal cortex, limbic system, and default mode network. These findings underscore how practices like meditation, mindfulness, and yoga can reshape neural pathways, fostering emotional regulation, resilience, and a sense of interconnectedness. This understanding of neuroplasticity aligns seamlessly with the holistic frameworks of Eastern traditions, which emphasize the integration of the body, mind, and spirit for optimal well-being.

This book, edited by Drs BN Gangadhar, Rajashree Ray, and Anju Dhawan, with contributions by experts in psychiatry and spirituality from around the world, thoughtfully addresses these intersections. The first section, which focuses on fundamental concepts, delves into the distinctions between religion and spirituality, the relationship between consciousness and spirituality, and the transcultural dimensions of spiritual experience. The inclusion of perspectives from positive psychology highlights how spirituality contributes to flourishing and resilience, offering a counterbalance to the reductionist tendencies of contemporary psychiatry.

The second section delves into spirituality across the lifespan, highlighting its relevance to various mental health conditions, including mood and anxiety disorders, psychosis, addiction, and suicidality. Here, neuroscience meets the wisdom of texts like the Bhagavad Gita, which provides profound insights into navigating existential dilemmas, cultivating equanimity, and transcending suffering. These teachings resonate deeply with the growing body of evidence showing that spiritual practices can enhance mental health by fostering neurocognitive flexibility, reducing stress reactivity, and promoting a sense of meaning and purpose.

The final section addresses broader topics, including spirituality's role in creativity, palliative care, criminality, medical education, and mental health services. Of particular importance is the integration of spirituality into the education of future mental health and medical professionals. In an era where burnout and compassion fatigue are pervasive, training clinicians to engage with the spiritual dimensions of care can foster empathy, resilience, and a deeper connection to their work. Furthermore, incorporating spiritual frameworks into medical education equips current and future mental health practitioners to address the diverse cultural and existential needs of their patients, fostering a more holistic approach to healing.

This volume is more than an academic endeavor; it is a call to action. By bridging the insights of neuroscience, psychiatry, and spirituality. This book challenges us to rethink the ways we understand and promote mental health. Their work underscores the need for a person-centered approach that goes beyond symptom reduction, recognizing the profound interconnections between the brain, mind, and spirit. Although heavily slanted to spirituality traditions from the east, especially India, the insights are applicable broadly across all spirituality traditions from around the world, and potentially motivate future empirical research into the rich interface between spirituality, science and health. As the complexities of the human mind continue to be elucidated by advances in psychiatry and neuroscience, the integration of spirituality offers a pathway to more compassionate, culturally attuned, and effective care. I believe this book will serve as a valuable resource for clinicians, researchers, educators, and all those interested in exploring the transformative potential of spirituality in mental health.

Finally, this book is a heartfelt tribute to the late Dr Avdesh Sharma, a visionary in the field of spirituality and mental health. Dr Sharma was not only a pioneer but also a cherished friend and mentor to many. His deep insights, compassionate approach, and unwavering commitment to integrating spirituality into mental health care continue to inspire generations of clinicians and researchers. His presence will be profoundly missed, but his legacy lives on through the work of his students, colleagues, and friends.

Matcheri Keshavan MD
Stanley Cobb Professor of Psychiatry
Harvard Medical School, USA

Message from the President of Indian Psychiatric Society (IPS)

It gives me immense pleasure to pen this message for the publication of the book, *Spirituality and Mental Health*. This endeavor represents a significant contribution to understand the intricate interplay between the mind, body, and soul—a triad that has fascinated thinkers, healers, and philosophers for centuries. As psychiatrists, we witness daily how the complexities of mental health influence every aspect of human life. In this context, spirituality emerges as an essential dimension that complements scientific approaches to healing. Exploring spirituality alongside psychiatry enables us to connect with the deeper aspects of humanity, fostering holistic healing, and well-being.

This book comes at a time when the world is navigating a mental health crisis. It emphasizes the importance of grounding our clinical practices in fundamental principles while integrating spiritual wisdom to address the unique challenges of modern life. I hope this compilation will serve as a beacon of knowledge for practitioners, students, and anyone interested in mental health and wellness. I extend my heartfelt congratulations to the contributors, editors, and organizers of this initiative, especially Dr Rajashree Ray for their dedication to this noble cause. May this book inspire its readers and contribute to a greater understanding of the profound connection between spirituality and mental health.

Laxmikant Rathi
DPM MD (Psychiatry)
Consultant Psychiatrist and Founder
Govardhan Hospital
Amravati, Maharashtra, India
President, Indian Psychiatric Society (IPS)

Message from President Elect of Indian Psychiatric Society (IPS)

I deem it an honor and pleasure to write this message for the upcoming book on *Spirituality and Mental Health* under the aegis of the Indian Psychiatric Society (IPS). The book is edited by a consummate group of psychiatrists working in this field in India. This is the enhanced edition of the book with expanded coverage both in terms of topics as well as authors. The contributors taken from across the globe have delved into the subject of spirituality and its interface with religion, science, consciousness, parapsychology, and yoga in relation to life and mental health across lifespan. Modern medicine and spirituality are not to be seen as an anathema but complimentary is the new wisdom that can make the practice of medicine holistic and also enhance the scope and value of therapeutic interventions for most mental disorders. This book will be an extremely valuable resource for psychiatrists, physicians, and all health/mental healthcare workers for embracing the principles and practice of spiritualism while treating or handling patients in distress due to disease or disaster.

I congratulate the team of editors and all the authors for having taken up this onerous task with great elan. I extend my best wishes for success of this book.

Savita Malhotra
MD PhD FAMS Hon Fellow American
College of Psychiatrists
Professor of Psychiatry
Former Dean and Head
Department of Psychiatry
Postgraduate Institute of
Medical Education and Research
Chandigarh, India
President Elect
Indian Psychiatric Society (IPS)

Message from the Desk of Hony General Secretary, Indian Psychiatric Society (IPS)

I am truly honored to write this message on the publication of the enhanced edition of the book *Spirituality and Mental Health* by the Indian Psychiatric Society.

Spirituality and mental health are deeply intertwined, offering a profound pathway to inner peace, resilience, and emotional well-being. Spirituality transcends religious beliefs, guiding us toward the pursuit of meaning, connection, and transcendence in life. It encourages introspection, alignment with our values, and mindfulness to navigate life's challenges with grace.

This edition is a reflection of the commendable efforts nearly 50 contributors from India and abroad, along with their dedicated teams, in presenting a comprehensive exploration of this vital subject. Their work captures advancements and insights into the relationship between spirituality and mental health.

I am confident this book will hold a special place in our libraries, serving as a source of guidance to find purpose in adversity, deepen connections, and foster compassion.

My heartfelt congratulations to the editorial team and all contributors for their dedication in bringing forth this valuable edition during ANCIPS 2025.

Amrit Pattojoshi
DPM MD
Professor and Head
Department of Psychiatry
Hi-Tech Medical College and Hospital
Bhubaneswar, Odisha, India
Hony General Secretary, Indian Psychiatric Society (IPS)

Message from Chairperson, Spirituality and Mental Health Section of Indian Psychiatric Society

Dear Readers,

Ours is a journey in life to find meaning, clarity, and peace amidst the turmoil in our thoughts and emotions. This book is a companion for this journey: Deepening the connection between spirituality and mental health—a connection that nourishes the soul and calms the mind.

Spirituality and mental health are closely interlinked, providing routes to inner peace, resilience, and a sense of purpose. Spirituality is not just religious practice but an exploration of meaning, connection, and transcendence in our lives. When we engage with our spiritual self, we foster emotional well-being and navigate life's challenges with greater clarity. This integration can lead to a more harmonious and fulfilling existence-through quiet introspection with nature, community, and the expression of creativity.

Indian Psychiatric Society (IPS) re-embarks on this journey to explore the synergy of spirituality and mental health to empower us to find meaning in experiences, connect genuinely with others, and embrace life's uncertainties with grace. This is the enhanced edition of the book on Spirituality and Mental Health, inspired by Dr Vinay Kumar, during his tenure as the President of Indian Psychiatric Society.

In these pages, you will find reflections to help you reconnect with your inner self, cultivate mindfulness, and embrace practices that lead to emotional well-being. May it inspire you to embrace your wholeness, find peace in your present moment, and foster a deeper connection with yourself and the world around you.

On behalf of the Specialty Section of Indian Psychiatry Section, we wish all of you success in your individual journeys.

Rajashree Ray
MD FRCPsych (UK) CCT (General Adult and Addiction Psychiatry, UK)
PGDMLE (NLSIU, Bangalore) PGMHSC (De Montfort Univ, UK)
Professor and Head
Department of Psychiatry
Gouri Devi Institute of Medical Sciences and Hospital (GIMSH)
Durgapur, West Bengal, India
Former Clinical Director and Consultant
Birmingham and Solihull Mental Health NHS Foundation Trust, UK
Honorary Member, World Psychiatric Association
Secretary, Section on Religion, Spirituality and Psychiatry, World Psychiatric Association

Spirituality and Mental Health Section of Indian Psychiatric Society

Preface

Mental health and spirituality are intertwined aspects of our human experience. Yet, they are often addressed in isolation, neglecting the profound impact each has on the other. During times when we navigate through the complexities of life, the strength of spirituality sustains us with solace and purpose. Similarly, the quality of our existence is determined by our emotional and psychological well-being. Taking cognizance of this, the Indian Psychiatric Society (IPS) has attempted to bridge this gap, offering an exploration of the intersections of spirituality and mental health. This exploration is particularly timely in an era marked by rapid societal change, technological advancements, and increasing disconnection. Book attempts to examine the various facets of spirituality through the lens of science.

Spirituality and Mental Health has been published by the Indian Psychiatric Society as an enhanced version of the book *Spirituality and Mental Health, Reflections of the Past, Applications in the Present, Projections for the Future,* published by Indian Psychiatric Society, in association with Medical Wing, Rajyoga Education and Research Foundation , Mount Abu in 2019, under the Editorship of Late Dr Avdesh Sharma. Since significant research has happened in this field in the last 15 years, it was felt that it is important to publish an enhanced edition of the book on Spirituality and Mental Health.

The current edition has three sections: The Fundamentals, Spirituality and Mental Health (Preventive and Therapeutic Aspects), and Beyond Clinical Practice. Each Section has 7 chapters, written by different authors. The Fundamentals section includes chapters on what spirituality is, its interface with religion, neuroscience, consciousness, positive mental health, yoga, and culture. The section on Spirituality and Mental Health (Preventive and Therapeutic Aspects) includes spirituality across lifespan, in pregnancy and maternal mental health, chapters on spirituality and various psychiatric disorders/conditions such as mood and anxiety-related conditions, addictive disorders, suicidality, in rehabilitation and palliative care, and using spiritual principles in psychotherapy. The third section on Beyond Clinical Practice adds an interesting dimension to the book and includes spirituality in relation to creativity, sensuality, sexuality, crime, and its application in mental health. Finally, the recent global initiatives for restoring spirituality have been discussed and the need for the integration of teaching spirituality in medical curriculum.

As you turn the pages ahead, you may find insights that resonate with your own experiences and answers to questions that you have wondered. We hope that mental health professionals find this book useful and that it generates further interest in this topic from clinical, academic, and research perspective.

BN Gangadhar
Rajashree Ray
Anju Dhawan

Acknowledgments

We express our deepest gratitude to all those who have contributed to the development and success of this book on Spirituality and Mental Health.

We sincerely acknowledge the invaluable contributions of the authors of the book, *Spirituality and Mental Health*, Reflections of the Past, Applications in the Present, Projections for the Future, published by Indian Psychiatric Society, in association with Medical Wing, Rajyoga Education and Research Foundation, Mount Abu in 2019, under the Editorship of Late Dr Avdesh Sharma, whose foundational work has greatly enriched this present volume. We extend our heartfelt thanks to the contributors of the present edition for their dedicated efforts and insightful contributions.

Our profound appreciation goes to the Executive Committee and the Publishing Sub-Committee of the Indian Psychiatric Society for commissioning this edition and for their unwavering support throughout the process. We also thank the members of the Spirituality Section and the Yoga and Mental Health Section of the Indian Psychiatric Society for their active involvement and encouragement.

We are especially thankful to Professor Matcheri Keshavan for graciously writing the foreword and adding immense value to this book. We also honor and express our gratitude to the family of late Dr Avdesh Sharma for their continued support and inspiration.

Our heartfelt thanks go to Dr Vinay Kumar and Dr PK Singh for conceptualizing and shaping the framework of this book, providing a strong foundation for its development.

We deeply appreciate M/s Jaypee Brothers Medical Publishers (P) Ltd, New Delhi, India for their professionalism and commitment in bringing this book to fruition.

Lastly, we extend our sincere gratitude to our families for their unwavering support, patience, and understanding, which have been instrumental in completing this work.

With deepest appreciation

Contents

SECTION 3: BEYOND CLINICAL PRACTICE

1 SECTION

The Fundamentals

1

CHAPTER

Spirituality: A Missing Dimension in Mental Health Care

Nikhil G Patel, Diane G Tillman

INTRODUCTION

Albert Einstein said, "Religion without science is blind and science without religion is lame". The quote reverberates in the hearts and minds of scientists and the religious leaders alike for past few centuries. In fact, the origin of the word "religion" comes from the old French or Latin term *Religare* which means "obligation, bond, reverence". The traditional Eastern Indian philosophy has a synonymous word namely *dharma* that literally means "to inculcate values or to perform duties as per the moral". Sometimes, the terms "religion" and "spirituality" are used interchangeably, but in their truest sense, spirituality transcends the confines of specific religious doctrines, such as Hinduism, Islam, Christianity, and others. The modern-day education teaches our students various forms of sciences namely the social science, the industrial science, the political science, and the computer science to name a few. It is intriguing that religious science or the spiritual science are a big miss from the mainstream educational system. It is also conspicuous in the modern-day medical science and more so in the field of neurosciences and behavioral sciences called neuropsychiatry and clinical psychology.

In the last few decades, positive contributions of spirituality have been increasingly acknowledged by the psychiatric community. No longer maligned as it was a century ago, spirituality as an important aspect of mental health is being explored by special committees in the American Psychiatric Association, the Indian Psychiatric Society, the Royal College of Psychiatrists in the United Kingdom, and the World Psychiatric Association, to name a few. Some psychiatrists and psychologists include it as a tool in their therapeutic practice.

Despite the advances in medicine and mental health care, the incidence of mental illness continues to increase around the world and an interesting observation that "Americans" mental health is at its lowest point in history, was made by David H Rosmarin.[1] As people feel more isolated than ever, they are less connected to each other and to something spiritual. A growing number of psychologists believe that religion and spirituality have tools that can help in today's mental health crisis.[2]

Of concern, it has been observed that the world is at a crossroads. Despite tremendous progress in science and medicine, we have not been able to eliminate distress. The utopian dream of achieving health, peace, and happiness—beyond physical and mental comforts—remains just that: a dream. It may not become a reality unless we integrate spirituality into our scientific endeavors.[3]

What is Spirituality?

Spirituality has been defined as "the individual's personal experience that provides a greater sense of inner peace, harmony, hopefulness, and compassion for others and oneself".[4] The term 'spiritus' in Latin means 'the breath' that is most vital to life. It involves the individual's experience of and relationship with a fundamental, nonmaterial aspect of the universe that may be referred to in many ways—God, Higher power, Mystery—whereby an individual finds meaning and connectedness to something greater than oneself".

The American Psychological Association defines spirituality as: "(1) A concern for or sensitivity to things of the spirit or soul, especially as opposed to materialistic concerns. (2) More specifically, a concern for God and a sensitivity to religious experience, which may include the practice of a particular religion but may also exist without such practice. (3) The fact or state of being incorporeal".[5]

The Royal College of Psychiatrists website comments "Spirituality can be an important, sometimes a central part of someone's life. It can offer real benefits for mental health. The sense of spirituality is deeply varied. For some, it is a private and personal matter, while for others, it is expressed within an established group or religious context. Generally, descriptions of spirituality encompass the idea of seeking the best relationship with oneself, with others, and with what may lie 'beyond'. From helping us to find meaning and purpose in life to giving us a sense of hope, spirituality can be the best support in the times of suffering and loss we all experience".[6]

A SPIRITUAL PERSPECTIVE AND BENEFITS OF MEDITATION

*M*ind is the "experiencer" of the inner and outer worlds. It is thus extremely necessary to include the spiritual dimension in all aspects of health, especially mental health. One of the main tasks of human endeavors is to regain our original, perfect condition of the soul".[3]

If we delve into the history of mankind, five thousand years ago, the land of Bharat (India) was completely happy, viceless, and spiritually elevated. The divine human beings sometimes referred to as "Gods and Goddesses" were completely nonviolent and like all virtuous deities like Sri Krishna, Sri Radhe, and Sri Ram. They practiced all moral and spiritual values in their thoughts, words, and deeds and never required to perform so-called external "religious" rituals to invoke God. It was actually the original eternal deity religion that lasted for about 2,500 years that is also known as golden Age, the *Satyug* and also described in Bible as paradise. Subsequently, a gradual erosion of values and morals cripped in and the gross and subtle forms of body-consciousness, sex-lust, anger, greed started intruding into the human beings. As a result, many seers, saints, religious leaders started preaching and practicing the path of devotion, asceticism, chastity, and sublimation. They all tried to elevate consciousness by invoking the Divine or God. Some of them adopted the teachings to go within through meditation or penance and some of them have combined the external rituals and prayers while trying to connect with the transcendent or the divine. The formal religions with specific names came into existence like Hinduism (originally called an "original eternal/*Sanatan* deity" religion), Judaism, Islam, Buddhism, Christianity, Jainism, Sikhism, or some minor less known paths like Sannyasa, Patanjali Yoga, Swaminarayan cult, the Art of Living, Isha Foundation, and Iyengar Yoga to name a few. The latest addition among them is a unique faith called the BKWSU which focuses on self-transformation and the inculcation of virtues through Raj Yoga Meditation, understanding that it is only with self-transformation that there will be transformation of the world into one of peace and well-being for all.

In Raj Yoga meditation, the soul is understood to be peaceful, loving, compassionate, powerful, pure, and happy in its original state. Human consciousness, or the soul in its true form, is full of virtues and free from negativity. While all souls inherently seek peace, over time as it becoming body-conscious, depletes spiritual energy. This gradual loss often leaves individuals overwhelmed by worries, fears, negativity, feelings of inadequacy, and even mental or psychosomatic illnesses.

In the teaching of Raja yoga meditation, three functions of the soul are described—the mind, intellect, and *sanskaras*/personality traits. The mind is like a screen, where we visualize things and experience our feelings. It is in the mind that we experience life. When the mind if full of pure vibrations of peace or love, the mind naturally slows down and is then ready to connect with the Highest One, the Supreme Soul. When stress or anger fills the mind, the whole person is negatively impacted. By learning and practicing this form of meditation, people seek to find happiness, reduce stress, and have more peace of mind.[7]

Raja Yoga meditation has potential impact on mental and emotional well-being and helps to lead a pure and elevated lifestyle. The basic principles of meditation involve relaxation, oxygenation, imagery, visualization, concentration, self-hypnosis, cognitive restructuring, peak experiences, and excretion of endorphins. More specifically, the process of meditation raises energy levels and strengthens the immune system to fight or ward off illnesses. It induces the relaxation response and associated psychophysiological processes. It acts on the Karmic/Sanskar levels to neutralize the causes and effects of illness. It enhances the positivity of the person about self and healing, thus setting off chain reactions of healing. It induces a connection to the source (God) to draw the power to heal and stimulates lifestyle changes, which are useful for self-healing, allowing external healing forces to act better. Practicing this meditative processes regularly for 20–45 minutes once or twice daily produces decreased heart rate and blood pressure; increased blood flow to the brain and heart; positive changes in EEG, EMG, and skin resistance; improved sleep, reduced irritability, anxiety and depression on rating scales, low frequency and duration of illnesses, decreased accidents and days lost at work, improved interpersonal relationships; improved scores on self-actualization inventories, and emotional and spiritual quotients.[8]

It is common for people learning Raja Yoga meditation to talk about their increased peace, serenity, contentment, and ability to stay more positive with their families and in the workplace. They suggested that in future, meditation may be a mainstream form of treatment rather than considered just a complimentary or alternative treatment.

Currently, studies are being conducted which contrast meditation as treatment in lieu of medication for patients with anxiety disorders. Mindfulness-based stress reduction (MBST) was a well-tolerated treatment option with comparable effectiveness to a first-line medication for patients with anxiety disorders. It was determined that MBST was "noninferior to escitalopram, a commonly used first-line psychopharmacological treatment for anxiety disorders".[9]

At this juncture, it is crucial to note that the addictions in the form of psychoactive substance abuse or dependence, a global menace is on the rise and the governments and the mental health professionals find it difficult to develop a multipronged approach to curb this menace. Raja Yoga meditation practiced regularly can be a standalone or an adjuvant modality to overcome even the hard drug abuse and dependence.[10]

During the COVID-19, spiritualists like BK Sister Shivani's approach to spirituality and self-improvement garnered widespread recognition for its practical relevance and transformative impact. Her method integrating spiritual principles with everyday challenges effectively addresses emotional and mental struggles in a relatable and logical manner. With the principles of Raj Yoga meditation, one can learn to identifying common pain points, such as negative thoughts, emotional distress, or strained relationships, it explores the results of that negative thought and how that creates further distress internally. It is possible to then consider an alternative way of thinking about the triggering event which is beneficial for the self in terms of more peaceful or loving vibrations, more positive action/karma, and internal locus of control. Over a period of time, it leads to a heightened sense of peace and harmony in noticeable improvements in relationships and emotional stability.

If we look at the essence of all religions, most share a belief in soul/spirit, the practice of virtues, and a Supreme Source. While different religions describe God differently, reports from people who have had Near-Death Experiences, no matter their faith or lack of faith, all describe experiencing a brilliant divine light and an overwhelming sense of peace and absolute, unconditional love.[11] Dr Raymond Moody, a psychiatrist, began exploring the phenomena during the mid-1970s during his medical residency. Is God a being of light with peace and unconditional love? As decades of research have continued, people continue to describe their powerful love-filled experiences with that Being of Light.[12]

Spirituality includes all-inclusive concepts of The Divine (God), the human soul and its journey of birth and rebirth from the highest deity form to an ordinary man, the cyclic form of the world drama,[7] the corporeal and the incorporeal worlds of the universe, the true history and geography that evolves in and around the land of Bharat (India). etc.[13] They also teach how the negative forces in the world are intensifying. And to counteract that and bring transformation, we must concentrate as never before on being the peace we want to see in the world, that is, being the change, we want to see within. They feel the global conversion from negative to positive energy can be created through a heightening of individual consciousness, an awakening inside the human spirit.

TWO DIMENSIONS OF MENTAL HEALTH

Mental health has two dimensions—the absence of mental illness and the presence of a well-adjusted personality that contributes effectively to the life of the community. The essential features of mental health are the "ability to take responsibility for one's own actions, flexibility, high frustration tolerance, acceptance of uncertainty, involvement in activities of social interest, courage to take risks, serenity to accept the things which we cannot change, courage to change the things which we can change, the wisdom to know the difference between the above, acceptance of handicaps, tempered self-control, harmonious relationships to self, others, including Nature and God".[14]

It is interesting to note that this description of mental health includes many qualities and virtues. Fortunate children have virtues modeled and reinforced by loving, supportive families. Others may learn about qualities and virtues from their teachers, therapist, close friends, colleagues, or mentors, or in a self-exploration process.

SPIRITUALLY-INFORMED THERAPIES

The number of mental health treatments including a spiritual aspect is growing. There are a variety of 12-step programs, such as alcoholics anonymous, narcotics anonymous, over-eaters anonymous and groups for adult children of alcoholics. Many mental health professionals recommend meditation and/or mindfulness courses for stress reduction. Compassion-focused therapy[15] and forgiveness therapy[16] are recent approaches that delve into spiritual ways of dealing with the self in a more positive and healing manner. Spiritually augmented cognitive behavior therapy is used by practitioners to effectively aid clients identify a spiritual or religious belief that is deeply meaningful to them, or helping them anchor into a value that they feel is most important.

SPIRITUAL CONCEPTS THAT ARE EASY TO APPLY IN MENTAL HEALTH CARE

- The impact of our thoughts on health and happiness has been demonstrated in numerous studies. This concept can be introduced to clients in a straightforward way by categorizing thoughts into five types—negative, wasteful, necessary, positive, and pure.
- Negative and intense thoughts can drain our physical, emotional, and spiritual energy, often leaving us feeling worse over time. On the other hand, positive and pure thoughts have a rejuvenating effect, boosting our energy and overall well-being. The more we focus on positive and pure thoughts, the better we tend to feel, both mentally and physically.
    - Identifying the core values through guided reflection, developing a couple affirmations based on their core values, and the natural qualities of the soul/spirit. These concepts are easily learned and are of benefit to people suffering with anxiety and depression, especially when combined with meditation.
- In ruminative disorders, it is important to help explore the root of frequent ruminative thoughts to find a positive powerful memory, value, belief, or affirmation that can be used in its place. The negative ruminative thoughts are replaced with positive effects during a guided reflection. If stuck in reliving a traumatic memory, it is useful to use the process of verbalization of what they would like the perpetrator to know. Then, when the negative memory comes again, it is used as a signal to tell that person mentally what he/she needs to know and go into their feeling of sureness and knowing their rights, and bring up the feeling of the values they have expressed, and stopping the negative thought.
- A spiritual perspective that is healthy and helpful to mental health is that each person is a soul/spirit and that we are all

part of one world family. This has profound implications for our relationships with others, once we truly understand this we are able to understand the importance of treating each person with respect and dignity. Many people are involved with groups that constrict circles rather than expanding circles of acceptance, compassion, and belongingness. The former is often fear and/or power based. Building exclusivity frequently pits "them" against "us" and creates artificial and sometimes demeaning and harmful divisions. These divisions can fuel fear, prejudice and violence, harmful to both the sender and receiver.

- Encourage gratitude and gratitude journals. Gratitude is well documenting as improving mental health by creating a more positive orientation to daily life.
- Encourage clients to journal with two voices, not just the voice of the part of the self that is hurt, traumatized or in sorrow. Help them find their wise core self and use that part of themselves to listen to and encourage the hurt part. They can do this by writing on the opposite side of the page.
- Explore virtues that they admire or would love to experience. It might be peace, contentment, benevolence, joy, love, resilience, compassion, universal brotherhood, or a myriad of others. Research on the positive effects of practicing and teaching hope is increasing.[17]

The 17 Sustainable Development Goals (SDGs) under United Nations' 2030 Agenda for Sustainable Development[18] to transform our world are—no poverty; zero hunger; good health and well-being; quality education; gender equality; clean water and sanitation; affordable and clean energy; decent work and economic growth; industry, innovation and infrastructure; reduced inequality; sustainable cities and communities; responsible consumption and production; climate action; life below water; life on land; peace and justice strong institutions; and partnerships to achieve the goal.

Hunger, ecological disasters, war, and corruption create the conditions for physical and mental illness like anxiety, depression, despair, and hopelessness. In addition, there is an enormous cost of hunger and war in terms of loss of life, the stunting of physical, emotional, and intellectual growth, long-term trauma, and loss of social productivity. With 108 plus million refugees and internally displaced people at this point in history, and with rampant violence, corruption and consequent trauma and subsistence poverty in some societies, the mental health needs appear unlimited. If we are to help them step forward positively in life, we need to simultaneously help them develop the social and emotional skills needed to create well-being for themselves and those around them.

PSYCHOSOCIAL EDUCATIONAL INTERVENTION AS MENTAL HEALTH CARE

Mental health care is important for refugees who have endured the trauma of war. Untreated, the cycle of trauma and violence often continues. A remarkable example is the curriculum designed by Tillman for refugees and children affected by war in the late 90s. This curriculum included training refugee teachers of the same culture in the first 9-day with 35 teachers in two Karen Tribe refugee camps of 11,000 people in a jungle in Thailand.[19] The refugee teachers participating in a values awareness exercise, named a Living

Value Education (LVE) program, were taught skills to create a values-based atmosphere, and underwent some of the activities they were going to do with their students. This was necessary for them to begin their own healing journey, trust the activities they were going to be asked to do with their students, and learn positive ways of interacting with the students. After 1 year of implementation by the 35 teachers, most of the young people engaged in the LVE activities never fought, unlike previously. They learned to value peace, were involved in activities to tell their own stories and learned conflict resolution. Learning social and emotional skills, relaxation-focusing exercises on filling self with peace, respect, and love improved their emotional well-being. After 2 years of implementation, the refugee educators reported that none of the students in the two camps of 11,000 fought. Instead of getting angry quickly and fighting, they were peaceful, concentrated better, asked questions of their teachers, and engaged in spontaneous and creative play. Their happiness was a sharp contrast to their state 2 years earlier. The values-based atmosphere in which everyone is treated in such a way that they feel loved, respected, valued, understood, and safe was healing. Creating a culture of peace, caring, and respect dramatically affected all involved in a very positive way, both adults and young people.

CONCLUSION

In conclusion, integrating spirituality into mental health care provides professionals with additional tools to support their clients. By incorporating spiritual practices and beliefs, clients can be guided to access positive spiritual resources that help them better understand and navigate issues and trauma. This integration allows individuals to connect with their soul's inherent qualities, build emotional and spiritual resilience through a relationship with the Supreme or Higher Power, and address the deeper need for purpose, meaning, and the pursuit of eternal truth.

It is essential for clients to explore their challenges and learn to lovingly accept and manage both positive and negative emotions. Except in cases of florid psychosis, combining psychology with spirituality enhances our ability to address issues at multiple levels. This includes preventing societal stressors and conflicts from worsening mental health and facilitating the healing of communities affected by trauma.

Ultimately, this approach not only helps individuals gain greater self-awareness and foster healthier relationships but also nurtures the development of kinder, more conscious human beings. Such individuals are more inclined to treat others with dignity and respect, contributing to a more compassionate and understanding society.

REFERENCES

1. Schiffman R. (2022). More psychologists are incorporating religion into their practices, The Washington Post. [online] Available from https://www.washingtonpost.com/religion/2022/09/23/psychotherapy-religion-spirituality/. [Last accessed December, 2024].
2. Rosmarin DH. Spirituality, Religion, and Cognitive-Behavioral Therapy. New York: Guilford: 2018.
3. Nirwair BJ. Inspirations. In: Sharma A (Ed). Spirituality & Mental Health: Reflections of the Past, Applications in the Present, Projections for the Future. Abu Road: Om Shanti Press; 2009. p. vii.
4. Das EM. Introduction. In: Sharma A (Ed). Spirituality & Mental Health: Reflections of the Past, Applications in the Present,

Projections for the Future. Abu Road: Om Shanti Press; 2009. pp. iv-v.
5. American Psychological Association. Definition of Spirituality. [online] Available from https://dictionary.apa.org/spirituality. [Last accessed December, 2024]
6. Royal College of Psychiatrists. Spirituality and Mental Health. [online] Available from https://www.rcpsych.ac.uk/mental-health/treatments-and-wellbeing/spirituality-and-mental-health. [Last accessed December, 2024]
7. Brahma Kumaris. (2023). Brahma Kumaris at the U.N. [online] Available from https://brahmakumaris.org. [Last accessed December, 2024]
8. Sharma A, Sharma SD. Meditation: The Future of Medication? In: Sharma A (Ed). Spirituality & Mental Health: Reflections of the Past, Applications in the Present, Projections for the Future. Abu Road: Om Shanti Press; 2009. pp. 569-84.
9. Hoge EA, Bui E, Mete M, Dutton MA, Baker AW, Simon NM, et al. Mindfulness-Based Stress Reduction vs Escitalopram for the Treatment of Adults with Anxiety Disorders, A Randomized Clinical Trial. JAMA Psychiatry. 2023;80(1):13-21.
10. Nikhil P, Barbara G. Meditation in a lived faith context as a therapeutic intervention for substance abuse, dependence and addiction: an empirical study. Arch Indian Psychiatr. 2005;7(1):52-6.
11. Moody RA. Life After Life. New York: Bantam Doubleday Dell; 1976.
12. Greyson B, Kelly EW, Kelly EF. Explanatory models for near-death experiences. In: Holden JM, Greyson B, James D (Eds). The Handbook of Near-Death Experiences: Thirty Years of Investigation. Santa Barbara, CA: Praeger/ABC-CLIO; 2009. p. 226.
13. Raja Yogi BK, Chander J. Eternal Drama of Souls, Matter and God Part II. Mount Abu: Om Shanti Press; 1998. pp. 201-18.
14. Verghese A. Spirituality and Mental Health. Indian J Psychiatr. 2008;50(4):233.
15. Gilbert P. Introducing Compassion-Focused Therapy. Adv Psychiatr Treat. 2009; 15: 199-208.
16. Enright RD, Fitzgibbons RP. Forgiveness Therapy: An Empirical Guide for Resolving Anger and Restoring Hope. Washington DC: American Psychological Association; 2015.
17. Doheny K. (2022). Is Hopefulness the Key to Better Mental and Physical Health? [online] Available from https://www.webmd.com/mental-health/news/20230823/cm/is-hopefulness-the-key-to-better-mental-physical-health. [Last accessed December, 2024]
18. United Nations. Sustainable Develop Goals to Transform Our World. [online] Available from https://www.un.org/development/desa/disabilities/envision2030.html. [Last accessed December, 2024]
19. Tillman DG. (2001). Educating for a Culture of Peace in Refugee Camps. [online] Available from https://www.tandfonline.com/doi/abs/10.1080/00094056.2001.10521673. [Last accessed December, 2024]

2 CHAPTER

Religion, Spiritual Traditions, and Theories

Ranjan Bhattacharyya, Aratrika Sen

INTRODUCTION

Religion and spirituality are often used interchangeably as synonymous words. Though not diagonally opposite, but still they held some minute differences. Religion is practiced by a wider segment, is more organized and community based, whereas spirituality comes from inner space of an individual though both have similar foundation.[1]

RELIGION

History of religion dates back to almost 5,200 years back, since when writing has been invented. Religious writings, scriptures, and books have been one of the major sources for historians to understand religion.[2] Writing played a crucial role in unifying religious texts across different eras and regions, while also aiding in the memorization of prayers and sacred guidelines.

Pioneer sociologist Émile Durkheim described religion as "things that surpass the limits of our knowledge" (1915). He gave the definition: "religion is a unified system of beliefs and practices relative to sacred things, that is to say, things set apart and forbidden—beliefs and practices which unite into one single moral community, called a church, all those who adhere to them" (1915).[3]

From the Latin "religio" (respect for what is sacred) and religare (to bind, in the sense of an obligation), the term religion describes various systems of belief and practice concerning what people determine to be sacred or spiritual. Throughout history, and in societies across the world, leaders have used religious narratives, symbols, and traditions in an attempt to give more meaning to life and understand the universe. Some form of religion is found in every known culture, and it is usually practiced in a public way by a group. The practice of religion can include feasts and festivals, God or gods, marriage and funeral services, music and art, meditation, or initiation, sacrifice or service, and other aspects of culture.

If we go through the timeline of religion, little can be known about the religion and religious practices in pre-historic era due to lack of writings. The source of information is mainly archaeological evidences. The timeline of progress of religion can be broadly divided into:

- Prehistoric era
- Ancient era
- Common era
- Middle ages
- Early modern era and modern era[4]

Important events in each time-period have been tabulated in the **Table 1**.

TABLE 1: Timeline of religion based on archaeological evidences.

Timeline	*Time period*	*Important events*
Prehistoric era (20,000–6,000 BC)	Middle paleolithic	Earliest known human burial in the Middle East (10,000 BC)
	40,000–6,500 BC	More evidence of burial practice Göbekli Tepe, oldest man-made sites of worship
Ancient era (6,000–100 BC)	2,635–2,610 BC	The oldest surviving Egyptian pyramid was commissioned by Pharaoh Djoser
	1,700–1,100 BC	The oldest of the Hindu Vedas (scriptures), the Rigveda was composed
	1,500 BC	The Vedic period began in India after the collapse of the Indus Valley civilization
	599–527 BC	The life of Mahavira, 24th and last Tirthankara of Jainism
	563/480–483/400 BC	Gautama Buddha, founder of Buddhism was born
Common era (100 BC to 405 AD)	7 BC to 30/33 AD	The life of Jesus of Nazareth, the central figure of Christianity
	250900AD	Classic Mayan step pyramids were constructed
Middle ages (500–1,500 AD)	410 AD	Decline of Western Roman Empire with onset of Dark Ages
	570–632 AD	Life of Prophet Muhammad of Islam
	716–936 AD	Migration of Zoroastrian communities from Persia to India
	788–820 AD	Life of Hindu saint, Adi Shankara (doctrine of Advaita Vedanta)
	1,206 AD	The Delhi Sultanate was established
	1,378–1,417 AD	The Roman Catholic Church split during the Western Schism
	1,469–1,539 AD	Life of Guru Nanak (Sikhism)
Early modern and modern eras (16th century to 21st century)	16th century: 1,526 AD	African religious systems introduced to the America
	17th century: 1,699 AD	Guru Gobind Singh Ji created the Khalsa in Sikhism
	18th century: 1,791 AD	Freedom of religion added to the Constitution of the USA (one of the first significant secular governments)
	19th century: 1,893 AD	Swami Vivekananda's first speech at the Parliament of the World's Religions, Chicago, brought the ancient philosophies of Vedanta and Yoga to the western world
	20th century:	
	1,917 AD	Onset of religious suppression in Russia (October Revolution)
	1,947 AD	Pakistan, the first nation-state in the name of Islam was created. British India was partitioned into the secular nation of India with a Hindu majority and the Muslim-majority nation of Pakistan (the eastern half of whom would later become Bangladesh)

Contd...

Contd...

	1,948 AD	The modern state of Israel was established as a homeland for the Jews
	1,959 AD	The 14th Dalai Lama fled Tibet amidst unrest and established an exile community in India
	21st century:	
	2,006 AD	Sectarian rivalries exploded in Iraq between Sunni Muslims and Shias, with each side targeting the other in terrorist acts, and bombings of mosques and shrines
	2,008 AD	Nepal, the world's only Hindu Kingdom, was declared a secular state by its Constituent Assembly after declaring the state a Republic on 28 May 2008
	2,011 AD	Civil war broke out in Syria over domestic political issues. The country soon split along sectarian lines between Sunni Muslims, Alawite, and Shiites

Classification of Religions

Academicians studying sociology have divided religions into three broad categories:

1. *World religions:* A term which refers to transcultural and international religions. Main religions under this category are five—Hinduism, Buddhism, Judaism, Christianity, and Islam, being known as the "Big Five".
2. *Indigenous religions:* It refers to culture-specific, or nation-specific religious groups.[5]
3. *New religious movements:* A new religious movement (NRM), as described by scholars, is a religious, ethical, or spiritual group or community with thoughts and practices of relatively modern origins. NRMs may be novel in origin or they may exist on the edge of a wider religion, in which case they will be distinct from already established denominations. Examples are ISKCON (International Society for Krishna Consciousness), Brahmo Samaj, etc.

World Religions

- *Christianity:* It is the world's largest and most widely spread religion with about 2.38 billion followers.
- *Islam:* It is the world's second largest religion with about 1.8 billion followers globally.
- *Hinduism:* It is the world's third largest religion, with over 1.2–1.35 billion followers. Hinduism has been called the oldest religion in the world.
- *Buddhism:* It is the world's fourth largest religion, with over 520 million followers (Buddhists).
- *Judaism:* It has its roots as an organized religion in the Middle East during the Bronze Age. Judaism's texts, traditions, and values strongly influenced later Abrahamic religions, including Christianity and Islam **(Table 2)**.

Table 2 gives the different aspects of some of the major religions of the world.[6-8]

TABLE 2: Classification of religion based on followers and their origin.

Religion	*Christianity*	*Islam*	*Hinduism*	*Buddhism*	*Judaism*
Followers	Christians	Muslim	Hindus	Buddhist	Jews
Number of followers worldwide	2.38 billion	1.8 billion	1.2 billion	362 million	14.5 million
Origin	Middle East (Israel/ Palestine)	Middle East (Saudi Arabia)	India	India	Middle East (Israel/ Palestine)
Founder	Jesus Christ	Muhammed	No founder	Gautam Buddha	Abraham Moses
Worship	Monotheistic Jesus is the son of God	Monotheistic "Allah" in Arabic	• Polytheistic (many gods) • Most important: Brahma Vishnu Maheshwara • Most worshipped God: Ganesha	Polytheistic (Buddha is not God—just a revered teacher)	Monotheistic God (Yahweh)
Places of practice	Church	Mosque	Temple	Monastery	Synagogue
Ultimate goal	Heaven	Spread message of Allah	Moksha	Nirvana/ Enlightenment	Live in harmony with God
Holy book	Bible	Quran	The Vedas	Tripitaka	Torah

Other religions of importance in India are as follows:

- *Sikhism:* Originated in Punjab region. Sikhism developed from the teachings of Guru Nanak (1469–1539), the first guru, and the nine Sikh gurus who succeeded him. The tenth guru, Gobind Singh (1666–1708), named the Sikh scripture Guru Granth Sahib as his successor, thus ending the line of human gurus and establishing the scripture as the 11th and last eternally living guru, a religious guide for Sikhs.
- *Jainism:* It is also known as Jain Dharma. The lineage of twenty-four Tirthankaras (supreme teachers of Dharma), with the first in the current time cycle being Rishabhadeva, holds the basis of Jainism. Parshvanatha and Mahavira are recognized as the twenty-third and twenty-fourth Tirthankaras in Jainism, a faith regarded as an eternal dharma. Its core principles include Ahimsa (nonviolence), Anekantavada (nonabsolutism), and Aparigraha (non-possessiveness).

Religion and Related Aspects

- *Law and religion:* The study of law and religion is a new field with involvements of department of law, sociology, and political science. Researchers in this relatively new discipline are focused on legal issues regarding religious freedom or legal understandings of religious phenomenon. Common topics include marriage, family, and human rights.

- *Science and religion:* Religion and science both offer explanations for why life and the universe exist. Science relies on evidence and observation. Religion relies on subjective belief in a supreme entity. There is evidence of both conflicts (creationism vs. evolution) and harmonious relationship between the two. The relationship has been dynamic and complementary since ages.
- *Health and religion:* Mayo Clinic researchers examined the association between religious involvement and spirituality, and physical health, mental health, health-related quality of life, and other health outcomes. The authors reported that: "Most studies have shown that religious involvement and spirituality are associated with better health outcomes, including greater longevity, coping skills, and health-related quality of life (even during terminal illness) and less anxiety, depression, and suicide."
- *Politics and religion:* Religion has a significant role in politics. Some countries even use religious terms in the country name like "The Islamic Republic of Iran". It has been seen that politics in Europe has much less influence of religion while in US, a president is less likely to be elected if the contestant is an atheist. Indian politics is also highly influenced by religion while politics in Japan and China has less influence of religion.
- *Violence and religion:* Anthropologist Jack David Eller asserts that religion is not inherently violent, arguing "religion and violence are clearly compatible, but they are not identical". He asserts that "violence is neither essential to nor exclusive to religion" and that "virtually every form of religious violence has its nonreligious corollary".[9,10]

SPIRITUALITY

Spirituality deals with the quality of being concerned with the spirit or soul rather than materialistic things. Traditionally, spirituality referred to a religious process of reformation which "aims to recover the original shape of man". There is no single accepted definition of spirituality; however, most experts have defined it in the light of self-realization. Houtman and Aupers suggest that modern spirituality is a blend of human psychology, mystical and rare traditions, and Eastern religions.[11]

- In modern times, the emphasis has been given on the subjective experience and the "deepest values and meanings by which people live", enhancing self-growth and transformation, which is distinct from religious rituals. It is a personal search for meaning in life or for experiencing the transcendent.
- Kees Waaijman described four forms of spiritual practices:
    1. Somatic practices, especially deprivation and diminishment. Deprivation deals with the purification of the body. Diminishment concerns with the putting back of self-oriented impulses. Examples include fasting and poverty.
    2. Psychological practices, for example meditation
    3. Social practices. Examples include the practice of obedience and communal ownership, ego orientedness into other orientedness.
    4. Spiritual. All practices aim at purifying ego centeredness and direct the abilities at the divine reality.

SPIRITUAL BUT NOT RELIGIOUS

Following the Second World War, spirituality began to diverge from traditional theistic religion, focusing more on personal experience rather than integrating the self into a wider religious framework. This shift gave rise to a new discourse that blended humanistic psychology, mystical and esoteric traditions, and Eastern religions, emphasizing self-discovery, free expression, and meditation as paths to uncovering the true self.

"Spiritual but not religious" (SBNR), also known as "spiritual but not affiliated" (SBNA), or less commonly "more spiritual than religious", is a popular phrase which gained popularity in the modern era. The term loosely defines the approach to self-identify spirituality, but not in the context of an organized religion. No single religion is viewed as the exclusive or most valuable path to spiritual growth. Historically, the terms "religious" and "spiritual" were often used interchangeably to encompass various aspects of religion. However, in modern usage, spirituality has become more closely associated with an individual's inner life, focusing on the well-being of the "mind-body-spirit," while religion is typically linked to institutional or communal practices. The distinction between spirituality and religion gained prominence in the late 20th century with the rise of secularism and the New Age movement. Difference between religion and spirituality has been explored in the late 20th century and been discussed by some authors like Chris Griscom and Shirley MacLaine.[12]

The SBNRs are categorized into five distinct categories by Linda A Mercadante:

1. Dissenters are individuals who deliberately choose to distance themselves from organized religion. Within this group, "Protesting Dissenters" are those who have left religious affiliations due to negative personal experiences. "Drifted Dissenters" are individuals who, for various reasons, lost connection with organized religion and chose not to return. Finally, "Conscientious Objector Dissenters" are those who openly question religious institutions, believing that religion is neither essential nor beneficial to personal spirituality.[13]
2. Casuals are individuals who view religious or spiritual practices as situational, primarily turning to them during times of crisis. For them, spirituality is not a core aspect of their lives but rather a tool to enhance health, alleviate stress, and provide psychological support when needed. Their approach is best described as a "healing" spirituality, focused on personal well-being and happiness.[14]
3. Explorers are individuals characterized by what Mercadante calls a "spiritual wanderlust." These spiritually curious individuals enjoy delving into various spiritual traditions, driven by an insatiable desire to learn and experience. Often described as "spiritual tourists", they take pleasure in the journey itself without feeling compelled to settle on or commit to a single spiritual path or practice.[15]
4. Seekers are individuals searching for a spiritual home but often struggle to move past their previous religious experiences. Embracing the "spiritual but not religious" identity, they are actively looking for a new form of spiritual or religious affiliation—whether through a different faith or an alternative spiritual community—that they can fully commit to.[16]
5. Immigrants are people trying to cope with a new spiritual world and its community. This process of adapting to the new practices is difficult and often disturbing for them.[17]

The intersection between religion and spirituality has been depicted in **Figure 1**.

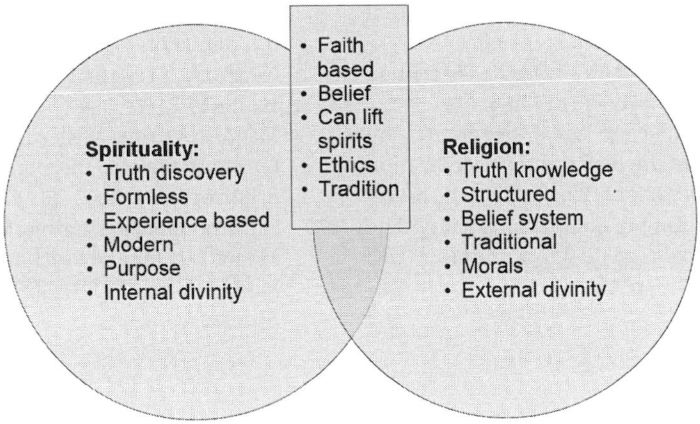

Fig. 1: Religion and spirituality: The intersection and commonalities.

CONCLUSION

Both religion and spirituality are required to withstand shock, personal loss and overcome a crisis during stressful situations. The mental health benefits of religious practices are multifold. At the individual level, it generates inner peace, tranquillity, calmness, makes life more meaningful and purposeful; on the other hand, it teaches an individual tolerance and reduces risk of alcohol and drug dependence and of suicides. At the community level, religious practices improve social connectedness, bonding, group cohesiveness, sense of belongings, and togetherness.

The sacred texts of Hinduism like Shrimad Bhagawat Gita, Vedas, Upanishad, etc. talk about liberation. Spirituality teaches us to think bigger than an individual, incorporates a healthy practice for the mind and body.

REFERENCES

1. Weber SR, Pargament KI. The role of religion and spirituality in mental health. Curr Opin Psychiatry. 2014;27(5):358-63.
2. Kugelmann R, Belzen JA. Historical intersections of psychology, religion, and politics in national contexts. Hist Psychol. 2009;12(3):125-31.
3. Kołodziej-Sarzyńska M, Majewska M, Juchnowicz D, Karakuła-Juchnowicz H. Risk factors of suicide with reference to the theory of social integration by Émile Durkheim. Psychiatr Pol. 2019;53(4):865-81.
4. Thomas G, Pluskowski A, Gilchrist R, García-Contreras Ruiz G, Andrén A, Augenti A, et al. Religious Transformations in the Middle Ages: Towards a New Archaeological Agenda. Med Archaeol. 2017;61(2):300-29.
5. Rayburn CA. Religion, spirituality, and health. Am Psychol. 2004;59(1):52-3; discussion 54-5.
6. Yeasmeen T, Kelaher M, Brotherton JML. Understanding the types of racism and its effect on mental health among Muslim women in Victoria. Ethn Health. 2023; 28(2): 200-16.
7. Patel P. Hinduism. Cancer Treat Res. 2023; 187:231-5.
8. Khoo T. Buddhism. Cancer Treat Res. 2023; 187:153-9.
9. Gonçalves JPB, Lucchetti G, Maraldi EO, Fernandez PEL, Menezes PR, Vallada H. The role of religiosity and spirituality in interpersonal violence: a systematic review and meta-analysis. Braz J Psychiatry. 2023; 45(2):162-81.
10. Beier M. Countering Anti-Semitism and Religious Violence. Psychoanal Rev. 2020; 107(1):1-34.
11. Dike CC, Briz L, Fadus M, Martinez R, May C, Milone R, et al. Religion, Spirituality, and

Ethics in Psychiatric Practice. J Nerv Ment Dis. 2022;210(8):557-63.
12. Hall EJ, Powell RA. Valuing the Spiritual. J Relig Health. 2021;60(3):1430-5.
13. Heelas P. The New Age Movement: The Celebration of the Self and the Sacralization of Modernity. Oxford: Blackwell; 1996, p. 60.
14. Carrette JR, King R. Selling Spirituality: The Silent Takeover of Religion. London, UK: Routledge; 2004. p. 41.
15. Mercadante LA. Belief without borders: inside the minds of the spiritual but not religious. New York, NY: Oxford University Press; 2014.
16. Wong YLR, Vinsky J. "Speaking from the Margins: A Critical Reflection on the 'Spiritual-but-not-Religious' Discourse in Social Work". Brit J Soc Work. 2009;39(7):1343-59.
17. Sangaramoorthy T, Carney MA. Immigration, Mental Health and Psychosocial Well-being. Med Anthropol. 2021;40(7):591-7.

CHAPTER 3

Neuroscience of Spirituality

E Mohan Das, Avinash De Sousa, Russell D'Souza

INTRODUCTION

What is spirituality and religion?

The word spirituality originated from *spiritualitas* (breath) is a complex phenomenon often mixed with religiosity. Both these phenomena are quite different. One can be spiritual without being religious and vice versa. Spirituality is a *"felt-sense"* or medium whereby individuals seek and express meaning and purpose by way of connecting to the moment, self, others, nature, and to the transcendent sacred figure which they believe in. Spirituality encompasses multiple positive emotions which provide a sense of inner peace and harmony. The positive emotions include love, hope, joy, compassion and empathy, trust, forgiveness, gratitude, and awe reflecting mainly the concept of eudemonic happiness.[1] Multiple cortical and subcortical structures are involved in spirituality.

Religion is derived from the Latin word *religare* (to bind together) which refers to an organized system of beliefs and practices. The degree of adherence to the organized religion is called religiosity or religious involvement.[2]

The chapter outlines an integrated overview of the neurobiology of spirituality incorporating neural substrates (although overlapping) of positive emotions.

What are spiritual practices?

Spiritual practices (activities associated with cultivating spirituality) include prayers, meditation, yoga, chanting, religious worship, and rituals. Spiritual experiences described are feeling of transcendence, tranquility or quietude, sense of joy and pleasure, feeling of detachment, feeling of union with God, visual experiences, analgesia, mystical and trance states. In extreme stages of spiritual practices, psychotic states may surface. Spiritual practices enhance physical functioning, self-esteem, drug compliance, and longevity. Beneficial effects of spiritual-religious practices have been seen documented to have anxiolytic, antidepressant, antisuicidal, and anticraving effects. Increased self-esteem and hope generated by spiritual exercises promote better functional ability and perceived health.[3]

SPIRITUALITY AND NEUROSCIENCE

Neurotheology or spiritual neuroscience is a discipline focusing on the neurological processes underlying spirituality, faith, mysticism, meditation, religiosity, and beliefs. The spiritual practices and experiences may reflect specific cognitive mechanisms. Neural explanations have been advanced in meditative practices and yoga. However, recent attempts focus on specific networks especially the frontopolar network and default mode network. Ferguson and co-workers (2022) have proposed a common brain circuit centered on the periaqueductal gray.[4] Considering multiple positive emotional phenomena embracing spirituality, various brain areas and multiple networks are involved.[5]

POSITIVE EMOTIONS AND NEURAL SIGNATURES

Love

Love encompasses at least three motivational behaviors—lust, attraction, and attachment. Over time passionate love may turn to compassionate love. Romantic love, maternal love, and compassionate love may underlie different neural mechanisms. Reward and motivation circuitries underpinning the neurobiology of love involve multiple brain areas like ventral tegmental area (VTA), nucleus accumbens, amygdala, hippocampus, and the orbitofrontal cortex (OFC). The amygdala assesses the pleasurable or aversive nature of experience.[6] The hippocampus records memories of an experience, including where, when, and with whom it occurred. The frontal cortex especially OFC and cingulate coordinates and processes all information and consequently determines the ultimate behavior. The striatum (caudate nucleus, putamen, and globus pallidus) responds to sexual arousal. Hypothalamic activation specific to romantic love could reflect the component of erotic arousal inherent to this sentiment. The inhibition of sympathoadrenal and stress response activity (HPA axis activity) via oxytocin engages in the formation of social attachment. Social interactions and attachments then activate endocrine or autoregulatory signaling systems that can further reduce stress and the related autonomic nervous system's involvement, thereby accounting for health benefits from loving relationships.[7] Compassionate love may involve the orbital part of the left inferior frontal gyrus, right cerebellum, bilateral middle temporal gyrus, bilateral insula, and the right caudate nucleus.[8]

Empathy

Empathy is a multi-faceted construct. Empathy is the ability to feel into. Empathy is a visceral feeling what another feels. Affective empathy is isomorphic to another person's affective state, elicited by the observation or imagination of another person's affective state. Cognitive empathy (perspective-taking) refers to the ability to recognize and understand another's mental state [part of theory of mind (ToM) or mentalizing].[9] Affective perceptual empathy involves areas like right dorsal anterior cingulate cortex, right anterior insula, right dorsomedial thalamus, and midbrain. Cognitive evaluative empathy recruits left OFC, left anteromedial cingulate, and left dorsomedial thalamus. In short, empathy involves multiple brain areas—inferior frontal gyrus, anterior cingulate, somatosensory cortex, amygdala, and insula. Mirror neuron system [posterior inferior frontal gyrus, lowest part of primary motor cortex, superior temporal sulcus (STS), inferior parietal lobule (IPL), and occipital area)] may be one of the operational mechanisms of empathy.[10] Empathy is the gateway to compassion.

COMPASSION

Compassion involves feeling for a person who is suffering and being motivated to act to help them. Researchers describe compassion as a cognitive, affective, and behavioral process involving five components, viz., recognizing suffering; understanding the universality of suffering in human experience; feeling empathy for the person suffering and connecting with the distress (emotional resonance); tolerating uncomfortable feelings aroused in response to the suffering person (e.g., distress, anger, and fear) so remaining open to and accepting of the person suffering; and motivation to act/acting to alleviate suffering.[11] Compassion recruits further brain areas than empathy: medial frontal cortex, subgenual anterior cingulate, ventral striatum including nucleus accumbens, globus pallidus, putamen, and VTA[12] **(Box 1)**.

Forgiveness

Activation specifically of the right angular gyrus of the temporoparietal junction. Empathy and forgiveness involve the activation of the left precuneus, the left superior frontal gyrus, right orbitofrontal gyrus, and posterior cingulate. Spirituality may enhance empathetic and forgivability judgments which might be helpful for evaluation of the self and others.[14]

BOX 1: Structures involved in the mirror neuron system.[13]

Brain structures involved in the mirror neuron system:

- Posterior IFG (BA 44, Broca's)
- Lowest part of primary motor cortex
- Superior temporal sulcus (STS)
- Inferior parietal lobule (IPL)
- Occipital area
- Primary motor cortex
- Supplementary motor area
- Amygdala

Morality and Trust

Moral cognition involves diverse cortical regions, viz., the anterior prefrontal cortex (aPFC), the medial and lateral orbitofrontal cortex (OFC: mOFC and lOFC), and dorsolateral prefrontal cortex (mostly the right hemisphere), the anterior temporal lobes (aTL) and the superior temporal sulcus (STS). Subcortical structures are also involved, viz., amygdala, ventromedial hypothalamus, septal area and nuclei, basal forebrain (especially the ventral striatum/pallidum and extended amygdala), and brainstem tegmentum. Positive decision to trust employs caudate and anterior paracingulate cortex whereas negative decision to distrust involves prefrontal cortex, insula, and amygdala[15] **(Table 1)**.

Gratitude

Ratings of gratitude would correlate with brain activity in circuits associated with moral cognition (medial prefrontal cortex, anterior cingulate cortex) with reward from the pleasure of receiving a benefit in social interactions (ventromedial prefrontal cortex) with social cognitive processes such as perspective-taking and theory of mind (dorsal medial prefrontal cortex) and basic emotion (insula).[16]

TABLE 1: Overlapping brain areas in morality and empathy.

Brain structures overlapping in morality and empathy:		
Theory of mind	*Empathy*	*Mirror neuron system*
• Inferior frontal gyrus • Orbitofrontal cortex • Superior temporal sulcus • Inferior parietal lobule • Precuneus	• Inferior frontal gyrus • Anterior cingulate cortex • Somatosensory area • Amygdala • Insula	• Inferior frontal gyrus • Superior temporal sulcus • Inferior parietal lobule • Occipital cortex • Primary motor cortex

Happiness/Joy

Spirituality envisages eudemonic happiness by finding meaning and purpose. Hedonic happiness is the pursuit of pleasure and the avoidance of pain. Major hotspots for pleasure are the rostro-dorsal part of the medial shell in nucleus accumbens and posterior ventral pallidum. Putative areas include mid OFC, insular cortex, and parabrachial nucleus of dorsal pons.[17]

NEURAL CIRCUITS INVOLVED IN SPIRITUALITY (TABLE 2)

Frontal Lobes

The frontal lobe, especially the prefrontal cortex (PFC), mediates both the preparedness of religious experience and conscious cognitive process involved in the appreciation of religious experience.[18] PFC is primarily concerned with executive functions. Certain prosocial behaviors such as empathy, perspective taking, forgiveness, and theory of mind (ToM) involve the PFC. Decision making and impulse control are also under the control of PFC. Afferent connections of dorsolateral prefrontal cortex (DLPFC) are from dorsofrontal and parietal area. Dorsal parafascicular thalamus, medial pars compacta of substantia nigra, raphe nucleus, and central midbrain tegmentum send afferent projections to DLPFC.[19]

Orbitofrontal cortex receives afferent inputs from superior temporal area, entorhinal cortex, amygdala, rostromedial parafascicular thalamus, medial pars compacta of substantia nigra, raphe nucleus, and central midbrain tegmentum. The medial PFC (mPFC) along with the posterior cingulate participates in self-reflective thought and this helps the person to have an insight into his own experience and the perception of self in relation to the divine being.[20]

The anterior cingulate cortex (ACC) has bidirectional connections with the prefrontal, premotor, motor cortical regions, and medial temporal cortical regions. In the medial temporal cortex, ACC is connected with the entorhinal cortex, and perirhinal cortex. In addition, it projects to the molecular layer of the CA1 subfield of Ammon's horn. ACC has four components with specific roles, viz., anterior (involved in executive functions), posterior (evaluative functions), dorsal (cognitive function), and ventral (emotional functions). ACC is involved in regulating autonomic functions and rational cognitive functions (reward anticipation, decision-making, empathy, error detection, anticipation of tasks, motivation, conflict monitoring, and reward-based learning).[21]

Neuroimaging studies have demonstrated activation of PFC during meditative/ spiritual practices. PFC provides cautious rationality to the emotional experiences surfacing from limbic system mastery. Religious experiences are cognitive processes, mediated by a pre-established neural circuit, involving DLPFC, dorsomedial frontal and medial parietal cortex.[22] The preparedness for religious experiences is mediated by the dorsomedial frontal cortex. The experience becomes religious by conscious identification of the experience. This cognitive process most probably involves the DLPFC and medial parietal cortex. The mPFC is needed to maintain balanced religious activities.[23]

Temporal Lobes

The temporal lobe is integral to auditory perception, receptive components of language, visual memory, declarative (factual) memory, and emotion. The role of temporal lobe inferred from the observation that temporal lobe epilepsy is characterized by religious experiences as part of the ictus

TABLE 2: Brain structures involved in spirituality.

Brain structure	*Role in spirituality*
• Ventral tegmental area (VTA) • Nucleus accumbens • Amygdala • Hippocampus • Orbitofrontal cortex (OFC)	Neural and reward circuits involved in the neurobiology of love
• Right dorsal anterior cingulate cortex • Right anterior insula • Right dorsomedial thalamus • Midbrain	Affective perceptual empathy
• Left orbitofrontal cortex • Left anteromedial cingulate • Left dorsomedial thalamus	Cognitive empathy
• Medial frontal cortex • Subgenual anterior cingulate cortex • Ventral striatum • Nucleus accumbens • Globus pallidus and putamen • Ventral tegmental area	Neural circuits that involve compassion
• Left precuneus • Left superior frontal gyrus • Right orbitofrontal gyrus • Posterior cingulate • Left angular gyrus	Circuits that involve empathy and forgiveness
• Anterior prefrontal cortex (aPFC) • Medial and lateral orbitofrontal cortex • Dorsolateral prefrontal cortex (right) • Anterior temporal lobes (aTL) • Superior temporal sulcus (STS) • Amygdala, ventromedial hypothalamus, septal area and nuclei, basal forebrain • Brainstem tegmentum	Neural circuits that involve morality and trust
• Medial prefrontal cortex • Anterior cingulate cortex	Moral cognition
• Ventromedial prefrontal cortex • Dorsolateral prefrontal cortex	Gratitude and its neural circuits
• Rostro-dorsal part of the medial shell in nucleus accumbens • Posterior ventral pallidum • Orbitofrontal cortex • Insular cortex • Parabrachial nucleus of dorsal pons	Neurobiology of happiness and joy
Dorsomedial prefrontal cortex	Preparedness for religious experiences
Medial prefrontal cortex	Balance of religious activity
Temporal lobe activation—medial	Hyper-religiosity
Precuneus and posterior cingulate cortex	Empathetic judgement and theory of mind
Reticular nucleus of thalamus	Focus and attention in meditative states

and the inter-ictal behavior. Activation of temporal cortical areas (left) is associated with hyper-religiosity in TLE.[24] Reported literature suggests that greater number of temporal lobe signs, like those associated with TLE (temporal lobe epilepsy), occur in normal individuals who hold above-average beliefs in spiritual and paranormal phenomena and/or are more prone to paranormal or transcendental experiences. Psychophysiological ictal phenomena, like hallucinations, dejà vu, depersonalization etc., are tagged to limbic system activation. The limbic marker hypothesis states that limbic system tags ordinary experiences as profoundly important, as detached, as united into a whole, and as joyous experiences. These form the basis of religious experience. Despite the evidence pointing to a temporal lobe involvement, there is no literature which shows that lesions or removal of temporal lobe resulted in a change in religious activity.[25]

Amygdala–Hippocampus Complex

Amygdala engages in emotional processing, fear conditioning, emotional memory, implicit processing and unconscious memory, and modulation of cognitive functions, such as attention, perception, and explicit memory. The central nucleus of amygdala (CeA) controls the behavioral (freezing), autonomic, and endocrine responses through its influence on hypothalamus.[26] Hippocampus participates in the formation of declarative memories. Physiological arousal, a component of emotion, affects hippocampal processing of memory. Moderate arousal can improve memory, but extreme arousal will impair memory. The hippocampal stimulation decreases cortical arousal and responsiveness.[27] The partial deafferentation of the right PSPL during meditation results in the stimulation of the right hippocampus which in turn influences the right lateral amygdala. Overstimulated amygdala becomes hyperactive leading to emotional intensity. This influences hypothalamic activity reflected by changes in autonomic nervous system (ANS). Sympathetic activation prepares the body for action. The meditative/spiritual activity results in parasympathetic overdrive leading to relaxation and tranquility (right lateral amygdala stimulating ventromedial hypothalamus). The sympathetic system is activated but to a lesser degree than parasympathetic, leading to raised perceptual sensitivity. However, in certain frenzied mystical states and possession states, there may be a sympathetic overdrive (via lateral hypothalamus). When sympathetic and parasympathetic systems fire simultaneously at maximum levels, a state of cosmic or "God" consciousness or probably "nirvana", or "anandamaya" may be attained.[28]

Parietal Cortex

Parietal cortex represents somatosensory cortex (primary and secondary), precuneus, parietal operculum, parietal lobules (superior and inferior), and angular gyrus. The posterior–superior parietal lobule (PSPL), a part of complex attentional network including PFC and thalamus, participates in the analysis and integration of higher order visual, auditory, and somesthetic information.[29] The PSPL helps construct a complex three-dimensional image of the body in space. These functions help distinguish self and the external world and a deafferentation of PSPL may result in an altered perception of self-experience during spiritual practices. Precuneus may be a part of the neural network subserving self-awareness and conscious experience. Precuneus together with the posterior cingulate cortex is specifically involved in processing intentions related to perspective-taking thereby playing a role in empathic judgment and theory of mind.[30]

Thalamus

The PFC activates the thalamus, especially the reticular nucleus of the thalamus during spiritual experiences. Thalamic reticular nucleus, a thin lamina of neurons located between thalamus and cortex, functions as an attentional gate, which regulates the flow of information between the thalamus and cortex. The reticular nucleus regulates thalamocortical transmission and the contents of consciousness.[31] The thalamus mediates the flow to the cortex of visuospatial information. When excited, the reticular nucleus via inhibitory GABAergic (gamma-aminobutyric acid) projections cuts the input via the lateral geniculate body (LGB) and the lateral posterior nucleus (LPN) to the striate cortex and the PSPL (especially right). This functional deafferentation enhances the sense of focus during meditation.[32]

NEUROCHEMISTRY OF SPIRITUALITY

Dopamine is associated with the gating of cortical-subcortical interactions, leading to an overall decrease in readiness for action that is associated with spiritual practices. Dopamine is integral to the reward pathway and plays a role in the positive emotional states associated with religious-spiritual practices. Changes in DA (dopamine) levels are positively correlated with variations in religiosity. Hypodopaminergic state in parkinsonism is associated with significant loss of religiosity. The mesoaccumbens DA system involved in reward circuits may influence the positive effects of spiritual practice.[33]

Research has reported activation of DA receptors in the striatum during meditation using [11C]Raclopride. Decrease in binding of injected [11C]Raclopride during meditation reflected the greater occupancy of DA receptors.[34] Repeat alleles of the dopamine D4 receptor gene (DRD4) were also correlated with spiritual acceptance.[35] The valine allele of COMT (catechol-O-methyltransferase), which confers higher levels of enzyme activity with the resultant decrease in extrasynaptic DA, is correlated with lower activity of DLPFC. Valine/methionine (Val/Met) COMT polymorphism has been correlated positively with suggestibility. However, a recent study of paranormal experience and COMT DA gene could not find any correlation with different COMT genotypes.[36]

During meditation, lateral hypothalamic activation releases serotonin through the raphe nucleus. $5HT_{2A}$ receptors are abundant in cortex, claustrum, and basal ganglia, whereas $5HT_{1A}$ receptors are rich in the hippocampus, septum, and amygdala. Reduced 5HT receptor density has been correlated inversely with self-transcendence a personality trait associated with spirituality.[37] Serotonergic deficiencies are associated with extreme religious beliefs and practices that resemble OCD symptoms and antiserotonergic drugs create mystical states and religious experiences. Extreme stages of spiritual practices may activate cortical $5HT_{2A}$ receptors. This activation along with its interplay on thalamocortical circuits leads to sensory flooding, cognitive fragmentation, and ego dissolution (psychotic phenomena). $5HT_{1A}$ activation may also contribute to the hallucinogenic effect.[38]

Melatonin surge during meditation is the result of lateral hypothalamic activation on pineal gland. Melatonin may partly account for the calmness and decreased pain observed during meditation.[39] Acetylcholine may enhance attentional processing and spatial orientation during progressive deafferentation of input to PSPL. However, the exact variation in acetylcholine during spiritual practices is not clear. Parasympathetic overdrive dampens PGN (paragigantocellular nucleus) and thereby reduces firing of LC. This results in reduced noradrenaline.[40]

Alteration of amino acid neurotransmitter levels may occur during meditation. The increased PFC activity produces an increase in the level of free synaptic glutamate in the brain. NAA (*N*-acetylaspartate) is a direct precursor for the enzymatic synthesis of the neuron-specific dipeptide *N*-acetylaspartylglutamate (NAAG), the most concentrated neuropeptide in the human brain. NAA in neuronal tissue can serve as a large reservoir for replenishing glutamate in times of rapid or dynamic signaling demands and stress. Glutamate activates the *N*-methyl-*D*-aspartate receptors (NMDARs). When NMDAR activation reaches a threshold, the brain might limit the production of *N*-acetylated-ά-linked-acidic dipeptidase, the enzyme that converts NAAG to glutamate. This prevents excitotoxicity. However, NAAG accumulation may contribute to dissociative, mystical, or psychotic states. Reticular nucleus activation may increase GABA.[41]

Parasympathetic activation, dampening PGN, leads to reduced LC (locus coeruleus) firing of the paraventricular nucleus (PVN) of the hypothalamus. This results in a decrease of CRH (corticotropin-releasing hormone) and cortisol. The decreased baroreceptor stimulation during parasympathetic overdrive may disinhibit the supraoptic nucleus, leading to the release of arginine vasopressin (AVP). AVP may have a role in arousal and learning mechanisms. Release of β-endorphin (BE) secondary to increased glutamate levels may contribute to euphoria and analgesia.

CONCLUSION

The neurobiology of spirituality is a complex and interdisciplinary field that explores the relationship between the brain and spiritual experiences. While spiritual experiences are deeply personal and often tied to cultural and religious beliefs, researchers have sought to understand the neural mechanisms underlying such experiences. It is important to note that the study of spirituality and the brain is still an evolving area, and there is not a single, universally accepted explanation. Some studies suggest that activity in the temporal lobes, particularly the right temporal lobe, may be associated with spiritual experiences while the frontal lobes, responsible for higher cognitive functions such as reasoning and decision-making, are also thought to play a role in shaping spiritual beliefs. Functional imaging studies show changes in activity in areas related to self-awareness, emotion, and perception. The question of whether spirituality is "located" in the brain is complex and does not have a straightforward answer. Spiritual experiences are highly subjective and can involve a wide range of cognitive, emotional, and perceptual aspects. While some researchers have explored the neural correlates of spiritual experiences, it is important to recognize that the nature of spirituality is multifaceted and often extends beyond the confines of specific brain regions.

REFERENCES

1. Lepherd L. Spirituality: Everyone has it, but what is it? Int J Nurs Pract. 2015;21(5):566-74.
2. Koenig HG. Religion, spirituality, and health: a review and update. Adv Mind Body Med. 2015;29(3):19-26.
3. Gottlieb RS. Spirituality: What it is and why it matters. Oxford: Oxford University Press; 2013.

4. Ferguson MA, Frederic LW, Schaper VJ, Cohen A, Siddiqi S, Merrill SM, et al. A Neural Circuit for Spirituality and Religiosity Derived from Patients with Brain Lesions. Biol Psychiatry. 2022;91(4):380-8.
5. Newberg A. Neurotheology: How science can enlighten us about spirituality. New York City: Columbia University Press; 2018.
6. Esch T, Stefano GB. The neurobiology of love. Neuroendocrinol Lett. 2005;26(3):175-92.
7. De Boer A, van Buel EM, Ter Horst GJ. Love is more than just a kiss: a neurobiological perspective on love and affection. Neuroscience. 2012;201:114-24.
8. Esch T, Stefano GB. The neurobiological link between compassion and love. Med Sci Monit. 2011;17(3):RA65.
9. Howe D. Empathy: What it is and why it matters. London: Bloomsbury Publishing; 2012.
10. Engen HG, Singer T. Empathy circuits. Curr Opin Neurobiol. 2013;23(2):275-82.
11. Strauss C, Taylor BL, Gu J, Kuyken W, Baer R, Jones F, et al. What is compassion and how can we measure it? A review of definitions and measures. Clin Psychol Rev. 2016;47:15-27.
12. Davidson RJ. The neurobiology of compassion. In: Germer CK, Siegel RD (Eds). Wisdom and Compassion in Psychotherapy: Deepening Mindfulness in Clinical Practice. New York City: The Guilford Press; 2012. pp. 111-8.
13. Rajmohan V, Mohandas E. Mirror neuron system. Indian J Psychiatry. 2007;49(1):66-9.
14. Farrow TF, Zheng Y, Wilkinson ID, Spence SA, Deakin JW, Tarrier N, et al. Investigating the functional anatomy of empathy and forgiveness. Neuroreport. 2001;12(11):2433-8.
15. Mendez MF. The neurobiology of moral behavior: Review and neuropsychiatric implications. CNS Spectr. 2009;14(11):608-20.
16. Yu H, Gao X, Zhou Y, Zhou X. Decomposing gratitude: Representation and integration of cognitive antecedents of gratitude in the brain. J Neurosci. 2018;38(21):4886-98.
17. Tanzer JR, Weyandt L. Imaging happiness: Meta-analysis and review. J Happiness Stud. 2020;21:2693-734.
18. Muramoto O. The role of the medial prefrontal cortex in human religious activity. Med Hypothes. 2004;62(4):479-85.
19. Rushworth MF, Kolling N, Sallet J, Mars RB. Valuation and decision-making in frontal cortex: one or many serial or parallel systems? Curr Opin Neurobiol. 2012;22(6):946-55.
20. D'Argembeau A. On the role of the ventromedial prefrontal cortex in self-processing: the valuation hypothesis. Front Hum Neurosc. 2013;7:372.
21. Stevens FL, Hurley RA, Taber KH. Anterior cingulate cortex: unique role in cognition and emotion. J Neuropsychiatr Clin Neurosc. 2011;23(2):121-5.
22. Van Elk M, Aleman A. Brain mechanisms in religion and spirituality: An integrative predictive processing framework. Neurosc Biobehav Rev. 2017;73:359-78.
23. Maselko J. The neurophysiology of religious experience. In: Pargament KI, Exline JJ, Jones JW (Eds). APA Handbook of Psychology, Religion, and Spirituality (Vol. 1): Context, theory, and research. Washington, DC: American Psychological Association; 2013. pp. 205-20.
24. Trimble M, Freeman A. An investigation of religiosity and the Gastaut–Geschwind syndrome in patients with temporal lobe epilepsy. Epilepsy Behav. 2006;9(3):407-14.
25. Devinsky O, Lai G. Spirituality and religion in epilepsy. Epilepsy Behav. 2008;12(4):636-43.
26. Rosen JB. The neurobiology of conditioned and unconditioned fear: a neurobehavioral system analysis of the amygdala. Behav Cogn Neurosc Rev. 2004;3(1):23-41.
27. Bartsch T. The Clinical Neurobiology of the Hippocampus: An integrative view (Vol. 151). Oxford: Oxford University Press; 2012.
28. Previc FH. The role of the extrapersonal brain systems in religious activity. Conscious Cogn. 2006;15(3):500-39.
29. Sereno MI, Huang RS. Multisensory maps in parietal cortex. Curr Opin Neurobiol. 2014;24:39-46.
30. Cavanna AE, Trimble MR. The precuneus: a review of its functional anatomy and behavioural correlates. Brain. 2006;129(3):564-83.
31. Pinault D. The thalamic reticular nucleus: structure, function and concept. Brain Res Rev. 2004;46(1):1-31.

32. Manuello J, Vercelli U, Nani A, Costa T, Cauda F. Mindfulness meditation and consciousness: An integrative neuroscientific perspective. Conscious Cogn. 2016;40:67-78.
33. Mohandas E. Neurobiology of spirituality. Mens Sana Monogr. 2008;6(1):63-83.
34. Dewey SL, Smith GS, Logan J, Brodie JD, Fowler JS, Wolf AP. Striatal binding of the PET ligand 11C-raclopride is altered by drugs that modify synaptic dopamine levels. Synapse. 1993;13(4):350-6.
35. Sasaki JY, Kim HS, Mojaverian T, Kelley LD, Park IY, Janušonis S. Religion priming differentially increases prosocial behavior among variants of the dopamine D4 receptor (DRD4) gene. Soc Cogn Affect Neurosc. 2013; 8(2):209-15.
36. Blum K, Thompson B, Oscar-Berman M, Giordano J, Braverman E, Femino J, et al. Genospirituality: Our beliefs, our genomes, and addictions. J Addict Res Ther. 2013; 5(4):162.
37. Karlsson H, Hirvonen J, Salminen JK, Hietala J. No association between serotonin 5-HT1A receptors and spirituality among patients with major depressive disorders or healthy volunteers. Mol Psychiatry. 2011;16(3):282-5.
38. Borg J, Andrée B, Soderstrom H, Farde, L. The serotonin system and spiritual experiences. Am J Psychiatry. 2003;160(11):1965-9.
39. Stehle JH, Von Gall C, Korf HW. Melatonin: a clock-output, a clock-input. J Neuro-endocrinol. 2003;15(4):383-9.
40. Decker AL, Duncan K. Acetylcholine and the complex interdependence of memory and attention. Curr Opin Behav Sci. 2020;32: 21-8.
41. McKenna MC. The glutamate-glutamine cycle is not stoichiometric: Fates of glutamate in brain. J Neurosc Res. 2007;85(15):3347-58.

4 CHAPTER

Spirituality and Science of Consciousness

Soumitra Ghosh, Vijay Gogoi

INTRODUCTION

The constructs of spirituality and consciousness are globally accepted concepts and have recently gained importance in understanding mental health. Conceptualizing the two has garnered considerable confusion and debate. Spirituality is a broad concept that involves a sense of connection to something greater than oneself. It is a deeply personal and subjective experience characterized by a search for meaning, purpose, and a sense of inner peace. It is about understanding the nature of existence and the purpose of life. It often involves exploring morality, ethics, and values and seeking a deeper connection with the universe or a higher power. For many people, spirituality is closely tied to religious beliefs and practices. However, it can also be a more secular pursuit involving meditation, mindfulness, and yoga. Ultimately, it is a way of exploring and understanding the inner self and the relationship between the self and the world around us. It can provide guidance, comfort, and meaning and help individuals develop a more profound sense of purpose and fulfillment. Consciousness, on the other hand, is being aware of one's surroundings, thoughts, emotions, and experiences. At its most basic level, it refers to the subjective experience of being alive and aware. It involves the ability to perceive, process, and respond to external stimuli, as well as the ability to generate thoughts, feelings, and emotions. It is often described as a continuum, ranging from low-level states of awareness, such as sleep and coma, to high-level states of alertness and self-awareness. Many others have divided it into different components, such as sensory consciousness (the ability to perceive and process sensory information), cognitive consciousness (the ability to think and reason), and affective consciousness (the ability to experience emotions). Nevertheless, to date, the nature and origin of consciousness are still the subjects of much debate and research. Some theories suggest that it emerges from complex interactions between different parts of the brain, while others propose it is a fundamental aspect of the universe. But how do the concepts of spirituality and consciousness relate to each other? Are these concepts universal, or do they vary across cultures?

DIVERSE UNDERSTANDING OF THE TWO CONSTRUCTS

Multiple social discourses around spirituality and consciousness exist, with commonalities and differences across international contexts. Western and Eastern concepts differ within these two highly ambiguous domains. Western religious traditions, such as Christianity and Judaism, tend to be theistic, believing in a personal God separate from the individual and focusing on prayer, worship, and devotion. Their spiritual traditions often have a hierarchical structure, with religious authorities such as priests and pastors guiding the spiritual development of their followers. In contrast, many Eastern spiritual practices, such as Buddhism and Taoism, are nontheistic, emphasizing the importance of personal experience and self-realization, with spiritual teachers serving as guides rather than authorities. For consciousness, western philosophical and scientific traditions prioritize analytical thinking and reductionism. They separate the mind from the body and see consciousness as a nonphysical entity. Thus, they focus on the neural and cognitive processes underlying consciousness and often seek to locate consciousness in specific brain regions. However, Eastern philosophical traditions emphasize nondualism, which sees the mind and body as interconnected aspects of a unified whole and sees consciousness as a more expansive and interconnected phenomenon.

Both constructs involve a deep exploration of the nature of subjective experience and the underlying mysteries of existence. They involve a process of self-exploration and introspection, seeking to understand the nature of self and its relationship to the world around us. They recognize the interconnectedness of all things and the nondual nature of reality and offer unique perspectives and tools for self-discovery, growth, and transformation. However, although closely related concepts, they have some differences too. Spirituality focuses on the search for meaning, purpose, and connection with something greater than oneself. It is often approached through religious or philosophical traditions and considered in the context of a particular culture or tradition. On the other hand, consciousness is more concerned with understanding the nature of subjective experience and the workings of the mind. It is often studied through scientific research, which is more universal, such as studies of brain activity, neuroimaging, and other empirical methods. However, there is potential for these two constructs to complement each other. Spirituality can provide insights into the subjective experience of consciousness, while the science of consciousness can provide a deeper understanding of the biological and psychological processes underlying spiritual experiences.

A diverse range of people across various fields of inquiry study spirituality and consciousness with different approaches and theories.[1] Psychologists are interested in studying spirituality and its relationship to mental health, well-being, and personal growth. They focus on understanding the contents of consciousness and the subjective experiences of individuals. Neuroscientists are interested in studying the neural correlates of spiritual experiences, investigating how different brain regions are activated and and relate to other aspects of cognitive function. Philosophers who discuss the nature of the self, and the existence of God, have developed various theories such as dualism, materialism, and panpsychism.

Anthropologists study the cultural and social dimensions of spirituality, including how spiritual beliefs and practices are shaped by cultural context and how they influence social norms and behavior. Sociologists study the role of spirituality in social organization, social stratification, and power dynamics. Cognitive scientists study the cognitive processes that underlie consciousness, such as perception, attention, and memory. Finally, artificial intelligence researchers study consciousness from a computational perspective, trying to understand how to create machines that exhibit consciousness and self-awareness. There are also various programs and institutes which are dedicated to the study of spirituality and consciousness. The Harvard Study of Adult Development is one of the longest-running studies of adult development ever conducted, spanning over 80 years and examining the factors contributing to health and well-being. The Templeton Foundation's Positive Psychology Research Program is on the intersection of spirituality and positive psychology. The National Institute of Health's Center for Complementary and Integrative Health has invested in complementary and alternative medicine research, including many spirituality-related practices.

SCIENCE OF SPIRITUALITY

The relationship between science and spirituality is complex, and there is an ongoing debate about whether science can fully explain spirituality. Some argue that spirituality is a purely subjective and personal experience that cannot be studied scientifically, while others believe the contrary. Researchers have used neuroimaging and other techniques to study the brain activity associated with spiritual experiences such as meditation, prayer, and near-death experiences.[2] They found that different brain regions are activated during spiritual experiences, including the prefrontal cortex, the amygdala, and the insula. Meditation and mindfulness practices are associated with increased activity in the prefrontal cortex, which is involved in attention, decision-making, and self-awareness. Religious experiences and prayer have been linked to increased activity in the limbic system, which involves emotions and memory. Studies also show that spiritual experiences can have a measurable impact on the brain's structure and function. Long-term meditation practice can lead to changes in the brain's gray matter density, particularly in regions associated with attention and emotional regulation. However, the subjective and varied nature of spiritual experiences often limits these studies. Aspects, such as the search for meaning, purpose, and connection with something greater than oneself, may lie beyond the scope of empirical science **(Fig. 1)**.

With the growing interest in the potential benefits of meditation and mindfulness practices for mental health and well-being, newer fields of study that attempt to integrate scientific research methods with various practices have gained popularity. Contemplative practices help develop deep concentration and quieten the mind amidst distractions in everyday life. Contemplative neuroscience is an emerging interdisciplinary field of research on contemplative practices that focuses on complex mental processes, states, and the contemplative context involving historical, cultural, and societal factors. Nevertheless, this, too, is plagued with the fundamental limitation of definitional clarity. One of the evolving concepts of contemplative science involves the metacognitive self-regulatory capacity of the mind (MSRC), which consists of interacting systems and processes of metacognition and attention, emotion regulation, and conceptual processing. Cumulative changes in the MSCM enable shifts in modes of existential awareness (MEA) modulated by motivational/intentional and contextual factors of contemplative practices. These MSRC changes and MEA shifts further modify the autonomic nervous system, mediating their impact on well-being.

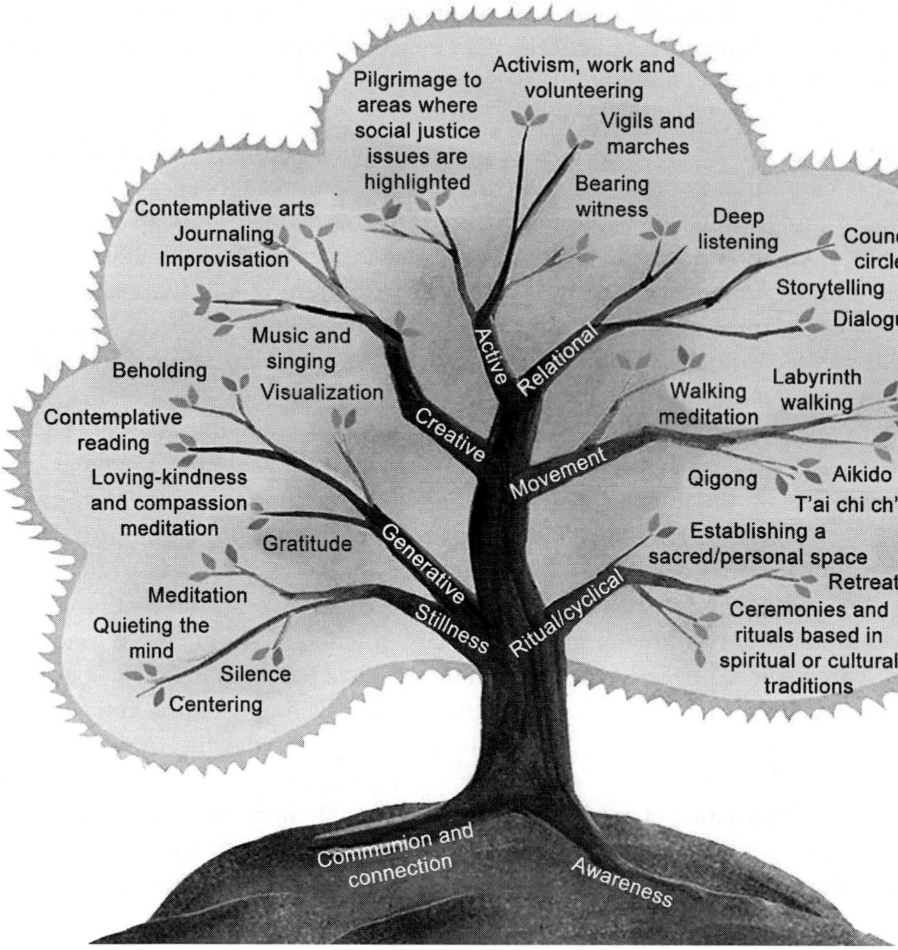

Fig. 1: The tree of contemplative practices.[3]

SCIENCE OF CONSCIOUSNESS

Consciousness too, is a complex and multi-dimensional concept that is difficult to define and measure directly. Several methods have been developed for assessing different aspects of consciousness, including its level, content, and quality. One of the most common ways to measure consciousness is through self-reporting, where individuals report their subjective experiences, thoughts, and feelings using scales or questionnaires. Another way to measure consciousness is by observing people's behavior and responses to stimuli. This might involve testing their ability to perceive and respond to visual or auditory stimuli or assessing their cognitive functions, such as memory and attention. Advances in brain imaging technology have made it possible to measure various aspects of consciousness using techniques, such as functional magnetic resonance imaging (fMRI), electroencephalography (EEG), and magnetoencephalography (MEG). These methods can measure brain activity patterns during sleep, wakefulness, or altered states of consciousness induced by drugs or meditation. In a clinical setting, it can be assessed using standardized neurological tests that measure a person's level of arousal, responsiveness, and orientation, for example, the Glasgow Coma Scale.

However, such techniques often fall short of measuring the myriad forms of consciousness each with its unique features and characteristics.[4] Wakefulness consciousness refers to the state of being awake and alert and is associated with high levels of attention, awareness, and responsiveness to external stimuli. Altered states of consciousness refer to any mental state that differs significantly from the normal waking state, such as sleep, hypnosis, meditation, and drug-induced states. Subliminal consciousness refers to mental processes that occur below the level of conscious awareness, such as automatic responses to stimuli, implicit memory, or nonconscious perception. Higher consciousness refers to expanded awareness and understanding beyond the individual self. It is often associated with spiritual or mystical experiences and is characterized by feelings of interconnectedness, compassion, and transcendence. Collective consciousness refers to the shared beliefs, values, and attitudes that shape a group or society's social identity and behavior. It is often associated with cultural or religious traditions and can influence the way people perceive and respond to the world around them. All these different types of consciousness reflect the complexity and diversity of human experience and highlight how consciousness shapes our perceptions, thoughts, and actions.

Apart from the conceptual understanding, consciousness is also difficult to study for several other reasons. First, consciousness is a subjective experience, meaning it is only accessible through introspection and self-report. This makes it difficult to measure or compare across individuals, as each person's experience of consciousness may be unique and challenging to quantify. Second, it is a multidimensional and dynamic phenomenon involving various cognitive and neural processes. These processes interact in complex ways, making isolating specific components or variables contributing to consciousness difficult. Third, depending on attention, motivation, emotion, and physiology, it can vary across time, context, and individuals. This variability makes it challenging to generalize findings across different contexts or populations. Finally, the brain is a complex and delicate organ, making it difficult to observe or manipulate neural activity associated with consciousness directly. Researchers must rely on indirect measures such as neuroimaging, which can be noisy, expensive, and may have limited spatial or temporal resolution. Despite these challenges, researchers in neuroscience, psychology, philosophy, and other fields continue to develop innovative methods and theories for studying consciousness to understand better the nature of subjective experience, perception, and cognition.

A review article by Takuya Niikawa[5] summarizes the various fundamental questions about consciousness and the scientific approaches to understanding it. The list of questions is categorized using a top-down approach based on traditional philosophical inquiries, while the list of approaches is constructed using a bottom-up approach by classifying existing methods based on methodological differences. The question list includes five fundamental categories: Definitional, phenomenological, epistemological, ontological, and axiological, with each fundamental category divided into more determinate questions. For example, "How should we define consciousness"?,

"What content, dimension, or structure does consciousness have?, "How do we know about our consciousness or others"?, "How is consciousness related in the world"?, or "What type of cognitive, epistemic, moral, or aesthetic value does consciousness enable its possessor to have"?

SCIENTIFIC THEORIES OF CONSCIOUSNESS

Many experiments were conducted to explain the neurobiological basis of consciousness. The Split-Brain Experiments[6] of the 1960s and 1970s, conducted on patients who had undergone split-brain surgery, in which the corpus callosum was severed, provided important insights into the functional differences between the left and right hemispheres of the brain and the role of consciousness in integrating information from both sides. In the 1980s, Benjamin Libet conducted a series of experiments in which participants were asked to make a voluntary movement (such as pressing a button) while their brain activity was monitored. The experiments found a delay between the time participants reported their intention to move and the time when brain activity associated with the movement was detected, suggesting that conscious awareness of the decision to move may arise after the decision has already been made. Near-death experiences (NDEs) are a controversial but fascinating area of research into consciousness. Studies have found that a significant proportion of people who have had NDEs report a range of subjective experiences, such as feelings of peace and transcendence, out-of-body experiences, and encounters with deceased loved ones or spiritual beings. While the exact nature and significance of these experiences are still debated, they provide important insights into the complex relationship between consciousness, the brain, and the wider universe.

The Global Workspace Theory (GWT),[7,8] proposed by Bernard Baars in the 1980s, posits that consciousness arises from integrating information across multiple brain regions, creating a "workspace" in which different types of information can be combined and processed. The global availability of information through this workspace is what we subjectively experience as a conscious state. According to the GWT, consciousness arises when sensory information is distributed and made available to multiple cognitive systems. These systems then collectively process this information, enabling functions like speech, memory recall, and decision-making. The most current understanding is named the Global Workspace Dynamics (GWD), where distinctive evidence-based approaches and theories are proposed that are in sync with each other. Evidence supports the role of corticothalamic systems and views the cortex as a unified oscillatory machine. However, some criticize that this theory or model explains the cognitive part of consciousness but fails to address the hard problem of answering what consciousness is.

The Attention Schema Theory (AST),[9] proposed by neuroscientist Michael Graziano in 2011, suggests that consciousness arises from the brain's ability to generate an attention schema. It states that the brain partly controls attention by constructing a descriptive and predictive attention model. It proposes that three different phenomena are linked by one mechanism. Firstly, attention is controlled by an internal model of attention. Just as the brain generates a body schema to control a specific movement, our brains also generate an attention schema to describe, predict, and control attention as directed toward items. Secondly, attention schema can also be constructed to model the attentional states of other people, thus helping to predict their behavior, similar to a component of the theory of mind. This brain's model of attention supplies information that people claim as consciousness.

Neural Correlates of Consciousness (NCC) is a scientific approach to identifying the specific neural activity associated with consciousness.[10,11] It states that consciousness is closely related to the activity of certain regions of the brain, such as the prefrontal cortex and the thalamus. By studying the neural activity in these regions, researchers may be able to identify the specific activity patterns associated with conscious experiences. Brain imaging techniques, such as fMRI and positron emission tomography (PET), have provided valuable insights into the neural correlates of consciousness. By measuring changes in blood flow and metabolic activity in the brain, researchers can identify the regions of the brain that are active during conscious experiences. For example, studies using fMRI have shown that the prefrontal cortex, which is involved in decision-making and working memory, is highly active during conscious experiences. Other studies have identified activity in the thalamus, which is involved in sensory processing, as well as the parietal cortex, which is involved in spatial awareness and body image. Content-specific NCCs are specific neurons or neuronal mechanisms that determine particular distinctions within an individual's conscious experience. For example, the NCC for experiencing the content of a face are the neurons that activate when a person observes, imagines, or dreams of a face. When artificially stimulated, this can cause the person to perceive a face, even if one is not present, and when blocked, they may not see a face even if one is present. The full NCC or the overall state of being conscious refers to the neural substrates that support conscious experiences as a whole, regardless of their specific content. It encompasses the sets of content-specific NCC for all possible contents of experience. It is important to differentiate the NCC from the background conditions for consciousness, which are factors that enable consciousness but do not directly contribute to its content, such as the presence of glucose and oxygen, the right neuromodulatory environment, and afferent inputs that maintain cortical excitability. However, delineating the neural correlates of every conscious experience is a daunting task. Marek Havlík, in a review article, has tried to describe the neural correlates for three types of consciousness; Background states of consciousness such as being awake, asleep, dreaming, and being in a coma or vegetative state; General stream of consciousness representing a general stream of mental states and ongoing subjective experience; and specific states of consciousness which refer to the specific mental states or contents of consciousness that occur in the stream of consciousness. He postulates that the endogenous activity of the brain and the Default Mode Network (DMN) represents a baseline of brain activity, and neural oscillations in these areas should be an essential component of all consciousness studies. The attempt also highlighted the importance of the precuneus, and posterior cingulum as opposed to the thalamus, which is considered an important area for consciousness.

Despite great advances in neurosciences, there still lies an explanatory gap as to why a particular set of neurons fire to produce a sense of experience while others do not. And this has been called the "*hard problem*" of consciousness. Instead of trying to answer the question as to how the brain creates an experience, the Integrated Information Theory (IIT), proposed by Giulio Tononi,[12,13] takes the other approach, starting by identifying the essential properties of the experiences (axioms) and inferring the properties of physical systems necessary for the properties of the experience (postulates). From these postulates are derived whether a particular system of elements possesses consciousness, how much, and of which kind. According to this theory, the axioms or the essential properties of any experience are (1) its intrinsic existence, meaning that the experience is real and, it is here and now. It exists from an intrinsic perspective and is independent of external observers; (2) composition of the experience with multiple phenomenological distinctions which can be elementary or higher-order, e.g., in one experience, we may identify a book, blue color, a blue book, etc.; (3) axiom of information states that experience is specific, composed of a particular set of phenomenal distinctions (qualia), which make it what it is and different from other experiences; (4) integration which states that experience is unitary and irreducible to noninterdependent, disjoint subsets of phenomenological distinctions. For example, we experience a whole visual scene and not independent experiences of the right or left visual field; (5) exclusion, meaning that the experience is definite in its content and spatiotemporal grain. The phenomenological distinctions are finite and neither less nor more, and they flow at a finite speed, neither slow nor fast. Corresponding to each axiom or essential properties of experience, IIT postulates that a physical substrate has a causal property that accounts for it, and consciousness is the capacity of the system to integrate the information. The theory suggests that the level of consciousness accessible to a system can be quantified by measuring the Φ (phi) value of a complex of elements within that system.[14] Despite significant interests and findings, this theory too is criticized by many as pseudoscience and for lack of evidence. These are just a few of the many theories and models that have been proposed to explain the scientific basis of consciousness. While each theory has its own strengths and weaknesses, they all contribute to our growing understanding of this complex phenomenon.

CONCLUSION

The study of spirituality and the science of consciousness represents an exciting and rapidly evolving field of inquiry. The emergence of contemplative neuroscience has provided a new perspective on the relationship between these two fields and has the potential to transform our understanding of the nature of consciousness and its relationship to the physical world. By integrating scientific research methods with contemplative practices, researchers may gain insights into the neural mechanisms underlying spiritual experiences and the potential benefits of spiritual practices for mental and physical well-being. As research in this field continues to expand, we may be able to unlock new insights into the fundamental nature of existence and human experience. Scientific study of consciousness has made significant progress in recent years, providing a basis for understanding the neural mechanisms that underlie consciousness. While there is still much to be learned about the basis of consciousness, continued research in this field has the potential to shed light on one of the most fundamental aspects of human experience.

REFERENCES

1. Pesut B, Fowler M, Taylor EJ, Reimer-Kirkham S, Sawatzky R. Conceptualising spirituality and religion for healthcare. J Clin Nurs. 2008;17(21):2803-10.
2. Mohandas E. Neurobiology of Spirituality. Mens Sana Monogr. 2008;6(1):63-80.
3. CMind. (2021). The Tree of Contemplative Practices. The Center for Contemplative Mind in Society. [Online] Available from https://www.contemplativemind.org/practices/tree [Last accessed December, 2024].
4. Bayne T, Hohwy J, Owen AM. Are There Levels of Consciousness? Trends Cogn Sci. 2016;20(6):405-13.
5. Niikawa T. A Map of Consciousness Studies: Questions and Approaches. Front Psychol. 2020;11:530152.
6. de Haan EHF, Corballis PM, Hillyard SA, Marzi CA, Seth A, Lamme VAF, et al. Split-Brain: What We Know Now and Why This is Important for Understanding Consciousness. Neuropsychol Rev. 2020;30(2):224-33.
7. Baars BJ, Geld N, Kozma R. Global Workspace Theory (GWT) and Prefrontal Cortex: Recent Developments. Front Psychol. 2021; 12:749868.
8. Bartolomei F, Naccache L. The global workspace (GW) theory of consciousness and epilepsy. Behav Neurol. 2011;24(1):67-74.
9. Wilterson AI, Kemper CM, Kim N, Webb TW, Reblando AMW, Graziano MSA. Attention control and the attention schema theory of consciousness. Progress in neurobiology. 2020;195:101844.
10. Overgaard M. The Status and Future of Consciousness Research. Front Psychol. 2017;8:1719.
11. Rees G. Neural correlates of consciousness. Ann N Y Acad Sci. 2013;1296(1):4-10.
12. Koch C. What Is consciousness? Nature. 2018;557(7704), S8-12.
13. Tononi G, Boly M, Massimini M, Koch C. Integrated information theory: from consciousness to its physical substrate. Nat Rev Neurosci. 2016;17(7):450-61.
14. Seth AK, Izhikevich E, Reeke GN, Edelman GM. Theories and measures of consciousness: an extended framework. Proc Natl Acad Sci U S A. 2006;103(28):10799-804.

5 CHAPTER

Spirituality for Self-development and Positive Mental Health

Sujatha D Sharma, Manasi Sharma

INTRODUCTION

Historical Background

Mankind's relationship with religion and spirituality (R/S) in their multifarious aspects, is deeply intertwined with the history of humanity itself. Both have evolved out of an overarching need for humans to understand their inner self, the meaning, and purpose of their existence, and sometimes also, how a connection with a higher power impacts that meaning. Religious and spiritual themes have been recurrent aspects of art, architecture, and lifestyle practices across cultures and societies. These themes have persisted and evolved across centuries and played an influential role in shaping the history of mankind and the world as it currently exists. While early philosophers explored these issues in their seminal works, psychologists such as William James, and Carl Jung, and humanists such as Victor Frankl, emphasized the spiritual dimension of human nature in their work, including the basis for suffering and striving, while examining the human psyche, and its manifestations in health, well-being, and pathology.

The early 20th century saw scientific growth in the fields of psychology and psychiatry, in understanding etiology, diagnosis, and treatment of mental disorders. These fields adopted the existing scientific paradigm that emphasized rigorous methodology in the observation and measurement of constructs. Thus, the insight and possible contribution from the fields of R/S were ignored by mainstream mental health studies and were seen as being in conflict with it.[1] Moreover, the complexities involved in constructing a universal understanding of R/S concepts and their interplay in impacting human behavior led to its denigration to the sidelines in the fields of psychology, psychiatry, and the neurosciences. This has been compounded by the fact that R/S cannot be easily reduced to simple and observable scientific constructs and is hence perceived to be beyond the scope of rigorous empirical study.

Later, with the advent of humanism-existentialism schools of psychology in the mid-1900s, spearheaded by Abraham Maslow, Carl Rogers, and Victor Frankl, psychology moved away from a focus on psychopathology towards models of growth, self-actualization, and positive mental health.[2-4] These paved the way for the emergence of newer movements in psychology and mental health that included transpersonal psychology and positive psychology.[5] The former explored the integration of spiritual and transcendent aspects of human experience or going beyond the individual self to encompass wider aspects of humankind and the cosmos.[6] The latter movement gained momentum with the work of Seligman and Csikszentmihalyi, which focused on the positive aspects of individuals and mandated the scientific study of "optimal human functioning," building upon the themes of earlier humanists, William James and Abraham Maslow.[7] Positive psychology examines the interface of positive mental states and various forms of well-being and also discusses the role of spirituality and transcendence in promoting well-being. These historical and foundational antecedes have opened the doors for the study of R/S constructs that contribute to individual and societal mental health and well-being.

CONCEPTUAL DEFINITIONS OF RELIGION AND SPIRITUALITY

Though often used together, and sometimes interchangeably, R/S are two very distinct, yet closely related constructs that are not entirely congruent. They can vary from highly personalized beliefs and practices to more collectivist and organized forms of instruction and systems. While religion typically implies social norms, beliefs, traditions, rituals, and ceremonies, spirituality has been seen to encompass deep-seated and holistic values, beliefs, experiences, and practices.[9] Both have overlapping characteristics as well, including giving a sense of purpose, belonging, support, and a way of life for the betterment of society. Although we use the collective term R/S throughout this chapter, we will define the concepts individually in this section and highlight key differences in their conceptualizations that should be noted.

Overall, spirituality is considered as something broader and more personal with religion being more institutional and communal. Religion is viewed by many as community-based spirituality, that also allows rites, rituals, and communal worship, whereas spirituality is very much rooted in individualistic thought and practice.[10,11] Both have generally been considered as having tremendous implications for the health and well-being of individuals and societies. They are available to anyone regardless of age, gender, income, social class, or other life circumstances.

Spirituality has been defined in various ways. It has been described as the personal quest for understanding the ultimate questions about life, meaning in life, and one's relationship with the sacred or transcendent.[12] It is also viewed as giving humanity its "humanism" and as giving meaning and direction to a person's life and as such, includes vital dimensions like the quest for purpose, self-transcending knowledge, meaningful relationships, love, and commitment, as well as (for some) a belief in and search for a sacred holy power higher than oneself.[13-16] More recent conceptualizations of spirituality describe it as a search for a universal truth, as an activity that leads people to discover meaning and significance in the world around them.[17] Spirituality has also been defined as experiencing transcendence through inner peace, harmony, and connectedness to others.[18] Spirituality has even been considered a personality trait, such that a greater degree of spirituality was related to better mental health, specifically reflected in lowered levels of neuroticism and greater extraversion.[19] These authors are of the view that spirituality may foster the mental health of people by making them less self-centered and more connected with a larger whole. Some individuals, however, have been known to possess and embody transcendent powers, which may go beyond the ambit of empirical study.

Religion on the other hand is seen as a shared set of institutional or communal beliefs, experiences, practices, and traditions related to a sacred God or transcendent higher power.[10] Thus, it is seen as often being practiced in a community, usually based on a specific set of rules and customs, often focusing on a belief in deities, gods, religious texts, and rituals. In religion, the organized and shared system of beliefs and practices through rituals and symbols may enable individuals to experience the transcendent.[9] Religiousness has also been studied as a cultural adaptation of personality traits, specifically agreeableness and conscientiousness, supported by a meta-analysis across 19 countries and regardless of age, gender, and context.[20]

In this chapter, we use 'Religion' as an umbrella term encompassing a broad array of sociocultural systems and faiths such as Christianity, Islam, Hinduism, Buddhism, Judaism, Bahá'í, Taoism, Confucianism, Jainism, Sikhism, Zoroastrianism, and traditional, indigenous, and folk religions (including African and Native American religions), along with several other religious sects. Each of these has a distinct set of beliefs and systems, however, we will be discussing the associations between religion, spirituality, and mental health in the broader sense, rather than specific sects.

CONCEPTUAL DEFINITIONS OF POSITIVE PSYCHOLOGY, POSITIVE MENTAL HEALTH, AND WELL-BEING

Before we delve into how R/S is associated with mental health and well-being, it is imperative to first understand these multi-dimensional concepts.

Positive Psychology

Although the current definition of mental health considers it more than the absence of mental illness, but rather a state of psychosocial well-being, the historical underpinnings of these concepts are complex. In the latter part of the 20th century, the fields of psychology and psychiatry were primarily focused on delineating, diagnosing, and treating mental illness, virtually ignoring the positive aspects of mental health and subjective well-being. It was Martin Seligman's clarion call for a "positive psychology" that would eventually set the stage for a scientific movement to readdress the imbalance in the prevailing notions of the psychology of illness and health.[7,21] Echoing the calls of his predecessors such as William James, Abraham Maslow, and Carl Rogers for psychology to move towards studying the positive aspects of human growth and potential as important aspects of positive mental health, Seligman is credited with catalyzing the field of positive psychology in 1998.[22] Positive Psychology is the field of psychological theory and research that focuses on individual traits or character strengths (e.g., intimacy, wisdom, integrity, and altruism), psychological states (e.g., contentment, joy), and social institutions that enhance subjective well-being and make life worth living.[23] It has been described as the study of conditions and processes that determine optimal human functioning and overall flourishing across individuals, communities, and contexts.[24] It also is the study of what helps people develop and nurture these positive attributes, psychological assets, and strengths. Its aim is to understand and foster the factors that allow individuals, communities, and societies to face hardships with resilience and thrive.[25] Thus, positive psychology has served to shift attention away from pathology, disease, and dysfunction in mental health to positive emotions, resilience, and optimal functioning. This shift has also catalyzed the field of mental health promotion as an integral feature of health promotion practices.[26]

Positive Mental Health

Common to both, mental health promotion and positive psychology, is the focus on 'positive mental health' including psychological assets and skills to promote and achieve a state of well-being.[27,28] Hence, positive psychology strategies would serve well to engage in public health interventions that would have positive mental health and well-being as desired outcomes.[25] According to the World Health Organization, positive mental health is viewed as a positive effect, a feeling of happiness that encompasses self-control, self-esteem, resilience in the face of adversity, the capacity to cope with life stressors, and productivity and contributions to society.[29] It is an overall state of well-being, pervasive across physical, psychological, social, and spiritual dimensions, and indicating a state of "flourishing," adequate management of stress, a realization of one's potential, being consistently productive, and having high life satisfaction. One of the earliest postulations of the concept of positive mental health came from Marie Jahoda in 1958 in her book "*Current Concepts of Positive Mental Health*" wherein she has described six major dimensions that characterized it as: attitudes towards the self; individual style and degree of growth; integration of personality; autonomy; perception of reality; and environmental mastery.[30] As these early concepts were considered too narrow in their scope, researchers expanded and modified Jahoda's conceptualization to include personality and coping styles;[31] a subjective sense of well-being;[32] love, wisdom, socio-emotional intelligence, and resilience;[33] or as a "salutogenic" approach focusing on optimism and coping skills employed.[34,35]

Well-being

Well-being, a key concept in positive psychology, manifests as a state of feeling healthy, happy, peaceful, and purposeful. Empirical studies of positive mental health concepts have identified two key dimensions of well-being as: (1) The "Hedonic' component that views well-being as the maximization of positive feelings and minimization of negative feelings and (2) the "Eudaimonic" component, which comprises of positive functioning and engagement leading to social well-being.[28,36-38] The term subjective well-being has been widely used in positive psychology to indicate high levels of positive affect, low levels of negative affect, and a high degree of satisfaction with one's life, and resonates with the hedonistic approach.[39] In contrast, the concept of psychological well-being, wherein people function to their maximum potential, is consonant with the concept of eudaimonism.[38,40]

Psychological or eudaimonic well-being, a determinant of positive mental health, has been conceived of having six components—autonomy, environmental mastery, personal growth, positive relationships, purpose in life, and self-acceptance.[36] This model of well-being has been subjected to extensive research.[36,37,39,41] It has also been suggested to include the dimension of spiritual well-being into this model.[42,43] It has been argued that while initial theoretical foundations of eudaimonic well-being conceived of the six-dimension model and did not include spirituality due to its nonscientific underpinnings, this omission is misguided and misconceived.[37] Spiritual well-being as a vital component contributing to positive mental health has been conceptualized, not as specific beliefs, practices, or relationships, but rather by the individual's spiritual pathways and destination that work in synchronicity with each other.[8] It has also been defined as being in a state that reflects positive feelings, cognitions, and behaviors in relationships with oneself, others, nature, and the transcendent. This is thought of as providing the individual with a sense of identity, purpose, wholeness, satisfaction, contentment, joy, love, inner peace, and harmony.[44] Similarly, religious/spiritual well-being has been also defined as the ability to experience and integrate purpose and meaning in life through a connectedness with oneself, with others, or with a power greater than oneself.[45]

THE INTERSECTION OF POSITIVE PSYCHOLOGY AND RELIGION/SPIRITUALITY

It is quite evident that both R/S and positive psychology have grappled with similar concepts such as quality of life, virtues, self-development, purpose and meaning of existence, contentment, hope, coping, and so on. Therefore, we can assume that the goals of human development, and psychological, and social well-being overlap and intersect within the fields of R/S and positive psychology.

Well-being, or the harmony of mind, body, and spirit, seems to be closely aligned to R/S. Literature in this burgeoning area of well-being has examined the role of religious/spiritual activities that lead to creating meaning, providing social support, and increasing positive emotions in determining subjective and psychological well-being.[46-48] Studies have also shown how R/S provides a framework for "flow," another aspect of well-being that is described as a subjective state where an individual gets immersed in an activity they are engaged in, oblivious to everything else.[49] Activities that individuals and communities engage in during R/S practices are thought to induce such a flow state.[50]

Studies have found associations between R/S and diverse aspects of well-being including increased hedonic well-being.[51] The overlap and similarities between the fields of positive psychology and R/S make a strong case for their integration, which would help them coevolve and contribute significantly to better scientific inquiry and study their individual and combined benefits to individuals and societies.[52] These authors make a persuasive case for this integration, citing key similarities such as (1) having similar aims advancing the scientific understanding of the human mind and behavior; (2) having similar historical and philosophical origins exploring the role of morality, ethics, and virtues in human flourishing; (3) laying similar emphasis on studying the subjective experiences of individuals and groups that increase resilience and enhance well-being; and (4) focusing on positive emotions, meaning-making, and fostering relationships across settings.[52] They further clarify that their concept of 'integration' does not indicate a merger, but rather fostering interconnections between these fields, to achieve more synergy and collaboration. This integration will mutually benefit both positive psychology and the R/S, as the former already has a substantial presence in empirical science and its applications.[53,54] The latter would benefit from the former's scientific rigor, methods, and measures, while also invigorating the field of positive psychology with its contribution to unraveling concepts such as meaning, identity, growth, and resilience.[55-58] Religion and spirituality can also shed light on how diverse cultures have adopted certain practices to nurture and enhance positive health, emotions, and relational well-being, and develop capacities to cope with adversity.[33,59] Ultimately, such integration would also benefit the field of psychology by creating a strong, diverse, yet unified psychology that enhances knowledge and improves the quality of life.[60]

There has been growing interest in including R/S as a key component in research in positive psychology.[52,61,62] They are gradually acquiring the place it deserves alongside positive psychology. There has been increasing focus on research that explores the relationship between R/S and various health indices as well as their contribution to mental health intervention programs, more specifically through the psychotherapeutic process.[8]

Religion/Spirituality and its Importance to Mental Health and Well-being

The relationship between spirituality, religion, and mental health is multifaceted, complex, and relatively unresearched, yet promising in terms of emerging evidence and growing interest in the significant influence of R/S on people's mental health.[10,11,63] This is not surprising considering how much R/S impacts various aspects of one's life—well-being, life satisfaction, inner stability, life goals, purpose, and our social connectedness with the outer world. It has been found that even after factoring in the influences of variables such as age, gender, and geographic location, those who subscribe to S/R beliefs and practices reported better physical and mental health than those who do not and were better equipped to cope with crisis, stress, and the uncertainties of life.[12] Studies have demonstrated the positive impact of R/S on outcomes such as subjective well-being, health-related quality of life, coping skills, recovery from mental illness, and reduced addictive or suicidal behaviors.[64-67]

A meta-analytic study reviewing the results of 31 studies of spiritual therapies with clients suffering from a variety of mental health problems (anxiety, depression, stress, and eating disorders) provides empirical evidence for the benefits that spiritually-oriented psychotherapy provides.[68] Another meta-analysis of 48 longitudinal studies that looked at the effects of R/S on positive mental health revealed a positive but small effect size for positive functioning (well-being, positive mood, and life satisfaction) and the lack of negative functioning (distress or negative mood).[69] Studies have also indicated the role of R/S in recovery from mental disorders including anxiety and depression,[9,68,70] post-traumatic stress disorder,[71] suicidal behaviors,[72] and schizophrenia.[73,74]

The strong, emergent empirical associations and positive benefits of R/S on psychological well-being, as well as in decreasing the magnitude of psychological distress have led to a healthy trend of integrating spirituality into mental health practice, including psychotherapeutic interventions[75] This can be postulated to happen in two ways. One is the direct and overt use of spiritual and religious practices in therapy, including prayer, meditation, and mindfulness to heal and transform the client.[1] The other is a more indirect approach where the therapist is open to discussion on spiritual issues or concerns that the client wants to bring up on their own.[76]

This awareness of the role and significance of R/S as a possible mediator in the psychotherapeutic process has also led to the birth and evolution of integrative practices such as mindfulness-based cognitive behavior therapy, mindfulness-based stress reduction,[77-79] transpersonal psychotherapy,[80] rational emotive spiritual therapy,[81] and cognitive augmented spiritual therapy.[82] These approaches perhaps go well beyond distress or symptom reduction to self-transformative processes, leading to greater self-awareness and personality growth. In the section below, we describe the role of various positive psychology constructs that have been studied as possible mediators or moderators of the association between R/S and well-being.

SPIRITUALITY AND POSITIVE MENTAL HEALTH: THE ROLE OF KEY MEDIATORS

Religion and spirituality have been described to impact overall health outcomes through the mediational pathways of proximate psychosocial and well-being variables, which affect physiological processes, such as blood pressure, cortisol levels, and immunity.[83] The way in which R/S impacts positive mental health may be through the mediating and moderating role of related concepts such as hope and faith, meaning and purpose in life, social support and connectedness, health-related behaviors, locus of control, coping styles, forgiveness, meditation and mindfulness, emotional regulation, self-actualization, and transcendence.[84-86] A review of the effect of R/S on the mental health of believers in their faith/practice showed that it can promote mental health through positive religious coping, positive beliefs, and community support. There was evidence also for the negative impacts on mental health, mediated by negative beliefs, miscommunication, and negative coping.[87] It additionally appears that R/S increased empowerment through internal resources (feeling of self-worth) and social resources (sense of belonging through community networks).[88] In the following section, we will explore some of these concepts and the pathways through which they influence positive mental health, including findings from evidence-based research.

Meaning and Purpose in Life

The relationship between various aspects of religion, spirituality, and positive mental health may be explained by a sense of purpose and meaning in life. Park and colleagues suggest a meaning systems framework to explain this, whereby people's core beliefs, goals, and values help them interpret their experiences and appraise the importance of objects, states, or people in their lives. These can help create a subjective sense of one's life purpose and connect it to a global understanding of the meaning of life. For some people, R/S forms a core part of their meaning system, influencing their values, beliefs, lifestyle, and goals.[89,90] Moreover, it is postulated that the higher-order need for growth and self-actualization among human beings may be supported by the constructive role of R/S in meeting this need.[91] Consequently, research over decades has linked meaning and purpose in life to reduced suffering, and higher psychological and physical well-being, including happiness and flourishing.[46,87,92,93] Finding a sense of meaning in life has been linked to higher positive affect, optimism, and life satisfaction.[94] Additionally, studies have found that the mediating role of purpose and meaning in life due to R/S was found to be significant during brief religious engagement[46] and persisted with prolonged engagement.[93]

Social Support and Connectedness

Aspects of religious and spiritual life, including attendance at religious events, spiritual talks, meditation practices, group retreats, pilgrimages, services, and ceremonies, all contribute to building social support networks. Importantly, these networks share common beliefs and value systems which increase a sense of connectedness and belonging, as well as a shared devotion to a higher power. There are various dimensions of social support that contribute to this, including the size of the social network, the type and frequency of social interactions, instrumental assistance or the tasks performed by the support network for the individual (such as transport and healthcare), and the individual's satisfaction with the quality of support.[95] A study comparing the mediating effects of secular social support (from friends and family) and religious social support (received from members of the religious congregation) found that although both forms of support were associated with less distress in the sample, only religious social support had a mediating effect on the association between group attendance and reduced distress.[96]

Locus of Control

The manner in which R/S influences mental health may depend on people's attributional style, which may stem from their locus of control.[97] An external locus of control implies a belief that outcomes are determined by external forces such as fate, luck, or figures of authority, whereas those with an internal locus of control believe that outcomes are largely due to their responses and actions and are thought to have a greater perceived sense of personal control.[98] Feelings of little or no control over one's life may be linked to distress, helplessness, and lower life satisfaction, whereas greater internal control over one's life outcomes and decisions may lead to higher self-esteem, mastery, and hope. For R/S however, the relationship may not be as straightforward and linear. While people who are religious or spiritual may have an external locus of control in terms of surrender to a God or Higher power, this may also increase their internal locus of control in terms of strength and resilience to make decisions and have faith and hope for positive outcomes. This implies 'collaborative control' whereby people work with others in their R/S group as well as with their belief in a higher power in order to take proactive action toward outcomes, including positive mental health.[99]

Religious and Spiritual Coping

Further, during times of stress, R/S provides key resources for coping and building coping styles, including reframing negative events using the frameworks provided by one's belief system, meditation and prayer, rites of passage, social support, rituals, and surrendering to a higher power. These forms of religious and spiritual coping have been found to be associated with a range of positive mental health outcomes, beyond the effects of secular coping methods.[100,59] Positive religious coping, wherein individuals resort to religious or spiritual resources to cope with negative life events and setbacks, has been widely investigated and found to have significant positive impacts on mental health and well-being, including for people who have experienced trauma and abuse.[101,102] Religiosity-related personality characteristics (such as agreeableness and conscientiousness) have been found to be uniquely related to cognitive coping styles such as positive reappraisal of difficult situations.[103] Moreover, for those exposed to stressful or traumatic life events that they have little to no personal control over, religious coping may be associated with better adaptive outcomes and reduced negative mental health outcomes.[75]

Self-regulation and Emotional Regulation

It has been found that R/S can help develop key life skills such as self-regulation and self-control, in an effort to build moral and ethical value systems and teach individuals to monitor and regulate their actions for the benefit of society as a whole. Self-regulation and self-control are inherent aspects of R/S, including a disciplined lifestyle and religious rituals like prayer, fasting, and meditation.[104] They proposed that R/S promotes positive life outcomes through the intermediate effects on self-control. Self-regulation is also seen to have an enabling and integral role in cultivating virtues and purposeful living, fostering self-development and well-being.[105] These skills are important in building one's internal locus of control, strength, life satisfaction, and prosocial behaviors, along with personality traits such as conscientiousness and goal motivation, a finding that was consistent across age, gender, country, and religion. [20,104]

Moreover, R/S may increase self-reflection and self-monitoring in daily life, which can lead to increased self-awareness and understanding. This in turn promotes one's self-concept, suggesting the positive impact of self-rumination in mediating happiness.[106] The need to understand the self, and find one's potential for self-development, appears to be mediated through improved self-monitoring that facilitates an awareness of one's mental state. This in turn primes meaningful self-rumination, self-growth, and self-development, accelerating the process of self-regulation.[107]

The other mechanism that may explain these positive impacts on subjective well-being is that of emotional regulation (modulation of emotional states as per environmental demands).[85] R/S may train people to be more evaluative of emotional events through constant cognitive appraisals. It has been found that people with greater religious/spiritual involvement and belief in a "higher power" tend to give more positive appraisals of their lives, despite the adversities they may encounter.[85,86] Yet other studies did not show evidence for the association between R/S and positive/negative affect.[107] Thus, being religious or spiritual does not necessarily influence one's affective experience.

Health-related Behaviors

Self-regulation due to R/S can also manifest as improved health-related behaviors and lifestyle factors, which may contribute to improved psychosocial and physical health outcomes. These may include following a daily routine, sleep hygiene, meditation and prayer, and avoidance of smoking, alcohol, and drug use.[108] Moreover, R/S practices have been associated with increased prosocial behaviors such as volunteering and helping others.[109-111] R/S have also been linked bi-directionally to various health issues including cancer,[112] both as increasing religiosity in them, as well through strong spiritual experiences that enhance life satisfaction over time in survivors, who had low life satisfaction at baseline.[113] Other studies have also enquired into the relationships between R/S and different health outcomes, physical, mental, and subjective well-being, quality of life, coping skills, recovery from mental illness, suicidal ideation, and addictive behaviors.[114]

Positive Emotions (Including Hope, Optimism, and Resilience)

Positive emotions are important psychological resources that a person builds up over time which aid in coping with stress and also lead to enhanced well-being.[115] Furthermore, R/S informs how a person thinks and appraises events that happen in their life and may influence the emotions that the person experiences related to these events.[116] Indeed, many forms of R/S actively elicit positive emotions such as love, peace, contentment, compassion, forgiveness, and gratitude through specific beliefs and practices.

In general, findings of researchers examining the relationships between R/S and positive emotions leading to enhanced coping and psychological well-being, have highlighted the role of daily spiritual experiences, positive religious coping, and religious participation as key aspects related to measures of positive emotions.[117] These authors postulate that their review of studies suggests that healthy R/S is related to increases in both positive emotions and resilience and that these mediators of well-being may also have a reciprocal influence on each other.

The bidirectional nature of the relationship between positive emotions and R/S has been addressed through another recent systematic review.[118] This study demonstrates that R/S practices produce positive emotions by allowing the expression of emotional experiences, such as acceptance of situations, cognitive appraisals, emotional regulation skills, prosocial behaviors, and embodied practices (such as physical motions, gestures, and postures).

Hope and optimism are interconnected positive emotions and indicate an expectation that positive outcomes will occur despite challenges. These concepts are also closely related to resilience, or the ability to bounce back from adversity. R/S may foster an optimistic outlook by providing individuals and communities with a sense of support, a framework for understanding their experiences and the world around them, a tool for coping with stressful situations, and maintaining a positive perspective even in difficult circumstances.[119,120]

Studies have also found that R/S promoted teleological explanations of events that occur in a person's life, including the self-transcendent type, which leads to the experiences of greater positive emotions.[121,85] Thus, from the above evidence, it is clear that positive emotions are consequential and valued by practitioners of R/S. They not only "feel good" but also lead to individual as well as collective well-being.

Self-transcendence

Many authors have stressed the central aspect of R/S as a belief in an absolute reality that is also sacred and transcending,[122] about a feeling that 'something other' than the self can be sacred,[14] and as a search for the sacred and the sacred understood as encompassing "God the divine and the transcendent."[15] Transcendence in this context has been viewed as both taking place within a person (self-realization, self-improvement, and personal development) as well as outside the person, directed to a higher energy or entity.[123] It has been well acknowledged for long that religious or spiritual practices lead to heightened experiences of positive emotions such as love, peace, joy, gratitude, and bliss, giving rise to feelings of self-transcendence and fostering well-being. Through cross-sectional studies, the relationship between R/S and well-being is seen as being mediated by self-transcendent positive emotions.[124] Similarly, it has been shown that spiritual practices such as loving-kindness meditation, increase a person's daily experience of positive emotions compounding over time, which helps build personal resources such as increased mindfulness and purpose in life, which in turn improves life satisfaction and well-being.[125]

It was the landmark work of the early exponents of positive psychology that borrowing from philosophical, religious, and cultural texts, proposed a model framework compiling a hierarchy of positive character strengths that comprised of 24 specific human qualities.[126] These "character strengths" are seen as consistent personality traits that are positive and are further organized into six virtues. Of these core character strengths, R/S or transcendence is one of them, which has been strongly linked to health and well-being.[9] However, while these conceptualizations and contributions were immensely important in bringing to the fore aspects that lead to a meaningful life and a flourishing society, the theoretical frameworks underlying the concept need to be developed further and validated.[127]

CONCLUSION

Religion, spirituality, psychology, and philosophy are disciplines that often draw from each other in diverse ways to aid human development. Although the importance of understanding religious and spiritual beliefs for promoting mental health and alleviating suffering has been acknowledged across cultures for a long time, tremendous strides have been made in recent decades in researching the associations between these disciplines. The overarching need for the integration of R/S with mental health practice for positive outcomes has been highlighted across contexts. This has opened the doors for a more inclusive attitude of incorporating aspects of R/S needs, beliefs, and practices of client populations for more holistic mental health care. This noteworthy stride has led to the refinement of methodological approaches, assessment tools, and outcome measures, which have significantly contributed to a more sensitized understanding of the role of R/S in alleviating suffering and promoting health. Concepts such as meditation and mindfulness have found a place in mainstream psychotherapies such as Mindfulness-Based Cognitive Behavior Therapy (CBT) and Mindfulness-Based Stress Reduction, which have considerable empirical evidence of their effectiveness.[77-79] Therapeutic interventions have emerged, such as transpersonal psychotherapy and rational emotive spiritual therapy, that have specific guidelines and recommended skills required to elicit and incorporate the client's spiritual and religious beliefs into clinical practice. Increasingly, the emphasis in spirituality research has expanded to include theoretical frameworks that address positive states of mind, psychological well-being, and the nature of their relationship with R/S. There is a growing need to explore the contribution of religious and spiritual beliefs to the field of positive mental health, specifically their role in preventive and promotive mental health interventions. R/S practices can also be understood as alternative approaches that not only aid the uptake of psychological interventions but also facilitate personal growth and development with long-term effects that may even go beyond what is achieved from psychiatric and psychological interventions.

The research findings and theoretical concepts described in this chapter demonstrate the value of religious and spiritual practices in alleviating suffering for people with a variety of mental health conditions while increasing hope and well-being by helping them cope with distress and building resilience through increased inner strength.[75] In fact, it has been argued that spiritual well-being is the missing dimension from the World Health Organization's definition of health.[128] This exclusion is primarily due to the challenges in the scientific inquiry, measurement of key constructs, the subjective nature of R/S concepts across contexts, and the high degree of variability in the methodologies and tools used to study these concepts. Moving forward, future research in areas of R/S and its relationship to personality development, mental health, and well-being needs to begin with examining various definitions and conceptualizations of R/S constructs. This should look at both the key distinguishing concepts of both R/S and their commonalities to arrive at a more holistic and integrative conceptualization of their key elements. This would further aid in the development of the appropriate tools for measurement and refine existing ones, resulting in improved indices, and more meaningful and psychometrically sound data.

We also described the role of potential key mediators in the association between R/S and mental health. Positive psychology constructs such as meaning and purpose in life, positive emotions, emotional regulation, resilience and coping, social support, positive emotions such as hope and optimism, and self-transcendence—are now emerging as possible mediating constructs between R/S and positive mental health and need to be more thoroughly investigated. This will synergistically impact both the fields of R/S and positive psychology by capitalizing on their mutual interconnectedness. More culturally and contextually driven research on these constructs and the mechanisms by which they impact the mental health of spiritually or religiously inclined persons can lead to an insightful understanding of oneself and our roles in societies and the world at large. This could be done by incorporating an anthropological and sociological lens in understanding the myriad ways in which culture shapes the individual and collective understanding of R/S and mental health and using these synergies to maximize the acceptability of psychosocial interventions across diverse cultural contexts.

There are various other factors that may impact these trajectories, and it may be beneficial to study the impact of R/S on proximal outcomes that further influence these key mediators. The authors of a meta-analysis of 48 longitudinal studies conclude that future research should focus on employing outcomes that are theoretically closer to R/S than distress and well-being, such as a sense of coherence, benefit finding, post-traumatic growth, sense of control, and spiritual well-being. They also suggest that such studies should examine the moderating effect of R/S on the relationship between stress conditions and mental health through well-controlled intervention studies.[69]

It should also be noted that the key constructs in R/S are often highly subjective and individualistic and are not always stable or fixed in people's lives but rather constantly evolving through changing life circumstances and personal growth. Mixed-methods research can aid the development of culturally and contextually relevant measures that capture the broad range of human experiences salient to people with religious and cultural beliefs.[129] Person-centered methods (in comparison to variable-centered methods) like latent profile analysis may shed light on the characteristics of individuals with varying degrees of religiosity and spirituality. Follow-up studies can also examine how religious and spiritual beliefs change (likely in a non-linear way), what factors lead to these changes, and the impact these changes have on mental health outcomes. Furthermore, as constructs of R/S and positive psychology overlap and interplay in determining states of positive mental health, subjective well-being, and self-development, the mostly correlational data, from the predominantly cross-sectional studies, need very cautious interpretation. Only methodologically refined longitudinal studies can help ascertain temporal ordering and causality. This becomes even more vital given the bidirectional nature of the impacts of these constructs on each other.

A comprehensive understanding of these factors and the complex interplay between R/S and mental health can be instrumental in developing targeted interventions that may be more feasible, resource-efficient, and culturally acceptable, especially since a large proportion of people globally seek religious leaders and traditional healers as their first point of contact for mental health issues populations.[130-132] Future research can also focus on examining how social and cultural factors (ethnicity, social class, religious affiliations, and culture) moderate the associations between R/S and mental health.

The time is opportune for a paradigm shift in looking at R/S as facilitators of embracing oneness and wholeness as opposed to separateness and fragmentation of human nature and existence. This calls for greater integration of the fields of positive psychology and those of R/S, as each of these focuses on increasing the flourishing and well-being of individuals and societies. As an existential crisis of the planet and humanity itself looms large ahead, only such a synergistic convergence of these fields and their resources will pave the way for building psychologically resilient, spiritually enriched, optimally functioning individuals and communities.

REFERENCES

1. Sharma P, Charak R, Sharma V. Contemporary Perspectives on Spirituality and Mental Health. Indian J Psychol Med. 2009; 31(1):16-23.
2. Maslow AH. A theory of human motivation. Psychological Review. 1943;50(4):370-96.
3. In: Rogers CR (Ed). On becoming a person. Oxford, England: Houghton Mifflin; 1961.
4. In: Frankl VE (Ed). The Unconscious God. New York: Simon and Schuster; 1985. p. 140.
5. In: Rowan J (Ed). The Transpersonal: Spirituality in Psychotherapy and Counselling, 1st edition. New York: Routledge; 1993. pp. 25-7.
6. Walsh R, Vaughan F. On transpersonal definitions. J Transperson Psychol. 1993; 25(2): 199-207.
7. Seligman ME, Csikszentmihalyi M. Positive psychology. An introduction. Am Psychol. 2000;55(1):5-14.
8. Pargament KI. Spiritually integrated psychotherapy: Understanding and addressing the sacred. New York, NY, US: Guilford Press; 2007. pp. xvi, 384.
9. In: Koenig HG, King DE, Carson VB (Eds). Handbook of religion and health, 2nd edition. New York: Oxford University Press; 2012; pp. xv,1169.
10. Hauck S, Cloninger CR. The key role of spirituality in positive psychiatry and psychology', in A. In: Moreira-Almeida A, Mosqueiro BP, Bhugra D (Eds). Spirituality and Mental Health Across Cultures. Oxford: Oxford University Press; 2021.
11. In: Moreira-Almeida A, Mosqueiro BP, Bhugra D (Eds). Spirituality and Mental Health Across Cultures. Oxford: Oxford University Press; 2021.

12. Koenig HG, McCullough ME, Larson DB. Handbook of Religion and Health. Oxford: Oxford University Press; 2001.
13. In: Eliade M (Ed). The Encounter between Contemporary Faiths and Archaic Realities. London: Harvill Press; 1960. p. 22.
14. Hardy A. The Spiritual Nature of Man. A Study of Contemporary Religious Experience. Tijdschrift Voor Filosofie., 1981;43(3):587-8.
15. Pargament KI. The Psychology of Religion and Spirituality? Yes and No. Int J Psychol Relig. 1999;9:3-16.
16. Swinton J, Pattison S. Spirituality. Come all ye faithful. Health Serv J. 2001;111(5786):24-5.
17. Woods TE, Ironson GH. Religion and Spirituality in the Face of Illness: How Cancer, Cardiac, and HIV Patients Describe their Spirituality/Religiosity. J Health Psychol. 1999;4(3):393-12.
18. Boswell GH, Kahana E, Dilworth-Anderson P. Spirituality and Healthy Lifestyle Behaviors: Stress Counter-balancing Effects on the Well-being of Older Adults. J Relig Health. 2006;45(4):587-602.
19. Cohen S, Wills TA. Stress, social support, and the buffering hypothesis. Psychol Bull. 1985;98(2):310-57.
20. Saroglou V. Religiousness as a cultural adaptation of basic traits: A five-factor model perspective. Personal Soc Psychol Rev. 2010; 14(1):108-25.
21. Seligman MEP. Positive psychology, positive prevention and positive therapy. In: Snyder CR, Lopez SJ (Eds). Handbook of Positive Psychology. New York, NY, US: Oxford University Press; 2002. pp. 3-9.
22. In: Hart R (Ed). Positive Psychology: The Basics. New York: Routledge; 2020.
23. In: VandenBos GR (Ed). APA dictionary of psychology, 2nd edition. Washington, DC, US: American Psychological Association; 2015. pp. xv,1204.
24. Gable SL, Haidt J. What (and Why) is Positive Psychology? Rev General Psychol. 2005;9(2): 103-10.
25. Kobau R, Seligman ME, Peterson C, Diener E, Zack MM, Chapman D, et al. Mental Health Promotion in Public Health: Perspectives and Strategies From Positive Psychology. Am J Public Health. 2011;101(8):e1-9.
26. Jané-Llopis E. Mental health promotion: concepts and strategies for reaching the population. Health Promot J Austr. 2007; 18(3):191-7.
27. In: Herrman H, Saxena S, Moodie R (Eds). Promoting mental health: concepts, emerging evidence, practice. Geneva: World Health Organization; 2005.
28. Barry MM. Addressing the Determinants of Positive Mental Health: Concepts, Evidence and Practice. International J Mental Health Promot. 2009;11(3):4-17.
29. World Health Organization. (2004). Promoting mental health: concepts, emerging evidence, practice: summary report. [Online] Available from https://iris.who.int/handle/10665/42940 [Last accessed December, 2023].
30. Jahoda M. The Psychological Meaning of Various Criteria for Positive Mental Health. In: Current concepts of positive mental health. New York, NY, US: Basic Books; 1958. pp. 22-64.
31. Leighton AH, Murphy JM. Primary prevention of psychiatric disorders. Acta Psychiatrica Scandinavica. 1987;337:7-22.
32. Bradburn NM. The structure of psychological well-being. Oxford, England: Aldine (The structure of psychological well-being). 1969;xvi, 318.
33. In: Vaillant GE (Ed). Spiritual evolution: A scientific defense of faith. New York, NY, US: Broadway Books; 2018. pp. xiii, 238.
34. Scheier MF, Carver CS. Optimism, coping, and health: assessment and implications of generalized outcome expectancies', Health Psychology: Official Journal of the Division of Health Psychol. 1985;4(3):219-47.
35. Antonovsky A. The salutogenic model as a theory to guide health promotion. Health Promot Intern. 1996;11(1):11-8.
36. Ryff CD. Happiness is everything, or is it? J Personal Soc Psychol. 1989;57(6):1069-81.
37. In: Ryff CD (Ed). Eudaimonic well-being: Highlights from 25 years of inquiry. Hoboken: John Wiley & Sons Ltd; 2018. pp. 375-5.

38. Ryan RM, Deci EL. On Happiness and Human Potentials: A Review of Research on Hedonic and Eudaimonic Well-Being. Ann Rev Psychol. 2001;52(1):141-66.
39. Deci EL, Ryan RM. Hedonia, eudaimonia, and well-being: an introduction. J Happ Studies. 2008;9(1):1-11.
40. Waterman AS. Two conceptions of happiness: Contrasts of personal expressiveness (eudaimonia) and hedonic enjoyment. J Personal Soc Psychol. 1993;64(4):678-91.
41. Keyes CLM. Mental Illness and/or Mental Health? Investigating Axioms of the Complete State Model of Health. J Consult Clin Psychol. 2005;73(3):539-48.
42. van Dierendonck D. The construct validity of Ryff's Scales of Psychological Well-being and its extension with spiritual well-being. Personality and Individual Differences. 2004;36(3):629-43.
43. Bożek A, Nowak PF, Blukacz M. The Relationship Between Spirituality, Health-Related Behavior, and Psychological Well-Being. Front Psychol. 1997;11.
44. Gomez R, Fisher JW. Domains of spiritual well-being and development and validation of the Spiritual Well-Being Questionnaire Personality and Individual Differences. 1991;35(8):1975-91.
45. Unterrainer HF, Huber HP, Sorgo IM, Collicutt J, Fink A. Dimensions of religious/spiritual well-being and schizotypal personality. Personal Indiv Differ. 2011;51(3):360-64.
46. Steger MF, Frazier P. Meaning in Life: One Link in the Chain From Religiousness to Well-Being. J Counsel Psychol. 2005;52(4):574-82.
47. Kashdan TB, Nezlek JB. Whether, When, and How Is Spirituality Related to Well-Being? Moving Beyond Single Occasion Questionnaires to Understanding Daily Process. Pers Soc Psychol Bull. 2012;38(11): 1523-35.
48. Villani D, Sorgente A, Iannello P, Antonietti A. The Role of Spirituality and Religiosity in Subjective Well-Being of Individuals With Different Religious Status. Front Psychol. 2019;10:1525.
49. Csikszentmihalyi M, Abuhamdeh S, Nakamura J. In: Csikszentmihalyi M (Ed). Flow and the Foundations of Positive Psychology: The Collected Works of Mihaly Csikszentmihalyi. Dordrecht: Springer; 2014. pp. 227-38.
50. Neitz MJ, Spickard JV. Steps Toward a Sociology of Religious Experience: The Theories of Mihaly Csikszentmihalyi and Alfred Schutz. Sociol Relig. 1990;51(1):15-33.
51. Greenfield EA, Marks NF. Religious Social Identity as an Explanatory Factor for Associations between More Frequent Formal Religious Participation and Psychological Well-Being. The Int J Psychol Relig. 2007; 17(3):245-59.
52. Davis EB, Worthington Jr EL, Schnitker SA, Glowiak KJ, Lemke AW, Hamilton C. Integrating Positive Psychology and the Psychology of Religion and Spirituality: Transcending Coexistence to Potentiate Coevolution. In: Davis EB, Worthington Jr EL, Schnitker SA (Eds). Handbook of Positive Psychology, Religion, and Spirituality. Cham: Springer International Publishing; 2023. pp. 3-19.
53. Rusk RD, Waters LE. Tracing the size, reach, impact, and breadth of positive psychology. J Posit Psychol. 2013;8(3):207-21.
54. In: Donaldson SI, Csikszentmihalyi M, Nakamura J (Eds). Positive Psychological Science: Improving Everyday Life, Well-Being, Work, Education, and Societies Across the Globe. United Kingdom: Routledge; 2020.
55. In: Pargament KI, Cummings J (Eds). Anchored by faith: Religion as a resilience factor', in Handbook of adult resilience. New York, NY, US: The Guilford Press; 2010. 193-210.
56. Park CL. Making sense of the meaning literature: An integrative review of meaning making and its effects on adjustment to stressful life events. Psychol Bull. 2010;136(2): 257-301.
57. In: Hays PA. Addressing cultural complexities in practice: Assessment, diagnosis, and therapy, 3rd edition. Washington, DC, US:

American Psychological Association; 2016. pp. vii, 355.
58. In: Tedeschi RG (Ed). Posttraumatic Growth: Theory, Research, and Applications. New York: Routledge; 2018.
59. In: Pargament KI (Ed). Religion and coping: The current state of knowledge, in The Oxford Handbook of Stress, Health, and Coping. New York, NY, US: Oxford University Press; 2011. pp. 269-88.
60. American Psychological Association. (2011). American Psychological Association Strategic Plan. [Online] Available from https://www.apa.org/about/apa/strategic-plan [Last accessed December, 2024].
61. In: Pargament KI, Mahoney A (Eds). Spirituality: Discovering and conserving the sacred', in Handbook of positive psychology. New York, NY, US: Oxford University Press; 2002. pp. 646-59.
62. Bellehumeur C, Malette J. Psychologie positive et spiritualité en psychothérapie: Presses de l'Université Laval. 2019.
63. Moreira-Almeida A, Neto FL, Koenig HG. Religiousness and mental health: a review. Braz J Psychiatry. 2006;28(3):242-50.
64. Mueller PS, Plevak DJ, Rummans TA. Religious involvement, spirituality, and medicine: implications for clinical practice. Mayo Clinic Proceedings. 2001;76(12):1225-35.
65. Miller WR, Thoresen CE. Spirituality, religion, and health: An emerging research field. Am Psychol. 2003;58(1):24-35.
66. Kharitonov SA. Religious and Spiritual Biomarkers in Both Health and Disease. Religions. 2012;3(2):467-97.
67. Unterrainer HF, Lewis AJ, Fink A. Religious/Spiritual Well-Being, Personality and Mental Health: A Review of Results and Conceptual Issues. J Relig Health. 2014;53(2):382-92.
68. Smith TB, Bartz J, Richards PS. Outcomes of religious and spiritual adaptations to psychotherapy: A meta-analytic review', Psychotherapy Research. 2007;17(6):643-55.
69. Garssen B, Visser A, Pool G. Does Spirituality or Religion Positively Affect Mental Health? Meta-analysis of Longitudinal Studies', The International Journal for the Psychology of Religion, 2021;31(1):4-20.
70. Baetz M, Griffin R, Bowen R, Koenig HG, Marcoux E. The association between spiritual and religious involvement and depressive symptoms in a Canadian population. J Nerv Ment Dis. 2004;192(12):818-22.
71. Shaw A, Joseph S, Linley PA. Religion, spirituality, and posttraumatic growth: a systematic review. Mental Health, Religion & Culture. 2005;8(1):1-11.
72. Lawrence RE, Oquendo MA, Stanley B. Religion and Suicide Risk: A Systematic Review. Arch Suicide Res. 2016;20(1):1-21.
73. Mohr S, Huguelet P. The relationship between schizophrenia and religion and its implications for care. Swiss Med Wkly. 2004;134(25-26):369-76.
74. Mohr S, Perroud N, Gillieron C, Brandt PY, Rieben I, Borras L, et al. Spirituality and religiousness as predictive factors of outcome in schizophrenia and schizo-affective disorders. Psychiatry Res. 2011;186(2): 177-82.
75. Sharma M, Fine SL, Brennan RT, Betancourt TS. Coping and mental health outcomes among Sierra Leonean war-affected youth: Results from a longitudinal study. Dev Psychopathol. 2017;29(1):11-23.
76. Tan S-Y. Religion in clinical practice: Implicit and explicit integration. In: Tan S-Y (Ed). Religion and the clinical practice of psychology. Washington, DC, US: American Psychological Association; 1996. pp. 365-87.
77. Kuyken W, Watkins E, Holden E, White K, Taylor RS, Byford S, et al. How does mindfulness-based cognitive therapy work? Behav Res Ther. 2010;48(11):1105-12.
78. Fjorback LO, Arendt M, Ornbøl E, Fink P, Walach H. Mindfulness-Based Stress Reduction and Mindfulness-Based Cognitive Therapy: a systematic review of randomized controlled trials. Acta Psychiatr Scand. 2011; 124(2):102-19.
79. Gu J, Strauss C, Bond R, Cavanagh K. How do mindfulness-based cognitive therapy and mindfulness-based stress reduction improve mental health and wellbeing? A systematic

review and meta-analysis of mediation studies. Clin Psychol Rev. 2015;37:1-12.
80. In: Suler JR (Ed). Contemporary Psychoanalysis and Eastern Thought. SUNY Press; 1993.
81. McKinney R. Introducing R.E.S.T. (Rational Emotive Spiritual Therapy): A 2,000 Year Old Healing Paradigm.
82. D'Souza RF, Rodrigo A. Spiritually augmented cognitive behavioural therapy. Australas Psychiatry. 2004;12(2):148-52.
83. In: Oman D, Thoresen CE (Eds). Do Religion and Spirituality Influence Health?', in Handbook of the psychology of religion and spirituality. New York, NY, US: The Guilford Press; 2005. pp. 435-59.
84. Diener E, Wirtz D, Tov W. New well-being measures: short scales to assess flourishing and positive and negative feelings. Social Indicat Res. 2010;7(2):143-56.
85. Ramsay JE, Tong EMW, Chowdhury A, Ho MR. Teleological explanation and positive emotion serially mediate the effect of religion on well-being. J Pers. 2019;87(3):676-89.
86. Vishkin A, Ben-Nun BP, Tamir M. Always Look on the Bright Side of Life: Religiosity, Emotion Regulation and Well-Being in a Jewish and Christian Sample. J Happin Studies. 2019;20(2):427-47.
87. Weber SR, Pargament KI. The role of religion and spirituality in mental health. Curr Opin Psychiatry. 2014;27(5):358-63.
88. Lim C, Putnam RD. Religion, Social Networks, and Life Satisfaction. Am Sociolog Rev. 2010;75(6):914-33.
89. Park CL. Religiousness/spirituality and health: A Meaning Systems Perspective. J Behav Med. 2007;30(4):319-28.
90. Park CL, Van Tongeren DR. Meaning as a Framework for Integrating Positive Psychology and the Psychology of Religiousness and Spirituality. In: Davis EB, Worthington Jr EB, Schnitker SA (Eds). Handbook of Positive Psychology, Religion, and Spirituality. Cham: Springer International Publishing; 2023. pp. 83-96.
91. Vilchinsky N, Kravetz S. How Are Religious Belief and Behavior Good for You? An Investigation of Mediators Relating Religion to Mental Health in a Sample of Israeli Jewish Students. J Scient Study Relig. 2005;44(4): 459-71.
92. Chamberlain K, Zika S. Religiosity, Life Meaning and Wellbeing: Some Relationships in a Sample of Women. J Sci Study Religion. 1988;27(3):411-20.
93. Kim ES, Chen Y, Nakamura JS, Ryff CD, VanderWeele TJ. Sense of Purpose in Life and Subsequent Physical, Behavioral, and Psychosocial Health: An Outcome-Wide Approach. Am J Health Promot. 2022;36(1): 137-47.
94. Zika S, Chamberlain K. Relation of hassles and personality to subjective well-being. J Personal Soc Psychol. 1987;53(1):155-62.
95. George LK, Ellison CG, Larson DB. Explaining the Relationships between Religious Involvement and Health. Psychol Inquiry. 2002;13(3):190-200.
96. Ellison CG, Levin JS. The religion-health connection: evidence, theory, and future directions. Health Educ Behav. 1998;25(6): 700-20.
97. Kirkpatrick BS, Phillip R, Shaver, Lee A. A General Attribution Theory for the Psychology of Religion. J Sci Study Religion. 1985;24(1):1.
98. Rotter JB. General Expectancies for Internal Versus External Control of Reinforcement. Psycholog Monog. 1966;80(1):1-28.
99. Fiori KL, Cortina KS, Brown E, Antonucci T. Locus of control as a mediator of the relationship between religiosity and life satisfaction: Age, race, and gender differences. Mental Health, Religion & Culture. 2003;9(3):239-63.
100. Pargament KI. The Psychology of Religion and Coping: Theory, Research, Practice. Guilford Press; 2001.
101. Cummings JP, Pargament KI. Medicine for the Spirit: Religious Coping in Individuals with Medical Conditions. Religions. 2010; 1(1):28-53.
102. Bryant-Davis T, Wong EC. Faith to move mountains: Religious coping, spirituality, and interpersonal trauma recovery. Am Psychol. 2013;68(8):675-84.

103. Schuurmans-Stekhoven JB. Conviction, character and coping: religiosity and personality are both uniquely associated with optimism and positive reappraising. Mental Health, Religion & Culture. 2018; 21(8):763-79.
104. McCullough ME, Willoughby BLB. Religion, self-regulation, and self-control: Associations, explanations, and implications. Psychol Bull. 2009;135(1):69-93.
105. Carver CS, Scheier MF. Optimism, coping, and well-being. In: Carver CS, Scheier MF (Eds). The handbook of stress and health: A guide to research and practice. Hoboken, NJ, US: Wiley Blackwell; 2017. pp. 400-14.
106. Elliott I, Coker S. Independent self-construal, self-reflection, and self-rumination: A path model for predicting happiness. Australian J Psychol. 2008;60(3):127-34.
107. Fabricatore AN, Handal PJ, Fenzel LM. Personal spirituality as a moderator of the relationship between stressors and subjective well-being. J Psychol Theol. 2000; 28(3):221-8.
108. Seybold KS, Hill PC. The Role of Religion and Spirituality in Mental and Physical Health. Current Direct Psychol Sci. 2001;10(1):21-4.
109. Einolf CJ. Gender Differences in the Correlates of Volunteering and Charitable Giving. Nonprofit and Voluntary Sector Quarterly. 2011;40(6):1092-12.
110. Einolf CJ. Daily Spiritual Experiences and Prosocial Behavior. Soc Indicat R. 2013; 110(1):71-87.
111. Taniguchi H, Thomas LD. The Influences of Religious Attitudes on Volunteering. Int J Volunt Nonprof Organiz. 2011;22(2):335-55.
112. McFarland MJ, Pudrovska T, Schieman S, Ellison CG, Bierman A. Does a cancer diagnosis influence religiosity? Integrating a life course perspective. Soc Sci Res. 2013; 42(2):311-20.
113. Rudaz M, Ledermann T, Grzywacz JG. Spiritual coping, perceived growth, and the moderating role of spiritual mindfulness in cancer survivors. J Psychosoc Oncol. 2018; 36(5):609-23.
114. Wagani R, Colucci E. Spirituality and Wellbeing in the Context of a Study on Suicide Prevention in North India. Religions. 2018;9(6):183.
115. Fredrickson BL. The role of positive emotions in positive psychology. The broaden-and-build theory of positive emotions. 2001;56(3): 218-26.
116. Fredrickson BL. How does religion benefit health and well-being? Are positive emotions active ingredients? Psychol Inquiry. 2002; 13(3):209-13.
117. Smith BW. Spirituality, resilience, and positive emotions', in The Oxford handbook of psychology and spirituality. New York, NY, US: Oxford University Press; 2012. pp. 437-54.
118. Van Cappellen P, Zhang R, Fredrickson BL. The Scientific Study of Positive Emotions and Religion/Spirituality. In: Davis EB, Worthington Jr. EL, Schnitker SA (Eds). Handbook of Positive Psychology, Religion, and Spirituality. Cham: Springer International Publishing; 2023. pp. 315-28.
119. Aglozo EY, Akotia CS, Osei-Tutu A, Annor F. Spirituality and subjective well-being among Ghanaian older adults: optimism and meaning in life as mediators. Aging Ment Health. 2021;25(2):306-15.
120. Lam C-Y, Chiu CPY, Lui KYM. Hope as a mediator of spirituality and subjective happiness among Chinese Christians in Hong Kong before and during the civil unrest: Implications for counselling practices. Asia Pacific J Counsel Psychotherapy. 2021;12(1): 3-21.
121. Stellar JE, Gordon A, Piff PK, Cordaro D. Self-transcendent emotions and their social functions: Compassion, gratitude, and awe bind us to others through prosociality. Emot Rev. 2017;9(3):200-7.
122. In: Eliade M (Ed). Myths, Dreams, and Mysteries: The Encounter Between Contemporary Faiths and Archaic Realities. New York: Harper and Brothers Publishers; 1961.
123. Heszen-Niejodek I, Gruszczyńska E. Wymiar duchowy człowieka, jego znaczenie w psychologii zdrowia i jego pomiar. [Spirituality as a human dimension, its importance in health psychology, and its

measurement]. Przegląd Psychologiczny. 2004;47(1):15-31.

124. Van Cappellen P. Religion and Well-Being: The Mediating Role of Positive Emotions. J Happ Studies. 2016;17(2):485-505.
125. Fredrickson BL, Cohn MA, Coffey KA, Pek J, Finkel SM. Open hearts build lives: Positive emotions, induced through loving-kindness meditation, build consequential personal resources. J Pers Soc Psychol. 2008; 95(5):1045-62.
126. Peterson C, Seligman MEP. Character Strengths and Virtues: A Handbook and Classification. Am J Psychol Assoc. 2004; 162(4):820-1.
127. Hauck S, Cloninger CR. The key role of spirituality in positive psychiatry and psychology', in A. In: Moreira-Almeida A, Mosqueiro BP, Bhugra D (Eds). Spirituality and Mental Health Across Cultures. Oxford: Oxford University Press; 2021.
128. In: Larson JS (Ed). The World Health Organization's Definition of Health: Social versus Spiritual Health Social Indicators Research. Philadelphia: Springer; 1996. pp. 181–192.
129. Cornah D. The Impact of Spirituality on Mental Health: A Review of the Literature. https://www.elament.org.uk/media/1204/impact-spirituality.pdf [Last accessed December, 2024].
130. Post BC, Wade NG. Religion and spirituality in psychotherapy: A practice-friendly review of research. J Clin Psychol. 2009;65(2):131-46.
131. Currier JM, Fox J, Vieten C, Pearce M, Oxhandler HK. Enhancing competencies for the ethical integration of religion and spirituality in psychological services. Psychol Serv. 2023;20(1):40-50.
132. Shafranske EP. The Scientific Study of Positive Psychology, Religion/Spirituality, and Mental Health. In: Davis EB, Worthington Jr. EL, Schnitker A (Eds). Handbook of Positive Psychology, Religion, and Spirituality. Cham: Springer International Publishing; 2023. pp. 345-58.

6 CHAPTER

Yoga and Spirituality

Bharath Holla, BN Gangadhar

INTRODUCTION

Spirituality, while deeply personal and somewhat complex to define, generally encompasses the pursuit of understanding life's deeper meanings and embracing a sense of interconnectedness, often coupled with a recognition of the sacred or divine. Originating from the Sanskrit root "Yuj," Yoga epitomizes "union," aiming to facilitate a harmonious integration of the mind, body, and spirit, articulated in the principle *"Samyoga yoga ityuktojivatmanaparamatmanoh"*, emphasizing the unison of individual and universal consciousness (Yoga Yajnavalkya 1.43). Thus, Yoga emerges as a pivotal pathway to spirituality.

Yoga guides individuals on an inward journey, meticulously outlined through its structured approach known as the "eight limbs" or "*angas*". This journey is categorized into external practices (*bahiranga*) which focus on principles of ethical living, physical postures, and breath control techniques; and internal practices (*antaranga*) which emphasize the deeper aspects such as sensory withdrawal, concentration, and meditation, ultimately culminating in spiritual realization. This systematic progression from external to internal practices could be perceived as a voyage from physical mastery to spiritual awakening, much like peeling the successive layers of an onion to reach its core. Each of these aspects serves as a prerequisite for the subsequent stage, sometimes simultaneously forming a scaffold for the practitioner's progression toward the more internalized facets of yoga.

Parallelly, Maslow's hierarchy of needs, which begins with addressing basic physiological needs and culminates in self-actualization, mirrors this journey, highlighting a pathway of reaching one's fullest potential through self-realization. Comparatively, the *Panchakosha* model elucidated in the *Taittiriya* Upanishad outlines a five-layered scheme of human existence encompassing physical, vital, mental, intellectual, and blissful dimensions. This model correlates strongly with the steps delineated in yoga, offering a structured pathway for individuals to evolve and reach a heightened state of consciousness—a spiritual transcendence.

From time immemorial, spirituality has been the cornerstone of Indian culture, transcending the boundaries of mere religion or belief systems to be a foundational aspect of life and philosophy in the region. This rich tapestry has been deeply embroidered with profound insights from thinkers such as Aurobindo and Vivekananda, who illuminated the world with the depths of Indian spiritual wisdom.

In Hinduism, the spirituality anchors itself in the concept of the unity of "*Atman*" (the individual soul) with "*Brahman*" (the universal spirit), a realization fostered through self-inquiry and contemplative practices, steering individuals toward liberation or *Moksha*. Buddhism, on the other hand, offers a pathway to enlightenment, or "*Nirvana*," urging individuals to navigate the "Middle Way"—a balanced pathway encapsulated in the Noble Eightfold Path and symbolically represented in the eight spokes of the Dharma Wheel, which advocates for moderation, avoiding both extreme indulgence and harsh asceticism.

Jainism extends the spiritual canvas, emphasizing non-violence and self-realization as avenues to attain "*Moksha*," fostering a deep sense of harmony with all beings. Meanwhile, Sikhism introduces a passionate devotion to God, coupled with an altruistic service to humanity, envisioning a state of eternal bliss known as "*Sach Khand*." Each of these doctrines, rich and distinct, contributes to the varied yet unified tapestry of Indian spiritual philosophy, offering diverse pathways to spiritual realization.

Swami Vivekananda, who was instrumental in introducing Indian philosophies such as Vedanta and Yoga to the Western world, emphasized yoga as not just a practice but a comprehensive lifestyle for spiritual enlightenment. He laid out four distinct paths toward this goal: (1) *Raja Yoga*, which empowers the person through meditation and mindfulness; (2) *Bhakti Yoga*, grounded in devotion and surrender; (3) *Karma Yoga*, focusing on selfless action and duty; and (4) *Jnana Yoga*, based on knowledge and discernment, each path uniquely designed to facilitate the union of individual consciousness with the universal spirit.

In the same spirit, philosopher and yogi Sri Aurobindo developed the concept of Integral Yoga, an evolutionary practice aiming to transcend the limitations of human consciousness and foster a divine life on earth. Aurobindo envisaged yoga as a dynamic tool for the transformation of human life into a divine existence, facilitating the elevation of human consciousness to a higher and spiritual plane. This robust framework accommodates various elements of yoga, harmoniously integrating them to nurture spiritual growth and foster a deeper understanding of one's intrinsic connection to the universal spirit.

Enriching the vibrant heritage of India, these philosophies resonate deeply within the spiritual dimensions of yoga. They illustrate the inherent unity in diversity, and demonstrate spirituality as a journey inward, a journey of discovering the profound interconnectedness of life.

Thus, yoga, deeply rooted in spirituality, provides not merely a structured approach to foster holistic health and well-being but also a pathway to realize the unity with the divine, an essence encapsulated in spirituality. Following the path carved by the "*angas*" offers individuals a structured approach to navigating life's complexities, fostering a state of harmony and eventual union with the universal spirit, embodying the pinnacle of spiritual pursuits. These elements of yoga resonate with the World Health Organization's holistic definition of health as a state of complete physical, mental, and social well-being and not merely the absence of disease.[1] One may note that the definition of health in Ayurveda, a much older health science, inherently included a spiritual dimension, characterized as a *"prasannaatmendriyamanah"*—a state of harmony and contentment involving the soul and the senses. This holistic view resonates strongly with the multifaceted therapeutic approaches seen in modern psychiatry, including the integration of yoga as a pathway to spiritual and mental well-being.

This chapter draws upon the profound wisdom from the authoritative texts such as Patanjali's *Yoga Sutras* and the *Bhagavad Gita*, delineating the multi-dimensional aspect of yoga that extends beyond a mere physical practice. It seeks to portray yoga as an encompassing philosophy, steering one toward deep spiritual realization. Yoga is a practical guide in the cultivation of an enlightened life. This disciplined approach to living, termed *"anushasana,"* is perceived as a deliberate cultivation of lifestyle with the anticipation of transformative outcomes.

As envisaged by revered Yogacharyas, "sadhana" signifies a dynamic, progressive enhancement in one's spiritual routine, nurturing a consistent growth that is both inward and expansive. It is a commitment to continual and sustained improvement, transforming the very fabric of one's being through deliberate and conscious efforts. In shedding light on the essence of all scriptures, we find a convergence in the teaching of Patanjali and the *Bhagavad Gita*. While the Patanjali's *Yoga Sutras* provide a systematic framework guiding individuals through a spiritual journey, the *Bhagavad Gita* contextualizes this elevated wisdom within the pragmatic dimensions of daily existence. It emphasizes a lifestyle rooted in the principles of yoga. Such a confluence of theoretical underpinnings and practical applications establishes a conducive environment for the seamless integration of yoga into routine life. This has substantial implications for its utility in mental health promotion and psychotherapeutic interventions,[2] thereby serving as a rich substrate for both personal and spiritual development.

YOGA SUTRAS OF PATANJALI: DEFINING THE PATH

The "*Yoga Sutras*" is a monumental work consisting of 196 cryptic aphorisms, or *sutras*, compiled by the sage, Patanjali. This seminal text forms the bedrock of classical yoga philosophy and its teachings continue to influence yogic practices worldwide. These short, thread-like sutras are condensed and cryptic, designed to be unpacked and explored with the guidance of a knowledgeable teacher. They form a comprehensive guide that touches on every aspect of the yogic path, providing a framework for practitioners to experience inner transformation and ultimately, liberation. These sutras are organized into four chapters (*Pada*)—*Samadhi Pada* (contemplation), *Sadhana Pada* (practice), *Vibhuti Pada* (manifestation), and *Kaivalya Pada* (liberation). Each sutra offers profound insights into the science and philosophy of yoga, providing a roadmap for personal development and spiritual awakening.

Samadhi Pada (Contemplation)

The first chapter of the *Yoga Sutras*, known as *Samadhi Pada*, lays the groundwork for the yogic journey, a process characterized by a progressively deeper immersion into the state of *Samadhi*, a pinnacle of concentrated meditation where the practitioner achieves unity with the object of their meditation. It represents a transcendental state of consciousness, fostering a sense of oneness and dissolution of the self.

YogashChittaVrittiNirodhah: Defining the Heart of Yoga

Almost the very first among the aphorisms in this chapter pronounces a foundational doctrine: "*YogashChittaVrittiNirodhah*," translating to "Yoga is the cessation of the fluctuations or modifications of the mind." This seminal phrase delineates yoga not merely as a bodily endeavor but a meticulous discipline aiming at reigning control over the mental oscillations.

Patanjali illumines the term *"Chitta"* which is most suitably translated to "mind space" or the psyche inclusive of various layers such as consciousness (*purusha*), intellect (*buddhi*), ego (*ahamkara*), and the mind (*manas*). This multi-dimensional entity is the theater of our experiences, perceptions, and cognitive processes, often visualized as a pool of water subject to constant ripples or *"Vrittis"*.

In this endeavor to unveil the complex dynamics of the mind, Patanjali identifies five distinct categories of *"Vrittis"* shaping our consciousness and perceptions at every moment. These are essentially the various forms that thoughts take in our minds and can either be detrimental or beneficial to one's mental state. *Pramana* refers to the correct knowledge or understanding one can have, which is grounded in reality and can be verified through direct perception, inference, or reliable testimony; *Viparyaya* representing incorrect knowledge or misunderstanding that is not based on the real nature of the subject. It encompasses all forms of misconceptions, illusions, or false beliefs; *Vikalpa*, the realm of imagination and fantasy unfounded in the sensory experiences. It is the mental construction of something that does not exist in the external world, a form of conceptualization that is not tied to real objects; *Nidra* which delineates the state of sleep where there is an absence of conscious content yet a potential for dreams to arise; and finally, *Smriti*, encompassing memory, a function that retrieves past experiences and impressions. Together, these *vrittis* sketch the intricate dynamics of the human mind, offering insights into its propensity for both correct and incorrect knowledge, vivid imaginations, and the realms of conscious and unconscious experiences.

One could venture to link these ancient conceptualizations of psyche's operation to insights provided by network neuroscience, a field that emphasizes the interconnectivity and dynamic interactions between different brain regions. For instance, "Pramana," which denotes correct knowledge, might involve the synchronized functioning of prefrontal cortex networks, facilitating rational thinking and decision-making processes. "*Viparyaya*," representing misconceptions, could be seen as arising from miscommunications between networks involving the temporal lobe, including the amygdala and hippocampus, which process emotions and memories. The *vritti* "*Vikalpa*," linked to imagination, could potentially be a product of interplays between networks rooted in the parietal lobe, fostering creativity, and abstract thinking. The "*Nidra*" state, associated with sleep, could relate to the deeply interconnected networks between the thalamus and brainstem, which are pivotal in governing sleep-wake cycles. Lastly, "*Smriti*," associated with memory, may implicate an intricate network involving the hippocampus, central to the formation and retrieval of memories. In offering these speculative connections, it is acknowledged that this approach is somewhat simplistic, it harmonizes with the profound insights of the *Yoga Sutras*, reflecting a concerted attempt to integrate ancient wisdom on human mind with modern scientific endeavors.

Journey to Samadhi: Bolstered by Effort and Detachment

In the closing discussions of the *Samadhi Pada*, Patanjali intricately describes the mechanisms to reach the pinnacle of yogic practice, *Samadhi*—a state of deep spiritual insight and tranquility. This zenith can be reached through two primary avenues—*Samprajnata* (conscious) and *Asamprajnata* (superconscious) *Samadhi.*

The *Samprajnata* path, which can be construed as the conscious road to *Samadhi,* is characterized by focused meditation where a conscious connection with the object of meditation is maintained, and distinct stages of concentration are experienced. Contrastingly, the *Asamprajnata* path leads to a superconscious state where there is a transcendence of all mental activities and a move toward a state of pure consciousness, free from the habitual patterns, and ruminations of the mind.

To tread on these paths and to arrive at these elevated states of consciousness, Patanjali emphasizes the duality of effort and surrender as the two core principles—*abhyasa* (consistent practice) and *vairagya* (dispassion or non-attachment). *Abhyasa* refers to the sustained effort needed to cultivate and maintain a focused and steady mind, a discipline that demands dedication and time. Meanwhile, *vairagya* invites practitioners to foster detachment, not only from material objects but from deep-seated desires and aversions, during the practice, enabling a freedom from the compulsions of the external world and encouraging an inward journey.

***Sadhana Pada* (Practice)**

In the *Sadhana Pada*, Patanjali delineates a strategic roadmap for inner transformation, articulating fundamental principles and structured approaches essential in navigating the yogic journey toward self-mastery and enlightenment. The discourse begins with the grounding techniques of *Kriya Yoga*, setting a robust foundation for practitioners. It then unfolds to reveal the five *Kleshas*, significant mental obstructions that need to be acknowledged and addressed in the spiritual pathway. Culminating this chapter is the intricate guide to self-realization embodied in the holistic practice of *Ashtanga Yoga*, offering an immersive pathway to enlightenment through a series of graduated steps (limbs). This section aids individuals in skillfully negotiating the spiritual terrain, providing them with the necessary tools to attain a higher state of consciousness.

The Three Pillars of Kriya Yoga

At the onset of the *Sadhana Pada* chapter, Patanjali presents *Kriya Yoga*, a foundational practice that is based on the trinity of tapas (austerity), *svadhyaya* (self-study), and *Ishvarapranidhana* (surrender to a higher power). *Tapas* refers to the rigorous discipline and austerity that are essential for spiritual growth. It is about fostering endurance, developing resilience, and cultivating a spirit of self-sacrifice to advance on the path of self-realization. *Svadhyaya* involves a deep introspection and study of oneself, a continual process of self-discovery that also encompasses the study of spiritual scriptures to attain greater understanding and wisdom. *Ishvarapranidhana* is the dedicated surrender to a higher power, fostering a deep sense of devotion and recognizing a force greater than oneself, which promotes humility and relinquishes the ego. This trifold approach serves as a preparatory stage, nurturing the ground for deeper yogic practices by developing discipline, self-awareness, and a transcendental connection.

The Panchakleshas: Five Obstacles to Spiritual Progress

As practitioners traverse the path of *Kriya Yoga* delineated in the *Sadhana Pada*, they will invariably encounter hurdles, primarily characterized by Patanjali as the "five *Kleshas*". These impediments to spiritual progress emerge from innate human tendencies and misunderstandings. First is *Avidya*, a foundational misconception that mistakes the transient as permanent, the impure as pure, and the painful as pleasurable, engendering a clouded perception of reality. This ignorance gives rise to *Asmita*, the egoism that fosters a heightened sense of individuality, drawing a wedge between the self and the universal consciousness, thus limiting a person's understanding and experience of the broader reality.

Following *Asmita*, *Raga* unfolds as an attachment to pleasurable experiences. This attachment engenders a vicious cycle of craving and discontent, continually veering individuals off the spiritual pathway. In contrast, *Dvesha* manifests as an aversion to discomfort and pain, incubating a life driven by fear and evasion, and consequently hampering personal growth and understanding. Lastly, the *Kleshas* bring forth *Abhinivesha*, a deep-seated and profound fear of death, cultivating an attachment to life that obstructs the ability to immerse oneself entirely in the present, stalling one's journey toward liberation. Understanding and mitigating these five *Kleshas*, therefore, stands central to advancing in one's yogic journey, fostering a pathway to liberation unfettered by these common human obstructions.

Ashtanga Yoga: The Eightfold Path to Self-realization

While the path of *Kriya Yoga* is beset with obstacles or *Kleshas*, Patanjali offers a structured pathway to maneuver through them—the *Ashtanga Yoga*, or the eight-limbed path. This framework comprises a series of steps (limbs) designed to cultivate discipline, focus, and ultimately, a deeper understanding of one's true nature.

The eight-limbed path starts with *Yama*, embodying ethical standards and integrity with a focus on our behavior and how we conduct ourselves in life. Following *Yama* is *Niyama*, which represents self-discipline and spiritual observances, encouraging us to cultivate habits that foster personal growth. *Asana*, the third limb, pertains to the physical postures practiced in yoga, aiming to develop discipline and concentration. *Pranayama*, the fourth stage, involves breath control, enhancing our ability to regulate our mental state through the breath. *Pratyahara*, the fifth limb, is the withdrawal of senses, allowing for internalization and a turning inward to foster deeper self-awareness. Following this, *Dharana* embodies the concentration stage, helping in fixing the mind onto one point, promoting mental stability and focus. *Dhyana*, the seventh stage, represents meditative absorption, a deep unbroken concentration where the sense of individuality dissolves. Finally, the journey culminates with *Samadhi*, the eighth limb, a state of ecstasy where the meditator merges with the point of focus, achieving a state of super-consciousness, and realizing the ultimate unity of all things. This step-by-step guide outlines a progressive path to self-realization, offering practitioners a tangible roadmap toward spiritual enlightenment.

***Vibhuti Pada* (Manifestation of Powers)**

The third chapter of the *Yoga Sutras*, the *Vibhuti Pada*, is often referred to as the "Chapter on Powers". It explores the extraordinary perceptual abilities, or siddhis, that may unfold as one deepens their yogic practice.

Samyama: The Mastery of the Mind

Patanjali takes us deeper into the yogic journey with the introduction of *Samyama*, a unified practice of *Dharana* (concentration), *Dhyana* (meditation), and *Samadhi* (a superconscious state). This triad represents a progressive journey where one starts from focused concentration, transitioning to meditation and finally culminating in a state of *Samadhi*, where the mind is absorbed entirely into the object of contemplation, representing a state of unity and oneness. It is through the disciplined and adept application of *Samyama* that a yogi can unlock potentials often deemed beyond normal human capabilities, unfolding a path to self-mastery and inner harmony.

Siddhis: The Extraordinary Abilities

Building upon the concept of *Samyama*, Patanjali introduces the potential attainments or *Siddhis*, the extraordinary capacities or "spiritual powers" that may emerge as one deepens their practice of *Samyama*. Patanjali elaborates on how these powers can be obtained, including through birth, the use of herbs, the practice of mantras, ascetic practices, or by achieving *Samadhi*. These *Siddhis* are numerous, illustrating a realm where the boundaries of the ordinary human experience can be transcended. However, Patanjali advises caution, noting that these *Siddhis*, although fascinating, can become a distraction on the path to liberation (*Kaivalya*), potentially fostering attachment and ego. Thus, a true yogi is encouraged to remain detached from these attainments, viewing them not as the end goal but as byproducts of a deeper spiritual evolution.

***Kaivalya Pada* (Liberation)**

The *Kaivalya Pada* is the final chapter of Patanjali's *Yoga Sutras*. It explores the ultimate goal of yoga—*Kaivalya*, often translated as liberation, isolation, or emancipation. This chapter takes a philosophical turn, delving into the process of liberation and the nature of existence.

The Path to Liberation: Right Knowledge and Virtuous Conduct

Patanjali emphasizes the integral roles of right knowledge and virtuous conduct in forging the path to liberation. Understanding the fundamental principles of reality, coupled with the cultivation of virtues such as compassion, truthfulness, and self-discipline, lay the groundwork for a practitioner to attain a state of complete detachment, clarity, and ultimate freedom.

Nature of Liberation: Understanding Kaivalya

In the *Kaivalya Pada*, Patanjali offers a profound explanation of the state of ultimate liberation termed as "*Kaivalya*". The *yogi* in this advanced stage of spiritual evolution comprehends the stark differentiation between the *Purusha*, the immutable eternal self, and *Prakriti*, the ever-changing material reality that encapsulates all forms and phenomena. This discernment signals the pinnacle of true knowledge, the shedding of all illusions tethered to the ephemeral world.

Patanjali explicates the transcendental journey where the yogi gradually breaks free from the clutches of ignorance (*avidya*), a foundational obstacle ingrained in human consciousness that breeds other afflictions (*kleshas*) and keeps one embroiled in the unyielding cycle of *karma*, birth, and rebirth. As *avidya* dissolves, it ignites the process of liberating the mind from its fluctuations and impurities, guiding it to return to its primal state—unmarked, pure, and tranquil.

At this juncture, the mind is no longer a slave to its oscillations; it halts, renouncing all its modified states and patterns it has accrued over lifetimes. The culmination of this intricate process is the attainment of *Kaivalya*, a state where the *gunas*, the fundamental forces steering the laws of nature, retreat, having fulfilled their designated roles in the grand cosmic play.

As the yogi reaches this paramount state, there remains no more karma to be manifested or worked upon, no more births to be taken, and no more experiences to be endured through the prism of duality. The yogi, now a seer, perceives reality in its most pristine form, resting in an unchanging, pure, omnipresent consciousness, which remains untainted and undistorted by time and space.

Patanjali underscores the ineffable nature of *Kaivalya*. It transcends the ambit of normal human experiences and reasoning, nestled in realms that words fail to describe, a space where boundless freedom, undying peace, and supreme bliss are not just pursued but are realized in their truest essence. *Kaivalya* is, therefore, not just a state of being but the zenith of yogic realization, an embodiment of supreme tranquility and the epitome of an awakened life, rejoicing in the pure, blissful, and eternal presence of the self **(Fig. 1)**.

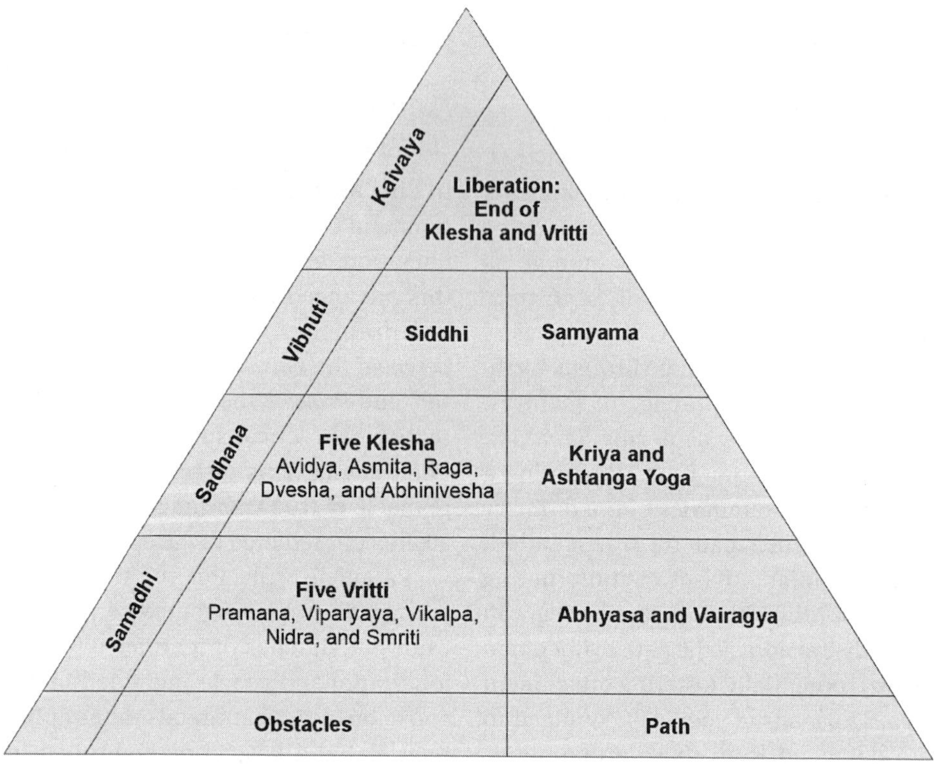

Fig. 1: Traversing the obstacles and paths of Patanjali's *Yoga Sutras*—a hierarchical ascension toward liberation. Refer to text for a more detailed description of each chapter (*Pada*).

Patanjali's Yoga Sutras: A Blueprint for Mastery

The principles and stages outlined in Patanjali's *Yoga Sutras* are universal and can be applied to any path in life, including professions. Take, for instance, the journey of becoming a doctor. The *Samadhi Pada*, the first section, corresponds to preclinical MBBS, where foundational knowledge is established, much like laying the groundwork for spiritual understanding. Next, the *Sadhana Pada* is akin to clinical postings, where theoretical knowledge is applied to real-world practice, mirroring the practical aspect of yoga. The *Vibhuti Pada* can be compared to the internship stage in medical education, where the practice deepens under direct supervision and students begin to experience the fruits of their efforts. Finally, the *Kaivalya Pada* symbolizes the full dedication to the profession, like a fully-fledged doctor, embodying the attainment of "*kaivalya*" or ultimate liberation in yoga. This analogy underscores the idea that the *yoga sutras* provide a universal guide for progression in any life endeavor.

BHAGAVAD GITA: YOGA IN ACTION

The *Bhagavad Gita*, often referred to as the *Gita*, is a 700-verse Hindu scripture that is part of the Indian epic *Mahabharata*. This sacred text provides profound philosophical insights through the discourse between Prince Arjuna and Lord Krishna, who serves as his charioteer. It offers not just a doctrine for religious belief, but a philosophical guide that addresses the complex dilemmas one faces in life.

In the dialogue, Krishna provides Arjuna with guidance on how to deal with moral dilemmas and make decisions that are based on duty (*dharma*) and righteousness (right conduct). The *Gita* embodies the concept of "Yoga in Action". It essentially encourages one to live a life that is harmoniously balanced between spiritual pursuits and worldly responsibilities. The teaching categorizes the paths to attain this balance into three primary *yogas*, explaining them as different avenues leading to the same ultimate goal—spiritual realization, or self-realization. The three paths of yoga are *Karma Yoga* (the path of selfless action), *Bhakti Yoga* (the path of devotion), and *Jnana Yoga* (the path of knowledge). It emphasizes that although the paths are different, they all lead to the same destination of spiritual realization. They provide a practical approach to spiritual wisdom, emphasizing the importance of acting in the world with detachment, devotion, and a deep understanding of the universal truth, that is beyond time, space, and causation.

Karma Yoga: The Yoga of Action

Karma Yoga, as delineated in the *Bhagavad Gita*, is fundamentally the spiritual discipline of selfless action. The term "*Karma*" translates as "action", while "Yoga" represents "union"—in this case, union with the divine. The essence of *Karma Yoga* lies in performing duties selflessly, without being attached to the fruits of the actions.

In the battlefield of Kurukshetra, Arjuna is initially unwilling to participate in the war due to the moral dilemma of fighting against his own kin. It is then that Krishna, in his role as the charioteer and guide, introduces the concept of *Karma Yoga*. He counsels Arjuna to fulfill his *Kshatriya* (warrior) duty as a fighter. Yet, he also emphasizes that Arjuna should remain detached from the outcome—success or failure should be the same to him. This, according to the *Gita*, is the true nature of action. Krishna explains that one has control over the actions they perform, but they have no control over the results. The fruits of the actions are not in human hands, and hence, humans should not bear the burden of the outcome. Krishna encourages Arjuna to surrender all his actions to God, performing his duty as a form of worship.

Moreover, the *Gita* makes it clear that avoiding action is not a solution. As living beings, action is a part of our nature and existence. However, it is the spirit behind the action that matters. Actions performed with selfless intent, without the expectation of rewards, purify the mind and lead to spiritual growth and realization of the self.

Therefore, *Karma Yoga* is a practical spiritual discipline that can be adopted by anyone, regardless of their walk of life. It provides a path to spiritual liberation that does not necessitate renunciation of worldly duties. Rather, it emphasizes the performance of these duties in a selfless, detached manner, making everyday life a path to spiritual growth and enlightenment.

Bhakti Yoga: The Yoga of Devotion

Bhakti Yoga, the yoga of devotion or divine love, is prominently detailed in the *Bhagavad Gita*. It is the path that entails love, reverence, and adoration toward God. The *Bhakti* path seeks to establish a personal relationship with the divine, surrendering oneself in pure love and devotion. This relationship can take various forms, from a loving parent-child relationship, as seen in the devotion of Yashoda (the foster mother) toward Krishna, to a relationship of a friend, like Arjuna to Krishna, or even a beloved, as seen in the love Radha bore for Krishna.

In *Bhakti Yoga*, the aspirant devotes their actions, thoughts, and feelings to God, seeing Him as the ultimate object of love and respect. God is perceived not as an abstract or distant entity but as a deeply personal and intimate presence. The devotee seeks to see God's manifestation in all things, embracing an attitude of universal love and acceptance. The practice of *Bhakti Yoga* involves various expressions of devotion, such as singing devotional songs (*bhajans*), reciting God's names (*japa*), listening to divine stories (*katha*), and performing ritual worship (*puja*). Yet, *Bhakti Yoga* goes beyond ritualistic practices; it is about cultivating an internal state of complete surrender and love toward the divine. The *Bhagavad Gita* states that through such pure, selfless devotion, the heart is purified. The veil of ignorance and illusion (*Maya*) is lifted, leading to the realization of the divine nature within oneself and all of creation. *Bhakti Yoga* promises the experience of divine love and bliss, the realization of oneness with the divine, and ultimately, liberation (*Moksha*).

Bhakti Yoga is, therefore, a path accessible to anyone, irrespective of their knowledge or capacities. It does not require complex philosophical understanding or physical practices but a sincere, loving heart. It is this universal accessibility and emphasis on love and devotion that have made *Bhakti Yoga* one of the most followed spiritual paths in India and beyond.

Jnana Yoga: The Yoga of Knowledge

Jnana Yoga, often termed the path of knowledge or wisdom, is a significant aspect of spiritual teachings outlined in the *Bhagavad Gita*. Unlike *Karma Yoga*, which focuses on selfless action, or *Bhakti Yoga*, which revolves around devotion, *Jnana Yoga* places emphasis on intellectual and philosophical inquiry. Its foundation lies in discerning between the eternal (unchanging and undying) and the ephemeral (changing and transient), leading to the realization of one's divine nature or the Self.

The practice of *Jnana Yoga* is not simply about acquiring intellectual knowledge or learning philosophical concepts, but it revolves around the profound experiential understanding of the truth. It involves a deep exploration into the nature of existence, understanding the distinction between the body, the mind, and the Self. It guides the practitioner toward self-realization, realizing that the true Self (*Atman*) is not distinct but is one with the universal spirit (*Brahman*). *Jnana Yoga*'s practice requires the cultivation of certain qualities. These include *Viveka* (discrimination between the real and the unreal), *Vairagya* (detachment from worldly desires), *Shatsampatti* (six virtues comprising tranquility, restraint, withdrawal, forbearance, faith, and focus), and *Mumukshutva* (intense longing for liberation).

In essence, *Jnana Yoga* represents a profound and rigorous path requiring intellectual sharpness and philosophical understanding. It is a method of exploration that guides practitioners to transcend the illusion of separateness, realize their true nature, and achieve union with the divine. Through *Jnana Yoga*, one realizes that they are not merely a body or a mind, but a part of the greater divine reality, ultimately leading to *Moksha*, liberation from the cycle of birth and death.

EMBODYING THE TEACHINGS OF THE *GITA* IN DAILY LIFE

The application of the *Bhagavad Gita*'s philosophies in everyday life transcends their interpretation as abstract concepts. At first glance, the *Gita* presents concepts such as the "Tree of Life" or the "upside-down eternal *Ashvattha* Tree" in an abstract, metaphysical manner, depicting an inverted tree with its roots above and branches below. However, on closer examination, this seemingly abstract concept manifests profound practical implications for daily life. The tree can also be understood through an analogy with the human body.

The roots of the tree, located upward, can be seen as the human brain. Just as the roots are the life source for the tree, the brain is the control center of our body, responsible for our thoughts, emotions, and actions. These thoughts and emotions can be the root cause of our suffering, but through wisdom and understanding, the brain can also be the source of wisdom and enlightenment. The branches of the tree, spreading downward and outward, represent our physical actions in the world, akin to how our limbs engage with the world around us. These actions, driven by our thoughts and emotions, can lead to various life experiences—some joyous, some challenging, echoing the principles of *Karma Yoga*. The leaves of the tree, symbolic of the holy scriptures, offer guiding wisdom, reflecting the path of *Jnana Yoga* or the pursuit of knowledge. Just like the leaves photosynthesize sunlight into energy for the tree, the wisdom we gain nourishes our minds, providing enlightenment and direction.

The act of understanding this metaphor and severing the tree with the "axe of detachment" indicates an intentional effort to break away from worldly illusions and false identities, much like consciously striving to detach from negative thought patterns that lead to suffering.

Summarily, the *Bhagavad Gita* presents numerous abstract concepts that intricately weave together the spiritual wisdom of *Karma*, *Bhakti*, and *Jnana Yoga*. However, these seemingly abstract notions offer a practical roadmap for individuals aspiring to integrate these philosophies into their everyday lives. By embodying the teachings of the *Gita*, individuals can navigate the journey toward spiritual realization, transforming abstract concepts into tangible practices for a fulfilling life **(Fig. 2)**.

TOWARDS AN INTEGRATIVE APPROACH: YOGA AND EASTERN PHILOSOPHIES AS EMERGING THERAPEUTIC FRONTIERS IN PSYCHIATRY

Despite advancements in psychopharmacology and psychotherapy, psychiatry has faced challenges in boosting the overall well-being and happiness of the general population, a situation further exacerbated by the coronavirus disease-2019 (COVID-19) pandemic.[3] This stagnation may arise from an undue focus on the negative aspects associated with mental disorders, neglecting the vital roles of nurturing positive emotions, fostering character development, and enhancing life satisfaction and spiritual growth.[4] It is in this context, it is essential to highlight that yoga is not just a pathway to spirituality but has become an integral tool in promoting mental wellbeing and managing psychiatric disorders in recent years.[2]

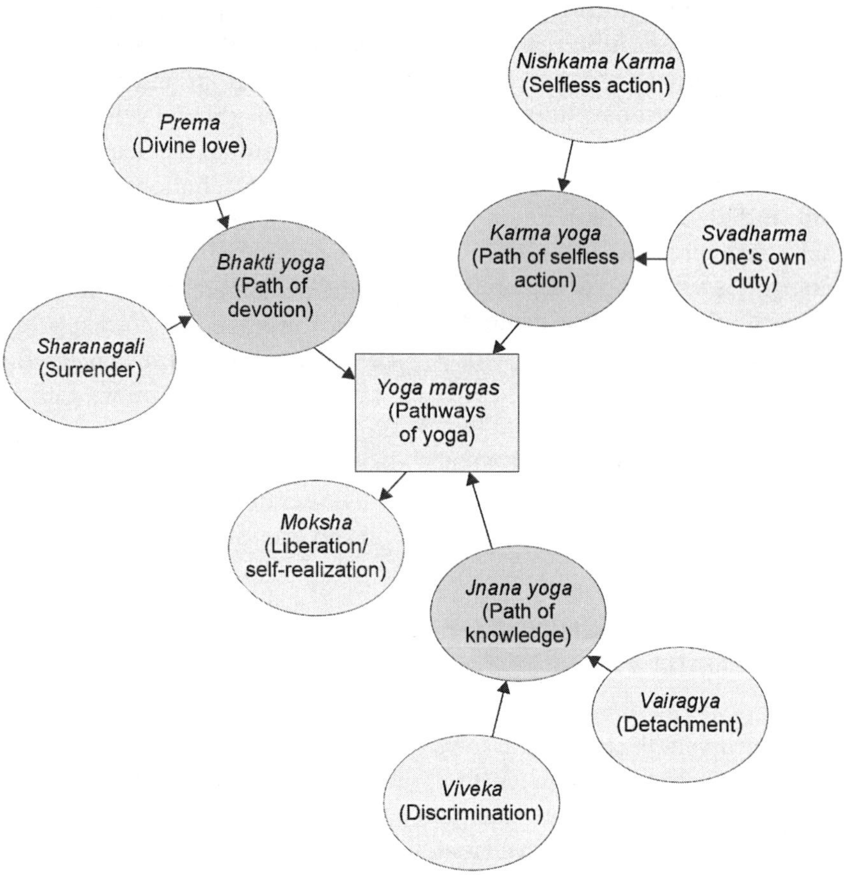

Fig. 2: A schematic representation of the paths of *Karma*, *Bhakti*, and *Jnana Yoga* as delineated in the *Bhagavad Gita*. The paths converge at the central node of *Yoga Margas*, highlighting the integrative approach in the journey toward *Moksha* or self-realization.

Recent research highlights the promising, yet underexplored, role of yoga in psychiatric therapy.[5] Research demonstrates yoga's efficacy as an effective antidepressant and its role as an adjunct intervention in treating schizophrenia, notably enhancing social cognition, reducing negative symptoms, and ameliorating facial emotion recognition deficits.[6] These beneficial effects potentially originate from yoga's capacity to enhance neuroplasticity and promote neurocognitive and mentalizing abilities, possibly through the reinforcement of prefrontal brain networks and the mirror neuron systems,[7] mediated by an increase in plasma oxytocin levels.[8]

The mirror neuron system is a neural circuitry that underpins our ability to understand and resonate with the emotions and actions of others. This system, stimulated through coordinated physical postures and meditative practices integral to yoga, facilitates the nurturing of social bonds grounded in empathy and understanding, encouraging a more profound interconnectedness with the wider community. Thus, yoga emerges as a powerful tool, not just in unifying the individual consciousness with the universal but in enhancing social connectedness, laying the grounds for relationships rooted in understanding, compassion, and mutual respect, fundamentally enriching the social fabric.

In recent years, scholars have highlighted a fruitful cross-pollination between age-old Eastern teachings and modern psychotherapy.[9] The *Bhagavad Gita*, for instance, serves as a reservoir of psychotherapeutic insights, illustrating metacognitive strategies that promote well-being, and laying the groundwork for several modern concepts in positive psychology, such as self-appraisal, intrinsic motivation, and the cultivation of compassion.[10] Furthermore, the *Gita*, along with other Eastern scriptures, portrays yoga as a multi-tiered approach to mental health prevention and holistic well-being, urging a harmonious integration of these ancient insights with contemporary psychotherapeutic models for a more comprehensive approach to mental health care.[11,12] This movement signals a hopeful trajectory toward a respectful collaboration and integration grounded in a broader awareness and a deeper understanding of both Eastern and Western perspectives in the evolving landscape of mental health interventions.

CONCLUSION

In conclusion, this chapter has ventured deep into the rich tapestry of yoga as elucidated in foundational texts such as Patanjali's *Yoga Sutras* and the *Bhagavad Gita*. We revisited the core tenets of the *Yoga Sutras*, appreciating the symbiotic relationship between the theory and practice of yoga. The *sutras* delineate a trajectory, from laying foundational knowledge in *Samadhi Pada* to the heights of liberation in *Kaivalya Pada*, mapping a practitioner's progressive journey toward inner harmony and self-mastery.

The *Bhagavad Gita* enriched our understanding, introducing us to the vibrant paths of *Karma*, *Bhakti*, and *Jnana Yoga*. These paths, while distinct, intertwine beautifully, allowing for a personalized journey that accommodates individual predispositions and inclinations. The text elucidates a synthesis of these pathways, advising a harmonious amalgamation of knowledge, action, and devotion, thereby encouraging a holistic and enriched life's journey toward spiritual realization.

This narrative showcases the yoga philosophy as not just a ritualistic practice but a lifelong journey. It is a guiding light steering individuals toward a path of deep spiritual realization and enlightenment. It helps one to celebrate the rich diversity in paths toward a common, revered destination of self-realization and inner peace.

It is evident that the philosophy of yoga stands not just as a testament to rich spiritual heritage but resonates deeply with modern mental health paradigms, potentially offering therapeutic pathways grounded in ancient wisdom. It portrays yoga not just as a practice but as a nurturing philosophy, a guide toward a harmonious life enriched with mental peace and spiritual depth.

The bond between yoga and spirituality highlighted in this chapter stands as a nurturing ground, urging one to cultivate a personal relationship with yoga's core. It beckons one to delve into its potential for enhancing mental well-being in the modern era, channeling age-old wisdom into today's lives, and promoting healing, harmony, and comprehensive health.

REFERENCES

1. World Health Organization. Constitution of the world health organization. In: World Health Organization: Basic documents. 45th edition. Geneva: World Health Organization; 1995.
2. Rao NP, Varambally S, Gangadhar BN. Yoga school of thought and psychiatry: Therapeutic potential. Indian J Psychiatry. 2013;55(Suppl 2):S145-9.
3. Keshavan MS. Building resilience in the COVID-19 era: Three paths in the Bhagavad Gita. Indian J Psychiatry. 2020;62(5):459-61.
4. Loninger CR. The science of well-being: an integrated approach to mental health and its disorders. World Psychiatry. 2006;5(2):71-6.
5. Varambally S, George S, Gangadhar BN. Yoga for psychiatric disorders: from fad to evidence-based intervention? Br J Psychiatry. 2020;216(6):291-3.
6. Bhargav H, George S, Varambally S, Gangadhar BN. Yoga and psychiatric disorders: a review of biomarker evidence. Int Rev Psychiatry. 2021;33(1-2):162-9.
7. Mehta UM, Keshavan MS, Gangadhar BN. Bridging the schism of schizophrenia through yoga-Review of putative mechanisms. Int Rev Psychiatry. 2016;28(3):254-64.
8. Jayaram N, Varambally S, Behere RV, Venkatasubramanian G, Arasappa R, Christopher R, et al. Effect of yoga therapy on plasma oxytocin and facial emotion recognition deficits in patients of schizophrenia. Indian J Psychiatry. 2013;55(Suppl 3):S409-13.
9. Tandon R. Asian philosophies and the practice of modern psychiatry. Asian J Psychiatr. 2023; 86:103700.
10. Keshavan MS, Tandon R. Eastern perspectives on mind and healing: Lessons from the Vedas and the Gita. Asian J Psychiatr. 2023; 85:103652.
11. Reddy MS. Psychotherapy - insights from Bhagavad Gita. Indian J Psychol Med. 2012; 34(1):100-4.
12. Keshavan MS. Psychotherapy teaching in an ancient case report: The Arjuna syndrome in the Bhagavad Gita. Asian J Psychiatr. 2023; 87:103743.

7 CHAPTER

Culture, Spirituality, Self, and Mental Illnesses

Dinesh Bhugra, Susham Gupta

INTRODUCTION

Human beings are born into a culture or a mixture of cultures, may grow up in different cultures, and work and play in yet other different cultures. Each culture has multiple aspects and facets to it. Including its core concepts, there are multiple microcultures. Each microculture contributes to multiple microidentities in an individual, and these are related to a number of factors including religion, gender, sexual orientation, etc. Throughout our development, we continue to absorb subtleties of each microculture we are exposed to. Our primary culture may overshadow secondary lessons from other microcultures. Cultures mold our cognitive and social development—the way we see the world or our worldview. Cultures also help us to develop and accumulate cultural capital, which we carry with us wherever we go. This cultural capital consists of our values related to culture but also concepts of religious values, educational attainments, dress, dietary habits, etc. Of course, some parts of cultural capital may well change easily and perhaps rapidly in response to exposure to other cultures leading to acculturation, but a core is likely to remain unchanged. Cultures not only help develop our worldview but also our identity and how we interact with others and mold our behaviors accordingly. Cultures teach us about what distress is, how pathological and deviant behaviors are, how we develop our explanatory models about the distress we experience, where we seek help from, and who the first person or port of call will be in times of distress. We learn how to dress, what to eat, and how to have our meals, i.e., table manners and live according to cultural norms and values with which we have become familiarized. Of course, this may well change according to circumstances and exposures to other cultures directly or through other means such as TV and social media.

Cultures help define what is normal and what is deviant and what is not and identify, mold and influence explanatory models of distress, which can be supranatural, natural, physical, medical, psychological, or social or a mixture of these. In mental illnesses, these models will dictate when, where, and how an individual seeks help. The models held by the family and the carers will also influence these pathways. In certain settings, especially when access to professional services is limited, individuals may seek help from religious leaders. Very often in the first instance, people will seek help, advice and suggestions from personal, and folk or social sectors. It is entirely possible that ability to pay for or afford private healthcare may lead to seeing advice from social or folk sector. Furthermore, these explanatory models may well influence development of healthcare services such as providing access to or delivery of alternate or complementary medicine such as homeopathy or Ayurveda in the Indian context. Thus, it is critical that service planners and those delivering it are cognizant of the cultural norms of populations they aim to serve. This will ensure that services are easily acceptable to the population. In addition, services must be easily accessible.

As described later in this chapter, in clinical practice of psychiatry often a biopsychosocial model of etiology and management is recommended but not always followed due to lack of trained personnel and limited resources. However, it is imperative that spiritual components are included as in many countries and settings, potential patients and their carers will look out for and seek help from spiritual resources.

DEFINITIONS OF CULTURE

Tylor (1871) described culture as a complex whole which includes knowledge, beliefs, arts, laws, morals, and customs, which may include capabilities and mindsets acquired from being a member of any culture.[1] Culture is a shared network of attributes, meanings, beliefs, norms, and values,[2] which are thus shared by a particular group of individuals. Interestingly, it is seen as a web culture created by human beings.[3] Kleinman (1996) defined culture as resulting from lived daily experiences, activities, communications, rhythms, rituals, and patterning of social relationships, which are likely to be strongly influenced by the typology of culture.[4] Cultures and individual members of that culture are interconnected in multiple identifiable and nonidentifiable ways. Cultures change individuals, and in return individuals change cultures, thereby confirming that cultures are not static and both bring about changes in the other. Individuals often have to follow the rules as set by cultures.[5] A broad classification of cultures is egocentric versus sociocentric[6] though it needs to be emphasized that not everyone in a single culture will imbibe and follow all the characteristics of that structure. Cultural characteristics can be molded by historical traditions in the same way a child's development affects their cognitive and social responses in their adulthood and beyond. Boas (1982) saw cultures to be a manifestation of social habits of a community,[7] whereas others have seen it an intervening variable between human organism and environment.[8]

Kirmayer (2018) illustrates various definitions of culture.[9] From traditional agriculture/agrarian societies to cultured states the term denotes multiple meanings. While the term is (agri)culture used in cultivation, it also reflects certain standards of conduct and refinement (often expected from rulers and those in positions of power) but may also identify a medium (a petri dish) where bacteria may grow as people will. Furthermore, culture is also used in upper classes as someone being described as cultured meaning that they had certain attributes. Cultures do provide a sense of belonging and a sense of purpose which give people's lives meaning and existential advantages. Of course, sometimes, some individuals may not feel a part of any culture and may therefore feel alienated, which may be attributed to personality traits. Having a common history, common heritage and language along with religious practices, individuals do carry socially transmitted aspects of the environment.[10] In addition to the places where we learn train and work are institutions which are not buildings but are formed of individuals who carry institutional memory with them. Institutions have their own cultures which are modifiable by individuals working there, but more importantly, such individuals have to abide by the institutional norms. Cultural characteristics can be molded by historical traditions in the same way a child's development affects their cognitive and social responses in their adulthood and beyond.

In its latest iteration, DSM-5 recognizes culture as systems of knowledge, concepts, rules, and practices, which are learnt and transmitted across generations.[11] Cultures have an extraordinary amount of influence on an individual's social and personal functioning. Cultures also set standards of actions and behaviors but also help interpret people's actions as normal, abnormal, or deviant. It is well recognized that cultures can precipitate, perpetuate, and influence presentation as well as therapeutic engagements, which influence outcomes of various psychiatric illnesses. Cultures and individual members of that culture are interconnected in multiple identifiable and nonidentifiable ways.

Certain types of psychiatric disorders are more common in some cultures rather than others. In a rather old study, Hupka et al. (1985) demonstrated that rates of morbid sexual jealousy were lower in communist countries.[12] Similarly, it has been demonstrated that egocentric cultures have higher rates of crime, divorce, and psychiatric disorders.[13] It is possible that cultural expectations of behaviors may lead to a variation in rates of certain psychiatric disorders. This is further complicated by issues related to Mental Health Acts in respective countries which decide the criteria for detention and forced treatments.

CONCEPTS OF SELF

The notions of self are very strongly linked with culture. What is self? Rosenberg (1979) uses the terms self and ego to refer to the inner nature or essential nature[14] as previously recognized by Fromm (1941, 1947).[15,16] Maslow (1954) also sees it in a similar vein and the self is both experience and construct (as well as context) of self-awareness.[17] This has to be seen as different from self-esteem. Rosenberg (1979) draws a distinction from the Freudian ego,[14] which according to Symonds (1951) consists of a set of intellectual processes,[18] which enable the individual to deal with reality primarily serving the interests of id.[14] Rosenberg (1979) defines self-concept as totality of the individual's thoughts and feelings with reference to themselves as an object.[14] This is also recognized as the realm of self-ideas. There are three components: The extant self (how the individual sees themselves), the desired self (how they would like to see themselves), and the presenting self (how they show themselves to others). Building on this, Rosenberg (1979) has described four principles which are worth noting as they do vary across cultures.[14] These include reflected appraisals (direct reflection), social comparisons, self-attribution, and psychological centrality. Thus, from a spiritual perspective, they will respond according to cultural context. In a sociocentric culture, they may be more aware of their extant self, whereas in egocentric cultures, it is possible that presenting self may be more significant.

Social identity in Rosenbergs view (1979) is related to categories which are based on gender, age, race, religion, family status, legal status, name etc.[14] Again, there are likely to be differences according to cultures. For example, in some South Indian communities, the individual's name includes village the family comes from, father's name, and then that of the child. Thus, the name itself indicates a number of identities and being classified in the context of socially defined categories. Social identity can be understood in the context of social status, membership of certain groups, etc. Membership of religion-based groups can offer support and a sense of purpose, which can contribute to better functioning. Organized religion more than spirituality can influence social identity which according to Rosenberg (1979) does not need to be logical.[14] On the other hand, these memberships may lead to extremist views in vulnerable individuals. Membership groups can become more complex as societies change and evolve and become more complex. Furthermore, in this context, religion plays a major role in identity even if the person is not religious in following rituals or attendance of religious events. In this role, another perspective of social labeling emerges, which can be personal, social, or legal labels.

Morris (1994) focuses on the concept of self,[19] which is clearly influenced by and related to cultural meaning systems.[20] This is a significant distinction in that the first conception of the person identifies the individual as a natural human being—the concept being universally organized. The second meaning, according to Morris (1994) is a cultural category which is articulated in the cultural representations of the community.[19] He points out that as a cultural category, the person is often clearly expressed in the ritual context often with an ideological function. Cultural representations are clearly embedded in lived experience. Morris (1994) goes on to describe third conception of the person as an individual self.[19] Smith (1978) and Marsella (1985) suggest that self-hood is an organizing tendency which offers structure and continuity to experience.[21,22] Thus, it is a process by which we come to know ourselves and the world around us. This undoubtedly is influenced by philosophical structures within a specific culture but also organized religion and its rites and rituals but also spirituality.

Harris (1989) draws a distinction between three levels of analysis of human beings and these are: Psychological, biological, and sociological domains of experience.[23] It is inevitable that psychological and sociological domains are going to be influenced by spirituality. As these three domains are crucial in our understanding of the etiology of psychiatric disorders and their management, it becomes critical to include spirituality both in the context of assessments and interventions.

It is well recognized through the work of Hofstede (1980/2000), Morris (1994), and others that how self is perceived and understood is because of a number of reasons of which religion is only one aspect which is often a key component of cultures.[6,19] These differences highlight various notions of the self across religions. Personal identity is fused with group affiliation but also at higher levels with family, caste, spirit, etc. Morris (1994) draws a clear distinction between Western concepts of person and the Eastern concept of the individual.[19] Western concept has been defined as having an analytic orientation tending toward the objectification of "external" objects as existing separately from the observer, thus implying a strong, rigid subject/object dualism.[24] This dualism can be seen in parallel with spirit and body which are often seen as separate and rigidly defined as if they do not talk to each other certainly in allopathic medicine.

As mentioned earlier, the Western conception of the self is individualistic and egocentric. It is also materialistic and rationalist.[19] This raises a rather difficult question to answer whether non-Western concepts are thus nonrationalist. As Morris (1994) goes on to challenge these perceptions including Cartesian mind-body dualism and argues that class differences may play a role too.[19] Citing Gould (1984) and Grimshaw (1986), he notes that the cultural hegemony of capitalism and bourgeois modes of thought and their inherent androcentric bias play a role.[25,26] This structure of the self in the West (bearing in mind that the West as an entity is often vague and huge and includes Western Europe, USA, Australia, and New Zealand) is seen as individuated, individualized, detached, separate, self-sufficient with a strong focus on autonomy. However, in large parts of the USA, Christian evangelism and other variants appear to be flourishing, which challenge some of these assumptions.

In the context of this chapter, we shall aim to focus on Hindu and Buddhist concepts of the self very briefly.

Hinduism is a philosophy and focuses on salvation (*moksha*) which emphasizes that the metaphysical conception of the self (as *atma*) is given priority, and self-realization is essentially a spiritual quest.[19] The four basic paths to salvation include knowledge (*gyana*), action (*karma*), devotion (*bhakti*), and spiritual discipline (*yoga*). This is of special interest as increasing evidence is beginning to emerge to illustrate the role yoga appears to play in managing some types of mental illnesses. Here, we are not looking at aspects of mental illnesses described in Ayurvedic texts. As Hinduism is more than simply an organized religion, it is difficult to distil its various tenets because it includes various strands, schools of thought and practice, themes, etc. Unlike philosophy in Greek and Roman times and in the West now, in India philosophy is essentially spiritual.[27] Morris (1994) argues that although Hinduism is not a philosophy in the Western sense, it has six orthodox systems of Indian philosophy.[19] Various components have been incorporated in Ayurvedic texts. Two selves are recognized in Hindu thought. These are material or phenomenal self and the inner self, which is formless, absolute, and immutable. The realization of the true self implies a detachment from the phenomenal world of becoming, not only from desires and material detachments but also from the flux of psychic life itself.[19] Three secular goals of life are *kama, artha,* and *dharma*. These are evident in arts and literature and may need to be included in management of certain psychiatric disorders. The four pathways into salvation mentioned above can be employed in culturally appropriate therapies. Traditionally this gives limited room for individuation and personal autonomy, but anecdotal clinical evidence suggests that this is beginning to change as cultures are changing. Marriott (1976) emphasizes that persons in South Asia are not individual (i.e., indivisible) but are dividual (meaning that they are divisible) and absorb heterogeneous material influences).[28] Self here is social collectivity, i.e., as collectivist or sociocentric which influences their identity, perception of the self, expectations of the others, and from the other.

Buddhism has been seen as a way of salvation and a way of life. Buddhism has a doctrine of "no-self", which is one of the three signs of being others, being nonpermanence, and suffering. Hence, this concept of no-self varies from traditional Western models of the self. Buddhism is atheistic and is unique in the history of human thought in denying the existence of both the soul (atman) and a god.[29,30] The doctrine of no-self in Buddhism is connected to the ideas of impermanence and suffering. The five components of the self and being are: Body, sense impressions, feelings, perceptions and consciousness, which are all impermanent.[19] These all constitute what can be described as the being. There is thus a need to overcome the egocentric consciousness.[31]

These two brief examples from Eastern religions illustrate how concepts of self vary, especially in the contexts of cultures. Cultures also therefore help mold concepts of spirituality which itself can be seen as collective or individualistic. The individual often views themselves as abstract categories as well as in the mirror of micro-identities. These abstract categories can be liberal, intelligent, kindly, brave, good, knowledgeable, skilled, outgoing, friendly, etc.[14] Rosenberg (1979) goes on to argue that the concepts of self can be abstract and may include attitudes, traits, abilities, values, preferences etc.[14,32] Thus simply looking at these components in the context of attitudes and values, spirituality can play a major role.

SPIRITUALITY

Religion and spirituality are important in mental health for a number of reasons. As Moreira-Almeida and Bhugra (2021) have defined spirituality as the relationship or contact with a transcendent realm of reality that is conceived, sacred, the ultimate truth or reality, they also highlight that religion and spirituality are important in managing mental illnesses for a number of reasons.[33] These reasons include the observation that religion and spirituality are important in large parts of the world. In the context of illnesses, especially mental distress, these are often the first step in help-seeking resources. These authors define religion as the institutional or communal aspects of spirituality as a shared set of beliefs, experiences, and practices related to the transcendent and the sacred. Higher levels of religious involvement (attending religious services), positive religious coping, and intrinsic religiosity have been shown to have lower rates of some psychiatric disorders such as depression, suicidal ideation, and alcohol abuse and have better quality of life. Religious gap between the health professional and the patient may well influence therapeutic engagement.

Both clinicians and patients understand and follow that mind and brain are different. Mind is related to soul or spirit, which in many cultures have very specific meanings. It has been argued that "our bodies are wired to benefit from exercising not only our muscles but our rich inner human core-our beliefs, values, thoughts and feelings".[34] Inevitably all of these are strongly influenced by cultures. These authors see medicine as a three-legged stool: Pharmacology, surgery, and intentional use of placebo effect. This raises key questions about how this model fits in with psychiatric illnesses. Beauregard and O'Leary (2008) point out that early in the twentieth century, medicine came down firmly against the idea that the mind influenced the body and sought to trace illness to single specific source.[35] These attitudes in allopathic medicine date back to Cartesian mind-body dualism. These authors place significant emphasis on the placebo effect which they also identify as remembered wellness.

Matthews et al. (1993) in a meta-analysis of 158 studies reported that religion played a positive clinical effect in 77% of studies.[36] Similar findings among older adults reported that religious activities such as meditation, prayer, and Bible study were associated with better survival rates. Helm et al. 2000 pointed out that older adults who participated in private religious activity before the onset of activities of daily living impairments had a survival advantage in comparison with those who did not.[37]

Spiritual assessment does not take long in clinical assessment and using cultural contexts and framework can be very helpful in improving engagement. In addition, spiritually integrated therapies can also help better therapeutic outcomes.[38]

CONCLUSION

Spirituality and religion form an integral part of people's lives in many countries and cultures and thus clinicians need to be aware of and sensitive to include these facets in assessments and management.

Ideal models of assessment in clinical psychiatry include biopsychosocial etiological factors and management. It is crucial to include spiritual assessment and thereafter work with religious and spiritual leaders to be able to offer optimal treatment to patients and support to their carers and families. The emphasis on social and spiritual factors may appear at odds to traditional assessments, but social factors such as attachment patterns in childhood influence brain development and poverty, unemployment, and overcrowding impact upon social functioning. Social factors also impact upon help seeking so perhaps the time is ripe for the profession to think outside the box and form partnerships in order to deliver the best treatments possible for patients with mental illnesses.

REFERENCES

1. Tylor EB. Primitive Culture, vols 1 and 2. London: John Murray; 1871.
2. DHHS. Mental Health, Culture, Race and Ethnicity. Rockville, MD: SAMSHA; 1999, 2001.
3. Geertz C. Myth, Symbol and Culture. NY: Norton Books; 1971.
4. Kleinman A. How is culture important for DSM-IV? In: Mezzich JE, Kleinman A, Fabrega H Jr, Parron DL (Eds). Culture and Psychiatric Diagnosis: A DSM-IV Perspective. American Psychiatric Association; 1996. pp. 15-25.
5. Haviland WA. Cultural Anthropology. Philadelphia, Penn: Pennsylvania State University. Pub Holt, Rinehart & Winston; 1990.
6. Hofstede G. Culture's Consequences. Beverly Hills, CA: Sage; 1980/2000.
7. Boas F. Race, Language and Culture. Chicago, Ill: University of Chicago Press; 1982.
8. Kroeber AL, Kluckhohn C. Culture: A Critical Review of Concepts and Definitions. Papers. Peabody Museum of Archaeology & Ethnology, Harvard University; 1952, 47(1), viii, 223.
9. Kirmayer L. Cultural psychiatry in historical perspective. In: Bhugra D, BHui K (Eds). Textbook of Cultural Psychiatry. Cambridge: Cambridge University Press; 2018. pp. 1-17.
10. Kuper A. Culture: The Anthropologist's Account. Camb, Mass: Harvard University Press; 2000.
11. APA. Diagnostic and Statistical Manual-5. Washington, DC: APPI; 2013.
12. Hupka RB, Buunk B, Falus G, Fulgosi A, Ortega E, Swain R, et al. Romantic jealousy and romantic envy: A seven-nation study. J Cross-Cult Psychol. 1985;16(4):423-46.
13. Maercker A. Association of cross-cultural differences in psychiatric morbidity with cultural values: A secondary data analysis. Ger J Psychiatry. 2001;4:17-23.
14. Rosenberg M. Conceiving the Self. Malabar, FL: Krieger; 1979.
15. Fromm E. Escape from Freedom. NY: Rinehart; 1941.
16. Fromm E. Man for Himself. NY:Rinehart; 1947.
17. Maslow A. Motivation and personality. NY: Harper; 1954.
18. Symonds P. The Ego and the Self. NY: Appleton-Century-Crofts; 1951.
19. Morris B. Anthropology of the Self: The Individual in Cultural Perspective. London: Pluto Press; 1994.
20. d' Andrade R. Culture meaning systems. In: Sheweder R, Levine R (Eds): Culture

Theory: Essays on Maid, Self and Evolution. Cambridge: CUP; 1984. pp. 88-122.
21. Smith MB. Perspectives on self-hood. Am Psychol. 1978;33:1053-63.
22. Marsella AJ. Culture, self and mental disorder. In: Marsella AJ, de Vos G, Hsu FLK (Eds). Culture and Self: Asian and Western Perspectives. NY: Tavistock; 1985. pp. 281-308.
23. Harris G. Concepts of Individual, Self and Person in Description and Analysis. Am Anthrop. 1989;91:599-612.
24. Johnson J. The Western concepts of self. In: Marsella AJ, de Vos G, Hsu FLK (Eds). Culture and Self: Asian and Western Perspectives. NY: Tavistock; 1985. pp. 91-138.
25. Gould CC. Beyond Domination: New Perspectives on Women and Philosophy. Ottowa: Rowman and Littlefield; 1984.
26. Grimshaw J. Feminist Philosophers. London: Harvester Wheatsheaf; 1986.
27. Radhakrishnan S. Indian Philosophy, vol. 1. New Delhi: OUP; 1933/2009.
28. Marriott MK. Hindu transactions: diversity without dualism. In: Kapferer B (Ed). Transaction and Meaning. Phil, Penn: Institute of study of Human Issues; 1976.
29. Conze E. Buddhism: Its Essence and Development. Oxford: Cassirer; 1951.
30. Rahula W. What the Buddha Taught. London: G. Frazer; 1959.
31. Wilber K. Up from Eden. Landon: RK&P; 1983.
32. Flavell JH. The development of inferences about others. In: Mischel T. (Ed). Understanding Other Persons. Oxford: Blackwell; 1974.
33. Moreira-Almeida A, Bhugra D. Religion spirituality and mental health: setting the scene. In: Monteiro-Almeida A, Mosqueiro BP, Bhugra D (Eds). Spirituality and Mental Health across Cultures. Oxford: OUP; 2021. pp 11-26.
34. Benson H, Stark M. Timeless Medicine: The Power and Biology of Belief. NY: Scribner; 1996.
35. Beauregard M and O'Leary D. The Spiritual Brain. NY: Harper One; 2008.
36. Matthews DA, Larson DB, Barry C. The Faith Factor: An Annotated Bibliography of Clinical Research on Spiritual Subjects, vol 1. NY: National Institute of Healthcare Research; 1993.
37. Helm HM, Hays JC, Flint EP, Koenig HG, Blazer DG. Does private religious activity prolong survival? A six-year follow-up study of 3,851 older adults. J Gerontol A Biol Sci Med Sci. 2000;55(7):M400-5.
38. Costa M de Abreu, Rosmarin DH. Spiritually integrated psychotherapy. In: Monteiro-Almeida A, Mosqueiro B P, Bhugra D (Eds.) Spirituality and Mental Health across Cultures. Oxford: OUP; 2021. pp. 383-94.

2

SECTION

Spirituality and Mental Health (Preventive and Therapeutic Aspects)

1 CHAPTER

Spirituality Across the Lifespan

Vishal Indla, Srividya Bellapukonda

INTRODUCTION

Spiritual dimension is important and relevant to almost all stages of life.

It starts with the "big questions" often posed in childhood, progresses to identity formation during adolescence, evolves into self-integration in adulthood, and culminates in a deeper existential exploration in later stages of life.

Spiritual health and well-being are acknowledged as fundamental rights in the UN Convention on the Rights of the Child and are widely regarded as an essential dimension of overall health.

Unlike other developmental domains such as physical, cognitive, or emotional growth, spiritual development often involves a conscious and deliberate act of choice. While few human development theories have addressed the spiritual dimension, those that do typically view spiritual development as a hallmark of the most advanced stages of adult growth.

James Fowler's faith development model serves as a key framework for understanding spiritual development across the lifespan. This model outlines seven universal stages, beginning with primal or undifferentiated faith in early childhood, which centers on security and trust. During adolescence, individuals typically progress to a synthetic-conventional faith, characterized by formal operational thinking, a focus on interpersonal relationships, a strong sense of belonging to groups, and conformity to societal norms. As individuals move through young adulthood and mid-life, they may advance through other stages, culminating in the rarely achieved universalizing faith in late adulthood—akin to enlightenment or transcendence.[1]

SPIRITUALITY IN ADOLESCENCE

During adolescence, individuals transit from the concrete religious impressions formed in childhood to a more reflective engagement with deeper existential and transcendental questions. Adolescents may be more likely than individuals in other age groups to engage in spiritual exploration, have a conversion experience, and make spiritual commitments that endure throughout the lifespan.[2]

At this stage of life, spiritual development plays a vital role in fostering positive youth development, shaping values, promoting civic engagement, and cultivating a sense of purpose and identity.

Spiritual health can be understood as the strength of an individual's connections across four key domains:

1. To oneself
2. To others
3. To nature
4. To the transcendent

The specific aspects of these dimensions may vary across spiritual traditions, shaped by cultural, environmental, and individual influences. They can also take both personal and institutional forms.

A universal pattern of spirituality emerged when spiritual health domains were assessed among thousands of adolescents across 12 countries. Both boys and girls consistently prioritized connections to self as the most important, followed by connections to others, nature, and finally, the transcendent. Notably, the perceived importance of connections to self was strongly associated with positive mental health outcomes. The connection to self also appeared to mediate associations between connections to others and nature with the mental health outcome.

Among the connection to self, there are two domains:

1. The importance of experiencing meaning or purpose in their lives
2. The importance of experiencing joy, pleasure, and happiness in life.

They may be working together synergistically so that the combined effect is strengthened. This sense of purpose is not only perceived to be highly important to the majority of adolescents but is strongly influenced by the connections young people have with the world around them.

The protective features of strong connections to others, to nature and to the transcendent act on mental health, individually or in composite, by changing or supporting the inner worlds of young people.[3]

There are different patterns of spiritual connectedness and three distinct patterns emerged in adolescents.

1. Adolescents with a "low and steady" profile of spiritual connectedness started low and remained low
2. Adolescents who were "decliners" started moderately high but declined significantly over the study period, with early adolescents experiencing steeper declines than middle adolescents.
3. A "high and steady" pattern with adolescents starting with high levels of spiritual connectedness and remaining so over the study period.

Specifically, just over four in 10 youth maintained high and steady levels of spiritual connectedness throughout early and middle adolescence. A similar percentage of youth showed a decline in spiritual connectedness across the adolescent years. Meanwhile, just over two in 10 youth reported low levels of spiritual connectedness, which remained low throughout the study period.

Overall, there was a general trend of spiritual connectedness declining over the course of the study. The three profiles—high and steady, decliner, and low and steady—differed in terms of coping, goal-directedness, caregiver-rated emotion management, and life satisfaction. Adolescents with high and steady levels of spiritual connectedness were more goal-directed, reported higher life satisfaction, demonstrated more effective coping strategies, and managed their emotions more effectively than youth in the decline or low and steady profiles.[4]

The relation of spiritual connectedness with goal orientation and emotional regulation points toward the consideration of spiritual connectedness as a potential intervention target in interventions seeking to improve adolescent adjustment.

Reflecting is one of the mechanisms to improve the spiritual development.

Reflection involves a cycle of consciously examining one's actions in relation to intentions, with the goal of expanding options and making decisions about more effective ways of acting.

Individuals must also reflect beyond immediate concerns to consider broader and contextual issues, such as the meaning of life, long-term plans, and identity formation. Reflection on spirituality encourages adolescents to build relationships with others, particularly those of different faiths. It propels them to search for meaning, belonging, and ultimate answers in life—central aspects of identity exploration during adolescence.

Reflections can be introduced when students of various faiths participate together in school or community projects such as environmental or service learning endeavors where they are encouraged to practically reflect on their learning experiences.

Some of the attitudes and procedures to promote reflection in the adolescents:

- Encouraging adolescents to ask questions and willing to respond to the questioning honestly and in a way which respects the adolescent's developing cognitive and emotional maturity.
- Make the adolescent aware that religion is a matter of faith
- Encourage attitudes of tolerance and understanding in relation to religious disagreement.

Through the three characters of reflection, that is open-mindedness, whole-heartedness, and intellectual responsibility, adolescents can transcend the self to reason critically about previously held values, beliefs, feelings, and behavior and become active agents in seeking their individual authenticity and wholeness.

Spiritual development through reflection can be promoted in school through various subjects across the curriculum, especially the arts—literature, poetry, drama, painting, and music.[5]

Following the spiritual education of students using the contemplative practices such as several types of body relaxation and movement practices, varieties of basic breathing practices, mindfulness meditation and guided meditation practices, a wide range of sensory awareness concentration practices and several social-emotional practices in educational settings, teachers noticed an atmosphere of peace and calm in the classroom and improvement in the attention levels of the students and their ability to focus in class. Teachers also reported a more positive change in how the children interacted with each other and the teacher. The findings again point toward the role of spiritual education for students.[6]

SPIRITUALITY IN YOUTH

During emerging adulthood, there is often a growing interest in exploring new forms of spiritual searching and practice. This is particularly evident among college students, who engage in spiritual activities as they seek purpose, meaning, fulfillment, depth, wholeness, and authenticity.

Youth spiritual development is viewed as the dynamic interplay of several underlying developmental processes.

- *Awareness of self and the world:* Developing an awareness of one's inherent strength. In some traditions, this process has to do with "awakening" to one's true essence or spirit. This also encompasses developing an awareness of the beauty, majesty, and wonder of the universe.
- *Connecting/belonging:* Developing the perspective that life is interconnected and interdependent.
- *Life of meaning and contribution:* Developing a life orientation grounded in hope, purpose, and gratitude.

The most important and potentially universal developmental elements of youth spiritual development include:

- Experiencing empathy, responsibility, and love for others, humanity, and the world.
- Finding significance in relationships with others, the world, or one's sense of the transcendent.
- Discovering, accepting, or creating deeper meaning in everyday experiences and relationships.
- Accepting, seeking, or experiencing a sense of purpose or meaning in life.
- Being present to oneself, others, the world, or one's sense of transcendent reality.
- Living with an awareness of something beyond the immediate concerns of daily life.
- Forming a worldview that addresses major life questions, such as the purpose of existence, life and death, and the nature of the divine or God.
- Engaging in relationships, activities, and practices that strengthen bonds with oneself, family, community, humanity, the world, or a transcendent belief.
- Living according to one's beliefs, values, and commitments in daily life.
- Cultivating hope, meaning, or resilience in the face of hardship, conflict, confusion, or suffering.

The linkage of youth spiritual development to outcomes was examined in four domains:

1. Academic (school engagement; achieving high grades)
2. Physical well-being (positive feelings about own health; avoiding health risk behaviors such as substance use and violence; resolving conflicts peacefully)
3. Psychosocial well-being (thriving; positive emotionality; feel emotionally safe and not picked on due to their religion); and
4. Civic engagement (hours volunteer/week; environmental stewardship).

Together, these served as core indicators of youths' well-being.

Youth with higher levels of spiritual development, were broadly associated with better concurrent developmental outcomes in the academic, physical, psychosocial, and civic domains.

The majority of youth pursued spiritual development without deep engagement in specifically spiritual or religious practices.

Those with the highest Youth Spirituality Development (YSD) Index scores reported better physical health, feeling healthier, happier and have better grades and a decreased likelihood of substance abuse than all other youth, and less engagement in violence than those with the lowest of YSD Index scores.[7]

Spirituality has been shown to reduce the likelihood of engaging in health-risk behaviors and is associated with higher levels of healthy behavior. Education plays a significant role in fostering spirituality.

A study revealed notable relationships between spirituality, health-related behaviors, and psychological well-being, particularly in relation to the type of education acquired. Both spirituality and health-related behaviors were directly linked to psychological well-being.

Spirituality demonstrated a positive relationship with health-related behaviors and had an indirect effect on psychological well-being through these behaviors. The relationship between spirituality and psychological well-being was stronger in students studying the human mind and spirit compared to those in other fields.

It seems that, in the human mind and spirit group, spirituality plays a greater role in influencing psychological well-being though the choice of the study group might be determined by a specific attitude toward spirituality and personal development.[8]

SPIRITUALITY IN ADULTHOOD

Adulthood is viewed as a developmental period rich with potential for spiritual growth, driven by neurological, cognitive, and socio-emotional maturation. Once key developmental tasks—such as forming an identity, establishing a family, and becoming actively involved in the workforce—are addressed, spirituality often emerges, marked by a deeper striving for meaning and self-transcendence.

During this stage of life, significant life events may prompt a search for spiritual development. There are two broad models of spiritual growth in the second half of adulthood:

1. The first model views spiritual growth as a positive outcome of the maturation process.
2. The second model sees the relationship between spirituality and older age more as one of constraints and adversity, rather than a natural progression of growth.

Unlike universal sequential stages or gradual maturation, spiritual development can occur through a more distinctive and non-linear process. This may include experiences such as radical religious conversion, where a person shifts from one set of religious beliefs to another, or the phenomenon of "quantum change," which involves a sudden spiritual realization and transformation.

Such examples can be found in religious, mystical, or transpersonal experiences, such as peak or near-death experiences. They can also result from post-traumatic growth, which refers to positive psychological changes following traumatic events such as loss, life-threatening illness, or severe addiction, and is often seen in programs such as Alcoholics Anonymous.[1]

The "growth" and "deficit or adversity" models of spiritual development are not mutually exclusive because a deficit may trigger growth.

There is a positive relationship between age and higher stages of faith development, which are marked by a sense of unity and personal transcendence. Older adults were found to be significantly more spiritual than their younger counterparts in early adulthood. Spirituality in older age was also correlated with the number of negative events experienced between adolescence and late middle adulthood (mid-50s to early 60s). Interestingly, spiritual development was linked to the experience of negative life events in the first half of adulthood, but not in the second half.

There is a relationship between spirituality and negative life events, such as conflict with a spouse, conflict with parents, and financial strain, particularly among women during the first half of the adult life cycle (teens to 40s).

Spirituality in older age was significantly predicted by religiosity, spirituality, and cognitive commitment (but not IQ) in early adulthood. It was also influenced by the number of negative life events experienced between early (30s) and middle (40s) adulthood.

This suggests that spirituality in older adulthood is highest among individuals who were cognitively committed as young adults and later experienced negative life events.

Additionally, there is a positive correlation between spirituality in older age and prior measures of cognitive commitment, especially for women. On the other hand, an absence of negative life events and low levels of cognitive commitment were not conducive to spiritual development.

SPIRITUALITY IN OLDER AGE

Both men and women showed a significant increase in spirituality from late middle adulthood (mid-50s to late 60s) to older adulthood (late 60s to mid-70s). There is a general tendency for individuals to become more focused on spiritual matters as they age.

This trend was particularly pronounced among women, who scored significantly higher than men on measures of spirituality in older adulthood. If the search for ultimate meaning in life is in any way influenced by an awareness of mortality, it is understandable that this quest would be intensified after the 50s.

Spiritual development in later life was more likely to occur in women who, as younger adults, were introspective, insightful, psychologically minded, unconventionally thinking, verbally fluent, and had broad interests.

The combination of high cognitive commitment in early adulthood and the experience of a significant number of negative life events from early to middle adulthood positively influenced levels of spirituality in older adulthood.

Spiritual development is particularly characteristic of individuals who have the psychological sensitivity and strength to transform personal pain and sorrow into a deeper understanding of life's mysteries.

Religiosity, a personality in early adulthood marked by cognitive commitment, and the experience of negative life events during early adulthood are all strong predictors of spiritual development 40 years later.[9]

Empirical studies have shown a clear connection between stressful life events and various forms of religious/spiritual involvement.[10]

The reason behind this connection can be explained as major life events can threaten or harm many objects of significance such as the sense of meaning, intimacy with others, personal control, physical health, and the sense of personal comfort.

Religious/spiritual methods of coping can affect the psychological, social, physical, and spiritual adjustment of people to crisis, for better or worse.

The factors in religious/spiritual copings used by adults who are dealing with a variety of life crises are:

- Spiritually-based coping (through the relationship with God, problems are reframed, limits of control are accepted, and guidance and reassurance are sought)
- Good deeds (efforts to live a better, more religiously integrated life)
- Discontent (expressions of anger, mistrust, and distance to God and the congregation)
- Religious support (attempts to obtain help from the clergy or congregation members)
- Pleading (attempts to bargain with God or obtain a miracle)
- Religious avoidance (religious activities to distract the individual from problems)[11]

Spiritual development is often linked to the later stages of adulthood, when individuals typically seek greater meaning in their lives and confront existential concerns related to the end of life.

This increased interest in spirituality is also evident in the growing availability of spiritually sensitive practices, such as spiritual care, which is particularly relevant for individuals nearing the end of life and their families, especially in the context of palliative care.

Contemporary psychologists often describe goal of religious and spiritual development as "successful aging" which includes: (1) a low probability of disease and related disability, with a life style that minimizes risk factors for problems, (2) a high physical and cognitive functional capacity, and (3) an active engagement with life, including good interpersonal relationships, productive activity that is socially valued, and resilience or rapid recovery from stress and other life changes.

While successful aging defines the goal of human life in terms of health, productivity, and social adaptation, spiritual maturity involves the development of a relationship with the transcendent or sacred that reflects positively on the welfare of others and ourselves.

These conceptions of spiritual maturity generally have two characteristics: (1) They include at least weak forms of transcendence as a necessary part of life and (2) they are holistic and encompass a wide variety of factors including relational, emotional, ethical, and cognitive strengths.[12]

Spirituality was an integral component of wisdom in religious scriptures and the items that were common to wisdom and spirituality included pro-social behaviors such as compassion and altruism, humility, gratitude, self-compassion, mindfulness, reverence for nature, nonviolence, ethical conduct, calmness, life satisfaction, and general sense of well-being.

Spirituality that is not directly related to wisdom but reports strong associations with greater well-being and mental health. A spiritual orientation can help people to cope with the consequences of a serious disease, thereby enhancing personal wellness. Thus, both wisdom as a whole and spirituality are associated with better mental health and well-being.[13]

Old age is a life period characterized by marked social and psychological transformations, where various social and contextual factors interact such as life conditions, family situation, support structures, and personal expectations.

The dimension of spirituality is fundamental to give meaning to life, to deal with adversity and the experience of the disease, and in aging people, simultaneously with the normal physical modifications.

The older adults defined spirituality in two ways—beliefs and harmonious reciprocal connectedness.

Beliefs address the older adults' views about belief in God and divine religions and on religious practices.

In terms of harmonious reciprocal connectedness, respondents defined spirituality as connection with God, self, and others and as dependence on nature in their statements.[14]

People create spirituality, give it a framework and use it as a coping mechanism for their successful, peaceful, happy, active, creative, and healthy aging with confidence.

Elderly living alone or only with the spouse are perceiving the meaning of spirituality and incorporating spirituality in their daily lives as a tool for learning, change, and adaptation for their active/creative/successful/peaceful and happy aging.

Following are some of the ways:

- Spirituality is perceived as a connection with something bigger than itself. This bigger entity was God for some respondents, *Guru* (teacher) for some and for some it was the universe or supernatural powers.
- Spirituality as a way of living—spirituality is connected with the inner genius.

- Living a peaceful and content life with non-violence is the crux of spirituality.
- Individuals have found a purpose or a duty they had to take care. This purpose of existence helps them to tackle loneliness and adjust through the old age.

  This "purpose" gives them a new strength and energy and fulfilling the "purpose" becomes their life. This spiritual belief of having a purpose in their lives allows them to live happier and fulfilling lives.
- *Karma* theory helps the elderly to understand their situation better and take positive actions too. They believe whatever they have done, good or bad, in this life or in the past lives have led them to this situation.

They do not feel grudges against people; instead, they try to do good karma to attain salvation.

Thus, spirituality has taught the elderly new ways of life to accommodate in a new situation. The process of accommodation is a continuous/ongoing process of learning.

Elderly take it as another phase of life accompanied by loneliness but overcome it by practicing spirituality and they are accepting it. It is an exploration of self. While exploring his or herself he or she identifies the positive characteristics of him or herself.

Through this positive identification, the elderly create a new type of actions and interactions that help them to modify their relationships with self and others.

When people begin to view everyone as a soul, it leads to a positive shift in their thought process and creates new connections. This acceptance helps them realize that they too have a purpose in life: "to achieve something new." This "something new" may involve self-exploration, re-engagement, or active aging.

There is a shift from a materialistic to a non-materialistic perspective. People no longer focus on the appearance of their bodies, but on how they look and feel from within. Their primary concern becomes the happiness of their soul, while external factors matter less.

Older individuals are increasingly moving toward inner transformation, giving their soul a new identity where bodily ailments, family issues, and societal pressures no longer hold as much significance. They begin to view themselves more positively. Spirituality has also helped them alleviate the anxiety associated with death and final rites.

Elderly individuals engaged in spiritual practices often find answers to why certain things are happening in their lives through spiritual discussions and activities, enabling them to overcome negative situations with greater ease. They explore spirituality not only to learn something new but also to re-engage with themselves.

Although the practices followed are different, all believe in spirituality as a meaningful engagement leading toward their active and happy aging.[17]

The importance of a holistic and individualized approach to positive aging is evident across various aspects of the aging process. Older adults identified several factors contributing to "successful aging," including maintaining a positive perspective, coping ability, active independence, meaningful relationships, freedom, a relationship with God, and a sense of spirituality.

Religion, spirituality, and belief were also found to provide social support, foster connectedness to others, and offer a sense of belonging to a community for older adults. These elements manifest in diverse ways in the everyday lives of older adults and play a significant role in shaping their experiences of aging.

Five significant themes emerge regarding the role of religion, spirituality, and belief in positive aging:

1. *Changing religious landscapes:* The perceived decline of traditional family values, shaped by religion, influences the positive aging of older adults. This highlights the need to consider not only health issues but also the impact of religion, spirituality, and belief in aging.
2. *Intrinsic personal and interpersonal nature:* Religion, spirituality, and belief are deeply personal and interpersonal for older adults, often intertwined with pro-social behaviors that shape their daily lives and interactions.
3. *Source of strength, comfort, and hope:* Religion, spirituality, and belief serve as powerful sources of strength, comfort, and hope, especially during health challenges and other difficulties of aging. These factors contribute to positive aging by offering a sense of peace and calm during illness.
4. *Social support and belonging:* Religion, spirituality, and belief provide vital social support through community and belonging. Being part of a religious or spiritual community helps older adults feel less isolated and more connected.
5. *Choice and holistic approaches:* The importance of choice and holistic approaches in integrating religion, spirituality, and belief into the lives of older adults is emphasized. This should be done in an individualized and person-centered way, recognizing that personal choice is key for positive aging. The role of religion and spirituality in health care, while debated, highlights that respecting the individual's choice may be crucial for fostering positive aging outcomes.

Overall, religion, spirituality, and belief can have numerous positive effects on older adults, including enhanced health and well-being, improved coping capacity, social support, and opportunities for societal participation.[18]

Several studies have shown the relationship between spirituality, quality of life, and mental health.

Spirituality is the only variable to have a direct effect on mental quality of life, emphasizing the role of spirituality on mental quality of life.[15]

Meaning of life and spiritual strength scored highest among the measures of quality of life. Spirituality is seen as a fundamental form of sustaining support. The spiritual contact and direction make it possible for the individual who is aging to reflect on him/herself.

Connection with a higher being, meaning in life, spiritual strength, faith, and spirituality showed significant correlations in the participants with more advanced age.[16]

CONCLUSION

Research suggests that cumulative effect of religion or spirituality has an effect on mortality confirmed this relationship between religion or spirituality and longer survival. At least 121 studies have examined relationships between religion, spirituality, and mortality. Most of these are prospective cohort studies, where baseline religion or spirituality (R/S) is assessed as a predictor of mortality during the observation period after controlling for confounders. Of those studies, 82 (68%) found that greater R/S predicted significantly greater longevity.

An increased survival of 37% was associated with religious, spiritual activities, which is highly significant and equivalent to the effects of cholesterol lowering drugs or exercise-based cardiac rehabilitation after myocardial infarction on survival.[19]

Thus, spirituality not only improves the quality of life, but also shown to extend the longevity of people.

REFERENCES

1. Russo-Netzer P. Spiritual Development. In: Arterberry ME, Fingerman KL, Lansford JE (Eds). SAGE Encyclopedia of Lifespan Human Development. SAGE Publications; 2017.
2. Good M, Willoughby T. Adolescence as a Sensitive Period for Spiritual Development. Child Develop Perspect. 2008;2:32-7.
3. Michaelson V, Šmigelskas K, King N, Inchley J, Malinowska-Cieślik M, Pickett W, et al. Domains of spirituality and their importance to the health of 75,533 adolescents in 12 countries. Health Promot Int. 2023;38(3):daab185.
4. Wright AW, Yendork JS, Kliewer W. Patterns of spiritual connectedness during adolescence: Links to coping and adjustment in low-income urban youth. J Youth Adolesc. 2018;47(12):2608-24.
5. Charlene T. Reflection for Spiritual Development in Adolescents. In: de Souza M, Leslie J. Francis LJ, O'Higgins-Norman J, Scott DG (Eds). International Handbook of Education for Spirituality, Care and Wellbeing: 3 (International Handbooks of Religion and Education). New York: Springer-Verlag Inc.; 2009.
6. Flanagan B, Nelson J, Mullally A. Spiritual Education: A Teacher Development Initiative. J Study Spiritual. 2012.
7. Scales P, Syvertsen A, Benson P, Roehlkepartain E, Sesma A. Relation of Spiritual Development to Youth Health and Well-Being: Evidence from a Global Study. In: Ben-Arieh A, Casas F, Frønes I, Korbin JE (Eds). Handbook of Child Well-Being. Springer Nature; 2013.
8. Bożek A, Nowak PF, Blukacz M. The Relationship Between Spirituality, Health-Related Behavior, and Psychological Well-Being. Front Psychol. 2020;11:1997.
9. Wink, Paul & Dillon, Michele. (2002). Spiritual Development Across the Adult Life Course: Findings from a Longitudinal Study. J Adult Develop. 2002;9:79-94.
10. Bearon LB, Koenig HG. Religious cognitions and use of prayer in health and illness. Gerontologist. 1990;30(2):249-53.
11. Pargament K, Ensing D, Falgout K, Olsen H, Reilly B, Haitsma K, et al. God Help Me: (I): Religious coping efforts as predictors of the outcomes to significant negative life events. Am J Commun Psychol. 1990;18:793-824.
12. Nelson JM. Religion, Spirituality, and Development in Adulthood. In: Nelson JM (Ed). Psychology, Religion, and Spirituality. New York, NY: Springer; 2009.
13. Jeste DV, Thomas ML, Liu J, Daly RE, Tu XM, Treichler EBH, et al. Is spirituality a component of wisdom? Study of 1,786 adults using expanded San Diego Wisdom Scale (Jeste-Thomas Wisdom Index). J Psychiatr Res. 2021;132:174-181.
14. Can Oz Y, Duran S, Dogan K. The meaning and role of spirituality for older adults: a qualitative study. J Relig Health. 2022;61(2): 1490-1504.
15. Lima S, Teixeira L, Esteves R, Ribeiro F, Pereira F, Teixeira A, et al. Spirituality and quality of life in older adults: a path analysis model. BMC Geriatr. 2020;20(1):259.
16. Chaves LJ, Gil CA. Older people's concepts of spirituality, related to aging and quality of life. Cien Saude Colet. 2015;20(12): 3641-52.
17. Kumari S, Sharma A. Spirituality: A tool for learning, change and adaptation of elderly in changing Indian family. Intern J Learn Change. 2018;10:33.
18. Malone J, Dadswell A. The Role of Religion, Spirituality and/or Belief in Positive Ageing for Older Adults. Geriatrics (Basel). 2018; 3(2):28.
19. Koenig HG. Religion, spirituality, and health: the research and clinical implications. ISRN Psychiatry. 2012;2012:278730.

2 CHAPTER

Spirituality in Pregnancy and Maternal Mental Health

Mrugesh Vaishnav, Suresh Sathe, Parth Vaishnav

INTRODUCTION

During pregnancy, spirituality play as a vital role, in supporting a mother's mental health, bringing a sense of purpose and peace. It aids in building emotional and mental well-being by lowering the levels of anxiety and stress strengthening the relationship between a mother and her child. Spiritual practices can be a source of strength for women by serving as a source of comfort along the whole journey.

PSYCHIATRIC DISTURBANCE DURING ANTENATAL PERIOD

Perinatal mental health is a pressing issue for maternity care providers worldwide, and it influences maternal health policy, professional assistance, and education. Depression and anxiety are the most frequent mental health issues during pregnancy, with roughly 12% of women suffering depression and 13% experiencing clinical anxiety at some point; many women experience both. Poor mental health is estimated to impact 15–25% of women during their childbearing years especially in underdeveloped countries.[1]

Maternal mental health during pregnancy has been linked to negative outcomes like premature labor, low-birth weight and early neonatal developmental difficulties, adolescent neurodevelopmental issues, and young adult mental and social problems.[2]

Prevalence of prenatal depression internationally indicated a range of 15–65%. Self-harm during pregnancy is a complicated cause of maternal deaths, particularly in females who have had mental health problems in the past.[2] A global survey found that the prevalence of suicide thoughts during pregnancy and after birth ranged between 5 and 14%.[3]

Indian Prevalence

The overall prevalence of prenatal depression ranged from 3.8 to 65%, whereas the overall anxiety ranged from 13 to 55%. Depression and anxiety are frequently co-occurring conditions, but the time of their onset is unknown. Few studies have found that high levels of prenatal anxiety can predict postpartum depression. Among the numerous psychosocial characteristics, insufficient social support was discovered to be a significant predictor of anxiety.[4]

Risk Factors

The most prominent risk factors identified in a meta-analysis of studies were pressure to have a male child, unemployment, financial difficulties, a history of miscarriage, marital conflict or poor relationship with the spouse, and a lack of recreational opportunities. Another key risk factor for prenatal depression that has been verified by several research is the presence of a prior history of abortion.[4]

Impact of Antenatal Depression and Anxiety

Aside from the potential impact on her children, a woman's mental health during pregnancy is strongly linked to other aspects of her health in general. A lack of social support directly correlates with the chance of experiencing despair, anxiety, and self-harm during the term. It is exacerbated by hormonal changes and can manifest as a period of increased risk in the presence of psychological health problems such as anxiety, sadness, and self-harm.[5]

Antenatal anxiety is characterized by overwhelming demands, fears, and doubts regarding pregnancy, labor, the newborn's well-being, and the couple's future parental and caring obligations.

Depression is the most common mental health condition during pregnancy, connected with side symptoms such as a discouraged state of mind, low confidence, lack of interest, perceptions of uselessness, peevish temperament, loss of food, feelings of weakness, and poor concentration abilities.[5]

SPIRITUALITY DURING PREGNANCY AND CHILDBIRTH

Given the numerous physical and psychological changes of pregnancy, severe health problems may emerge if this period is not managed effectively (WHO, 2018).[5] Antenatal care is a comprehensive approach to care that includes physical, psychological, social, and spiritual care.[2] Spiritual midwifery reflects the existential relevance and meaningfulness of process of birth.[1] Wojujutari (2018) explored the topic of ritualizing pregnancy and labor as a spiritual experience, including the five facets of spirituality (moral, majestic, mystical, concerns of meaning, and merging with the other or something outside of self).[6]

Offering spiritual support during labor decreases cesarean section incidence and the usage of intrapartum analgesia and prevents many problems and assistive treatments.[3] Nodoushan et al. (2020) discovered that the majority of pregnant women had high levels of stress and low levels of spiritual and psychological well-being increase the risk of preterm delivery and unsafe births.[7] There is an inverse link between spirituality and stress during pregnancy.[2]

In Brazil, Piccinini et al. (2021) found that negative religious and spiritual coping were associated with higher levels of depressive, anxious, and stress symptoms as well as worse physical and psychological quality of life.[8]

- *Spiritual experiences:* Athan et al. (2015) discovered that women who held attributions of God as loving, knowable, and residing within the self-experienced lower levels of anxiety, depression, and perceived stress, as well as higher levels of social support.[9]
- *Spiritual intelligence:* Spiritual intelligence is another concept associated with spirituality. Results of the study by Wojujutari et al. (2018) showed the significant moderation role of the spiritual intelligence on the relationship between psychological well-being and maternal psychosocial adjustment.[6]
- *Spiritual well-being:* Spirituality is regarded a vital aspect of the quality of life and a central factor for mental health during pregnancy.[10]
- *Maternal-fetal attachment:* The link between maternal-fetal attachment and spiritual well-being revealed a

positive correlation.[11] In a study among primiparous women and their infants, maternal religious attitudes affect fetal mental health by employing particular newborn mental health indicators.[12]

- *Postpartum depression:* Spirituality was regarded one of the linked factors that reduce the prevalence of postpartum depression.[2] Higher levels of spirituality linked to better maternal mental health and emotional wellness after childbirth; psychosocial resources of mastery, self-esteem, and optimism.[13]
- *Social support and religious devotion:* Social support and religious devotion influence depression symptoms during pregnancy and after childbirth. The effect of spirituality on mother mental health throughout pregnancy and in the postpartum period is significantly visible.[14]

PSYCHOLOGICAL WELL-BEING DURING PREGNANCY AND CHILDBIRTH

Stress during pregnancy affects women's physical and psychological well-being. Spirituality provides pregnant women with the ability to mitigate stress and its consequences and adapt well during difficult times.[2]

There is a substantial influence for spirituality and psychological well-being in lowering pregnancy-specific stress.[15] Dilgony et al. (2016) also validated the same results[16] as spiritual well-being predicts pregnancy-related stress.[17] In contrast, Mann et al. (2010) revealed that religiousness and spirituality related to greater reported stress.[18]

- *Psycho-spiritual transcendence:* Women regarded their experiences of agony after childbirth as a time for psycho-spiritual transcendence, highlighting the need to engage spirituality in maternity care.[2] Submission to God makes it easier to overcome pregnancy and childbirth; spiritual stories boost confidence and motivation. Women possess a powerful ability to improve their spirituality.[15,19]
- *Life satisfaction*: Positive strong correlations between life satisfaction, social support, and spiritual well-being, accounting for the mediating role of social support.[20]
- *Spiritual counseling:* A substantial benefit of spiritual care education on postpartum stress disorder was seen in women with preeclampsia along with improved sleep quality and reduced the severity of insomnia throughout pregnancy.[2] Giving spiritual care during antenatal care can be useful in sustaining maternal psychological well-being.[2]

ECOLOGY OF BIRTH

The ecology of childbirth conceptual framework highlights human relationships with one another and the environment **(Fig. 1)**. The framework of ecology consists of six components—contextuality, embodiment, relationality, temporality, spatiality, and mystery.[1]

- *Context:* Cultural and spiritual characteristics, people (family and carers), venues of care, and how care is administered all contribute to the setting in which childbirth takes place. It is clear that the circumstances of delivery experiences will always influence childbirth feelings.[1]

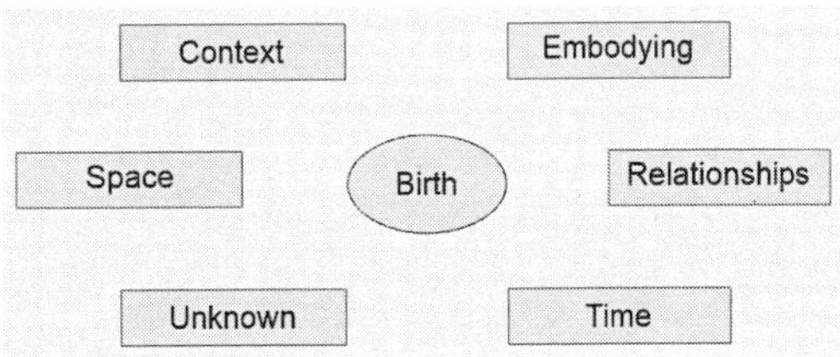

Fig. 1: Ecology of childbirth.
Source: Crowther S, et al.[1]

- *Space:* Bennington (2010) highlights various levels of energy that arise throughout delivery experiences, including environmental energy, location and space of birth, and the sociocultural milieu that surrounds birth. Mitchell's (2012) study emphasizes women's desire to find space in their delivery experience to relax and assimilate their experiences.[21]
- *Embodying:* Maternity care professionals must be aware of the physical and emotional demands of pregnant women.[2,22] Disregarding physical demands interferes with relationships and the ability to adapt to the changes that occur during childbirth[5] especially if there is lack of familial support, poverty, and a traumatic birth.[22] Mitchell (2012) discovered that physical connection and touch are significant.[23]
- *Relationships:* Equally important is relationships and kinship as weaker interpersonal connections are connected with lower chance for spiritual growth.[2] Women who felt alone, detached, uncared for, and unsupported by family were left feeling powerless and helpless.[22]
- *Clock time and felt time:* Temporality is a component of the delivery experience, consisting of clock time and felt time. Women need time to reflect on their past, present, and future relationships.[17] Childbirth is a unique time that requires inward development and invites women to become themselves. Being called to be externalized early may disrupt the "going inside" process of transformation and impair emotional wellbeing.[17]
- *Unknown:* Mitchell's (2012) study demonstrates how mothers struggle to find time for themselves to assimilate what is happening to them throughout the unpredictable childbearing year. Time is required to treat spiritual welfare, and how recognizing this requirement may lessen risk and need for scientific interventions.[23]

A NEW CONCEPTUAL MODEL (FIG. 2)

Orem (2001) recognizes three components of well-being—contentment, pleasure, and happiness. Orem's conceptual approach

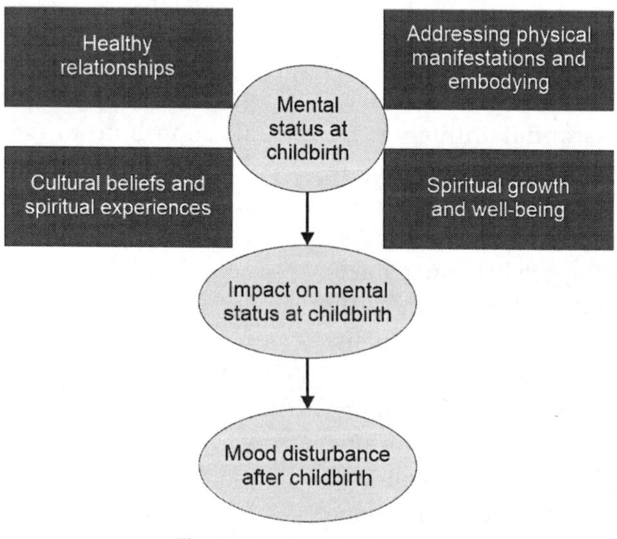

Fig. 2: A conceptual model.
Source: Crowther S, et al.[1]

allows us to think about delivery in a broader context than the narrow biomedical focus. A new conceptual model has formed based on the four themes highlighted using the ecology of childbirth framework.[1]

SPIRITUALITY AND COPING

Spirituality is an important subject to explore; it is more than just an esthetic aspect of human life; it is regarded as a fundamental component of human well-being and holistic treatment. Several difficulties, such as cesarean section, the usage of intrapartum analgesia and supportive techniques, and the prevalence of postpartum depression, should be minimized when offering spiritual support.[24]

THE STRUCTURAL MODEL

Pregnancy-specific Stress

The psychological and physical changes linked with them can generate various levels of anxiety and stress in women.[15] Almost 25% of women suffer some level of stress during their pregnancy which can contribute to complications during pregnancy and childbirth.[25] Stress and anxiety levels fluctuate throughout pregnancy.[26] Preterm birth, low birth weight, spontaneous miscarriage, and newborn abnormalities are some of the negative pregnancy outcomes that can result from these strains and tensions, depending on their duration and intensity.[25]

Spirituality and Stress Management

Increasing spirituality is advocated as a stress management and treatment method, as it constitutes a healthy lifestyle.[27] Monotheistic spirituality promotes health and gradually reduces hazardous behaviors.[28] Spirituality can relieve stress by making people feel peaceful, in control, independent, and purposeful.[15] Spirituality dramatically affects both physical and mental health.[15] Spirituality protects against stress during pregnancy.[29]

Health and Well-being

Health and well-being are fundamental components of an individual's identity, influencing all elements of life.[30] Individuals with a low sense of well-being adversely evaluate their life events and experience more negative emotions such as worry, melancholy, and rage.[31] There is a substantial relationship between life skills, anxiety, depression, and mental health and well-being.[32]

Spirituality and Psychological Well-being

Pregnancy-related stress can result in irreparable repercussions such as miscarriage, preterm delivery, and hypertension. Spirituality and psychological well-being influence pregnancy-related stress in beneficial manner.[15]

Fear of childbirth appears to stem from uncertainty about the birth process.[33] A quarter of women fear labor to varying degrees because they fear pain, losing control, and episiotomy which may have an negative impact on the mother and the infant.[34-37]

Social and Psychological Factors

A wide range of variables, including psychosocial, spiritual, and demographic traits, are linked to negative experiences and a fear of giving birth.[38,39] Mothers who have greater spiritual well-being and social support are better able to tolerate the pain of labor, which in turn reduces fear and improves the childbirth experience.[40-42]

Negative Impact of Religiosity

Religious beliefs could have the opposite effect by pushing people to stop receiving treatment or delaying their prompt referral for illness prevention.[43] Individuals with stronger spiritual beliefs had a worse prognosis and worse condition than other patients.[44]

MATERNAL ANXIETY

Pregnant women's fear and experience of birthing are correlated with their spiritual well-being and perception of social support. Therefore, reducing fear and the negative effects of labor can be achieved by implementing programs that provide spiritual and familial support, resulting in a happy childbirth experience.[36]

Maternal Anxiety and Pain

A woman's pregnancy is a wonderful time in her life and a physiological phenomenon as giving birth is a significant event in her life.[45] When it comes to enduring the pains of pregnancy and labor, every pregnant lady behaves differently from other pregnant women **(Fig. 3)**. Numerous variables influence this response **(Box 1)**.[46]

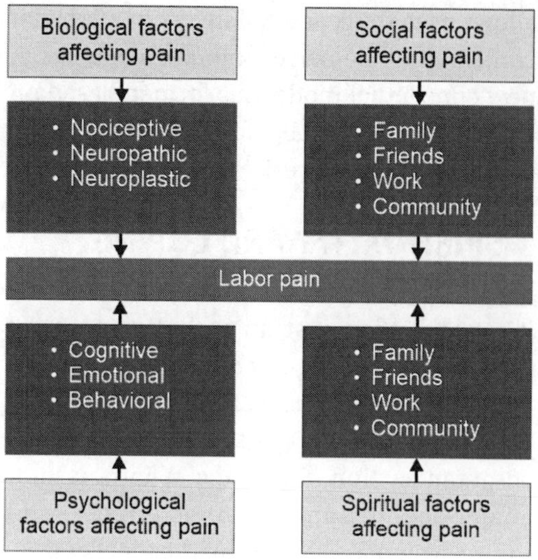

Fig. 3: Labor pain in pregnant mother.
Source: Dehestani H, et al.[45]

BOX 1: Factors affecting maternal anxiety during pregnancy.

- Education
- Economic situation
- Unplanned pregnancy
- History of miscarriage
- Vaginal bleeding
- Fever

Source: Ding X, et al.[46]

Pregnant women typically experience anxiety, insomnia, frequent awakenings, sleep deprivation at night, and effective sleep deprivation starting in the 12th week of pregnancy and continuing for the first 2 months following delivery. These issues with sleep patterns either result from anxiety or are the cause of anxiety.[47]

Maternal Anxiety and Fetal Cortisol

Anxiety is a psychological state brought on by coping with perceived or actual stressors.[48] The health of the mother and fetus may be significantly impacted by anxiety reduction techniques throughout pregnancy.[49]

The mother's anxiety and depressive state during her pregnancy raise the fetal levels of cortisol and adrenal secretion, which directly affects the mood of the child negatively.[45] Maternal anxiety influences the fetal heart rate variability.[50] Stress and bad experiences of mothers had during their pregnancies negatively affect the newborn's psychological development, motor-behavioral development, and physical growth.[51] Over 80% of pregnant women with low-risk pregnancies feel anxious at some point throughout their pregnancy.[52]

Dealing with Maternal Anxiety

Yoga, gentle physical activity, and massage might help lessen anxiety in mothers while also improving the quality of pregnancy outcomes.[53] Learning relaxation skills can help women prioritize their overall health, leading to healthy childbirth and childrearing.[54] Family physicians frequently overlook patients spiritual well-being.[55]

Women who have experienced physical harm and suffering also prefer to be religious because religion enables them to cope with the anguish and sorrow brought on by their illness.[56]

Women with Childhood Maltreatment Histories

A mother experiences major changes during the postpartum period, which makes her more susceptible to psychopathology. If mother who has gone through a lot of physical, emotional, and social changes could lower her quality of life and put her at risk for postpartum depression; especially mothers who experienced traumatic events and maltreatment in past.[57]

RELIGIOSITY AND SPIRITUALITY

Spirituality and religiosity are related, although they differ both conceptually and experimentally. It was proposed that spirituality typically refers to broader views and experiences, whereas religiosity concerns actions connected to formal traditions. It is possible to be spiritual without being religious, and vice versa. While many people identify as both religious and spiritual, not all do.

- *Religiosity and spirituality (R/S) and mental well-being*: A favorable correlation between R/S and mental well-being. In diverse communities and cultures, higher R/S was linked to improved mental health, like decreased prevalence of anxiety, sadness, and other stress-related mental diseases.
- *R/S and quality of life:* Given that many traditions place a high value on motherhood, childbirth, and the family, R/S encounters may be particularly pertinent for postpartum women. R/S may operate as modifying or directing elements to help avoid postpartum depression and/or improve quality of life.
- *R/S and postpartum phase:* A high correlation between postpartum mental health issues and women's childhood trauma experiences, such as abuse, neglect, or severe household dysfunction. R/S may be protective against postpartum depression symptoms.
- *R/S and resilience:* R/S were proposed as potential strategies to support stress resistance in trauma survivors from early life and may occasionally act as a moderator on the emergence of posttraumatic reactions in victims of childhood abuse.
- *R/S and childhood abuse:* A history of childhood abuse is a known risk factor for postpartum mental health and since R/S has been found to be one possible defense against abuse.
- *R/S and forgiveness:* The findings of Jonathan E Handelzalts et al. shown benefits for forgiveness rather than a more general feature of religion on postpartum depression and life quality.[57]

FEAR OF CHILDBIRTH

During reproductive years, a woman must cross an existential threshold by becoming pregnant and giving birth.[58] Women's expectations and experiences with pregnancy and childbirth range from joy and belief to fear and anxiety.[59] Fear of childbirth (FOC) is a prevalent issue among pregnant women because birthing is an unpredictable process that cannot be entirely controlled or known in advance.[37]

Research indicates that 26–45% of pregnant women experience moderate FOC,[37] while 8–27% experience severe FOC.[37]

In a study, nearly 10–14% of Turkish pregnant women have FOC at a clinical level, according to studies conducted there.[37]

Fear of childbirth has multiple causes and is influenced by psychological, obstetric, and sociodemographic factors. According to studies, factors influencing FOC include age, education level, planned versus unplanned pregnancies, history of miscarriages and treatments, and knowledge about childbirth.[37] Another obstetric trait linked to FOC is parity. Research indicates that nulliparas encounter FOC as a result of insufficient experience and associated uncertainty,[60] multiparas who have had difficult birth experiences in the past also suffer from FOC.[37]

The idea that pregnancy and labor are spiritual experiences and that women must prepare for childbirth by maintaining their spiritual health has gained prominence in recent years.[61] According to King (2008), spirituality is the ability to use spiritual elements including self-reflection, understanding the purpose of life, understanding oneself, and achieving higher spiritual states.[62]

Though spirituality was first linked to religion because religious leaders emphasized it, it is now a more expansive term than just religious observance.[37] Religion is a system that provides adherents with a way of life through the concept of god and sacred ideals. Religion is a ceremonial teaching, not spirituality.[63] One way to characterize religion is as a facet of spirituality, but religion cannot be the exclusive domain of spirituality. Whether or not they adhere to the official requirements of a particular religion, everybody have a spiritual side.[37]

SPIRITUAL WELL-BEING

Spiritual well-being facilitates coping with stress and increases psychological well-being by positively affecting mental health. It is reported in the literature that those with high spirituality levels better adapt to conditions and difficulties of life.[37] Spiritual well-being is linked to psychological health, happiness, and stress levels. Anxiety of birth diminishes as spiritual well-being rises.[37]

Fear of Childbirth and Psychological Well-being

Psychological well-being is described as spiritual, emotional, and mental well-being and is linked to positive feelings that impact mental and physical health.[44] Pregnant women are more likely than nonpregnant women to face psychological issues such depression and anxiety, which have a positive correlation with FOC. Women with high levels of psychological well-being can manage their challenges even when they are not in the best mental or emotional states of their lives.[37]

Fear of Childbirth and C-sections

Fetal discomfort, hemorrhage, interrupted delivery, protracted or quick delivery, and issues with mother–infant attachment are all known effects of FOC. FOC has been shown to have a negative impact on birth satisfaction, negatively impact acceptance of the role of pregnancy and motherhood, and increase preference for optional C-sections when there are no medical indications.[37]

Predictors of Fear of Childbirth

Predictors of FOC, relationships with prevalence, some psychosocial factors, sociodemographic and obstetric factors, and assessing the impact of childbirth education and health professional support have been the main subjects of research on FOC.[37]

Spiritual Health and Fear of Childbirth

Pregnant women have a higher frequency of false positives (FOC); on the other hand, those who have good spiritual and psychological health also have lower FOC. When combined with psychological well-being, spiritual well-being raised the variance explained by FOC to 24% from 18% when considered alone.[37]

By offering customized training programs and prenatal trainings that take into account the concepts of psychological well-being and spiritual well-being that are associated with the FOC, it is possible to ensure an increase in coping with the FOC, a decrease in the desire for optional cesarean sections, and a more positive birth experience for women.[37]

ABORTION

Emotional Sequelae of Elective Abortion

Many women who have abortions face long-term emotional, spiritual, psychological, and interpersonal challenges after the procedure; these issues can include complex grieving, depression, PTSD, and relationship problems. Estimates of these difficulties vary.

The dynamics of postabortion syndromes are further clarified by models of perinatal loss that include development, drive, object interactions, and narcissism. Postabortion sequelae are often generated and concealed in large part by feelings of guilt and shame. It makes sense to at least consider the possibility that guilt and shame, particularly shame, are involved when emotional phenomena are so obscure.[64]

There is no doubt that postabortion syndromes do occur, even though the true (and likely unknown) prevalence of these syndromes is unknown.[65]

Postabortion symptoms are probably underreported by at least as much of a margin because of guilt.[64] Furthermore, ''significant suffering can be present in women who have functioned well for long periods''.[66] Clinicians have a significant role in preventing, detecting, and treating this suffering.[64]

Spiritual Intelligence and Postabortion Depression

Miscarriage, also known as spontaneous abortion (SA), is a frequent pregnancy-related problem defined as the loss of pregnancy before 20 weeks gestation in the absence of voluntary medical or surgical intervention to terminate the pregnancy. About 15–27% of women aged 25–29 have SA. The prevalence among women over the age of 45 can reach 75%.[67]

As a major stressor, SA can impair physical and emotional health, to the point where almost all women who have SA experience grief.[67] Post-SA depression normally diminishes in 3–4 months, but it might linger for a year and lead to clinical depression, which requires treatment.[67,68] Although women of diverse races and moral traits show essentially identical responses to SA, their coping techniques differ.[69]

Their religiosity is a major contributing factor to this disparity. Spirituality is utilized as a coping method to deal with and manage challenging situations.[70] Fetal death can generate a major spiritual crisis for the affected women,[71] religious and spiritual principles are employed to deal with abortion.[69] Spirituality can help people respond positively to grief.[72]

ROLE OF HEALTH CARE PROVIDERS

Health Promotion Behaviors

There is indirect, strong positive influence of spiritual well-being on pregnant women's health promotion behaviors via the mediatory function of anxiety and planning-preparation coping. The mechanistic effect of spirituality on anxiety or planning-preparation coping, as well as the mediatory effects on healthy behaviors, is well understood. However, there are some assumptions in the interpretation of the impacts.[73]

- First, the level of anxiety is linked to both spirituality and good behaviors. Research has found that spirituality is connected with decreased levels of anxiety and perceived stress.[74] State anxiety predicted poor healthy behaviors of pregnant women, including healthy nutrition, physical activity, and health responsibility.[75]
- Second, spirituality promotes pregnant women's well-being. Individuals with more spirituality manage better with difficult life, have a sense of control, and higher hope.[76] Individuals with higher spirituality have greater social support and less social anxiety.[73]
- Third, improving planning-preparation copings can increase pregnant women's spiritual well-being and healthy behaviors. It appears that spirituality helps women boost their preparation to plan solutions to deal with difficult situations.[77]

Spirituality and Problem-solving

Evidence suggests that spirituality is strongly associated with problem-solving methods among pregnant women.[78] These findings highlight the role of anxiety and coping plans in mediating mechanisms that explain how spiritual well-being influences pregnant women's health-promoting behaviors.

Health care workers could emphasize the beneficial impacts of spiritual well-being on anxiety and pregnant stress reduction, as well as the promotion of healthy behaviors. Educating women and their partners about the significance of spiritual well-being in reducing anxiety and promoting planning-copings may be an effective motivator for improving health promotion behaviors during pregnancy.[73]

SPIRITUAL COUNSELING

Elevated sensations of depression and anxiety during pregnancy are linked to later child overall emotional and behavioral issues.[79] Spiritual counseling can help pregnant women handle their perceived stress and anxiety. As a result, spiritual counseling is advised as a complimentary and helpful solution for managing psychological difficulties in pregnant women.

The Effect of Spiritual Counseling on Stress and Anxiety in Pregnancy

A randomized controlled trial by Masoumeh Haghighat et al. recruited 112 pregnant women who visited health centers in Maragheh, Iran, between 2016 and 2017.

The participants were divided into two groups—control and intervention **(Table 1)**. Before and 4 weeks after the intervention, individuals were interviewed and given a sociodemographic questionnaire, the perceived stress scale, and the Spielberger state-trait anxiety inventory (STAI). 55 participants in the counseling group and 56 in the control group were followed up and analyzed until the end of the study.

TABLE 1: Effect of spiritual counseling on stress and anxiety in pregnancy.

Group	*Number of patients*
Control	56
Intervention (spiritual counselling)	55

Source: Haghighat M, et al.[80]

Results:

Stress ***(Fig. 4)***

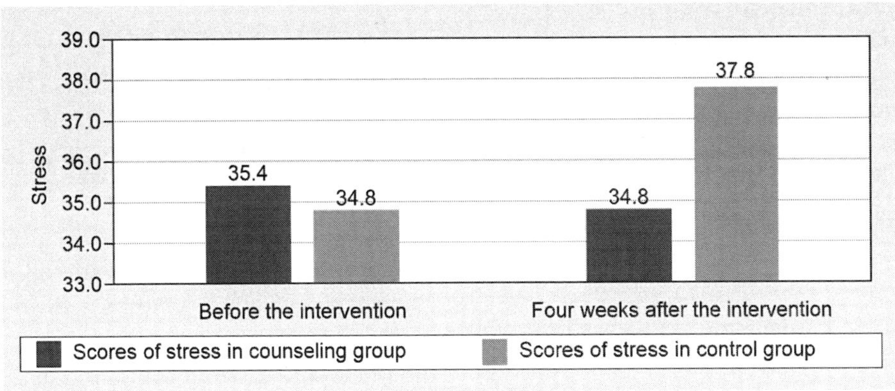

Fig. 4: Stress.

State anxiety ***(Fig. 5)***

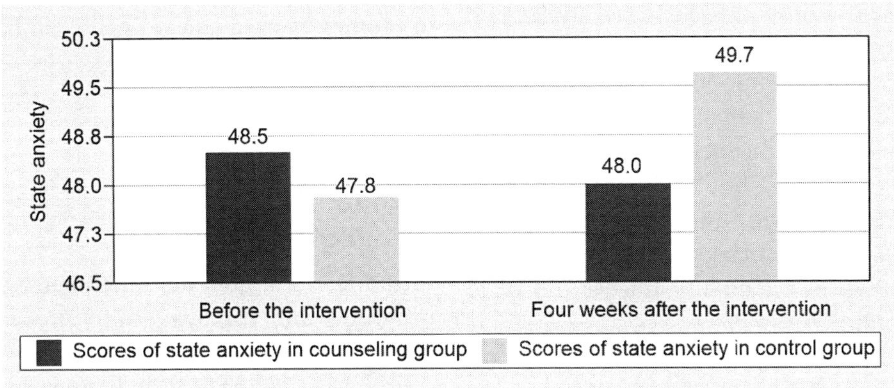

Fig. 5: State anxiety.

Trait anxiety ***(Fig. 6)***

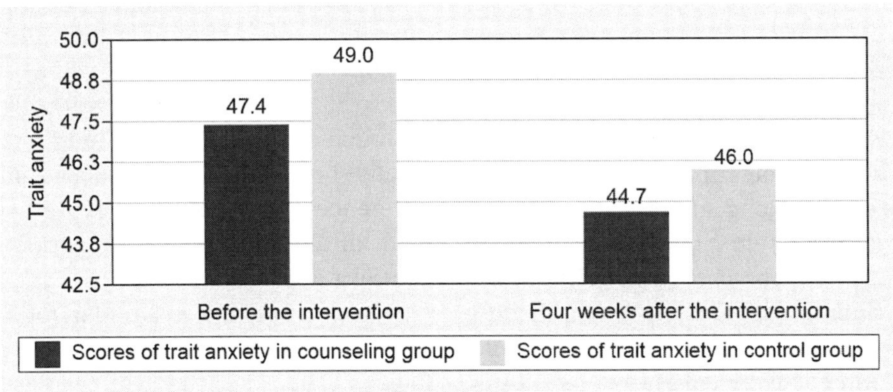

Fig. 6: Trait anxiety.

Spiritual counseling can control perceived stress and state anxiety of pregnant women. Therefore, spiritual counseling is recommended as a complementary and effective intervention in controlling the psychological problems of pregnant mothers.[80]

SPIRITUAL INTELLIGENCE

Recently, psychologists presented the novel notion of spiritual intelligence (SI) as a crucial role in mental health.[67] SI, one of the seven categories of intelligence, mixes spirituality and intelligence to create a new construct.[67] It is described as the awareness of the world and the role of humans in it.[67] SI involves using one's spiritual resources to make decisions, address existential questions, and solve daily problems. It provides people a profound insight into life events and makes them resistant to their consequences.[67]

Spiritual intelligence not only improves physical health, but also helps people properly cope with unpleasant conditions such as grief. It brings satisfaction in life and enhances life quality and psychosocial functioning.[67]

Effects of religiosity and spirituality on posttraumatic stress disorder have been investigated in some;[67] however, due to heterogeneity in the methodology of these studies, no firm conclusion concerning the impact of spirituality on post-SA mental problems can be reached.[81] Furthermore, the findings of these investigations are contradictory.[43] Some research found a substantial association between SI and mental health among nurses, instructors, and students. As a result, it may also be useful in relieving post-SA psychological difficulties.[67]

Spiritual intelligence acts as a defense mechanism, protecting women from mental health issues after sexual assault. As a result, establishing and implementing SI promotion techniques can help to prevent and treat psychological issues following SA.[67]

MINDFULNESS-BASED CHILDBIRTH AND PARENTING EDUCATIONAL PROGRAM

The mindfulness-based childbirth and parenting educational program increases the self-efficacy of nulliparous pregnant women.[82] This is compatible with the work of Hamzekhani et al.[83] According to the findings of this study, self-efficacy scores increased in the intervention group compared to the pre-study group following the mindfulness-based childbirth and parenting teaching program.[83]

The educational intervention is effective in promoting pregnant women's self-efficacy for childbirth and reducing their perceived pain and anxiety in the first two stages of labor.[84]

Prenatal Scheduled Training Programs

Introduction of prenatal scheduled training programs and the availability of adaptive techniques for nulliparous pregnant women, such as breathing skills, distraction from pain, sedation, and recognition of pain status, might lead to high self-efficacy and reduction anxiety about delivery.[83] In a study by Ip et al., the intervention group got two 90-minute sessions of the instructional program between 33 and 35 weeks of gestation, with follow-up examinations completed 48 hours later. The results showed that there was no significant difference in the perceived self-efficacy of labor in the postintervention period of the control group.[83]

Melender et al. also found in their study that most individuals were afraid because of their previous experience with childbirth, lack of prior information and knowledge about childbirth, and uncertainty about midwives and obsessive-compulsive labor.[85] There is a significant change in knowledge, evaluation of behavioral outcomes, behavioral attitudes, and reinforcement of pregnant women's intentions and performance, demonstrating the usefulness of educational interventions during pregnancy.[86]

Expectation of Self-efficacy

A significant difference between the expectation of delivery outcome and the self-efficacy expectation of labor in the active phase of labor is observed in various studies.[87,88] In childbirth classes, it is important to consider not only the effectiveness of coping techniques and labor, but also the individual's conviction in their own abilities.[89]

MINDFULNESS-BASED TRAINING IN WOMEN WITH GESTATIONAL DIABETES

The prevalence of anxiety during pregnancy is roughly 18%.[90] Various studies suggest that anxiety during pregnancy can have a direct impact on the fetal growth pattern and the duration of the pregnancy.[91] It has negative effects like preterm labor and poor birth weight.[92] Anxiety also increases the secretion of stress hormones, which can impair fetal brain development between weeks 12 and 22.[93] Maternal anxiety during pregnancy accounts for 15% of children's anxiety disorders and cognitive delays.[94,95] Some of the reasons of anxiety disorders in pregnant women include early maternal age, primiparity, genetic anxiety, physical disease,[96] history of preterm labor, and a high risk of fetal abnormalities.[97]

A common medical problem during pregnancy is gestational diabetes, defined as carbohydrate intolerance that is diagnosed and begins during pregnancy.[97] The prevalence of gestational diabetes varies from 1 and 14% in different parts of the world.[96]

Fetal consequences of gestational diabetes include macrosomia, birth trauma, hypoglycemia, hypocalcemia, hyperbilirubinemia, and respiratory distress syndrome. Future maternal problems include hypertension, premature labor, hydramnios, cesarean birth, and type 2 diabetes.[98]

Pregnant women with diabetes require special care, since it has a significant impact on their physical and mental health and raises their anxiety.[99] The prevalence of anxiety among diabetic patients is 20% higher than nondiabetics.[100] Nonpharmacological therapies, including as cognitive-behavioral therapy (CBT) and spiritual trainings, have been used to reduce anxiety during pregnancy.[101] Recently, mindfulness-based therapies have been created and used to manage psychiatric difficulties during pregnancy.[102] Mindfulness is cognizant of and paying attention to what is going on right now. It is regarded one of the cognitive-behavioral therapies of the third wave, and it is a type of meditation.[103] Mindfulness-based interventions consist of mindfulness-based stress reduction (MBSR) and mindfulness-based cognitive therapy (MBCT).[104]

MINDFULNESS-BASED INTERVENTIONS IN DIABETES

Researchers have examined the impact of mindfulness-based therapies on anxiety reduction in a variety of populations, including nondiabetic pregnant women and diabetic pregnant women.[101] Several researches have been conducted to evaluate the effect of mindfulness training on self-efficacy and fear of childbirth in pregnant women.[105]

A recent study on women aged 20–40 years with type 2 diabetes found that a MBSR program was helpful in decreasing anxiety, stress, and HbA1C, as well as enhancing self-esteem.[106] Another study demonstrated that the MBSR method is useful for diabetics who suffer from emotional issues, anxiety, and depression and can improve their health.[107]

Mindfulness-based counseling is an excellent method for reducing anxiety in pregnant women with gestational diabetes. As a result, mindfulness-based counseling can improve the mental health of pregnant women with gestational diabetes.[101]

PRENATAL YOGA-BASED INTERVENTIONS

Pregnancy is a period of significant physiological, social, and emotional changes, which can lead to prospective mothers experiencing low back pain, pelvic discomfort, anxiety, depression, post-traumatic stress, and changes in quality of life.[25,26]

Both parents frequently have psychological disorders, particularly anxiety and depression.[27] Concretely, roughly 13% of pregnant women are diagnosed with depression, which increases to 22% during the first year of postpartum.[28] Anxiety symptoms are also a serious worry, with a prevalence ranging from 18% in the first trimester of pregnancy to 25% in the third.[29] Prenatal posttraumatic stress disorder reaches 3.3% in community samples, increasing to 4.0% during postpartum.[108] Physical activity is a viable way to alleviate these psychological issues during the prenatal or postnatal period.[109,110]

Yoga is a mind–body–spirit practice that emphasizes breathing exercises, meditation techniques, and physical postures.[111] Interest in yoga-based therapies among pregnant women has expanded tremendously, with fascinating results in improving numerous outcomes throughout pregnancy (e.g., interpersonal connections, labor pain, or quality of life).[112,113] Prenatal yoga therapies are regarded safe and innocuous, and they appear to be more beneficial than other physical activities such as walking or regular prenatal exercises.[114,115] Several systematic studies including meta-analysis have recently investigated its effectiveness in changing maladaptive psychological symptoms during pregnancy.[109]

Olga Villar-Alises et al. conducted a comprehensive review and meta-analysis to summarize the impact of prenatal yoga therapies on pain, psychiatric symptoms, and quality of life during pregnancy. Most meta-analyses (93%) found that prenatal yoga-based interventions are more beneficial than control interventions (such as social support, health education, or no intervention) in lowering anxiety, depression, and stress symptoms. However, the overall methodological quality of systematic reviews was rated as severely inadequate, and primary study overlap was quite high (CCA = 16%). Overall, prenatal yoga-based therapies may enhance the mental health of pregnant mothers.[116]

GARBH SANSKAR

The phrase "Garbh Sanskar" is derived from the Sanskrit words "Garbh," which means "womb," and "Sanskar," which refers to the process of imprinting the fetus inside the mother's womb. The idea behind this concept is that a child's mental and physical development begins while they are still in their mother's body and can be influenced by a range of inputs, including the mother's thoughts, feelings, and behaviors. Garbh Sanskar, an ancient technique, has been practiced in India for many years.[117]

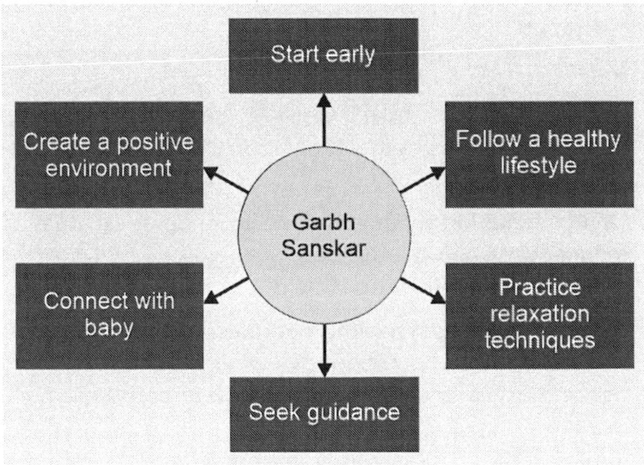

Fig. 7: Recommendation for practicing Garbh Sanskar.
Source: Verma P, et al.[117]

During Garbh Sanskar, several rites and customs were observed to protect the fetal health and development, which was formerly regarded to be an important component of pregnancy. These activities included reciting mantras, performing specific yoga movements, and eating nourishing foods.[117]

It is crucial to note that, while Garbh Sanskar is becoming increasingly popular, there is still a lack of strong scientific data to support its efficacy **(Fig. 7)**.

As a result, it is critical to use caution when engaging in Garbh Sanskar activities and to contact with a certified healthcare expert before making any significant changes to your diet or exercise routine while pregnant **(Table 2)**.[117]

PREGNANCY YOGA

Yoga is a mind-body discipline that originated in India as part of ancient Indian philosophy. It comprises physical postures (asana), breathing exercises (pranayama), concentration and meditation (dhyana), and contemplation.[118]

Yoga has been shown to reduce depressive symptoms, stress and salivary cortisol levels, anxiety levels, help women adopt more conscious and healthy behaviors, pain associated with pregnancy, α-amylase levels, increase birth self-efficacy, sleep quality of pregnant women, fear of delivery, postpartum maternal and fetal complications, preterm birth rate and delivery period,[19] and vaginal delivery rate. Enhanced spirituality in pregnant women was linked to reduced stress and more health-promoting behaviors.[118]

Yoga is stated to be an evidence-based complementary therapy for improving physical and psychological health during pregnancy (normal and high-risk), delivery, and the postpartum period.[118]

Some pregnant women have reported that yoga practice helps them feel more empowered and develop stronger coping techniques to manage their fear of childbirth.[116]

SELF-COMPASSION

Spiritual well-being and increased resilience directly reduce pregnant women's health worry. Self-compassion, on the other hand, helps pregnant women lower their health concerns both directly and indirectly. Teaching pregnant women self-compassion could help them lessen their health worries.[119]

TABLE 2: Garbh Sanskar therapies.

Therapy	*Details*
Prenatal yoga and exercise	Prenatal yoga sessions and activities created exclusively for pregnant women can help improve physical fitness, flexibility, and overall well-being throughout pregnancy
Meditation and mindfulness	Using meditation and mindfulness techniques can help expectant moms relax, reduce stress, and create a positive mindset, resulting in a tranquil and caring environment for the fetus
Nutritional guidance	Seeking advice from healthcare professionals and nutritionists to maintain a well-balanced and nutritious diet while pregnant. This involves ingesting foods rich in critical nutrients and avoiding hazardous toxins
Music therapy	Listening to soothing and tranquil music, specifically intended for the prenatal period, can have a favorable impact on both the mother and the fetus, encouraging relaxation and emotional well-being
Positive affirmations and visualization	Using positive affirmations and visualization techniques to foster a positive mindset and establish a link with the unborn child. This entails repeating positive affirmations and visualizing a healthy, happy pregnancy and birthing experience
Emotional bonding	Talking, singing, and reading aloud can help develop a deep attachment and promote a sense of security for the unborn child
Supportive environment	Creating a helpful and loving environment with the participation of the partner, family, and loved ones. This includes offering emotional support, understanding, and encouragement to the expectant mother throughout her pregnancy experience
Positive thinking	The mother is urged to keep a cheerful attitude and prevent negative thoughts and emotions. The mother's thoughts and feelings are supposed to have a significant impact on her child's mental and emotional well-being
Massages	Massages can help to enhance blood circulation, relieve stress and anxiety, and promote relaxation. Garbh Sanskar often includes Ayurvedic treatments with herbal oils. Ayurvedic massages, also known as abhyanga, are said to be beneficial to pregnant women
Mantras	Mantra recitation is thought to improve the fetal mental and spiritual growth
Aromatherapy	Certain scents are thought to have a beneficial effect on the developing fetus. For example, the scent of jasmine is thought to encourage relaxation and lessen anxiety
Positive affirmations	Pregnant women should repeat positive affirmations to themselves, such as "I am healthy, and my baby is healthy." This is supposed to help establish a happy outlook and minimize stress

MINDFULNESS INTERVENTIONS DURING PREGNANCY

In an analysis of 230 studies, Leandro Lucena and colleagues discovered that mindfulness therapies were effective in treating stress, anxiety, and depression. Mindfulness was also useful in pregnant women who had a history of depression or were currently suffering depression.[120]

One recent meta-analysis revealed that mindfulness interventions (MBIs) may complement and extend the existing range of effective therapies for clinical and subthreshold prenatal depression and anxiety.[121]

EFFECTS OF A PRENATAL MINDFULNESS PROGRAM

Mindfulness prenatal programs are handy and effective ways to reduce stress, anxiety, and depression throughout the perinatal period.[122] A study by Zarenejad M et al. found that mindfulness reduces anxiety in pregnant mothers. Mindfulness programs can reduce maternal anxiety and improve pregnancy and delivery outcomes.[123]

CONCLUSION

- Perinatal mental health, including depression and anxiety, is a significant issue for pregnant women worldwide.
- Depression and anxiety affect approximately 12% of pregnant women, with many experiencing both.
- Poor mental health during pregnancy can lead to negative outcomes for both the mother and the child, including premature labor, low-birth weight, developmental difficulties, and mental and social problems later in life.
- The prevalence of prenatal depression internationally ranges from 15 to 65%, with self-harm being a significant cause of maternal deaths.
- Risk factors for prenatal depression include pressure to have a male child, unemployment, financial difficulties, history of miscarriage, marital conflict, and a lack of recreational opportunities.
- The ecology of childbirth conceptual framework provides a comprehensive perspective on the relationships between humans, themselves, and the environment during childbirth.
- Lack of social support is strongly correlated with despair, anxiety, and self-harm during pregnancy.
- Spiritual care, including spiritual midwifery, is an important aspect of antenatal care and can have positive effects on maternal and fetal outcomes.
- Spiritual experiences and spiritual intelligence can play a role in reducing anxiety, depression, and stress during pregnancy.
- Maternal–fetal attachment and maternal religious attitudes can affect fetal mental health.
- Higher levels of spirituality are associated with better maternal mental health and emotional wellness after childbirth.
- Stress during pregnancy can be mitigated through spirituality, leading to better psychological well-being.
- Spiritual counseling and education can have positive effects on stress and anxiety during pregnancy and postpartum.

REFERENCES

1. Crowther S, Stephen A, Hall J. Association of psychosocial–spiritual experiences around childbirth and subsequent perinatal mental health outcomes: an integrated review. J Reprod Infant Psychol. 2020;38(1):60-85.
2. Brinkley RL. (2004). The Correlation Between Perceived Stress and Health Promoting Self-care Behaviors in High-risk Third Trimester Pregnancies. [online] Available from https://www.semanticscholar.org/paper/The-Correlation-Between-Perceived-Stress-and-Health-Brinkley/6fd891d988d189344ee8442c78b507042d9fcef9. [Last accessed December, 2024]
3. OBoyle C, Brady V, Timmins F. Making space for spirituality in childbirth. J Clin Nurs. 2017;26(19-20):2823-5.
4. Sahoo S, Gill G, Sikka P, Nehra R. Antenatal depression and anxiety in Indian women:

a systematic review. Ind Psychiatry J. 2023; 32(2):222-33.

5. World Health Organization. WHO recommendations on antenatal care for a positive pregnancy experience [Internet]. Geneva: World Health Organization; 2016.
6. Wojujutari AK, Teslim Alabi O, Emmanuel AT, Olugbenga OM. Spiritual Intelligence and Mindfulness as Moderators of Relationship between Psychological Well-Being and Psychosocial Adjustment of Pregnant Women. J Womens Health Care. 2018;7(3):1-5.
7. Nodoushan RJ, Alimoradi H, Nazari M. Spiritual Health and Stress in Pregnant Women During the Covid-19 Pandemic. SN Compr Clin Med. 2020;2(12):2528-34.
8. Piccinini CRP, De Castro Almeida V, Da Silva Ezequiel O, De Matos Fajardo EF, Lucchetti ALG, Lucchetti G. Religiosity/Spirituality and Mental Health and Quality of Life of Early Pregnant Women. J Relig Health. 2021;60(3):1908-23.
9. Athan A, Chung S, Sawyer Cohen J. Spiritual beliefs of mothers with potentially distressing pregnancies. Spiritual Clin Pract. 2015;2(3):216-32.
10. Nourimand F, Forouhari S, Jahromi BN, Asadi N, Abbasi Z, Beygi Z, et al. (2020). Studying the correlation between spiritual well-being and religious attitude with mental health and quality of life in pregnant women. [online] Available from https://www.researchgate.net/publication/358643658_Studying_the_correlation_between_spiritual_well-being_and_religious_attitude_with_mental_health_and_quality_of_life_in_pregnant_women. [Last accessed December, 2024]
11. Tork Zahrani S, Haji Rafiei E, Hajian S, Alavi Majd H, Izadi A. The Correlation between Spiritual Health and Maternal-Fetal Attachment Behaviors in Pregnant Women Referring to the Health Centers in Qazvin, Iran. Int J Community Based Nurs Midwifery. 2020;8(1):84-91.
12. Dokuhaki S, Ghodrati F. (2019). Investigation of Relationship between Maternal Religious Attitude and Mental Health of Infant at Birth. [online] Available from https://womenshealthbulletin.sums.ac.ir/article_45781.html. [Last accessed December, 2024]
13. The Community Child Health Network (CCHN), Cheadle ACD, Dunkel Schetter C. Mastery, self-esteem, and optimism mediate the link between religiousness and spirituality and postpartum depression. J Behav Med. 2018;41(5):711-21.
14. Clements AD, Fletcher TR, Childress LD, Montgomery RA, Bailey BA. Social support, religious commitment, and depressive symptoms in pregnant and postpartum women. J Reprod Infant Psychol. 2016;34(3):247-59.
15. Dolatian M, Mahmoodi Z, Dilgony T, Shams J, Zaeri F. (2017). The Structural Model of Spirituality and Psychological Well-Being for Pregnancy-Specific Stress. [online] Available from https://www.researchgate.net/publication/316498751_The_Structural_Model_of_Spirituality_and_Psychological_Well-Being_for_Pregnancy-Specific_Stress. [Last accessed December, 2024]
16. Dilgony T, Dolatian M, Shams J, Zayeri F, Mahmoodi Z. (2016). Correlation of spirituality and psychological well-being with pregnancy-specific stress. [online] Available from https://journals.sbmu.ac.ir/en-jrrh/article/view/15565. [Last accessed December, 2024]
17. Lundgren I. (2002). Releasing and relieving encounters. Experiences of pregnancy and childbirth. [online] Available from https://www.diva-portal.org/smash/get/diva2:161654/FULLTEXT01.pdf. [Last accessed December, 2024]
18. Foruzandeh N, Shahrekord University of Medical Sciences, Foruzandeh M, Shahrekord University of Medical Sciences, Darakhshandeh S, Shahrekord University of Medical Sciences, et al. The Role of Spiritual Well-being in Predicting Pregnancy-Specific Stress. J Health Care. 2019;20(4): 292-300.
19. Mutmainnah M, Afiyanti Y. The experiences of spirituality during pregnancy and child birth in Indonesian muslim women. Enferm Clínica. 2019;29:495-9.

20. https://www.shbonweb.com/articlecited.asp?issn=2589-9767;year=2020;volume=3;issue=4;spage=152;epage=157;aulast=Olatunji;type=0;aid=SocHealthBehav_2020_3_4_152_294533
21. Bennington L. (2010). The relationship among maternal infant bonding, spirituality, and maternal perception of childbirth experience. [online] Available from https://scholarscompass.vcu.edu/etd/2242/. [Last accessed December, 2024]
22. Hanely J, Brown A. Cultural Variations in Interpretation of Postnatal Illness: Jinn Possession Amongst Muslim Communities. Community Ment Health J. 2014;50(3):348-53.
23. Mary M. Narrative accounts of women who use complementary and alternative medicine in pregnancy: 'Forewarned, forearmed and relaxed'. [online] Available from https://uwe-repository.worktribe.com/output/942480/narrative-accounts-of-women-who-use-complementary-and-alternative-medicine-in-pregnancy-forewarned-forearmed-and-relaxed. [Last accessed December, 2024]
24. Abu-abbas M, Ayasreh IR, Sumaqa YA, Alhamory S, Al Tarawneh TR, Abudari MO, et al. (2023). Spirituality and Psychological Wellbeing During Pregnancy and Childbirth: A Review of the Literature. [online] Available from https://jrtdd.com/index.php/journal/article/view/1715. [Last accessed December, 2024]
25. Loomans EM, Van Dijk AE, Vrijkotte TGM, Van Eijsden M, Stronks K, Gemke RJBJ, et al. Psychosocial stress during pregnancy is related to adverse birth outcomes: results from a large multi-ethnic community-based birth cohort. Eur J Public Health. 2013; 23(3):485-91.
26. Öhman SG, Grunewald C, Waldenström U. Women's worries during pregnancy: testing the Cambridge Worry Scale on 200 Swedish women. Scand J Caring Sci. 2003;17(2):148-52.
27. Rohit V. Lifestyle: A Comparative Study of the Arts and Science college students. [online] Available from https://www.academia.edu/71349066/Lifestyle_A_Comparative_Study_of_the_Arts_and_Science_college_students?uc-sb-sw=77576935. [Last accessed December, 2024]
28. Schieman S, Bierman A, Ellison CG. Religion and Mental Health. In: Aneshensel CS, Phelan JC, Bierman A (Eds). Handbook of the Sociology of Mental Health [Internet]. Dordrecht: Springer Netherlands; 2013. pp. 457-78.
29. Lucero SM, Pargament KI, Mahoney A, DeMaris A. Links between religious and spiritual coping and adjustment among fathers and mothers during first pregnancy. J Reprod Infant Psychol. 2013;31(3):309-22.
30. Fisher JW. (2003). Gomez, R. & Fisher, J.W. (2003) Domains of spiritual well-being and development and validation of the Spiritual Well-Being Questionnaire. Personality and Individual Differences 35(8): 1975-1991. [online] Available from https://www.researchgate.net/publication/256499063_Gomez_R_Fisher_JW_2003_Domains_of_spiritual_well-being_and_development_and_validation_of_the_Spiritual_Well-Being_Questionnaire_Personality_and_Individual_Differences_358_1975-1991. [Last accessed December, 2024]
31. Diener E, Oishi S, Lucas RE. Personality, Culture, and Subjective Well-Being: Emotional and Cognitive Evaluations of Life. Annu Rev Psychol. 2003;54(1):403-25.
32. Goyal M, Singh S, Sibinga EMS, Gould NF, Rowland-Seymour A, Sharma R, et al. Meditation Programs for Psychological Stress and Well-being: A Systematic Review and Meta-analysis. JAMA Intern Med. 2014;174(3):357.
33. Wigert H, Nilsson C, Dencker A, Begley C, Jangsten E, Sparud-Lundin C, et al. Women's experiences of fear of childbirth: a metasynthesis of qualitative studies. Int J Qual Stud Health Well-Being. 2020;15(1):1704484.
34. Molgora S, Fenaroli V, Saita E. The association between childbirth experience and mother's parenting stress: The mediating role of anxiety and depressive symptoms. Women Health. 2020;60(3):341-51.
35. Fenaroli V, Molgora S, Dodaro S, Svelato A, Gesi L, Molidoro G, et al. The childbirth experience: obstetric and psychological

predictors in Italian primiparous women. BMC Pregnancy Childbirth. 2019;19(1):419.
36. Hosaini S, Yazdkhasti M, Moafi Ghafari F, Mohamadi F, Kamran Rad SHR, Mahmoodi Z. The relationships of spiritual health, pregnancy worries and stress and perceived social support with childbirth fear and experience: A path analysis. Kassa ZY, editor. PLoS One. 2023;18(12):e0294910.
37. Bilgiç G, Çıtak Bilgin N. Relationship Between Fear of Childbirth and Psychological and Spiritual Well-Being in Pregnant Women. J Relig Health. 2021;60(1):295-310.
38. Phunyammalee M, Buayaem T, Boribo-onhirunsarn D. Fear of childbirth and associated factors among low-risk pregnant women. J Obstet Gynaecol. 2019;39(6):763-7.
39. Mozingo JN. Pain in labor: a conceptual model for intervention. JOGN Nurs J Obstet Gynecol Neonatal Nurs. 1978;7(4):47-9.
40. Siddall PJ, Lovell M, MacLeod R. Spirituality: what is its role in pain medicine? Pain Med Malden Mass. 2015;16(1):51-60.
41. Grossoehme DH, Friebert S, Baker JN, Tweddle M, Needle J, Chrastek J, et al. Association of Religious and Spiritual Factors with Patient-Reported Outcomes of Anxiety, Depressive Symptoms, Fatigue, and Pain Interference Among Adolescents and Young Adults with Cancer. JAMA Netw Open. 2020;3(6):e206696.
42. Dolatian M, Mahmoodi Z, Alavi-Majd H, Moafi F, Ghorbani M, Mirabzadeh A. Psychosocial factors in pregnancy and birthweight: Path analysis. J Obstet Gynaecol Res. 2016;42(7):822-30.
43. Rabiepour S, Etesami E. (2022). Analyzing the Relationship Between Spiritual Well-being and Fear of Childbirth in Pregnant Women. [online] Available from https://philpapers.org/rec/RABATR-2. [Last accessed December, 2024]
44. Beery TA, Baas LS, Fowler C, Allen G. Spirituality in persons with heart failure. J Holist Nurs Off J Am Holist Nurses Assoc. 2002;20(1):5-25; quiz 26-30.
45. Dehestani H, Moshfeghy Z, Ghodrati F, Akbarzadeh M. The Relationship of Spiritual Health and Mother's Forgiveness with Her Anxiety in the Labor of the Pregnant Women. Int J Womens Health Reprod Sci. 2018;7(2):174-9.
46. Ding X, Mao L, Ge X, Xu S, Pan W, Yan S, et al. [Course and risk factors of maternal pregnancy-related anxiety across pregnancy in Ma' anshan city]. Wei Sheng Yan Jiu. 2015;44(3):371-5.
47. Punamäki RL, Repokari L, Vilska S, Poikkeus P, Tiitinen A, Sinkkonen J, et al. Maternal mental health and medical predictors of infant developmental and health problems from pregnancy to one year: Does former infertility matter? Infant Behav Dev. 2006; 29(2):230-42.
48. Faisal-Cury A, Menezes P, Araya R, Zugaib M. Common mental disorders during pregnancy: prevalence and associated factors among low-income women in São Paulo, Brazil: Depression and Anxiety during Pregnancy. Arch Womens Ment Health. 2009;12(5):335-43.
49. Hall WA, Hauck YL, Carty EM, Hutton EK, Fenwick J, Stoll K. Childbirth Fear, Anxiety, Fatigue, and Sleep Deprivation in Pregnant Women. J Obstet Gynecol Neonatal Nurs. 2009;38(5):567-76.
50. Akbarzadeh M, Dokuhaki A, Joker A, Pishva N, Zare N. Teaching attachment behaviors to pregnant women: a randomized controlled trial of effects on infant mental health from birth to the age of three months. Ann Saudi Med. 2016;36(3):175-83.
51. Dokuhaki A, Akbarzadeh M, Pishva N, Zare N. A study of the effect of training pregnant women about attachment skills on infants' motor development indices at birth to four months. Fam Med Prim Care Rev. 2017;2:114-22.
52. World Health Organization. (2008). Maternal mental health and child health and development in low and middle income countries: report of the meeting, Geneva, Switzerland, 30 January - 1 February, 2008. [online] Available from https://iris.who.int/handle/10665/43975. [Last accessed December, 2024]

53. Saisto T, Toivanen R, Salmela-Aro K, Halmesmäki E. Therapeutic group psycho-education and relaxation in treating fear of childbirth. Acta Obstet Gynecol Scand. 2006; 85(11):1315-9.
54. Bastani F, Hidarnia A, Kazemnejad A, Vafaei M, Kashanian M. A Randomized Controlled Trial of the Effects of Applied Relaxation Training on Reducing Anxiety and Perceived Stress in Pregnant Women. J Midwifery Womens Health. 2005;50(4):e36-40.
55. Mueller PS, Plevak DJ, Rummans TA. Religious Involvement, Spirituality, and Medicine: Implications for Clinical Practice. Mayo Clin Proc. 2001;76(12):1225-35.
56. Al Zaben F, Khalifa DA, Sehlo MG, Al Shohaib S, Binzaqr SA, Badreg AM, et al. Religious involvement and health in dialysis patients in Saudi Arabia. J Relig Health. 2015;54(2):713-30.
57. Handelzalts JE, Stringer MK, Menke RA, Muzik M. The Association of Religion and Spirituality with Postpartum Mental Health in Women with Childhood Maltreatment Histories. J Child Fam Stud. 2020;29(2): 502-13.
58. Nilsson C, Hessman E, Sjöblom H, Dencker A, Jangsten E, Mollberg M, et al. Definitions, measurements and prevalence of fear of childbirth: a systematic review. BMC Pregnancy Childbirth. 2018;18(1):28.
59. Mazúchová L, Škodová Z, Kelčíková S, Rabárová A. (2017) Factors associated with childbirth-Related fear among Slovak women. [online] Available from https://cejnm.osu.cz/artkey/cjn-201704-0006_factors-associated-with-childbirth-related-fear-among-slovak-women.php. [Last accessed December, 2024]
60. Toohill J, Fenwick J, Gamble J, Creedy DK, Buist A, Ryding EL. Psycho-Social Predictors of Childbirth Fear in Pregnant Women: An Australian Study. Open J Obstet Gynecol. 2014;04(09):531-43.
61. Abdollahpour S, Khosravi A. Relationship between spiritual intelligence with happiness and fear of childbirth in Iranian pregnant women. Iran J Nurs Midwifery Res. 2018; 23(1):45.
62. King DB. (2008). Rethinking Claims of Spiritual Intelligence: A Definition, Model, and Measure. A Dissertation Presented in Partial Fulfillment of the Requirements for the Degree of Master of Science, Peterborouge. [online] Available from https://www.scirp.org/reference/ReferencesPapers?ReferenceID=1597063. [Last accessed December, 2024]
63. Como JM. Spiritual practice: a literature review related to spiritual health and health outcomes. Holist Nurs Pract. 2007;21(5): 224-36.
64. Whitney DK. Emotional Sequelae of Elective Abortion: The Role of Guilt and Shame. J Pastor Care Couns Adv Theory Prof Pract Sch Reflective Publ. 2017;71(2):98-105.
65. Harris AA. Supportive Counseling Before and After Elective Pregnancy Termination. J Midwifery Womens Health. 2004;49(2): 105-12.
66. Butler C. Late psychological sequelae of abortion: questions from a primary care perspective. J Fam Pract. 1996;43(4):396-401.
67. Moafi F, Momeni M, Tayeba M, Rahimi S, Hajnasiri H. Spiritual Intelligence and Post-abortion Depression: A Coping Strategy. J Relig Health. 2021;60(1):326-34.
68. Janssen HJEM. A Prospective Study of Risk Factors Predicting Grief Intensity Following Pregnancy Loss. Arch Gen Psychiatry. 1997; 54(1):56.
69. Van P, Meleis AI. Coping with Grief After Involuntary Pregnancy Loss: Perspectives of African American Women. J Obstet Gynecol Neonatal Nurs. 2003;32(1):28-39.
70. Callister LC, Khalaf I. Spirituality in Childbearing Women. J Perinat Educ. 2010;19(2): 16-24.
71. Klass D, Goss R. The politics of grief and continuing bonds with the dead: The cases of Maoist China and Wahhabi Islam. Death Stud. 2003;27(9):787-811.
72. Whitaker C, Kavanaugh K, Klima C. Perinatal Grief in Latino Parents. MCN Am J Matern Nurs. 2010;35(6):341-5.
73. Chehrazi M, Faramarzi M, Abdollahi S, Esfandiari M, Shafie Rizi S. Health promotion

behaviours of pregnant women and spiritual well-being: Mediatory role of pregnancy stress, anxiety and coping ways. Nurs Open. 2021;8(6):3558-65.

74. Shattuck EC, Muehlenbein MP. Religiosity/Spirituality and Physiological Markers of Health. J Relig Health. 2020;59(2):1035-54.
75. Omidvar S, Faramarzi M, Hajian-Tilak K, Nasiri Amiri F. Associations of psychosocial factors with pregnancy healthy life styles. PloS One. 2018;13(1):e0191723.
76. Vasegh S, Rosmarin DH, Koenig HG, Dew RE, Bonelli RM. Religious and spiritual factors in depression. Depress Res Treat. 2012; 2012:298056.
77. Faramarzi M, Amiri FN, Rezaee R. Relationship of coping ways and anxiety with Pregnancy Specific-stress. Pak J Med Sci. 2016;32(6):1364-9.
78. Faramarzi M, Pasha H, Khafri S, Heidary S. The Factor Structure and Psychometric Properties of the Persian Version of the Revised Prenatal Coping Inventory (Nu-PCI). J Clin Diagn Res JCDR. 2017;11(3):QC17-20.
79. Leis JA, Heron J, Stuart EA, Mendelson T. Associations Between Maternal Mental Health and Child Emotional and Behavioral Problems: Does Prenatal Mental Health Matter? J Abnorm Child Psychol. 2014;42(1):161-71.
80. Haghighat M, Mirghafourvand M, Mohammad-Alizadeh-Charandabi S, Malakouti J, Erfani M. (2018). The Effect of Spiritual Counseling on Stress and Anxiety in Pregnancy: A Randomized Controlled Clinical Trial. [online] Available from https://www.proquest.com/openview/534d66add4b6e13ebd05bb699ce5342b/1?pq-origsite=gscholar&cbl=105757. [Last accessed December, 2024]
81. Becker G, Xander CJ, Blum HE, Lutterbach J, Momm F, Gysels M, et al. Do religious or spiritual beliefs influence bereavement? A systematic review. Palliat Med. 2007;21(3):207-17.
82. Khoshayand N, Amanelahi A, Haghighizadeh MH, Abbaspoor Z. (2019). Effectiveness of Mindfulness-based Childbirth and Parenting Educational Program on the Self-efficacy of Nulliparous Pregnant Women: A Randomized Clinical Trial Study. [online] Available from https://www.jrmds.in/articles/effectiveness-of-mindfulnessbased-childbirth-and-parenting-educational-program-on-the-selfefficacy-of-nulliparous-pregnant-women-a-25961.html. [Last accessed December, 2024]
83. Hamzekhani M, Hamidzade A, Rahimparvzar SFV, Montazeri AS. (2014) Effect of Computerized Educational Program on Self-Efficacy of Pregnant Women to Cope with Childbirth. [online] Available from https://www.researchgate.net/publication/307823325_Effect_of_Computerized_Educational_Program_on_Self-Efficacy_of_Pregnant_Women_to_Cope_with_Childbirth. [Last accessed December, 2024]
84. Ip WY, Tang CS, Goggins WB. An educational intervention to improve women's ability to cope with childbirth. J Clin Nurs. 2009; 18(15):2125-35.
85. Melender H. Fears and coping strategies associated with pregnancy and childbirth in Finland. J Midwifery Womens Health. 2002;47(4):256-63.
86. Ali KJ, Fatemeh S, Seyed Mansour K. Effectiveness of Educational Program Based on the Theory of Reasoned Action to Decrease the Rate of Cesarean Delivery Among Pregnant Women in Fasa, Southern Iran. J Educ Community Health. 2014;1(1):62-71.
87. Khorsandi M, Ghofraniour F, Hiadarnia A, Faghihzadeh S. (2009). Effects of childbirth education classes on self-efficacy of nulliparous women in coping with labour pain. [online] Available from https://www.researchgate.net/publication/268103737_Effects_of_childbirth_education_classes_on_self-efficacy_of_nulliparous_women_in_coping_with_labour_pain. [Last accessed December, 2024]
88. Ip WY, Chan D, Chien WT. Chinese version of the Childbirth Self-efficacy Inventory. J Adv Nurs. 2005;51(6):625-33.
89. Rastegari L, Mohebbi P, Mazlomzadeh S. (2013). The effect of childbirth preparation training classes on perceived self-efficacy

in delivery of pregnant women. [online] Available from https://www.researchgate.net/publication/288706146_The_effect_of_childbirth_preparation_training_classes_on_perceived_self-efficacy_in_delivery_of_pregnant_women. [Last accessed December, 2024]
90. George A, Luz RF, De Tychey C, Thilly N, Spitz E. (2013). Anxiety symptoms and coping strategies in the perinatal period. [online] Available from https://bmcpregnancychildbirth.biomedcentral.com/articles/10.1186/1471-2393-13-233. [Last accessed December, 2024]
91. Fink NS, Urech C, Cavelti M, Alder J. Relaxation During Pregnancy: What Are the Benefits for Mother, Fetus, and the Newborn? A Systematic Review of the Literature. J Perinat Neonatal Nurs. 2012;26(4):296-306.
92. Field T, Diego M, Hernandez-Reif M, Figueiredo B, Deeds O, Ascencio A, et al. Comorbid depression and anxiety effects on pregnancy and neonatal outcome. Infant Behav Dev. 2010;33(1):23-9.
93. Weinstock M. The long-term behavioural consequences of prenatal stress. Neurosci Biobehav Rev. 2008;32(6):1073-86.
94. Okour AM, Badarneh R. Spousal violence against pregnant women from a Bedouin community in Jordan. J Womens Health 2002. 2011;20(12):1853-9.
95. Brownridge DA, Taillieu TL, Tyler KA, Tiwari A, Ko Ling Chan, Santos SC. Pregnancy and intimate partner violence: risk factors, severity, and health effects. Violence Women. 2011;17(7):858-81.
96. American Diabetes Association. Diagnosis and Classification of Diabetes Mellitus. Diabetes Care. 2010;33(Supplement_1):S62-9.
97. Cunningham FG, Leveno KJ, Bloom SL, Spong CY, Dashe JS, Hoffman BL, et al. Williams Obstetrics, 24th edition. (2014). [online] Available from http://repository.stikesrspadgs.ac.id/44/1/Williams%20Obstetrics-1376hlm.pdf. [Last accessed December, 2024]
98. Sun Y, Zhao H. The effectiveness of lifestyle intervention in early pregnancy to prevent gestational diabetes mellitus in Chinese overweight and obese women: A quasi-experimental study. Appl Nurs Res. 2016;30:125-30.
99. Murphy NM, McCarthy FP, Khashan AS, Myers JE, Simpson NAB, Kearney PM, et al. Compliance with National Institute of Health and Care Excellence risk-based screening for Gestational Diabetes Mellitus in nulliparous women. Eur J Obstet Gynecol Reprod Biol. 2016;199:60-5.
100. Li C, Barker L, Ford ES, Zhang X, Strine TW, Mokdad AH. Diabetes and anxiety in US adults: findings from the 2006 Behavioral Risk Factor Surveillance System. Diabet Med J Br Diabet Assoc. 2008;25(7):878-81.
101. Hamidi F, Javadnoori M, Hosseinifard S, Nikbakht R. The effectiveness of mindfulness-based training on anxiety in pregnant women with gestational diabetes. Fam Med Prim Care Rev. 2020;22(4):279-83.
102. Yazdanimehr R, Omidi A, Sadat Z, Akbari H. The Effect of Mindfulness-integrated Cognitive Behavior Therapy on Depression and Anxiety among Pregnant Women: A Randomized Clinical Trial. J Caring Sci. 2016;5(3):195-204.
103. Robins JLW, Kiken L, Holt M, McCain NL. Mindfulness: an effective coaching tool for improving physical and mental health. J Am Assoc Nurse Pract. 2014;26(9):511-8.
104. Baer RA. Mindfulness training as a clinical intervention: A conceptual and empirical review. Clin Psychol Sci Pract. 2003;10(2):125-43.
105. Byrne J, Hauck Y, Fisher C, Bayes S, Schutze R. Effectiveness of a Mindfulness-Based Childbirth Education pilot study on maternal self-efficacy and fear of childbirth. J Midwifery Womens Health. 2014;59(2):192-7.
106. Vala M, Razmandeh R, Rambol K, Esfahani EN, Ghasemabadi RG. (2016). Mindfulness-based Stress Reduction Group Training on Depression, Anxiety, Stress, Self-confidence and Hemoglobin A1c in Young Women with Type 2 Diabetes. [online] Available from https://ijem.sbmu.ac.ir/browse.php?a_id=1941&sid=1&slc_lang=en. [Last accessed December, 2024]

107. van Son J, Nyklíček I, Pop VJ, Blonk MC, Erdtsieck RJ, Pouwer F. Mindfulness-based cognitive therapy for people with diabetes and emotional problems: long-term follow-up findings from the DiaMind randomized controlled trial. J Psychosom Res. 2014;77(1):81-4.
108. Yildiz PD, Ayers S, Phillips L. The prevalence of posttraumatic stress disorder in pregnancy and after birth: A systematic review and meta-analysis. J Affect Disord. 2017;208:634-45.
109. Nakamura A, Van Der Waerden J, Melchior M, Bolze C, El-Khoury F, Pryor L. Physical activity during pregnancy and postpartum depression: Systematic review and meta-analysis. J Affect Disord. 2019;246:29-41.
110. Cai C, Busch S, Wang R, Sivak A, Davenport MH. Physical activity before and during pregnancy and maternal mental health: A systematic review and meta-analysis of observational studies. J Affect Disord. 2022; 309:393-403.
111. Taneja D. Yoga and health. Indian J Community Med. 2014;39(2):68.
112. Curtis K, Weinrib A, Katz J. Systematic Review of Yoga for Pregnant Women: Current Status and Future Directions. Evid Based Complement Alternat Med. 2012;2012: 1-13.
113. Jiang Q, Wu Z, Zhou L, Dunlop J, Chen P. Effects of Yoga Intervention during Pregnancy: A Review for Current Status. Am J Perinatol. 2014;32(06):503-14.
114. Dennis CL, Falah-Hassani K, Shiri R. Prevalence of antenatal and postnatal anxiety: Systematic review and meta-analysis. Br J Psychiatry. 2017;210(5):315-23.
115. Kwon R, Kasper K, London S, Haas DM. A systematic review: The effects of yoga on pregnancy. Eur J Obstet Gynecol Reprod Biol. 2020;250:171-7.
116. Villar-Alises O, Martinez-Miranda P, Martinez-Calderon J. Prenatal Yoga-Based Interventions May Improve Mental Health during Pregnancy: An Overview of Systematic Reviews with Meta-Analysis. Int J Environ Res Public Health. 2023;20(2):1556.
117. Verma P, Shukla A. (2023). Garbh Sanskar: Preparation of Motherhood. [online] Available from https://ijip.in/articles/garbh-sanskar-preparation-of-motherhood/. [Last accessed December, 2024]
118. Koçak DY, Akarsu RH. (2023). The effect of pregnancy yoga on spiritual well-being: A randomised controlled trial. [online] Available from https://dergipark.org.tr/en/pub/yobusbf/issue/79535/1206419. [Last accessed December, 2024]
119. Afrashteh MY, Bitarafan L. (2021). Relationship between Spiritual Well-Being and Resilience with Health Anxiety in Pregnant Women: The Mediating Role of self-Compassion. [online] Available from https://hehp.modares.ac.ir/browse.php?a_id=51660&slclang=en&sid=5&printcase=1&hbnr=1&hmb=1. [Last accessed December, 2024]
120. Lucena L, Frange C, Pinto ACA, Andersen ML, Tufik S, Hachul H. Mindfulness interventions during pregnancy: A narrative review. J Integr Med. 2020;18(6):470-7.
121. Leng LL, Yin XC, Ng SM. Mindfulness-based intervention for clinical and subthreshold perinatal depression and anxiety: A systematic review and meta-analysis of randomized controlled trial. Compr Psychiatry. 2023;122:152375.
122. Pan WL, Lin LC, Kuo LY, Chiu MJ, Ling PY. Effects of a prenatal mindfulness program on longitudinal changes in stress, anxiety, depression, and mother-infant bonding of women with a tendency to perinatal mood and anxiety disorder: a randomized controlled trial. BMC Pregnancy Childbirth. 2023;23(1):547.
123. Zarenejad M, Yazdkhasti M, Rahimzadeh M, Mehdizadeh Tourzani Z, Esmaelzadeh-Saeieh S. The effect of mindfulness-based stress reduction on maternal anxiety and self-efficacy: A randomized controlled trial. Brain Behav. 2020;10(4):e01561.

3 CHAPTER

Association between Spirituality, Mood, and Anxiety Disorders

Kishan Porandla, Sai Krishna Puli, Vishnu Vardhan M, Sphurti Pusukuri

INTRODUCTION

The United Nations and world community have acknowledged our Indian national wisdom, "Yoga," by announcing "June 21" as International Yoga Day. The word "yoga" means "union," that is, the union of cosmic consciousness with one's own personal consciousness. Yoga helps a person grow from "I" to "We," that is, from being self-centered to a global human being.[1] The "union" could also mean, for a psychiatrist, the unification of thought and affect as well as mind and body, which may have therapeutic value in both illness and wellness domains.

Yoga is a systematic, scientific method with a spiritually approaching practice to help the human consciousness (self) get command over the mind and body (prakriti) and get coherence between the self and mind-body complex.

By practicing yoga, a human being (self) can achieve the highest coordination with the mind and body. By the practice of yoga, the person not only gets coherence at the individual level ("I"—the limited self) but also one would get coherence with the world citizens irrespective of caste, creed, language, nationality, race, or religion, thereby an individual evolves from "I" to "WE."[1]

Yoga is a method given by ancient Rishis to the human race which refers to one of India's wisdom traditions, used for millions of years to study, explain, and experience the mysteries of mind and human nature.

It is not a religion but an experiential philosophy and spiritual procedures of sanatana dharma (eternal duty/dharma) using the symbols and metaphors that originated in the Indian subcontinent. Yoga is a way of life that spiritually transcends all religions. It can be practiced by any person belonging to any religion or belief system to improve one's fitness to practice one's own religion by increasing neurobiological fitness to the maximum. This facilitates the individual to become a spiritual human being. Yoga is applied successfully to different psychiatric disorders around the world, and several studies published in well-established journals have reported promising results in the last three decades. These significant scientific and statistical evidences are forcing the scientists of mind, that is, psychiatrists and other mental health professionals, to pay attention to this evidence and encourage them to integrate yoga and spirituality into mental health services in both illness and wellness. For all practical reasons, yoga and spirituality are put in use by several psychiatrists, taking into consideration their recognized benefits in promoting good health through its effects on the mind and therapeutic role in alleviating symptoms through neurobiological changes.[2]

Yoga has been widely used as an intervention along with conventional therapies and also exclusively in less severe to severe mental illnesses. While the exact mechanisms of yoga are not fully understood for modulating these therapeutic and biological effects, certain findings are relevant. Yoga involves imitating the therapist's movements and postures during the learning process. This practice will promote mirror neuron activity that is involved in social cognition.[3] Yoga practice typically involves being mindful while performing asanas. In traditional Ashtanga yoga, mindfulness is illustrated as dharana and dhyana. Practices of mindfulness showed positive effects on neuroplasticity and increased the density of gray matter.[4]

The cognitive benefits of yoga can be explained by the neuroplastic effect.

STRESS THEORY—WELLNESS

"Stress" can be defined as a condition that disturbs or is likely to disrupt a person's normal psychological or physiological functioning. Stress is described by the body as something (real, physical, or imagined) that threatens the life of a person, putting into practice a sequence of reactions that seek to reduce the impact of stress and restore homeostasis.

STRESS-DISTRESS

"Acute-chronic stress versus wellness"

Various neurotransmitters respond to stress. Stress causes the release of catecholamines through the locus coeruleus and autonomic nervous system by activating noradrenergic neurons in the brain. In response to stressors, increased serotonin production has been documented in the serotonergic systems of the brain, as well as increased dopaminergic neurotransmission in the mesofrontal pathways. Stress not only brings about changes in the neurotransmitter system but also in the endocrine and immune systems. Adrenocorticotropic hormone (ACTH) is released from the anterior pituitary in response to corticotropin-releasing factor (CRF) secreted from the hypothalamus. The adrenal cortex is in turn stimulated by ACTH, which leads to the synthesis and release of glucocorticoids. The immune system's functioning is inhibited by glucocorticoids. Stress may also lead to immune activation through a variety of pathways, such as the release of humoral immune factors (cytokines) and interleukins. Human biology/physiology, behavior, emotional, and cognitive processes are also influenced by stress. Stress and negative emotion will decrease human cognition by increasing the volume of the amygdala and decreasing the volume of the hippocampus, causing changes in behavior (as established in rat and human experiments). The hippocampus and the hypothalamic-pituitary-adrenal (HPA) axis are involved in the feedback regulation of cortisol, which is the body's primary stress hormone. Epinephrine and norepinephrine release is regulated by the locus coeruleus, amygdala, adrenal gland, and the sympathetic nervous system (SNS). Stress modulates synaptic plasticity in the hippocampus. Specific cognitive deficits in spatial learning and memory are seen due to the effect of chronic stress on structural synaptic plasticity, which causes atrophy of apical dendrites in pyramidal hippocampal neurons. Ultrastructural changes reported as a result of acute and repeated stress include decreased expression of brain-derived neurotrophic factor (BDNF).

Yoga and spirituality are ways to live a stress-free life. It trains us in how to live without stress and develop better coping mechanisms. Therefore, it has preventive value for both physical diseases of the body and psychological disorders of the human being. This is the basis of "Ashramam life." In India, under the guidance of gurus in various ashrams, a lifestyle without shrama, an effortless way of living, is followed, which is the key factor of Himalayan wellness. Indian stress-free living, which is a tradition of ancient Indian culture, has been practiced in India for decades.[5]

YOGA AND SPIRITUALITY IN NEUROTIC DISORDERS

The positive benefits of yoga and spirituality have been extensively investigated and demonstrated in areas of various milder forms of mental illness, such as anxiety and depression. Yoga reduces stress and is part of several stress management packages.[6] The practice of hatha yoga decreases body weight, improves the pattern of respiratory function, decreases the respiratory rate, increases the expansion of the chest, increases vital capacity, increases breath holding time, and also increases resistance to physical stress.[7] Khalsa (2004), in his article on yoga, views that yoga is becoming therapeutic for various psychiatric conditions such as depression and anxiety, other medical conditions of cardiovascular origin such as hypertension and heart disease, and respiratory illnesses such as asthma and diabetes.[8] Hartfiel et al. published a paper on yoga's role in increasing levels of psychological well-being by reducing perceived stress and back pain and increasing work performance.[9] Subhadra Evans, PhD, published a paper on yoga and proved its capacity to cure chronic pain conditions.[10] A number of research studies have shown downregulation of the HPA axis and the SNS and reinforce the theory that yoga practice increases physical and mental well-being, resulting in tremendous health benefits.[11] Arambula et al., in their study, argued that there is more alpha-EEG activity in occipitoparietal areas and an increased skin conductance level during meditation.[12]

Yoga has proven its benefits for anxiety, not only in the nonclinical population but also in the clinical population.[13] Kirkwood et al. published positive results in anxiety disorders, such as specific anxiety disorders, especially in OCD.[14] Obsessive-compulsive disorder was treated with kundalini yoga, and the results were promising.[15]

Recent reports suggest that yoga has been successful in reducing functional pain in somatoform disorders.[16] The Sudarshan Kriya Yoga (SKY) programme, a yogic breathing treatment, is giving positive results in stress management, anxiety disorders, post-traumatic stress disorder (PTSD), depression, and the management of war victims and victims of natural disasters.[17]

NEUROTIC DISORDERS MANAGEMENT

We are able to treat neurotic disorders with wonderful molecules, but the present psychotherapeutic modules are not very promising. We are practicing Jacobson's progressive muscle relaxation training (JPMR) for relaxing the body to relax the mind. But in my many years of therapies of relaxation even though behavior therapies are relatively better promising, I found something was missing.

Poorna Kshama Therapy[1]

I found that the "Poorna Kshama therapy" of Indian origin is highly effective. Here the therapist guides the client to imagine mother's/father's figure and excuses them for any mistakes done in their lives and gets excused by them for wrong things done by him. He was trained to excuse and get excused by all fellow beings, both males and females, of the whole world who are counter parts of the father figures (males) and mother figures (females), with the "Poorna Kshama" guilt goes off. Inhibitions, suppressions, and immature defenses disappear. Healthy attachments and object relationships and views set in. Internal space opens, and inner relaxation pervades.

In the wellness domain, human beings are neurotically conditioned by civilization, unfortunately forgetting that civilization is a creation of man and becoming victims of civilization with good and bad attributes, leading to guilt and aggression (suicide and homicide). According to Sigmund Freud, religion is a product of the neurotic tendencies of human beings. In "Poorna-Kshama therapy," the Indian concept of "Mathru devo bhava, Pithru devo bhava, Acharya devo bhava, and Athidi devo bhava" is used. Our so-called present civilization evolved from the past masters of the world. Masters include both opposing philosophies, such as negative, positive, or shukracharya, and Brihaspati groups over the generations, which are all conditionings to the human race. Caste, religion, language, regional attachments, and nationalities are all inevitable creations of past masters. The client evolves by understanding the inevitability of masters and their relative contributions to civilization. In the extreme wellness domain, he understands the relativity of civilization, the relativity of negative and positive philosophies of the world, and considers the mother, father, and teacher as Mathru devo bhava, Pithru devo bhava, and Acharya devo bhava. He also realizes that the prakriti is the ultimate guru, and the inner guru awakens. He sees mother, father, and teacher (guru) unconditionally and can excuse everyone, and the client evolves to the stage that "everything is okay".[1]

Spirituality and Yoga in Mood Disorders

Specific forms of yogasanas, such as Sudarshan Kriya and Sahaja Yoga, have been tested with positive findings for depression management.[18,19] Studies with different clinical outcomes suggest that patients have benefited from a reduction in depression scores following yoga. Such studies were inspired by the finding that yoga led to a sense of well-being and decreased dysphoria in psychologically stable participants. Yoga was almost as effective as an antidepressant drug (imipramine) in a randomized comparison.[20] Yogasana-based therapy alone reduced depression to remission levels.[20] These therapeutic effects are also linked to changes in some biomarkers. Smaller amplitudes in the event-related potential (P300) suggest lowered mentation in depression. Following 3 months of therapy with yoga as the sole intervention, this physiological marker was "normalized" to a higher value in depressed patients.[21] Yoga therapy improved serum levels of BDNF in depressed patients who, as a group, had lower levels of BDNF. Interestingly, BDNF response has also been correlated with the therapeutic effects of antidepressant drugs and electroconvulsive therapy. These biological effects, as mentioned above, are correlated with the antidepressant effects of yoga.[14] The cortisol-reducing properties of yoga indicate attenuation of the HPA axis, which in depression and other stress-related states is otherwise overactive.[14]

Magnetic resonance spectroscopy (MRS) of the brain shows elevated gammaaminobutyric acid (GABA) levels after an active yoga session.[22] GABAergic medications are known to have mood-stabilizing effects. This could be yet another yoga mechanism explaining therapeutic effects in depression and anxiety. One of the yoga procedures includes chanting "OM." From functional magnetic resonance imaging studies, there is some evidence that chanting OM is known to deactivate those brain regions (implied in emotions), probably through vagal afferent stimulation.[23]

Vagal nerve stimulation is used in depression as an invasive treatment. Sharma et al. conducted a study of sahaja yoga in depressive disorders and found that HAM-A and HAM-D scores were significantly improved in patients with sahaja yoga.[24] Streeter et al. concluded that the brain GABA level increases in experienced yoga practitioners after a yoga session. This indicates that yoga practice should be investigated as a therapy for conditions with reduced levels of GABA, such as depression and anxiety disorders. Yoga increases GABA levels.[25]

Preventive and Promotive Methods for Mood Disorders Management

We are able to treat mood disorders with wonderful molecules of antidepressants, antipsychotics, and mood stabilizers. But the present-day psychotherapeutic modules of different schools are not able to give promising results. Probably this inability in my routine practice forced me to search for something better, resulting in my presenting a paper titled "Psychotherapy for Mood Disorders by Using the Mrityunjaya Mantra" (A Biopsychosocio-spiritual Approach) in the Annual Conference of the IPS AP Chapter at Kurnool.

This helps the client to live with the negative and positive emotions and thoughts with detachment and helps the client against depression and mania. The therapist empowers the client to behave with cleverness to deal with the mind, which is full of negative or positive thoughts and emotions. Here the client gets awareness on how the self-attaches with the negative thoughts and emotions, which leads to depression. He detaches from those thoughts and emotions and escapes from depression. The client also understands how the self attaches to positive thoughts and emotions, causing mania like states; if the client detaches from that, he escapes from mania. Through self-awareness, the client gets the ability to handle the mind with relative attachment or detachment by fine-tuning.

Individuals in the normal domain of the human being naturally try to evolve to grow with the balanced emotions of relative positive and relative negative thoughts. The present civilization of the world divides the world into negative and positive dichotomies. The "Mrutyanjaya sloka" makes the client understand the dichotomy of the world and the relative positive and negative emotions attached to it. He learns to live without polarization and dichotomies of emotions. Thereby, the client will not become the victim of the mind and will become the master of balancing this mental dichotomy. This allows the human being to evolve into extreme wellness in the emotional domain. This is the way shown by our Indian Rishis to overcome bipolar thinking and bipolar mood disorders.

At the Annual Conference of the Indian Psychological Society, Andhra Pradesh division, at Kurnool, first author presented a paper entitled "Psychotherapy for Mood Problems Using the "Mrityunjaya Technique" (Biopsychosocio-spiritual Approach)."[1,26] Mrityunjaya mantra (mantra yoga) helps the client to live separately from negative and positive emotions and thoughts, thereby aiding clients to battle depression and mania. The therapist empowers the client to deal with a mind that is full of negative or positive thoughts and emotions in a clever manner. Here, the client becomes conscious of how the self attaches to the negative thoughts and emotions that lead to depression. One detaches from these negative thoughts and escapes from depression. The client also understands how the self attaches to positive thoughts and emotions that cause mania like states, from which he can escape if he relatively detaches himself. Through self-awareness, the client obtains the ability to handle the mind through fine-tuning the relative attachment or detachment. This is the way shown by our Indian Rishis to overcome bipolar thinking and bipolar mood disorders.[27]

CONCLUSION

In conclusion, spirituality plays a significant role in influencing mood and anxiety disorders, offering potential for healing and emotional balance. By fostering a sense of meaning, connection, and inner peace, spiritual practices may complement traditional therapies, providing a holistic approach to managing mental health. More research is needed to deepen this understanding.

REFERENCES

1. Porandla K. Psychiatric care: Illness to wellness. APJ Psychol Med. 2013;14(2):75-84.
2. Rao NP, Varambally S, Gangadhar BN. Yoga school of thought and psychiatry: Therapeutic potential. Indian J Psychiatry. 2013;55(6):145-9.
3. Mehta UM, Thirthalli J, Aneelraj D, Jadhav P, Gangadhar BN, Keshavan MS. Mirror neuron dysfunction in schizophrenia and its functional implications: A systematic review. Schizophr Res. 2014;160(1-3):9-19.
4. Hölzel BK, Carmody J, Vangel M, Congleton C, Yerramsetti SM, Gard T, et al. Mindfulness practice leads to increases in regional brain gray matter density. Psychiatry Res. 2011; 191(1):36-43.
5. Kishan P. Yoga and spirituality in mental health: Illness to wellness. Indian J Psychol Med. 2020;42(5):411-20.
6. Sharma M. Yoga as an alternative and complementary approach for stress management. J Evid Based Complementary Altern Med. 2013;19(1):59-67.
7. Udupa KN. The scientific basis of yoga. JAMA. 1972;220(10):1365.
8. Khalsa SB. Yoga as a therapeutic intervention: a bibliometric analysis of published research studies. Indian J Physiol Pharmacol. 2004; 48(3):269-85.
9. Hartfiel N, Burton C, Rycroft-Malone J, Clarke G, Havenhand J, Khalsa SB, et al. Yoga for reducing perceived stress and back pain at work. Occup Med. 2012;62(8):606-12.
10. Evans S, Subramanian S, Sternlieb B. Yoga as treatment for chronic pain conditions: A literature review. Int J Disability Hum Dev. 2008;7(1):25-32.
11. Ross A, Thomas S. The health benefits of yoga and exercise: A review of comparison studies. J Altern Complement Med. 2010;16(1):3-12.
12. Arambula P, Peper E, Kawakami M, Gibney KH. The physiological correlates of Kundalini Yoga meditation: a study of a yoga master. Appl Psychophysiol Biofeedback. 2001;26(2):147-53.
13. Kirkwood G, Rampes H, Tuffrey V, Richardson J, Pilkington K. Yoga for anxiety: A systematic review of the research evidence. Br J Sports Med. 2005;39:884-91.
14. Thirthalli J, Naveen GH, Rao MG, Varambally S, Christopher R, Gangadhar BN. Cortisol and antidepressant effects of yoga. Indian J Psychiatry. 2013;55(Suppl 3):S405-8.
15. Shannahoff-Khalsa DS. An introduction to kundalini yoga meditation techniques that are specific for the treatment of psychiatric disorders. J Altern Complement Med. 2004; 10(1):91-101.
16. Sutar R, Desai G, Varambally S, Gangadhar BN. Yoga therapy, a novel treatment option

for somatoform disorders: a case study. Int J Public Ment Health Neurosci. 2015;2:7-10.
17. Brown RP, Gerbarg PL. Sudarshan kriya yogic breathing in the treatment of stress, anxiety, and depression: Part I—neurophysiologic model. J Altern Complement Med. 2005; 11(1):189-201.
18. Cramer H, Lauche R, Langhorst J, Dobos G. Yoga for depression: A systematic review and meta-analysis. Depress Anxiety. 2013; 30:1068-108.
19. Louie L. The effectiveness of yoga for depression: A critical literature review. Issues Ment Health Nurs. 2014;35:265-76.
20. Janakiramaiah N, Gangadhar BN, Murthy PN, Harish MG, Subbakrishna DK, Vedamurthachar A. Antidepressant efficacy of Sudarshan Kriya Yoga (SKY) in melancholia: A randomized comparison with electroconvulsive therapy (ECT) and imipramine. J Affect Disord. 2000;57:255-9.
21. Gangadhar BN, Naveen GH, Rao MG, Thirthalli J, Varambally S. Positive antidepressant effects of generic yoga in depressive out-patients: A comparative study. Indian J Psychiatry. 2013;55(Suppl 3): S369-73.
22. Streeter CC, Whitfield TH, Owen L, Rein T, Karri SK, Yakhkind A, et al. Effects of yoga versus walking on mood, anxiety, and brain GABA levels: A randomized controlled MRS study. J Altern Complement Med. 2010; 16(11):1145-52.
23. Kalyani BG, Venkatasubramanian G, Arasappa R, Rao NP, Kalmady SV, Behere RV, et al. Neurohemodynamic correlates of "OM" chanting: A pilot functional magnetic resonance imaging study. Int J Yoga. 2011; 4(1):3.
24. Sharma VK, Das S, Mondal S, Goswampi U, Gandhi A. Effect of sahaj yoga on depressive disorders. Ind J Physiol Pharmacol. 2005;49: 462-8.
25. Streeter CC, Jensen JE, Perlmutter RM, Cabral HJ, Tian H, Terhune DB, et al. Yoga asana sessions increase brain GABA levels: A pilot study. J Altern Complement Med. 2007; 13(4):419-26.
26. Porandla K. Comprehensive psychotherapy (CPT) for mood disorders by using Mruthyunjaya Mantra (bio-psycho-spiritual approach). 28th APSYCON, Kurnool, Andhra Pradesh, 2008.
27. Kishan P, Preeti G, Cheriyala S, Kambhampati S. Comprehensive Psychotherapy for Mood Disorders by using Mrityunjaya Mantra (Bio Psycho Socio Spiritual Approach). Telangana J IMA. 2021;1(2):36-40.

4 CHAPTER

Spirituality and Addictive Disorders

Sumegha Mittal, Anju Dhawan

INTRODUCTION

Addiction is one of the major social and medical problems of this era. The International Society of Addiction Medicine (ISAM) includes a spiritual dimension in its definition of addiction in addition to psychological and biological dimensions of substance use disorders. Spirituality has been known to be helpful in the prevention, treatment, and rehabilitation of addiction/substance use disorders.[1]

One of the most obvious limitations of the literature is that religion and spirituality are often entangled together with a lack of clarity of definitions, thus leading to what is often called and conceptualized as religiosity/spirituality (R/S) for the purpose of research.

ROLE OF RELIGION/ SPIRITUALITY IN PREVENTION OF SUBSTANCE USE

Spirituality and religious practices have a role in prevention of alcohol and other substance use disorders. Most substance use starts in adolescence, which is developmentally a time of transition and is marked by risk taking behaviors that can extend up to adulthood. Prevention of substance use in this vital stage of life is important and spiritual/religious practices and beliefs can play an important role.

Involvement in spiritual and religious practices has been correlated with positive health behaviors including avoidance of substance. Koenig et al. in 2012 completed a systematic review and found 278 studies which assessed the relationship between faith and religion and included 145 studies of good research quality. More than 90% of the studies found higher level of religiosity and spirituality were associated with decreased alcohol use and dependence while only one study reported that involvement in spirituality contributed to higher substance use.[2] A review of the research in the field of mental health showed that higher levels of religious involvement may be positively associated with indicators of psychological well-being, evidenced, in part, by reductions in depression, suicidal thoughts, and drug and alcohol use or abuse (Moreira-Almeida et al., 2006).[3]

Participation in spiritual, faith communities, and having faith in god and offering prayers have been suggested by evidence to be associated with less likelihood of abusing drugs and alcohol and engaging in related criminal activity.[4] The National Centre on addiction and substance abuse conducted a 2-year study in Columbia university in 2001 that gave a strong evidence that teenagers who held strong religious/spiritual beliefs were three times less likely to smoke, five times less likely to binge alcohol and eight times less likely to use marijuana compared to those who did not have religious/spiritual inclination. Attending to spiritual/religious activities was also associated with lesser substance use as compared to those who never attended the R/S services.[5] Similar findings were reciprocated in another large study conducted among American youth aged 12–17 years by Ford and Hill, 2012.[6] Adolescents with higher religiosity (including religious attendance, involvement, and reliance on religious beliefs in decision making) had better mental well-being, lesser likelihood of depression and had a negative attitude toward substance use. The adolescents were also reported to have better resilience in stressful situations and were less likely to use drugs and alcohol as a coping mechanism for stress. The relationship between stress, spirituality, and substance use was also analyzed in 6–8th grade private school students at Johns Hopkins School of Public Health and Center for the Prevention of Youth Violence. Stress was a predictor of substance use in adolescents as reported in other studies, but a stronger association was the role of spiritual involvement in prevention of substance use and coping with stress.[7]

Adolescents who have been involved in spirituality have been shown by Yeterian 2018[8] to be lesser involved in heavy alcohol drinking even when compared with those who were more religious at baseline. The review showed some contradictory findings and reported that higher involvement in the R/S was associated with marijuana use and correlated marijuana use with better spiritual experiences.

Research suggests that there are four main motives for problematic alcohol and drug use in youth—coping, enhancement, social, and conformity (peer pressure). Although coping with difficult states such as anxiety, depression etc. is an important motive for initiation but most of the currently available prevention programs are based on the addressing the environmental conditions such as peer influence. More effective strategies that target the coping skills such as emotion regulation, distress tolerance can address the alcohol and other drugs use problem more effectively than short lasting approaches addressing only the environment. Evidence suggests that deficits in emotional regulation and self-regulation of distress (distress tolerance) are strongly related to patterns of alcohol and other drug (AOD) use in young adults.[9] Emotional regulation can be enhanced by meditation which helps to non-judgmentally attend to present emotions and emotional experiences by being a witness to one's emotions and thoughts. This helps to enhance competence in handling stressful situations.

Spirituality could help to have a deeper connection with one/higher-self and experience positive emotions without using substances for their acute effect and could thus help in prevention of substance use. Spirituality could also help to increase social and emotional support by enhancing the sense of belongingness and help to find meaning and support in difficult/traumatic situations.[10] People with religious or spiritual coping seek support and meaning when faced with adverse situations as compared to those with negative religious coping.[11]

Effect of religiosity on prevention of substance use in adolescents was also studied as a multidimensional construct in African American youth of Philadelphia aged 13–20 years. Proximity to religious institutions as well as religiosity subdivided into three separate dimensions were studied which included (social religiosity, perceived social support, and private religiosity). The results suggested that at least two dimensions of religiosity were protective against one type of substance use. For instance, social religiosity was protective against cannabis use, perceived religious support against nicotine use and proximity to religious institutions might be protective against alcohol use. However, in this study, private religiosity was not protective against any substance use.

Pokhrel et al. studied if spirituality had a protective effect on alcohol and tobacco use behavior across different countries. The study compared the effect of spirituality in Russian and American adolescents. In American adolescents, spirituality was protective against substance use while in Russian high school students there was no relationship between spirituality and substance use. Authors suggested that spirituality as a protective factor varies across cultures and cannot be attributed as a universal protective factor against substance use.[12]

ROLE OF SPIRITUALITY IN RECOVERY FROM SUBSTANCE USE DISORDER

Addiction is defined as a recurring and relapsing illness and recovery is thought to be difficult in patients dependent on drugs/substances. Although addiction is a chronic illness, there are deficits in the currently available treatment approaches for recovery from addiction. Spiritual-based approaches tailored to different cultures can address these deficits and promote recovery from addiction.[13] Recovery from addiction is much more than mere abstinence from substance use as dependence on drugs affects many functional domains of life (e.g., familial, social, psychological, occupational, etc.). One more concept for securing sustained recovery is recovery capital. Recovery capital was defined by Granfield and Cloud as the internal and external resources (e.g., peer and cultural support, spirituality, religiosity, meaning of life, and 12-step affiliation) that a person can use to sustain recovery from drugs and also find purpose and meaning of life.[14,15] Spiritual affiliation helps to increase recovery capital which can improve the ability to handle stressful situations in the path of recovery and enhance life satisfaction and help to sustain recovery from substance use disorders.[16]

12-Step Facilitation

The first and the most widely studied approaches have been 12-step programs. Psychiatrist Marc Galanter studied the spiritually based 12-step programs which are based on the model of Alcoholics Anonymous (AA) founded by Bill Wilson and Dr Bob Smith in 1938. AA views recovery as "spiritual awakening" and has been reconfigured for numerous behavioral and chemical addictions, which are collectively known as 12-step facilitation (TSF). These fellowships now include groups for behavioral addictions, such as Gambler's anonymous, sex addict's anonymous, overeaters anonymous, and recovering couples anonymous (for sex addiction).

Does TSF make a difference? That depends on what is being measured. Project MATCH found that TSF produced an outcome comparable to cognitive behavioral therapy and motivation enhancement.[17] A review by Kaskutas (2009) found that higher levels of TSF attendance was related to higher rates of abstinence.[18] There have been many criticism in the AA research which includes self-selection bias of the subjects in the study, lack of comparison or control group in the study, blinding of the groups and only few studies mention about the drop out or attrition bias, selective reporting or reporting bias, comparability of the cohorts for baseline characteristics and outcome measures etc. A recent Cochrane review of Twenty-seven trials (21 RCTs, 5 non-randomized studies and 1 purely economic study) in 2020 involving 10,565 people took into account also the methodological factors while selecting articles of AA research for the reviews and concluded that there is a high-quality-evidence by experimental studies that clearly demonstrated the effectiveness of manualized AA or TSF approaches for achieving abstinence and reducing alcohol dependence or associated problem as compared to other established treatments such as cognitive behavioral therapy (CBT) in most of the outcome measures. Non-manualized AA or TSF approaches may also be as effective as other treatment approaches.[19] Other studies have also found that AA also leads to better outcomes through increasing spirituality/religiosity and by reducing negative affect.[20] The research may be summed up in one of the more popular AA *slogans, "It works if you work it."*

Possible Mechanisms by which Alcoholics Anonymous Works

Most physicians and addiction experts regard AA as an important part of treatment for alcoholism and related addictions based on their clinical experience. Aside from the spiritual teachings, experts find the social support and therapeutic milieu TSF can provide to be very helpful. AA helps to provide support in the form of a mentor, groups which are available on hourly or daily basis. These groups are easily accessible and affordable as they are free of cost. Sponsors also help to sustain the AA activities. A large community of AA members and mentors helps the fellow mates on the path of recovery. The group discussion helps to address factors associated with abstinence such as identifying high risk situations, how to handle high risk situations by learning from the experience of other members in the group and sharing own experiences. Sharing of addiction and recovery experiences instils hope and provides practical skills to stay sober and also evokes a sense of empathy and belonging. AA addresses an important factor in relapse that is peer group, which plays a vital role in recovery and maintaining abstinence by providing an alternate low risk peer group and a new social circle. AA groups offer one-line slogans that help in handling craving and facing different life challenges. AA helps individuals recover by enhancing self-efficacy, coping skills, and motivation and provides workbooks and discussion on these topics. The concrete changes happen through belief in the 12-step philosophy (acceptance of powerlessness, belief in a higher power, etc.) and most importantly AA states that spiritual awakening results in change in attitude and behavior. Strict rules for recovery, helping others by mentoring, and anonymity are key ingredients of the Fellowships. TSF helps to bring about emotional, behavioral, and cognitive changes. Studies report that AA can be helpful in maintaining abstinence for longer period in those who are continuously engaged with AA, attend regular meetings and are committed for abstinence and avoiding high risk situations. Earlier AA texts suggest that TSF groups are not supportive of medical and professional approaches but currently, TSF groups also support the disease model of addiction and medical treatment. Hence, social support (mentorship, sponsorship), fellowship, reducing stigma, easy accessibility, affordability, altruism, an organized 12-step spiritual philosophy, behavioral and attitudinal changes, an inclusive approach for other contemporary treatments, and a spiritual foundation appear to be the key elements of TSF.[21]

Yoga and Addiction

Yoga is considered a means of enhancing spiritual growth or connecting with the self. Literature has recently shown strong evidence of the role of yoga in the treatment of chronic illnesses. Discipline of yoga can play an important role in addressing the burden of substance use disorders.

Mechanism of how yoga can be helpful in substance use disorder: Yoga can be helpful in two phases of substance use disorders—firstly, during the detoxification period. The initial detoxification phase of drug cessation is usually a stressful period and can lead to increased sympathetic activity such as tachycardia, increased breathing rate etc., with depressant drugs such as alcohol, benzodiazepines, and opiates. Yoga techniques are known to increase the vagal or para-sympathetic activity that may be helpful in reducing these signs and symptoms. Yoga practices might also be helpful in prevention of relapse by enhancing the ability to handle distress and enhance emotional regulation.

Kuppili et al. (2019)[22] did a systematic review to study the effect of yoga in the management of substance use. A total of 314 studies were initially screened for inclusion in the study but only 16 studies met the inclusion criteria. Authors included 12 randomized studies, four non-randomized intervention studies, studies on females, adolescents, males done in different settings, both outpatient and inpatient. Studies were done on nicotine, alcohol, opioid, and cocaine use disorders only. There were no studies on stimulants, hallucinogens, and cannabis use disorders.

Studies on the effect of different yoga therapies such as *Hatha yoga, Sudarshan kriya yoga, vinyasa yoga* on substance use disorders were analyzed. The duration of yoga intervention, number of sessions, format of therapy (individual or group sessions) was also variable in the review. Studies had different active control groups such as physical exercise, reading material, wellness program, and no-active control groups leading to difficulty in comparison and interpretation of the results. Different outcome variables measured by self-report questionnaires for anxiety, depression, mood, quality of life, abstinence, and craving were used in the studies.

Results of the review found that most of the studies were done on nicotine use disorder and suggested that yoga has a role in abstinence from substance use and also reduces craving. Yoga therapy was effective in short term but studies with larger sample size and longer follow-up are warranted to demonstrate the long-term effects of yoga therapy. The authors reported that yoga has a potential role as an adjunct treatment to conventional treatment.

Another systematic review on yoga and substance use by Walia et al. (2021)[23] included only randomized controlled trials published between 2013 and 2021. A total of eight randomized controlled studies were included. The studies on yoga, breathing exercises as well as meditation were included. Studies which combined yoga with other interventions were excluded. Six studies had mentioned about the substance use studied which included smoking, alcohol, and opioids but two studies did not define which substance use disorder was studied. The study population included prisoners and the general population. Different interventions were studied such as *Hatha yoga, Iyengar yoga,*

Sudarshan kriya yoga, breathing exercises, and mindfulness-based relapse prevention. Wide range of control groups were included in six studies such as health education, counseling manuals, group wellness material on health topics, recreational activities while two studies did not have any active control group but used only treatment as usual. The review suggested that yoga intervention both as an adjunct treatment to standard treatment as well as independent treatment can improve outcome in substance use disorders. Both direct (abstinence rate, decrease in substance use, decrease in craving) and indirect outcomes (anxiety, posttraumatic stress disorder, stress, mood, criminal activity, mindfulness, and quality of life) were measured using standardized tools. However, there were lot of variabilities in the studies and most of the studies were not blinded.

Hatha Yoga

Bock et al. (2012)[24] studied the role of *hatha yoga* as a complementary treatment for smoking cessation in females. 55 females who were receiving cognitive behavior therapy were randomized in two groups of *hatha yoga* and group wellness activities. The *hatha yoga* arm received twice weekly 1-hour yoga sessions for a period of 8 weeks while the group wellness arm was shown videos on various health-related topics. Results showed that women in the yoga group at 7 days had higher abstinence rate than controls and effect was sustained at 3 months and 6 months. Yoga group also had favorable effects on other outcome measures such as anxiety and perceived health and well-being but had minimal effect on depression.

A pilot randomized controlled trial was done by Uebelacker et al. (2019)[25] to assess the acceptability and feasibility of *hatha yoga* program to treat chronic pain in patients on opioid agonist therapy for opioid use disorder. In the study, 40 patients on opioid maintenance therapy methadone or buprenorphine were recruited and randomized into yoga group and health education group for 12 classes. Initial acceptability of yoga and health education was 50% and 65% respectively. Participants in the yoga group also did home practice of yoga, with a mean of about 2.67 per week. There was a decrease in anxiety, sadness, irritability, fatigue, and chronic pain with both *hatha yoga* and health education group after intervention. There was significant reduction in pain and anxiety in the yoga group as compared to the health education group.

A randomized controlled trial was done on people living with human immunodeficiency virus (HIV) and substance use problems after re-entry from jail and prisons. Stress and substance use was quite high and the risk of relapse was high during this period. Wimberly et al. (2018)[26] randomized the patients into *hatha yoga* group along with standard treatment and standard treatment group to explore the potential role of *hatha yoga* in reducing stress and substance use. Participants in the first group were given weekly, 90-minute yoga intervention for 3 months. The change in stress and substance use measured by Perceived Stress Scale and Timeline Follow Back Scale respectively was significant in the yoga group at all the three time points—1 month, 2 months, and 3 months after intervention.

Yogic Breathing Practices

Kochupillai et al. (2005) studied the efficacy of *Sudarshan kriya yoga* in 82 participants who had completed the 6-day workshop which taught life skills and *Sudarshan kriya* (a rhythmical breathing process). The participants were encouraged to continue their daily home practice of *Sudarshan kriya.* A questionnaire was used to assess the pattern and amount of tobacco use at baseline, day 6, 2 weeks, 3 weeks, 2 months, 3 months, and 6 months. A total of 34 participants followed up at 6 months and 17 of them were abstinent. Among smokers with cancer, *Sudarshan kriya* was associated with smoking cessation and the efficacy of *Sudarshan kriya* was comparable to Bupropion (drug approved for smoking cessation) as intention to treat analysis showed success rate of 21% with *Sudarshan kriya.*[27]

The results of the effect of *Sudarshan kriya* on quitting tobacco was supported by a study by Rawat et al., 2011. The participants who were heavy smokers and used >10 cigarettes per day and willing to quit smoking were recruited. The participants were divided into two treatment groups, one group received *Sudarshan kriya yoga* and the other group only yoga. The results of the study showed that *Sudarshan kriya* reduced smoking, increased abstinent rates and also enhanced motivation to quit smoking as compared with yoga group only.[28]

Depression is a common comorbidity in alcohol-dependent patients. Depression predicts relapse by >50% in early stage of treatment of alcohol dependence. In a randomized controlled trial, Vedamurthachar (2006) studied the antidepressant effects of *Sudarshan kriya* in alcohol-dependent patients. 60 alcohol-dependent patients who were admitted to a tertiary hospital and detoxified in the first week were recruited and randomized in the *Sudarshan kriya* and treatment as usual group. Beck's depression inventory was used to assess for depression at baseline and 2 weeks after the *Sudarshan kriya*. Assays of morning plasma cortisol, adrenocorticotropic hormone (ACTH) and prolactin were also measured at baseline and at the end of 2 weeks. Beck Depression Inventory (BDI) scores improved in both the groups, but the improvement was significantly more in the *Sudarshan kriya* group. Similarly, plasma cortisol and ACTH reduced in both the groups at 2 weeks as compared to baseline but significantly more in SKY group. Symptomatic improvement in depression (BDI) was seen to correlate with the reduction in stress hormone (plasma cortisol and ACTH).[29,30]

Dhawan (2015)[31] studied the role of yogic breathing (*Sudarshan kriya*) in improving the quality of life of opioid-dependent patients on long-term buprenorphine maintenance therapy. The study was conducted in 84 patients who were following up for treatment and WHO-QOL brief scale and urine drug tests were done at baseline and 3 and 6 months. There was improvement in all four (physical, psychological, environmental, and social) QOL domain scores in the *Sudarshan kriya* group at 6 months.

Yogic breathing technique's role in smoking craving, negative affect, and smoking behavior was studied by Lotfalian (2019).[32] 60 participants who met the eligibility criteria were recruited and randomized into three groups by web-based randomization into (1) 20 participants opted for mindfulness yogic breathing (to consciously breath by slight constriction of the throat and bring attention back to the breath whenever mind wanders, (2) 20 participants were in cognitive strategy group (to think about the long-term consequences of substance use), (3) 20 participants opted for no treatment. The intervention was given for 20 minutes in each group. Self-report measures about smoking behavior, Fagerström test for nicotine dependence (FTND), mindfulness, and negative affect was done before and after intervention in two sessions and reminders were given to practice the techniques. Yogic breathing and cognitive strategy both reduced craving and perceived nicotine withdrawal but only breathing group reported improvement in negative effect. Yogic breathing technique reduced the smoking two times more than the other two groups. Neither of the group showed any effect on mindfulness.

Similar results of effect of yogic breathing on smoking cessation were found in a study by Shahab et al. in 2013.[33] 96 participants were recruited and randomized into yogic breathing exercise and video control group (video of breathing exercise was shown but no suggestion was given to practice). The intervention was given for 10 minutes in each group and subjects in the breathing group were asked to practice the technique to control the urges of craving. The yogic breathing technique performed better than the video control group in controlling the urges, but the effects were not sustained over 24 hours because of poor adherence to the practice of yogic breathing.

Transcendental Meditation

Transcendental meditation is a simple and effortless mantra-based meditation technique. The technique is taught by a certified trainer and has to be practiced 20 minutes daily twice a day. The technique helps to achieve a state of rest with alertness and allows the mind to settle down in a state of transcendental consciousness.

Gryczynski (2018)[34] conducted an open label study to assess the role that transcendental meditation could play as a relapse prevention strategy in treatment of alcohol use disorder. 60 newly admitted patients were recruited from the hospital and were divided in two groups. Group 1 was on treatment as usual which received medical-assisted withdrawal treatment, structured activities, group, and individual counseling using cognitive-behavioral and 12-step approaches, relapse prevention. The other group received both—treatment as usual and transcendental meditation (taught by a certified practitioner over 4 days, 1 hour session in each day). A 20-minute mantra-based meditation was taught, and the meditation was then practiced in group setting and the participants were advised to practice it twice a day for next 3 months. Patients were assessed at baseline and 3-months post discharge on measures which included a Timeline Follow Back (TLFB) interview of alcohol consumption, TM practice questionnaire, TM experience questionnaire (perceived helpfulness for managing stress, cravings, and alcohol use, at follow-up only), Addiction Severity Index-Lite, Perceived Stress Scale; Kessler-6 Psychological Distress Scale, Alcohol Urge Questionnaire, and Craving Experience Questionnaire. As compared to baseline at 3-month follow-up integrating TM into the treatment of alcohol use disorder patients was feasible, acceptance of TM was high and >60% had good adherence and practiced TM twice a day. Relapse to any form of drinking or heavy drinking was less as compared to the treatment as usual group. TM practice was also associated with decreased craving, alcohol use, and distress.

A meta-analysis was done by Alexander (1994)[35] on the studies related to TM and substance use. 19 studies which included >4,500 subjects were included in the review. 13 out of 19 studies were either uncontrolled studies or involved yoked-peer control with random assignments. The studies included a range of participant groups such as students, general population, prisoners, and Vietnam veterans. Only six studies were randomized controlled studies. The authors found that TM helps to reduce negative psychological outcomes such as anxiety, anger, depression, and hostility in heavy alcohol users. TM technique also helped to improve positive psychological outcomes such as self-concept and internal locus of control. The authors reported that these factors might have mediated in reduction of alcohol use, cigarette, and illicit drug use with transcendental meditation at 10-month follow-up.

In another randomized waitlisted controlled trial by Haaga (2011)[36] on the effect of TM on substance use in college students, 295 students showed interest and were eligible as per the inclusion criteria selected. Preintervention and 3 months post intervention assessments were done for substance use (self-report) and adherence to the TM technique. The results of the study found no effect of TM in reduction of smoking and drug use but showed significant decrease in alcohol use only among males.

Mindfulness-based Meditation

Mindfulness training can address the dysregulation in reward learning and executive functioning and produce significant therapeutic effects on substance use disorders and prevent relapse. There are various mindfulness-based interventions which address stress, negative affect, substance use impulses (e.g., first generation mindfulness-based interventions (MBIs)-mindfulness-based stress reduction (MBSR), mindfulness-based cognitive therapy (MBCT) and, newer MBI's [mindfulness-based relapse prevention (MBRP)], mindfulness-oriented recovery enhancement (MORE). Mindfulness techniques help to enhance awareness of the person-specific substance use patterns, compulsive and impulsive use and helps in emotional control which is a common reason for self-medicating using drugs.

Mindfulness-based techniques consist of two main steps—focused attention and open monitoring. Mindfulness training involves improved attention by mindfulness breathing and body scan meditation and open monitoring which involves increased awareness of the present moment, emotions, thoughts, bodily sensations, or other perceptual experiences. MBIs are usually delivered in group formats over 8 weeks. In the sessions, clients meditate for 30–45 minutes followed by a daily audio-guided practice for 45 minutes. Participants are trained in mindful breathing and body scan meditation by a trained clinician. The regular practice of mindfulness techniques helps to develop traits to be mindful in everyday life by neuroplastic changes in brain by regular practice.[37-39] MBSR was the first mindfulness-based technique introduced in 1980s at University of Massachusetts Medical School by Kabat-Zinn. MBSR helps to manage cravings and negative emotional states and helps to disengage from compulsive addictive behaviors by accepting the problems instead of trying to modify or suppress them.

Mindfulness-based cognitive therapy was formulated to treat chronic conditions which are associated with relapses like depression. MBCT principles were later adapted into similar programs specifically targeting addictive disorders. Based on the success of MBSR many MBIs were specifically designed for substance use disorders (SUD) such as MBRP and MORE, mindfulness training for smokers (MTS), moment-by-moment in women's recovery (MMWR). MBRP is a manualized, structured protocol that combines MBSR and Marlatt's cognitive behavior relapse prevention programs. This technique combines MBSR and Marlatt's Cognitive Behavior Relapse Prevention programs. Participants are trained to identify high risk situations by cultivating mindfulness or awareness of internal (e.g., emotions, thoughts, and sensations) and external cues (e.g., environmental) rather than instinctively using these substances and practice (by in-vivo and imaginative exposures) without automatically avoiding or escaping from the situation. Participants are taught to become mindful of the present moment despite the unpleasant sensation to make a less impulsive decision. The mindfulness training helps the clients to increase awareness of physical, emotional cognitive and/or craving states and accept the situation without reacting.[40]

Korecki et al. conducted a systematic review of all the manualized treatment for substance use disorders. A total of 902 peer reviewed published articles from 2016 to 2020 were selected by search and 30 articles which met the inclusion criteria were included. The review included peer reviewed randomized controlled trials although most of them were small size RCT and with shorter follow-up. The review analyzed the effect on different MBIs [MBSR, MBRP, MORE, MTS, and mindfulness-based addiction therapy (MBAT)] in different populations, e.g., stimulant dependents, comorbid psychiatric disorders, and substance use. Different techniques had different duration of MBI sessions; modified protocols included shorter mindfulness-based sessions for 75 minutes instead of 120 minutes, >8 weeks sessions and adjunctive treatment modalities such as combined effect on mindfulness-based intervention with acceptance and commitment therapy and additional role of transcranial direct current stimulation (TDCS). Secondary analysis of the studies which studied the effect of MBIs on treatment outcome showed that MBIs are more helpful in patients with high addiction severity and comorbid psychiatric disorders such as depression, anxiety etc.[37] The results of the review found that MBIs are as effective as other existing evidence-based treatments. MBIs can help with reducing craving for substance use, reducing frequency and quantity of drug use, improved abstinence rate and reduced other substance-related problems. But the review had certain limitations which included small size RCTs with short follow-ups. These lead to limited generalizability, results with small effect size and large confidence intervals, lack of stringent controls, and uniformity in the mindfulness interventions.

Weiss de Souza[41] conducted a controlled pilot study in 88 participants to assess the feasibility and effectiveness of MBRP as an adjunct treatment to standard treatment for smoking cessation. They received MBRP session in group format over 8 weeks. Each session was 2 hours long and comprised a primary topic, guided meditation, exercises, discussions, and homework review. Participants were given audio recordings for daily practice at home and they had to keep a record of the lapses and relapses. In the MBRP group, abstinence was higher than the standard treatment in the maintenance phase. The participants in MBRP group also had reduction in craving and better mindfulness based on the Five Facet Mindfulness Questionnaire-Brazil than the usual treatment.

In another controlled randomized trial in 70 opioid-dependent patients referred for long-term methadone maintenance treatment in Iran the efficacy of MBRP on the impulsivity and relapse was compared with treatment as usual. The participants were given 8-week MBRP therapy and were followed up at 2 months. Participants in the MBRP arm reported lower impulsivity on the Barrett's impulsivity scale and high abstinence rate both post treatment and at 2 months follow-up compared to the standard treatment arm.[42]

A study by Zemestani et al. in 2016[43] randomized 74 alcohol-dependent patients with comorbid depression in two groups—MBI and standard treatment. Similar to other studies intervention was given for 8 weeks and assessment was done with Beck Depression Inventory, Beck Anxiety Inventory, Penn Alcohol Craving Scale at baseline, 8 weeks after intervention, and 2 months after that in follow-up. MBRP group had significantly lower scores on all the three scales at follow-up. The study gave a strong base for further studies that MBRP could be effective in treatment of comorbid drug dependence and other psychiatric disorders such as depression, anxiety.

In another study, participants with opioid use disorders and chronic pain on methadone maintenance therapy were randomized in two groups. One group received manualized 8-session group therapy intervention MORE involving training in mindfulness (enhanced awareness and self-control over craving and non-reactivity to emotional and physical pain), reappraisal (to promote emotional regulation), and savoring skills (to remediate deficits in natural reward processing) to address OUD and chronic pain. Ecological monitoring assessment was done and pain, craving, and negative affect showed improvement in the MORE group as compared to the treatment as usual group. MORE therapy also led to better self-control over emotions and craving.[44]

A large randomized controlled trial was conducted to compare the effect of MORE, CBT, and treatment-as-usual (TAU) in 180 male patients with comorbid substance use disorders and psychiatric disorders. With all the three treatment modalities there was decrease in craving. Patients who received MORE had more reduction in craving than the CBT group and also showed improvement in post-traumatic stress disorder (PTSD) symptoms as compared to the other groups.

Newer modalities, MBAT and MTS cessation, are based on MBCT and MBSR respectively. Kober and colleagues conducted a randomized controlled trial to study the effect of MTS and CBT [American Lung Association's Freedom from Smoking (FFS) program] in smoking cessation. In this study, 23 participants were recruited from another RCT and were randomized into the two treatment groups and compared the change in stress reactivity and neural activity during stressful scripts during the treatment and in follow-up after 3 months. In the study both the treatments were found to reduce smoking, but the MTS was more effective (statistically significant) in reducing smoking and abstinence and the effects of MTS were maintained in long term during the follow-up. Functional magnetic resonance imaging (fMRI) studies were done to see the neural activity during stressful situations. The study reported that MTS group did not show any increase in neural activity in stressful situations in contrast with the FFS group which had greater neural activity in several regions of brain which includes the left amygdala, anterior, middle, and posterior insula, and bilateral portions of para-hippocampal gyrus and hippocampus, putamen, thalamus, midbrain, and cerebellum. Mindfulness therapies might be helping in smoking cessation by increasing the ability to handle stressful situations.[45]

BIOLOGICAL CORRELATES OF ROLE OF SPIRITUALITY IN SUBSTANCE USE

12-Step Facilitation

Studies have also found biological correlates of spirituality that might be helpful in understanding recovery from addiction. In an experimental study by Miller, responses to an individualized-guided neuroimaging task were compared between personally experienced spiritual experiences with neutral-relaxing and stressful experiences by using functional magnetic resonance imaging. There was reduced activation of parietal cortex in spiritual conditions in contrast with the neutral and stressful experiences.[46] Ventral Fronto-Temporal Network has also been found to be associated with engagement in spiritual condition and intrinsic spirituality distinct from engagement during the stress or neutral-relaxing conditions.[47] Cortical and subcortical regions are found to be activated in people exposed to early life trauma and are predisposed and more likely to engage in substance use. Intrinsic spirituality has been found to be inversely correlated with the activation of these regions and can play a vital role in prevention and treatment of addictive disorders.[48,49] Galanter et al.[50] conducted a study in long-term members of AA who reported no craving after joining AA and spiritual awakening to find the associated neural correlates. As compared to after reading passive irrelevant news or passive viewing, craving following prayers was associated with areas involved with attention and emotional control by decreased activation of default mode network and self-referential processing areas of brain. The study has paved way for further research in studying neural networks engaged in role of spirituality in recovery from substance use. The research on associated neural correlates with spiritual experiences might be helpful in better personalized psychological treatment for patients engaged in medication focused treatment programs.

Mindfulness-based Interventions

According to *yogis*, every sensory experience leads to impression on the mind and the craving for the same impression leads to addiction. The current addiction treatment research also predicts the role of learning and memory in addiction. Meso-limbic system and dorsal striatum regions are involved in learning and storage of memory of addictive disorders.[51] The neurobiological mechanism by Miller et al.[46] has described addiction as a "reward deficiency syndrome" and hypodopaminergic state leads to craving and motivation to regular use of drugs and also leads to relapse. Holistic modalities such as yoga and meditation which lead to long-term high dopaminergic state or dopamine homeostasis can favor long-term benefits in the treatment of drug dependence. Yoga practices can help in becoming more aware of the emotions and are also helpful to handle stress and negative emotional states and help in reducing stress hormone cortisol. Regular practice of yoga can be helpful in reducing cortisol hormone and ACTH as demonstrated in a study on alcohol-dependent patients by Sampedro-Piquero et al. (2019).[52]

Tang et al. (2016) found that brief mindfulness training [integrative body-mind training (IBMT)] had an impact on improved stress reduction and better emotional regulations in both smokers and non-smokers. These changes were then neurobiologically correlated and smoker group had reduced ACC (anterior cingulate)/mPFC (medial prefrontal cortex) activity in the self-control network before training, and these deficits were ameliorated after training as compared to non-smokers.[53]

CONCLUSION

Spirituality has a different meaning for everyone but mostly describes as connection of one-self with the higher-self. In the literature, concepts of spirituality and religion are used interchangeably. Prevention of substance use is an important area focused by different stakeholders to decrease the burden of substance use. Religion and spiritual beliefs can play a significant role in prevention of substance use by helping in emotional regulation, distress tolerance, and enhancing social and emotional support. The role of spirituality in recovery from addictive disorders has been documented in literature for many decades. 12-step facilitation and alcohol anonymous groups laid the foundation for the role of spirituality in management of alcohol and drug dependence. Recent literature has also found biological correlates of how spirituality helps in recovery from addictive disorders. Different spiritual practices such as yoga and meditation are increasingly recognized for their role in the treatment of addiction. Most of the studies have studied these as adjunct treatments to existing standard treatment. They can help to break the cycle of stress, negative emotion by enhancing self-awareness and self-control. This has generated greater scientific interest to conduct research on the role of different yoga, meditation, and breathing techniques in the long-term treatment of substance use disorders. Different mindfulness-based techniques tailored to address the factors involved in relapse from substance use have been developed like mindfulness-based stress reduction and mindfulness-based relapse prevention, mindfulness-based cognitive therapy, mindfulness based-assisted therapy, mindfulness training for smoking cessation. There is growing empirical evidence and conceptual underpinnings for mindfulness-based interventions in the treatment of addiction. Meditation and breathing techniques such as transcendental meditation, *Sudarshan kriya yoga* and other yogic breathing techniques have also shown promising results in recovery and treatment of addiction. However, there are some important factors to be considered in the existing literature as it involves different yoga and meditation practices, duration of the techniques is variable, expertise of the instructor, and most importantly inclination of subjects may be variable as is the daily home practice of the meditation technique. There is a need for larger studies with longer follow-up and suitable active control group. Further studies are required to firmly establish the role of different spiritual practices in different types of addiction.

REFERENCES

1. de Rezende-Pinto A, Moreira-Almeida A. Guidelines for integrating spirituality into the prevention and treatment of alcohol and other substance use disorders. Brazilian Journal of Psychiatry. 2023;45(3):274-9.
2. Koenig H, Koenig HG, King D, Carson VB. Handbook of Religion and Health. Oxford University Press, USA; 2012. p. 1186.
3. Moreira-Almeida A, Neto FL, Koenig HG. Religiousness and mental health: a review. Braz J Psychiatry. 2006;28(3):242-50.
4. Johnson BR, Pagano ME, Lee MT, Post SG. Alone on the Inside: The Impact of Social Isolation and Helping Others on AOD Use and Criminal Activity. Youth Soc. 2018;50(4):529-50.

5. The National Center on Addiction and Substance Abuse (CASA). So Help Me God Substance Abuse, Religion and Spirituality. 59 p. [online] Available from https://www.centeronaddiction.org/addiction-research/reports/so-help-me-god-substance-abuse-religion-and-spirituality. [Last accessed December, 2024].
6. Ford JA, Hill TD. Religiosity and Adolescent Substance Use: Evidence From the National Survey on Drug Use and Health. Subst Use Misuse. 2012;47(7):787-98.
7. Debnam K, Milam AJ, Furr-Holden CD, Bradshaw C. The Role of Stress and Spirituality in Adolescent Substance Use. Subst Use Misuse. 2016;51(6):733-41.
8. Yeterian JD, Bursik K, Kelly JF. "God put weed here for us to smoke": A mixed methods study of religion and spirituality among adolescents with cannabis use disorders. Subst Abuse. 2018;39(4):484-92.
9. Aldao A, Nolen-Hoeksema S, Schweizer S. Emotion-regulation strategies across psychopathology: A meta-analytic review. Clin Psychol Rev. 2010;30(2):217-37.
10. Carrico AW, Storholm ED, Flentje A, Arnold EA, Pollack LM, Neilands TB, et al. Spirituality/religiosity, substance use, and HIV testing among young black men who have sex with men. Drug Alcohol Depend. 2017;174:106-12.
11. Medlock MM, Rosmarin DH, Connery HS, Griffin ML, Weiss RD, Karakula SL, et al. Religious coping in patients with severe substance use disorders receiving acute inpatient detoxification. Am J Addict. 2017;26(7):744-50.
12. Tortolero SR. New Dimensions for Adolescent Substance Use Prevention. J Prim Prev. 2012;33(5):223-4.
13. Yel D, Bui A, Job JS, Knutsen S, Singh PN. Beliefs About Tobacco, Health, and Addiction Among Adults in Cambodia: Findings from a National Survey. J Relig Health. 2013;52(3):904-14.
14. Granfield R, Cloud W. Coming clean: Overcoming addiction without treatment. New York, NY, US: New York University Press; 1999. xxi, p. 296.
15. World Health Organization. (2020). International Standards for the Treatment of Drug Use Disorders. [online] Available from https://www.who.int/publications-detail-redirect/international-standards-for-the-treatment-of-drug-use-disorders [Last accessed December, 2024].
16. Laudet AB, White WL. Recovery Capital as Prospective Predictor of Sustained Recovery, Life satisfaction and Stress among former poly-substance users. Subst Use Misuse. 2008;43(1):27-54.
17. Tonigan JS, Miller WR, Connors GJ. Project MATCH client impressions about Alcoholics Anonymous: Measurement issues and relationship to treatment outcome. Alcohol Treat Q. 2000;18:25-41.
18. Kaskutas LA. Alcoholics Anonymous Effectiveness: Faith Meets Science. J Addict Dis. 2009;28(2):145-57.
19. Kelly JF, Humphreys K, Ferri M. Alcoholics Anonymous and other 12-step programs for alcohol use disorder. Cochrane Database Syst Rev. 2020;3(3):CD012880.
20. Kelly JF, Hoeppner B, Stout RL, Pagano M. Determining the Relative Importance of the Mechanisms of Behavior Change within Alcoholics Anonymous: A Multiple Mediator Analysis. Addict Abingdon Engl. 2011;107(2):289-99.
21. Kelly JF, Magill M, Stout RL. How do people recover from alcohol dependence? A systematic review of the research on mechanisms of behavior change in Alcoholics Anonymous. Addict Res Theory. 2009;17(3):236-59.
22. Kuppili PP, Parmar A, Gupta A, Balhara YPS. Role of Yoga in Management of Substance-use Disorders: A Narrative Review. J Neurosci Rural Pract. 2018;9(1):117-22.
23. Walia N, Matas J, Turner A, Gonzalez S, Zoorob R. Yoga for Substance Use: A Systematic Review. J Am Board Fam Med. 2021;34(5):964-73.
24. Bock BC, Fava JL, Gaskins R, Morrow KM, Williams DM, Jennings E, et al. Yoga as a Complementary Treatment for Smoking Cessation in Women. J Womens Health. 2012;21(2):240-8.

25. Uebelacker LA, Van Noppen D, Tremont G, Bailey G, Abrantes A, Stein M. A pilot study assessing acceptability and feasibility of hatha yoga for chronic pain in people receiving opioid agonist therapy for opioid use disorder. J Subst Abuse Treat. 2019;105: 19-27.
26. Wimberly AS, Engstrom M, Layde M, McKay JR. A randomized trial of yoga for stress and substance use among people living with HIV in reentry. J Subst Abuse Treat. 2018;94: 97-104.
27. Kochupillai V. Effect of Rhythmic Breathing (Sudarshan Kriya and Pranayam) on Immune Functions and Tobacco Addiction. Ann N Y Acad Sci. 2005;1056(1):242-52.
28. Rawat H, Vedamurthachar D, Rawat L, Rawat DR. How Sudarshan Kriya helps to reduce the habit of smoking and motivate to quit smoking. Intern J Pharma Sci Rev Res. 2011;6(2):27-9.
29. Varambally S, Gangadhar BN. Yoga: A spiritual practice with therapeutic value in psychiatry. Asian J Psychiatry. 2012;5(2):186-9.
30. Vedamurthachar A, Janakiramaiah N, Hegde J, Shetty T, Subbakrishna D, Sureshbabu S, et al. Antidepressant efficacy and hormonal effects of Sudarshana Kriya Yoga (SKY) in alcohol dependent individuals. J Affect Disord. 2006;94(1-3):249-53.
31. Dhawan A, Chopra A, Jain R, Yadav D, Vedamurthachar. Effectiveness of yogic breathing intervention on quality of life of opioid dependent users. Int J Yoga. 2015;8(2):144-7.
32. Lotfalian S, Spears CA, Juliano LM. The Effects of Mindfulness-Based Yogic Breathing on Craving, Affect, and Smoking Behavior. Psychol Addict Behav. 2020;34(2):351-9.
33. Shahab L, Sarkar BK, West R. The acute effects of yogic breathing exercises on craving and withdrawal symptoms in abstaining smokers. Psychopharmacology (Berl). 2013;225(4):875-82.
34. Gryczynski J, Schwartz RP, Fishman MJ, Nordeck CD, Grant J, Nidich S, et al. Integration of Transcendental Meditation® (TM) into alcohol use disorder (AUD) treatment. J Subst Abuse Treat. 2018;87:23-30.
35. Alexander CN, Robinson P, Rainforth M. Treating and Preventing Alcohol, Nicotine, and Drug Abuse Through Transcendental Meditation: A Review and Statistical Meta-Analysis. Alcohol Treat Q. 1994;11(1-2):13-87.
36. Haaga DAF, Grosswald S, Gaylord-King C, Rainforth M, Tanner M, Travis F, et al. Effects of the Transcendental Meditation Program on Substance Use among University Students. Cardiol Res Pract. 2011;2011:537101.
37. Korecki JR, Schwebel FJ, Votaw VR, Witkiewitz K. Mindfulness-based programs for substance use disorders: a systematic review of manualized treatments. Subst Abuse Treat Prev Policy. 2020;15(1):51.
38. Grodzicki J, Galanter M. Spirituality and Addiction. Subst Abuse. 2005;26(2):1-4.
39. Garland EL, Howard MO. Mindfulness-based treatment of addiction: current state of the field and envisioning the next wave of research. Addict Sci Clin Pract. 2018;13:14.
40. Alsubaie M, Abbott R, Dunn B, Dickens C, Keil TF, Henley W, et al. Mechanisms of action in mindfulness-based cognitive therapy (MBCT) and mindfulness-based stress reduction (MBSR) in people with physical and/or psychological conditions: A systematic review. Clin Psychol Rev. 2017; 55:74-91.
41. Weiss de Souza IC, Kozasa EH, Bowen S, Richter KP, Sartes LMA, Colugnati FAB, et al. Effectiveness of Mindfulness-Based Relapse Prevention Program as an Adjunct to the Standard Treatment for Smoking: A Pragmatic Design Pilot Study. Nicotine Tob Res. 2020;22(9):1605-13.
42. Yaghubi M, Zargar F, Akbari H. Comparing Effectiveness of Mindfulness-Based Relapse Prevention with Treatment as Usual on Impulsivity and Relapse for Methadone-Treated Patients: A Randomized Clinical Trial. Addict Health. 2017;9(3):156-65.
43. Zemestani M, Ottaviani C. Effectiveness of Mindfulness-Based Relapse Prevention for Co-occurring Substance Use and Depression Disorders. Mindfulness. 2016;7(6):1347-55.
44. Garland EL, Hanley AW, Kline A, Cooperman NA. Mindfulness-Oriented

Recovery Enhancement reduces opioid craving among individuals with opioid use disorder and chronic pain in medication assisted treatment: Ecological momentary assessments from a stage 1 randomized controlled trial. Drug Alcohol Depend. 2019;203:61-5.

45. Kober H, Brewer JA, Height KL, Sinha R. Neural Stress Reactivity Relates to Smoking Outcomes and Differentiates between Mindfulness and Cognitive-Behavioral Treatments. NeuroImage. 2016;151:4-13.
46. Miller L, Balodis IM, McClintock CH, Xu J, Lacadie CM, Sinha R, et al. Neural Correlates of Personalized Spiritual Experiences. Cereb Cortex. 2019;29(6):2331-8.
47. McClintock CH, Worhunsky PD, Xu J, Balodis IM, Sinha R, Miller L, et al. Spiritual experiences are related to engagement of a ventral frontotemporal functional brain network: Implications for prevention and treatment of behavioral and substance addictions. J Behav Addict. 2019;8(4): 678-91.
48. Potenza MN, Hong KI, Lacadie CM, Fulbright RK, Tuit KL, Sinha R. Neural Correlates of Stress-Induced and Cue-Induced Drug Craving: Influences of Sex and Cocaine Dependence. Am J Psychiatry. 2012;169(4):406-14.
49. Elsey J, Coates A, Lacadie CM, McCrory EJ, Sinha R, Mayes LC, et al. Childhood Trauma and Neural Responses to Personalized Stress, Favorite-Food and Neutral-Relaxing Cues in Adolescents. Neuropsychopharmacology. 2015;40(7):1580-9.
50. Galanter M, Josipovic Z, Dermatis H, Weber J, Millard MA. An initial fMRI study on neural correlates of prayer in members of Alcoholics Anonymous. Am J Drug Alcohol Abuse. 2017;43(1):44-54.
51. McLellan AT, Lewis DC, O'Brien CP, Kleber HD. Drug Dependence, a Chronic Medical Illness Implications for Treatment, Insurance, and Outcomes Evaluation. JAMA. 2000;284(13):1689-95.
52. Sampedro-Piquero P, J Santín L, Castilla-Ortega E. Aberrant Brain Neuroplasticity and Function in Drug Addiction: A Focus on Learning-Related Brain Regions. In: Palermo S, Morese R (Eds). Behavioral Neuroscience. Intechopen; 2019.
53. Tang YY, Tang R, Posner MI. Mindfulness meditation improves emotion regulation and reduces drug abuse. Drug Alcohol Depend. 2016;163 Suppl 1:S13-8.

5 CHAPTER

Spiritual Dimensions in Addressing Suicidality

Shubhangi R Parkar, Sunil Kuyare

INTRODUCTION

Suicide is a significant global health issue that affects individuals across all socioeconomic, cultural, and geographical boundaries. Tackling this problem requires a united effort and open discussions. However, fear, stigma, and shame often prevent people from seeking help or talking about it. Suicide is defined as a deliberate act of taking one's own life. According to the World Health Organization, it involves self-inflicted harm, injury, or poisoning carried out with the intent to die.[1] Every year, more than 800,000 people die by suicide worldwide, accounting for 1.3% of all deaths.[1]

In India, the situation is equally alarming, with the country recording the highest number of suicides globally. Data from the National Crime Records Bureau indicates an increase in suicide rates from 9.9 per lakh population in 2017 to 12.4 per lakh population in 2022.[2] Among individuals aged 15–39 years, suicide is the leading cause of death. Stigma surrounding suicide, combined with inconsistent reporting practices, contributes to underreporting, which masks the true extent of its impact as a public health crisis. Although suicide is not classified as a disease, it remains a profoundly tragic outcome with complex causes and continues to be a leading cause of death worldwide. In many countries, prevention efforts have not significantly reduced suicide rates. Developing culturally sensitive intervention strategies could play a crucial role in preventing these devastating losses.

COMMON RISK FACTORS AND WARNING SIGNS

Suicide risk arises from a combination of complex factors, both psychological and social. Individuals diagnosed with psychiatric conditions such as major depressive disorder, bipolar disorder, schizophrenia, anxiety disorders, or personality disorders face a heightened risk of suicidal behaviour.[3] Adverse childhood experiences, including physical or emotional abuse, neglect, or exposure to violence, can further amplify this vulnerability. Additionally, substance abuse, particularly involving alcohol or drugs, often worsens mental health challenges and contributes to suicidal tendencies.[4] Chronic medical conditions, such as cancer, HIV/AIDS, or persistent pain, frequently lead to feelings of despair and hopelessness.[5] Social isolation, marked by a lack of supportive relationships, loneliness, or a sense of disconnection from others, is another significant contributor.[6] These aspects highlight the need for holistic interventions that address not just the individual's mental and emotional well-being but also their broader sense of meaning, connection, and belonging. Spirituality emerges as a culturally sensitive and effective approach in this context, especially in societies where spiritual beliefs and practices are deeply ingrained in daily life.

THEORIES AND MODELS EXPLAINING SUICIDAL BEHAVIOR

Various theories and models have been developed to understand suicidal behavior, reflecting societal, psychological, and biological dimensions. Emil Durkheim (1897/1951) identified different types of suicide—egoistic, altruistic, anomic, and fatalistic—based on the degree of social integration and regulation.[7] He argued that societal factors, such as the strength of community bonds and the influence of collective norms, play critical roles in shaping suicide rates. Shneidman's psychache theory (1998) proposes that the primary driver of suicide is an overwhelming desire to escape intolerable psychological pain, often stemming from unmet psychological needs such as achievement, affiliation, or connection, rather than an explicit intent to die.[8] Similarly, Joiner's interpersonal-psychological theory (2005) identifies three critical factors contributing to suicide: A sense of being a burden, a lack of belonging or social connection, and the acquired capacity to overcome the fear of death through repeated exposure to distressing experiences.[9]

The popular diathesis-stress model examines how genetic or biological predispositions interact with environmental stressors to elevate suicide risk. This model also highlights the dynamic interplay between internal and external factors, with spirituality playing a key role in shaping responses to stress and reducing or increasing suicide risk. Expanding on this, O'Connor's (2011) Integrated Motivational-Volitional (IMV) model outlines three phases: The premotivational phase, involving background vulnerabilities; the motivational phase, focusing on the formation of suicidal intent; and the volitional phase, highlighting factors that facilitate suicidal actions, such as impulsivity or access to lethal means.[10] Baumeister's theory (1990) suggests that adopting a passive mindset may lead individuals to perceive themselves as victims rather than active agents in their lives, contributing to suicidal ideation.[11] Additionally, Beck and colleagues' hopelessness theory suggests that suicide is often driven by feelings of hopelessness—the belief that one's life will never improve, no matter what actions are taken.[12] This pervasive sense of hopelessness serves as the primary motivating force behind suicidal behavior. By combining these multifaceted perspectives, they provide a holistic approach to understanding and addressing suicide risk.[13]

SPIRITUALITY AND SUICIDE

Religion and spirituality have significant impacts on people's lives across the world. While the relationship between religion, spirituality, and suicide is intricate, research suggests that spiritual experiences and religious involvement can have positive effects on mental health. Several studies indicate that religiosity is associated with lower rates of mental illness and suicide.[14] Spiritual practices such as mindfulness, meditation, and other religious rituals have been shown to reduce stress, anxiety, and depression, which can contribute to suicide prevention. Further research is necessary to explore the connection between religiosity and suicide more deeply, which can help shape effective psychiatric interventions. Spirituality can play a dual role in suicidal behavior, both as a protective factor and, in some cases, a contributing factor.

Protective Role

Spirituality can provide individuals with a sense of purpose, connection, and hope, which are vital in reducing the risk of suicidal thoughts and behaviors. Strong spiritual beliefs and practices offer emotional support during times of crisis, enabling individuals to better cope with stress and adversity. A study by Talib and Abdollahi (2015) highlights the importance of spirituality as a protective factor against hopelessness, depression, and suicidal behavior among Malaysian adolescents.[15] Many spiritual or religious teachings explicitly discourage suicide, framing it as morally or ethically wrong, which can serve as a deterrent to suicidal ideation. Research has found that higher levels of spirituality are linked to lower rates of depression, anxiety, and suicide attempts, underscoring its protective role.[16]

Contributory Role

However, in certain situations, spirituality can exacerbate suicidal behavior. Feelings of spiritual failure, guilt, or shame—often stemming from a perceived inability to adhere to religious or spiritual norms—can worsen emotional distress. In rigid or punitive spiritual environments, individuals facing crises or uncertainties may feel alienated, intensifying feelings of worthlessness.[17] Moreover, spiritual beliefs can sometimes be misinterpreted in ways that justify suicide, such as viewing it as a means of achieving transcendence or escaping suffering.

SPIRITUALITY AND CULTURAL VARIATIONS

The concept of spirituality is diverse and subjective, fluctuating greatly across cultures and individuals. Notwithstanding these differences, spiritual beliefs and practices share a common impact on mental health. Research acknowledges that both religion and spirituality influence mental health in discrete ways. Recent literature distinguishes between spirituality and religion.[18] Religion is defined as an organized system of rituals, beliefs, practices, and symbols aimed at fostering closeness to the sacred. Spirituality, on the other hand, is understood as a personal quest for understanding life's ultimate questions. While the relationship between religion and mental health has been extensively studied,[19] the connection between spirituality, mental illness, and suicide remains understudied. Most research has focused on the association between religion and suicidal ideation and attempts, leaving a significant knowledge gap in the realm of spirituality and suicidal behavior. The impact of spirituality on suicidal behavior differs broadly across cultural and individual contexts.[20] In some cultures, deeply interwoven spiritual practices with daily life provide a robust buffer against suicidal behavior.

SPIRITUAL STRUGGLES AND SUICIDAL IDEATION

Spiritual struggles, such as feeling disconnected from a higher power or experiencing spiritual despair, are strongly linked to suicidal ideation.[21] These struggles are often marked by existential crises, guilt, or feelings of abandonment, which can worsen hopelessness and psychological distress. Following are significant aspects of spiritual struggles and their links to suicidal ideation:[17,21-23]

- *Disconnection from a higher power:* Studies indicate that spiritual disconnection is significantly correlated with depressive symptoms, which are major predictors of suicidal ideation. For individuals whose faith traditionally provides emotional support and purpose, this disconnection can amplify feelings of despair.

- *Existential and spiritual despair:* Spiritual despair emerges when individuals question life's purpose or feel that suffering has no meaning. This despair can also result from perceived failures to adhere to spiritual or moral values.
- *Guilt and perceived spiritual failure:* Devastating guilt due to perceived moral or spiritual disobedience may lead individuals to feel unworthy or fear divine punishment. For some, such emotions may contribute to the belief that suicide is the only means of escaping suffering or reconciling with perceived failure.
- *Conflict with religious teachings or communities:* Spiritual struggles can also arise from conflict with religious communities or the inability to reconcile personal views with institutional doctrine. This conflict can increase feelings of alienation and contribute to suicidal thoughts.
- *Unresolved spiritual conflicts:* Individuals experiencing spiritual struggles are more likely to express suicidal ideation compared to those without such struggles.[22] Unresolved spiritual conflicts are also associated with an increased risk of depressive episodes, which mediate the relationship between spiritual struggles and suicidal thoughts.[21]

ASSESSMENT AND INTERVENTION STRATEGIES

A precise assessment is crucial in addressing suicidal behavior, and several psychiatric rating scales help identify its various clinical dimensions. Frequently used psychometric tools such as the Hopelessness Depression Symptom Questionnaire-Suicidality Subscale (HDSQ-SS), Sheehan Suicidality Tracking Scale (S-STS), and Acquired Capability for Suicide Scale (ACSS) assess suicidal ideation and past attempts. The Beck Scale for Suicide Ideation (BSS) measures the intensity of suicidal thoughts, while the Suicide Behaviors Questionnaire-Revised (SBQ-R) evaluates both past and potential future behaviors. The Ask Suicide-Screening Questions (ASQ) is a quick screening tool used in emergencies.[24] Additionally, spiritual tools, such as the Spiritual Well-Being Scale (SWBS)[25] and Religious Coping Scale (RCOPE),[26] integrate holistic care by assessing spiritual distress and support. An exploratory study by Kopacz et al. (2015) evaluated a spiritual distress scale used by chaplains to identify veterans at risk for suicide.[27] The scale assessed factors such as guilt, grief, anger, hopelessness, and lack of purpose. Together, these tools enhance emotional risk identification and intervention in clinical practice.

Spiritual-based Interventions

Spiritual-based interventions can complement traditional strategies for addressing suicidal behavior by addressing existential concerns and fostering hope.

- Pastoral counseling integrates spiritual guidance with psychological support, providing a safe space for individuals to explore their struggles and find solace in faith during times of crisis.[28]
- Mindfulness and meditation practices, rooted in spiritual traditions such as Buddhism, can enhance emotional regulation and reduce suicidal ideation. They facilitate in reducing symptoms of stress, anxiety, and depression, all of which are important in addressing suicidal ideation.[29]

- Engagement with faith-based communities offers social support and a sense of purpose, helping mitigate feelings of isolation and helplessness.[30]
- Spiritual counseling plays a vital role in helping individuals address deep emotional pain, in the context of suicidal ideation, where unresolved emotional conflicts and feelings of worthlessness can intensify despair. By offering a safe space for individuals to explore their feelings and spiritual struggles, counselors help them reframe their experiences, fostering a sense of inner peace, and acceptance.[31]
- Forgiveness-based interventions grounded in many spiritual traditions, including Christianity, Buddhism, and others may involve structured practices such as prayer, meditation, or guided reflection, which allow individuals to confront their emotional pain and find meaning in their suffering.[32]
- Spiritual distress and interventions facilitate the role of spirituality in health, and including how addressing spiritual distress (e.g., guilt and alienation) can improve mental well-being and reduce suicidal risk.[33]
- Narrative and meaning-making therapies can further support recovery by allowing them to reconstruct their personal stories and find purpose in their experiences, which can counteract spiritual despair.[34] By integrating these approaches, spiritual care enhances holistic well-being and supports recovery from suicidal crises.
- Faith-based communities can offer social support, emotional reassurance reducing isolation, and improving mental health outcomes for individuals besieged with suicidal ideation.[30]

Spiritual Therapy with Psychological Support

Spiritual therapy, often referred to as spiritual counseling or care, represents a blend of spiritual guidance and psychological support aimed at addressing emotional and existential distress. This approach is particularly effective for individuals grappling with suicidal ideation or crises of meaning, as it seeks to reestablish connections with their core values and sense of purpose. By offering a compassionate and nonjudgmental environment, spiritual therapy fosters emotional recovery through practices such as forgiveness and reconciliation. Its integration with mental health care creates a holistic framework that aligns with the World Health Organization's definition of health, emphasizing resilience-building and alleviating symptoms of depression and anxiety, which are critical risk factors for suicide.[20,35]

In therapy, spirituality emerges as both a foundation for healing and a route to personal development. During the early stages of treatment, practices such as mindfulness meditation, gratitude exercises, and faith-based counseling provide grounding and help individuals navigate immediate psychological challenges. These approaches, as highlighted by researchers such as Koenig (2012), are shown to enhance emotional stability and resilience.[30] Kabat-Zinn (1990) further illustrates the benefits of mindfulness in cultivating present-moment awareness and stress regulation.[36] As mental stability improves, spirituality often transitions from a coping strategy to a means of self-discovery. Frankl's (1992) existential framework, for instance, suggests that exploring one's spiritual beliefs can lead to profound personal transformation and a renewed sense of purpose.[37] Advanced practices such as transcendental meditation, engaging with philosophical texts, and acts of altruism further support this growth by deepening the individual's connection to meaning and purpose. Pargament (2007) describes such spiritually integrated approaches as essential for addressing both short-term challenges and long-term existential aspirations.[38] Collectively, these insights underscore the dynamic interplay between spirituality and mental health, highlighting its dual role in fostering immediate recovery and long-term growth.

Mental Health Conditions and Spiritual Void

Mental health conditions such as depression and substance abuse, which are significant risk factors for suicidal behaviors, often stem from a complex interplay of biological, psychological, and social factors. An emerging perspective, however, highlights a potential link between these issues and a spiritual void—a profound sense of disconnection from meaning, purpose, and inner fulfillment. This perspective suggests that individuals facing such challenges may also be grappling with existential questions or a sense of emptiness, arising from a lack of spiritual engagement or connection.

Depression and Spiritual Void

Depression is frequently characterized by feelings of hopelessness, worthlessness, and helplessness, all of which contribute to an increased risk of suicide. Frankl, in his seminal work Man's Search for Meaning (1992), argued that a lack of meaning in life—a hallmark of spiritual void—can lead to existential frustration and psychological distress.[37] Spirituality, by providing a framework to understand suffering and foster hope, can help address the underlying causes of these feelings. Supporting this view, Koenig et al. (2012) found that individuals with higher levels of spiritual well-being were less likely to experience depression and reported better overall mental health outcomes.[39]

Substance Abuse and the Search for Meaning

Substance abuse often emerges as a maladaptive coping mechanism for stress, trauma, or a sense of inner emptiness and frequently precedes suicidal behavior. Jung (1976), a pioneer of modern psychotherapy, suggested that addiction may stem from a spiritual void, describing it as a "thirst for wholeness".[40] Jung posited that individuals struggling with addiction are often searching for transcendence or spiritual fulfillment in destructive ways. This notion is reflected in contemporary recovery programs such as Alcoholics Anonymous (AA), which place spirituality at the core of their approach. Research by Miller (1998) supports this idea, showing that spiritual interventions in addiction treatment enhance recovery outcomes by fostering a sense of connection, hope, and purpose.[41] The integration of spiritual and religious paths from Indian culture into addiction treatment offers a holistic and transformative approach. By addressing the physical, emotional, and spiritual dimensions of addiction, these practices not only help individuals overcome dependency but also guide them toward a fulfilling and purpose-driven life.

Addressing the Spiritual Void

A spiritual void can manifest as a lack of connection not only to a higher power but also to one's inner self, community, or the natural world. Effective interventions to address this void often incorporate practices such as mindfulness, meditation, yoga, and participation in spiritual or faith-based communities. These practices have been shown to significantly enhance mental health outcomes. For example, a meta-analysis by Leamy et al. (2011) identified spirituality as a critical factor in personal recovery from mental health conditions, helping individuals rebuild a sense of meaning, purpose, and resilience.[42]

HOLISTIC APPROACHES TO TREATMENT

Integrating spirituality into mental health care provides a holistic framework for healing. Pargament (2007) emphasized that spiritual guidance complements traditional therapeutic approaches by addressing the existential dimensions of mental health issues.[38] When individuals reconnect with their spiritual beliefs or explore new pathways to meaning, they often report enhanced emotional well-being and reduced reliance on maladaptive behaviors such as substance abuse. This integration highlights the transformative potential of spirituality in fostering not only recovery but also long-term emotional resilience.

Cultural Sensitivity and Spiritual Frameworks

Cultural sensitivity and awareness are essential when addressing suicide and spirituality, as cultural backgrounds directly influence individuals' spiritual beliefs, practices, and attitudes toward mental well-being. Spirituality often intersects with cultural norms, determining how individuals view life's meaning, cope with crises, and responds to suicidal ideation. For example, some cultures emphasize community and collective resilience through religious practices, while others may prioritize individual spirituality or meditation. Understanding these cultural nuances ensures that interventions are respectful and tailored to the individual's beliefs and practices, avoiding spiritual frameworks that may inadvertently alienate those seeking help. Research has shown that culturally appropriate approaches foster trust and engagement in treatment, significantly enhancing suicide prevention strategies.[43] In some cases, incorporating rituals or working with spiritual advisors familiar with a community's traditional practices can be instrumental in addressing spiritual despair and nurturing hope.

Suicide Prevention and Spirituality

Spirituality plays a vital role in suicide prevention by instilling hope, fostering a sense of purpose, and nurturing connections, all of which counteract despair and social isolation. Practices such as prayer, meditation, and participation in spiritual communities provide emotional support and effective coping strategies. Spiritual frameworks help individuals find meaning amidst challenges, enabling them to reframe adversities and build resilience. Furthermore, spiritual care interventions address deep-seated feelings of guilt, shame, and existential distress, contributing to emotional recovery and healing.

When integrated into mental health care, spirituality enhances holistic well-being and reduces suicide risk. Empirical evidence underscores its significance: Research by Miller et al. (2014) on the offspring of depressed parents found a remarkable 90% reduction in the risk of recurrent major depression among those who valued spirituality or religion, linked to structural changes in the brain.[44] Similarly, the Nurses' Health Study revealed that women who attended weekly religious services had an 84% lower risk of suicide compared to nonattendees.[16] For high-risk individuals, even simple posthospitalization interventions—such as sending supportive postcards—were shown to significantly reduce suicide rates, as demonstrated by Motto and Bostrom (2001).[45] These findings highlight spirituality's potential to complement clinical strategies, offering a multidimensional approach to suicide prevention.

CONCLUSION

Suicide is a critical public health concern that requires urgent attention, innovative solutions, and a steadfast commitment to preventing these tragic losses while promoting mental well-being. Spiritual care is an invaluable resource in suicide prevention. By addressing existential concerns, fostering hope, and providing a sense of connection, it creates a foundation for healing and resilience. Hope and resilience are cornerstones of spiritual care, and maturity in facing life's challenges is encouraged through practices such as storytelling, spiritual rituals, and mindfulness. These practices encourage individuals to view challenges as opportunities for personal growth, empowering them to endure and overcome life's adversities. Mental health professionals and spiritual care providers must collaborate to offer holistic, person-centered care that is tailored to the unique needs of each individual. Future research should focus on developing spiritually integrated interventions and exploring the complex interplay between cultural background, spiritual struggles, and suicidal behavior.

REFERENCES

1. World Health Organization. (2021). WHO/MSD/MER/19.3. Suicide in the world: Global Health Estimates. [online] Available from https://iris.who.int/bitstream/handle/10665/326948/WHO-MSD-MER-19.3-eng.pdf [Last accessed December, 2024].
2. National Crime Records Bureau (NCRB). (2022). Accidental Deaths & Suicides in India (ADSI) 2022. [online] Available from https://www.ncrb.gov.in/uploads/nationalcrimerecordsbureau/custom/adsiyearwise2022/ 1701611156012ADSI2022 Publication2022.pdf [Last accessed December, 2024].
3. Moitra M, Santomauro D, Degenhardt L, Collins PY, Whiteford H, Vos T, et al. Estimating the risk of suicide associated with mental disorders: A systematic review and meta-regression analysis. J Psychiatry Res. 2021;137:242-9.
4. Darke S, Ross J, Lynskey M. Suicidal behaviors among individuals with substance use disorders. J Subst Abuse Treat. 2010;38(2): 147-55.
5. Ehde DM, Dillworth TM, Turner JA. Cognitive-behavioral therapy for individuals with chronic pain: efficacy, innovations, and directions for research. American psychologist. 69(2);153.
6. Calati R, Ferrari C, Brittner M, Oasi O, Olié E, Carvalho AF, et al. Suicidal thoughts and behaviors and social isolation: A narrative review of the literature. J Affect Disord. 2019; 245:653-67.
7. Durkheim E. Suicide: A Study in Sociology. Glencoe, IL: Free Press; 1897/1951. Translated by Spaulding JA and Simpson G.
8. Shneidman ES. Further reflections on suicide and psychache. Suicide Life Threat Behav. 1998;28:245-50.
9. Joiner TE. Why people die by suicide. Cambridge, MA: Harvard University Press; 2005.
10. O'Connor RC. The integrated motivational-volitional model of suicidal behavior. Crisis. 2011;32(6):295-8.

11. Baumeister RF. Suicide as escape from self. Psychol Rev. 1990;97(1):90-113.
12. Abramson LY, Alloy LB, Hogan ME, Whitehouse WG, Gibb BE, Hankin BL, et al. The hopelessness theory of suicidality. In: Joiner TE, Rudd MD (Eds). Suicide Science: Expanding the Boundaries. Kluwer Academic/Plenum Publishers; 2000. pp. 17-32.
13. Selby EA, Joiner TE Jr, Ribeiro JD. Comprehensive Theories of Suicidal Behaviors. In: Nock MK (Ed). The Oxford Handbook of Suicide and Self-Injury. Oxford University Press; 2014.
14. Dunbar R. Religiosity and religious attendance as factors in wellbeing and social engagement. Religion, Brain & Behavior. 2020;11(1):17-26.
15. Talib MA, Abdollahi A. Spirituality Moderates Hopelessness, Depression, and Suicidal Behavior among Malaysian Adolescents. J Relig Health. 2017;56:784-95.
16. VanderWeele TJ, Li S, Tsai AC, Kawachi I. Association Between Religious Service Attendance and Lower Suicide Rates Among US Women. JAMA Psychiatry. 2016; 73(8):845-51.
17. Exline JJ, Rose ED. Religious and spiritual struggles. In: Paloutzian RF, Park CL (Eds). Handbook of the psychology of religion and spirituality, 2nd edition. The Guilford Press; 2013. pp. 380-98.
18. Pargament KI. Psychology of religion and coping: Theory, research, and practice. The Guilford Press; 1997.
19. Verghese A. Spirituality and mental health. Indian J Psychiatry. 2008;50(4):233-7.
20. Koenig HG. Religion, spirituality, and mental health. J Clin Psychol. 2015;71(1):1-13.
21. Noth I, Lampe J. Religious and Spiritual Conflicts: A Psychological Perspective. Pastoral Psychol. 2020;69:135-47.
22. Upenieks L. Religious/spiritual struggles and suicidal ideation in the COVID-19 era: Does the belief in divine control and religious attendance matter? Psychol Religion Spirituality. 2022;14(3):338-50.
23. Lemke AW, Davis EB, Voytenko VL, Cowden RG, Chen ZJ, McConnell JM, et al. Religious/Spiritual Struggles and Suicide Ideation Among Adult Psychiatric Outpatients: A 12-Month Longitudinal Study. J Affect Disord Rep. 2023;14:100640.
24. Kreuze E, Lamis DA. A Review of Psychometrically Tested Instruments Assessing Suicide Risk in Adults. Omega (Westport). 2018;77(1):36-90.
25. Paloutzian RF, Ellison CW. (1982). Spiritual Well-Being Scale (SWBS) [Database record]. APA Psyc Tests.
26. Pargament KI, Koenig HG, Perez LM. The many methods of religious coping: Development and initial validation of the RCOPE. J Clin Psychol. 1998;54(6):519-43.
27. Kopacz MS, Hoffmire CA, Morley SW, Vance CG. Using a Spiritual Distress Scale to Assess Suicide Risk in Veterans: An Exploratory Study. Pastoral Psychol. 2015;64:381-90.
28. Pargament KI, Exline JJ. The psychology of religion and coping: Theory, research, practice. Guilford Press; 2006.
29. Goyal M, Singh S, Sibinga EMS, Gould NF, Rowland-Seymour A, Sharma R, et al. Meditation programs for psychological stress and well-being: a systematic review and meta-analysis. JAMA Intern Med. 2014;174(3):357-68.
30. Koenig HG. Religion, spirituality, and health: The research and clinical implications. ISRN Psychiatry. 2012; 2012:278730.
31. Richards PS, Bergin AE. Handbook of Psychotherapy and Religious Diversity. American Psychological Association; 2000.
32. Enright RD, Fitzgibbons RP. Forgiveness Therapy: An Empirical Guide for Resolving Anger and Restoring Hope. American Psychological Association; 2000.
33. Pargament KI, Hahn J. Spirituality and health: The research and clinical implications. Am Psychol. 2002;57(1):1-4.
34. White M, Epston D. Narrative Therapy: The Construction of Meaning. Norton & Company; 1990.
35. Rosmarin DH, Krumrei EJ, Pargament KI. Spiritual coping and mental health. In: Paloutzian MA, Park CL (Eds). Handbook of Psychology, Religion, and Spirituality. New York, NY: Guilford Press; 2009. pp. 561-79.

36. Kabat-Zinn J. Full Catastrophe Living: Using the Wisdom of Your Body and Mind to Face Stress, Pain, and Illness. New York, NY: Delacorte Press; 1990.
37. Frankl VE. Man's Search for Meaning: An Introduction to Logotherapy, 4th edition (I. Lasch, Trans.). Beacon Press; 1992.
38. Pargament KI. Spiritually Integrated Psychotherapy: Understanding and Addressing the Sacred. Guilford Press; 2007.
39. Koenig HG, King DE, Carson VB. Handbook of Religion and Health. Oxford University Press; 2012.
40. Jung CG. Modern Man in Search of a Soul. New York: Harcourt Brace; 1976.
41. Miller WR. Spirituality in addiction treatment: The struggle for integration. Addiction. 1998; 93(7):979-90.
42. Leamy M, Bird V, Le Boutillier C, Williams J, Slade M. Conceptual framework for personal recovery in mental health: Systematic review and narrative synthesis. Br J Psychiatry. 2011; 199(6):445-52.
43. Teo DCL, Duchonova K, Kariman S, Ng J. Religion, Spirituality, Belief Systems and Suicide. In: Alfonso CA, Chandra PS, Schulze TG (Eds). Suicide by Self-Immolation. Springer, Cham; 2021.
44. Miller L, Bansal R, Wickramaratne P, Hao X, Tenke CE, Weissman MM, et al. Neuroanatomical correlates of religiosity and spirituality: a study in adults at high and low familial risk for depression. JAMA Psychiatry. 2014;71:128-35.
45. Motto JA, Bostrom AG. A randomized controlled trial of postcrisis suicide prevention. Psychiatry Serv. 2001;52:828-33.

6 CHAPTER

Spirituality in Palliative Care

Uday Chaudhuri, Abhay Dey, Swati Banerjee, Hiya Dey

"You matter because of who you are. You matter to the last moment of your life, and we will do all we can, not only to help you die peacefully but also to live until you die".

INTRODUCTION

This in essence sums up the core responsibilities of physicians and other caregivers to the dying (in Palliative care) and also to the seriously ill who need to recover and be brought back to at least a semblance of role-functioning (rehabilitation).

World Health Organization (WHO) defines palliative care as "an approach that improves the quality of life of patients and their families facing the problems associated with life-threatening illnesses, through the prevention and relief of suffering by means of early identification and impeccable assessment and treatment of pain and other problems, physical, psychosocial and spiritual".[1]

Although being recognized as an essential domain in palliative care, the spiritual domain is still the most neglected component of palliative care.

"Spirituality is the dimension of human life that relates to the way people in a community experience, express or seek meaning, purpose, and transcendence and the way they connect to the moment, to the self, to others, to nature, to the significant and/or the sacred"—as defined by Spirituality Reference Group of the European Association of Palliative Care.[2]

Although it is a theoretical concept, its broadness and uniqueness makes it difficult to be defined. Spirituality may described as the deepest part of who we are, the concern with ultimate questions, the need to find meaning, purpose and fulfillment in life, suffering and death. The most accepted definition of spirituality across the literature is "the aspect of humanity that refers to the way individuals seek an express meaning and purpose, and the way they experience there connectedness to the moment, to self, to others, to nature, and to the significant or sacred" (Puchalski et al., 2009).[3]

The classical example of spiritual questioning is the *Bhagavad Gita*.[4] If read carefully we can find Arjuna, the great warrior, was distressed with the decision to fight with his near and dear ones, for his kingdom. He was in search of the meaning of waging the war in Kurukshetra. He said he did not want to fight for the plot of land and was willing to sacrifice everything. Krishna stood by his side with care, compassion, and empathy. The spiritual awakening that happened to Arjuna through the discourse helped him to fight the war.

Similarly, scriptures such as Patanjali Yoga sutras, the Upanishads, and many other religious treatises address these spiritual issues that arise in individuals with changing life events.

In Indian mythology, we have come across the story of King Parikshit. A saint cursed him to be killed by a snake named Takshak within 7 days. King Parikshit who was enjoying the lavish comforts of his kingdom suddenly had the urgent wish to know "then what was the meaning of all these riches he was enjoying". He started asking "Then what is the meaning of this life". It was then that Saint Shuka gave a discourse known as "Bhagavad" which helped ease his suffering.

THE SPIRITUAL PAIN

Life is eventful and each event affects and transforms our belief system to some extent. When someone receives a life-threatening diagnosis with a poor prognosis, he starts questioning the meaning and purpose of life. Everybody has this quest. But the urgency in the above population increases.

To give a brief experience of spiritual pain, we would like to do an experiment now:

Imagine a deeply poignant scenario, reflective of the vulnerabilities many people face in the twilight of their lives, particularly those living with conditions like dementia. It paints a picture of profound physical, emotional, and existential challenges that demand not only compassion but also a deep understanding of the individual's inner world.

Imagine being in such a state—where memory fades, independence erodes, and trust in one's surroundings becomes fragile. The simple act of navigating familiar spaces becomes daunting, and the once-intimate sense of control over one's life dissipates. This leads to feelings of helplessness, insecurity, and loneliness. The emotional toll of these experiences is immense, compounded by the fear of abandonment and the stigma of dependency.

Such a situation calls for a profound shift in how society, families, and caregivers approach aging and dementia. Empathy, patience, and a genuine commitment to preserving dignity become paramount **(Fig. 1)**.

Here are some ways to address these challenges:

- *Creating a safe and familiar environment:*
  - Ensure that living spaces are designed to be dementia-friendly, minimizing disorientation and frustration.
  - Use labels, familiar objects, and routines to help maintain a sense of stability.
- *Strengthening emotional connections:*
  - Encourage meaningful interactions with family and caregivers, prioritizing quality time and understanding the emotional needs of the individual.
  - Support visits from friends and community members who show genuine compassion.
- *Providing comfort and security:*
  - Address fears of theft or loss by maintaining transparency and involving the individual in their care decisions whenever possible.
  - Use gentle reassurances and tactile support to alleviate feelings of insecurity.
- *Enhancing dignity and autonomy:*
  - Involve the individual in daily tasks they can still perform, fostering a sense of purpose.
  - Respect their preferences and choices, even in small matters.
- *Incorporating spiritual and emotional support:*
  - Engage in conversations about meaning, purpose, and spiritual concerns if the individual is open to them.

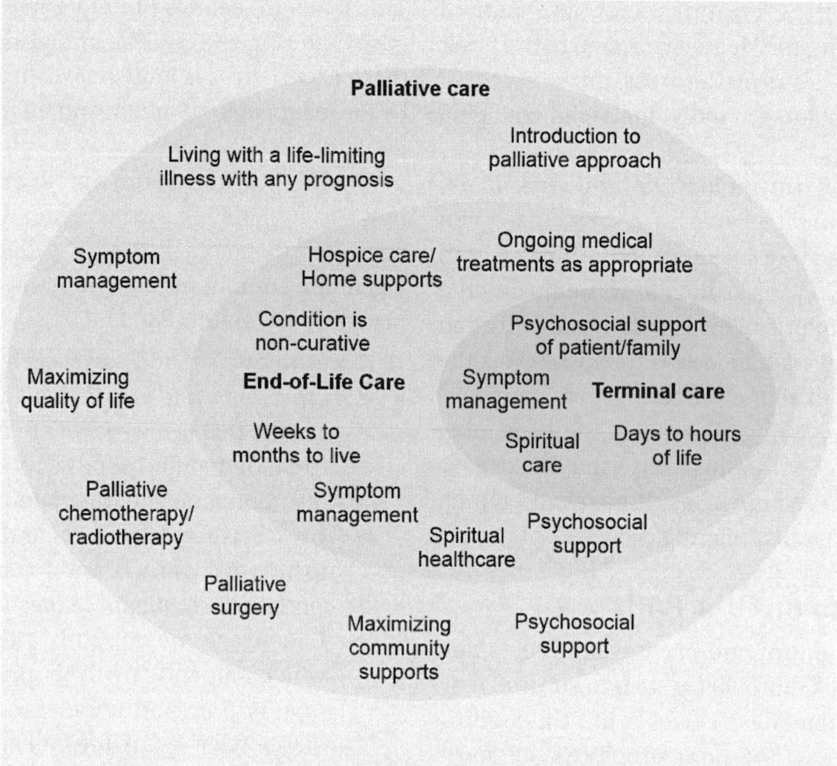

Fig. 1: The phases and layers of care.

Source: Wong T, Cowden RG, Yu TTF, Arslan G. Existential Wellbeing in Palliative Care: A Paradigm of Existential Positive Psychology. Public Health and Health Services. 2024.[5]

    - Create moments of peace and mindfulness, helping them find solace amidst their struggles.
- *Building a support system for caregivers:*
    - Families often need emotional and practical support to provide compassionate care without feeling overwhelmed.
    - Community programs and resources can offer respite care, counseling, and training.
    - Addressing the fear, isolation, and dependence that often accompany dementia requires us to extend not just care but an unwavering commitment to preserving the humanity and dignity of those affected. It reminds us that, while the mind may falter, the need for love, connection, and respect remains unchanging.

Imagine yourself in this way for a moment. How do you feel? The first question "Why me?" Then "What was the purpose of this life" and most significant is "What is the purpose of this suffering"—the search starts.

Thus life-changing events are not only characterized by physical pain but spiritual distress as well. Spiritual distress involves deep inner questioning and loss of purpose and meaning in life. Victor Frankl[6] stated, "Man is not destroyed by suffering: He is destroyed by suffering without meaning".

CURRENT SCENARIO

Recent studies have revealed that patients with advanced cancer report having hidden pain and suffering—not recognized by their family or healthcare professionals which left them alone and isolated.

Modern healthcare professionals are well-equipped to address the physical pain and discomfort experienced by patients. However, many struggle to address spiritual pain effectively. This challenge arises partly because most doctors are neither deeply familiar with religious scriptures nor attuned to the nuances of local cultures. As a result, spiritual and religious concerns are often dismissed as superstitions or regarded as mere consolation, a last resort when all other treatments fail. Furthermore, the discomfort associated with discussing deeply personal matters can make these conversations uneasy for both doctors and patients. Consequently, doctors may resort to making assumptions about a patient's belief system, often failing to acknowledge or address the patient's underlying distress.

Advancements in modern medicine have fostered an aura of invincibility, sometimes creating the illusion of immortality. Yet, the immutable laws of nature cannot be defied—everything that lives must eventually die. Even vast galaxies and intricate galactic systems are subject to the cycle of death and rebirth, a fundamental law of the universe. To navigate the morbid fear and despondency associated with mortality, one must turn to the insights of spirituality. For patients and their families, confronting the stark reality of life's impermanence can lead to profound resentment and despair, especially when the inevitability of physical death becomes undeniable.

Growing evidence has supported the benefits of providing spiritual care at the end of life on clinical outcomes, highlighting the importance of its integration in palliative care intervention. A spiritual outlook can help people accept the inevitable and face death with equanimity or even welcome death as in the story of Nachiketa in Vedas. A research was carried out at PPCS (Pain and Palliative Care Service) at the NIH Clinical Center in survives of life-threatening cancer and cardiac conditions. Many participants found that spirituality help them to adjust to their life-threatening illnesses. Participants utilize spirituality in a variety of context: forming greater connections with a higher power, people, their work, and their own lives. This spiritually-related connections gave participants greater meaning and purpose.[7,8] As Daniel Sulmasy writes—"At the end of life when the *milieu interior* can no longer be restored, healing is still possible, and the healing profession has a role". As Sulmasy[9] points out that to die believing that one's life and death have been of no use is the ultimate indignity. To die believing that there is no meaning to life, suffering, and death is abject hopelessness as he points out. To die alone and unforgiven is utter alienation. To ignore these questions at the time when their answers are urgently sought is to abandon the patent at the time of greatest need. As Teilhard de Chardin (1960)[10] puts it, besides the *milieu interior* there is also the *milieu divin*. Mental health professionals must accept the challenge and help the patients in their darkest hour. These profound questions can haunt even atheists at the time of impending death. Spiritual principles can offer succor and solace to patients and their relatives in these situations. Clinicians should not thrust their religious beliefs on their patients and guard against being seen as proselytizing but should be alert to the need to help where sought for.

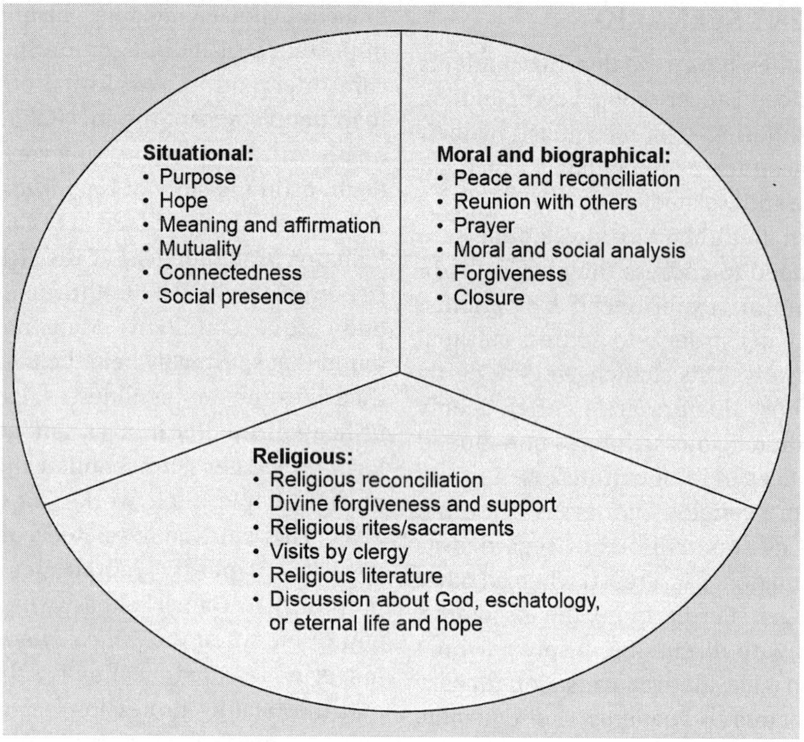

Fig. 2: Dimensions of spiritual need.[11]

Source: Kellehear A. Spirituality and palliative care: a model of needs. Palliative Medicine, 2000;14(2):149-55.

ADDRESSING THE ISSUE

It requires the cultivation of a lot of compassion and empathy to "get into the shoes" of the suffering person **(Fig. 2)**.

- Establishing rapport with the patient
- Good communication skills
- Keeping an open mind
- Respecting the patient's individuality
- Healthcare professionals should be made aware of the spiritual needs of the patient as shown below:
  - Enquiry into the terminal illness understanding of the patient:
    - "How do you describe your current health status".
    - Examination of patient's and family's hope.
  - Enquiry into the preferred place of death which is usually at home in the presence of near and dear ones.
  - *Understanding their religious beliefs*:
    - A brief RCOPE tool may be used
    - Enquiry into the belief in their God
    - Seeking a closer connection with God
    - Feeling abandoned by their God, the disease is a punishment from their God
    - Karma principle
    - Asking for forgiveness of their sins
  - Use of spiritual assessment tools such as FICA (faith, importance, community, and address) and SPIRIT.
  - Active listening

- *Management:* As per studies conducted:
    - *Being there:* The caregiver listened and bore witness to the patient's suffering
    - Helping patients to find peace, mitigating their fears: through hope, empowerment, and compassion
    - *As an art form:* Visual or auditive (music in its varied genres) arts
    - Facilitation and articulation of experience
    - Music therapy, dance movement therapy
    - Yoga and meditation
- Addressing spiritual pain in palliative care is an art. It is like handling a castle of cards. A little inattention can hurt the sentiments of the patient.
- Disappointment is normal. Expert help can always be obtained. Just being aware that the issue is a spiritual one is a great achievement. If confused, just sitting in silence with the patient and lending a listening ear, keeping all personal judgments away can help in healing. There are many reasons why caregivers often avoid the spiritual component of holistic care.
- Lack of training
- Comparatively lower spiritual interest and inclination in mental health professionals
- Fear of infringing ethical barriers and lack of time.

But spiritual care is an important component of care and cannot be wished away. In Gallup polls[12] it was found that 95–99% of Americans believe in God, 89% pray to God, and about one-third of Americans consider religion to be the most important dimension in their lives (Princeton Religion Research Center,1996). Similarly, India is a secular country but its long history bears testimony to a core of essential spirituality in its thinkers and writers, and spirituality permeates the daily lives of most of its people. Professionals caring for Illness and healing must take note of this.

Conclusion

Palliative care encompasses addressing the physical, psychosocial, and spiritual pain of both patients and their families. Neglecting the spiritual component leaves the care incomplete. Many individuals with advanced illnesses have emphasized the importance of having their spiritual needs acknowledged and addressed by healthcare professionals. Even small gestures—such as acts of kindness, a warm and compassionate presence, or an empathetic connection—can have a profound impact.

Developing competence in taking a spiritual history and integrating it into care plans is increasingly recognized as an essential skill for professionals in palliative care. Mental health practitioners need not feel overburdened by the intricacies of spiritual healing. Instead, they can involve clergy members and social workers as integral parts of the care team, ensuring a holistic approach to the care pathway for terminally ill patients.

SPIRITUALITY IN ADDICTION REHABILITATION

Spirituality is a strong force to fight addiction. We all know about 12-step programs in AA (Alcoholics Anonymous).[13] Here the spiritual step taken involves the prayer "God, please grant me the serenity to accept the things I cannot change, the courage to do the things I can, and the wisdom to know the difference".

CONCEPT

- Spirituality is a dimension difficult to define.

- Spirituality in Rehabilitation mainly points towards the idea of a higher power. Spirituality will always help different people in different ways. However, at its root, it signifies a movement towards Soul and spirit and away from material things.
- Spirituality can mean a connection to nature or the universe, something that binds all living things/beings together. People will define spirituality in a way that has meaning for them. Connecting with a higher power provides strength to help overcome difficult times.

UTILITY

Spirituality can help in several ways:

- Healing
- Strength in times of difficulty
- Gratitude
- A sense of purpose
- Modeling and teaching empathy
- Creating a healthy lifestyle, to cultivate meaningful connections and sustained recovery.
- The holistic approach teaches the clients the skills to protect their minds, body, and spirit.
- Spiritual rehabilitation is nothing but—"Healing inside out".

Spiritual rehabilitation as an alternative recovery method has started to be successful for alcohol addiction. It is an understanding and a connection to something that is bigger than us. Spirituality in rehabilitation is a personal search for meaning in life and a connection with something greater than ourselves. It is "to get quiet and to be present at the moment". It is the "Search for meaning in life". It includes prayer, meditation, and mindfulness.

REALITY

Spiritual rehabilitation is an alternative recovery method that has shown to be successful for drug and alcohol deaddiction. Addicts often go through the recovery process several times without success before finding their way to lifelong recovery.

Exploring the spiritual dimension is now being found to be beneficial in other disorders as well. Byrd (1988)[14] studied the effect of prayer using a Coronary Care Unit population and found individuals for whom prayers were said by an outside group did significantly better than a group of people who did not receive any prayers. In another study individuals treated with Christian-based psychotherapy recovered from depression significantly faster than those who received standard secular CBT (Propst, Ostrom, Watkins, Dean, and Mashburn,1992).[15] A group of people with a diagnosis of schizophrenia was less likely to be rehospitalized if they continued to participate in religious worship following reintegration into the community (Chu and Klein, 1985).[16] These results seem to suggest that religion and by extension its core of spirituality can play an important role in treatment and also decrease the likelihood of rehospitalization. Sylvia Mohr and others writing in the Am J Psychiatry, 2006, described a study to assess the role of religion as a mediating variable in the process of coping with psychotic illnesses. They found that in some patients with schizophrenia, religion instilled hope, purpose, and meaning in their lives (71%), whereas in lesser numbers it induced spiritual despair (14%). Patients also reported that religion lessened (54%) or increased (10%) psychotic and general symptoms. They pointed out that the results of their study highlight the clinical significance of religion in the case of patients with schizophrenia. They advocated a highly sensitive approach to each patient's individual story. Scott, Agresti, and Fitchett (1998),[17] investigated the role of spirituality with a group of people primarily diagnosed with an affective disorder and found that the closer individuals felt, the more satisfied with life they felt. The current research in contemplative neuroscience has also found the positive role of contemplative practices such as mindfulness-based meditation, tai chi, or yoga, most of which have roots in spiritual thinking and practices.

CONCLUSION

Fighting addiction is often an uphill battle, but spirituality can serve as a guiding light in the darkness when all else seems to fail. By adopting a "Spiritual Model of Care", patients often begin to see hope and a path to recovery. Key components of this model include modeling and teaching, empathy, trauma resolution, and fostering a healthy lifestyle to cultivate meaningful connections and promote spiritual healing. This approach has proven helpful not only in addiction recovery but also in treating other mental health conditions.

Science, at its core, is the search for truths that already exist in nature, waiting to be discovered and applied for the betterment of humanity and all living beings on this planet. Spirituality, in essence, shares this purpose—it is also a quest for truth, albeit on a conceptual and experiential level. The role of healers is to help their patients heal, and they must overcome biases and stigmas, embracing all proven methods that can aid in recovery. Spirituality is a beacon of light, offering holistic healing in both rehabilitation and palliative care.

Psychiatry has evolved from an illness-focused model to one that emphasizes wellness. While modern medical technology offers incredible advancements, clinicians must not lose sight of the soul of psychiatry—acknowledging the uniqueness of each individual's life story. A resilience-based mindset must be fostered to help patients bounce back from adversity.

The recovery process requires a comprehensive approach—transforming and saving lives through the science of medicine, the art of therapy (psychotherapy), and the compassion, loving-kindness, generosity, and humility of spirituality, all complemented by a philosophy of healing grounded in respect and dignity.

The principles of positive psychology of Martin Seligman and others need to be encouraged so that patients can move from patienthood to personhood towards human excellence.

WHO defines health not as the absence of disease and infirmity but as a harmonious state of well-being, physical, mental, and social well-being. Today positive Psychiatry and science and art of well-being are added with research and application of contemplative Neurosciences for well-being as a marker of overall human flourishing. May we conclude with a peace prayer from Upanishad.

Om Shaantih Shaantih Shaantih" "(Let all sentinel beings be happy, may all be cured of illness, let all see the auspicious, let no one suffer, Om shanti, shanti, shanti".)

REFERENCES

1. https://www.who.int/europe/news-room/fact-sheets/item/palliative-care
2. EAPC Spiritual Care Reference Group - https://eapcnet.eu/eapc-webinar-spiritual-care/
3. Puchalski C. Spiritualityinhealth:therole of spiritualityincritical care.
4. https://shop.advaitaashrama.org/product-category/books/scriptures/bhagavad-gita/
5. Providence Health Care - https://images.app.goo.gl/hrJzwPc2SRUgxMzS7
6. FranklVE.Man'sSearchforMeaning.New York: SimonandSchuster; 1984.
7. Skeath P, Norris S, Katheria V, et al . The nature of life-transforming changes among cancer

survivors. Qualitative Health Research. 2013; 23:1155 -67.

8. William YC. et al. Spirituality in the context of life-threatening illness and life-transforming change: Palliative and Supportive Care, 2014, Cambridge University Press, 2014.
9. Sulmasy DP. A Biopsychosocial-Spiritual Model for the Care of Patientsat the End of Life. The Gerontologist. 42;24-33.
10. Pierre Teilhard de Chardin: Divine Milieu https://books. google.co.in/ books/about/ Divine_Milieu.html?id=BgwZEQAAQBAJ & printsec =frontcover&source =kp_read_ button & hl=en&newbks=1&newbks_redir =0&gboemv=1&redir_esc=y#v=one page& q&f=false
11. Kellehear A. Spirituality and Palliative Care: a model of needs. Palliative Medicine, 2000; 14(2):149-55.
12. Princeton Religious Research Center (1996). Religion in America. Princeton, NJ: The Gallup Poll.
13. Alcoholics Anonymous, 4th Edition. https:// images.app.goo.gl/VVeSVdEzd Nf29tkW8
14. Byrd K. Positive therapeutic effects of intercessory prayer in a coronary care unit population. Southern Medical Journal. 1988;81(7):826-9.
15. Propst LR, Ostrom R, Watkins P, Dean T, Mashburn D. Comparitive efficacy of religious and non-religious cognitive - behaviour therapy for the treatment of clinical depressionin religious individuals. Journal of Consulting and Clinical Psychology. 1992:60;94-103.
16. Chu CC, Klein HE. Psychosocial and environmental variables in outcome of black schizophrenics. Journal of the National Medical Association. 1985;77: 793-6.
17. Scott ER, Agresti AA, Fitchett G. Factor analysis of the "Spiritual Well-Being Scale" and its clinical utility with psychiatric inpatients. Journal for the Scientific Study of Religion. 1998;37(2):314-21.

7 CHAPTER

Bhagavad Gita and Psychotherapy

Prasad Rao Gundugurthi, Simhachalam Gurugabelli, Umadevi Avasarala

INTRODUCTION

Old Hindu scriptures such as *Vedas, Upanishads,* and the *Puranas* like *Mahabharata, Ramayana,* and *Bhagvat. Bhagavad Gita* (the *Gita*, a celestial poem) also part of Mahabharata offers important knowledge in understandings of how mind functioning was presented. The description of body and mind dichotomy though initially in 19th century was presented, it can be seen in Hindu scriptures they were discussed anciently.[1] Modern mental health in ways that are complementary, in recent times were often influenced by those derived from Western psychology and practiced in western hemisphere. Mental health is defined not merely as the absence of ill-health, according to World Health Organization definition. Being positive in attitude is being promoted in addition to treating the disorders of mind and mental health, early detection and curing the disturbances is part of modern psychiatry. Psychological disturbances as measured by understanding psychopathology of the patients and diagnosing the mental disturbances is essentially phenomenological is practiced world over.

Psychopathology is viewed as resulting from too much or misplaced attachment and a faulty concept of self-leading to an excessive focus on resolving the conflict of mind.[2,3] The past century has witnessed the development of progressively refined approaches to psychotherapy mainly in the Western hemisphere, beginning with psychoanalysis in the early 20th century, and followed by behavioral, existential, cognitive, and interpersonal approaches. The Hindu way of practicing is much more eclectic, is currently practiced by many countries across the world by Hindus who have migrated from predominantly Asia which includes India, Nepal, Bhutan, Vietnam, Cambodia, and few more Asia-Pacific countries which arose >3 millennia ago in Indian continent, the psychological thoughts from Hindu offers insights that differ in important ways from western psychology. Although different aspects of Hindu thought were influenced by a number of well-known psychologists of 19th century such as Carl Jung and Abraham Maslow. The Hinduism as practiced and Hindu practices were researched on emotions and its disorders have been elucidated by many scholars and some attempts were done over the many decades to utilize the concepts in psychiatric treatments, especially psychotherapies. Some convergences between Hindu thinking and current models of psychotherapy suggest the fruitfulness of integrating these diverse approaches for the patients benefits in their culturally practices incorporating in psychotherapy.

Hinduism by far is practiced by billions across the world and possibly the world's third largest religion, with over 1 billion people practicing this religion in India and in Nepal, Vietnam, and Cambodia. About >60–70 million practicing Hindus are living outside India. Unlike many other religions, "Hinduism" is not the original name for this religion. Ancient Persians referred to people living on the banks of river Sindhu (Indus) as "Hindus".

Since the ancient times people in the Indian subcontinent simply called their way of life as "Sanatana dharma," which simply means "the eternal laws of living." Hinduism encompasses numerous related religions which have their origin from Hindus in some way are Sikhs, Jains traditions that share common elements but do not require a unified set of beliefs or practices to be followed. Many Hindu scriptures have developed over its long history including the *Vedas*.

The *Vedas* were believed to be composed many a centuries beginning probably around 1500 BC, and the *Upanishads*, which are the terminal portions of the Vedas may be dated around 800 BC. Around the time of the later Upanishads, there are four Vedas *(Rig Veda, Yajur Veda, Sama Veda,* and *Atharva Veda)*. The Vedas are taught not by textual but by teacher to pupil directly, hence called *apurusheyas*, and subsequently *aranyas* with further explanations, proceed to more explanatory hymns.

There are many commentaries of *Bhagavad Gita* or simply called *Gita*. In this chapter we predominantly relied on the *Bhagavad Gita* commentary by Prabhu Pada (Prabhu Pada et al. 2015); as we know *Gita* is a part of Mahabharata. The *Gita*, discussed in few chapters of the *Mahabharata*, is a 700-stanza poem which can be considered a brief summary of earlier Hindu scriptures and on the psychology and used by many schools of psychology.

The *Bhagavad Gita*, which literally discusses Lord Shri Krishna's verses, is taught by Lord Shri Krishna when Arjuna, in the battlefield of Kurukshetra, is in deep sorrow and is in a dilemma whether to fight the war against his blood relatives, and is fighting and winning the war worth it when he is facing his own relatives. The *Mahabharata* is a Hindu epic purana katha about the essentially a human behavior in myriads of forms, very much similar to behavior of modern people.

GITA: THE ESSENCE

Deeply sorrowful when faced with the moral dilemma of fighting against his own family, Arjuna is torn between his duty and the personal cost of victory. In *Gita*, a part of chapter in *Mahabharata*, Lord Krishna dispels Arjuna's doubts and imparts profound wisdom. The *Gita* comprises 18 chapters, beginning with *Vishada Yoga*. In this initial chapter, Arjuna grapples with the grief of potentially losing loved ones and the sins associated with his actions. In essence an intense emotional distressed Arjuna, the warrior hero, in acute depression and anxiety, Lord Krishna informs of his Avtar, takes his student, the beloved one too, the Lord explains therapeutically in the midst of battle between the Pandavas (the good people) versus Kauravas side (the bad people) and the content spiritually connects the distressed to divine lord.[4,5]

The *Mahabharata*, the world's longest poem of about 124,000 stanzas, possibly happened, according to the epic, in the present Asia in Indian subcontinent, most likely compiled about 200–500 BC. It is important to understand that many psychological models on mental health therapies might have few commonalities, and as we practice few cultural issues in practice, we see many models of modern western global psychology models do have few commonalities and few uniqueness in Hindu modeled psychotherapies may be similar to other psychotherapeutic models. The focus of this chapter is mainly on trying a model of mental health models based on *Gita*. The abundant philosophical, theological, and spiritual insights that can be gained or utilized in the *Gita* for larger spiritual and personality growth are beyond the scope of this chapter, and we recommend interested readers to authoritative texts elsewhere.[6-10]

We discuss how models of Western psychology work when applied to insights from our Hindu scriptures.

Concept of Human Psyche According to Some Hindu Scriptures

Let us understand the nuances about concept of the mind as understood in Hindu scriptures particular reference to *Gita*. The definition of positive mental health, as outlined in the *Gita*, there are clear steps of progression which is present in 18 chapters in sequential order where Lord Krishna takes Arjun to make him understand that he is in stressful crisis situation. There is a detail of his disturbed mind, and for the all people in stress how they go through was explained in the first two chapters where we find symptoms of anxiety and panic descriptions compassionately explained and made aware and comforting words to progress further to understand the intense psychological state, after making aware the psychology of self, reality of life at that point, Lord Krishna goes on to detail the responsibilities with an emphasis that nobody should run in regular life and more so in crises, away from responsibility especially during crises. These texts help cultivate positive mental well-being, focusing on an integrated psychobiological approach represented by the eight steps of yoga. Finally, traditional *Gita* is discussed considering the relevant Western psychological research to demonstrate how dialogue and empirical study can enrich both traditions.

The other concepts of Hinduism Samkhya, Nyaya, and Yoga offer an even richer contribution to the understanding of the human psyche.[4-16]

HISTORICAL AND COMPARATIVE PSYCHOTHERAPEUTIC PERSPECTIVES IN HINDU TRADITION

Nature of Psyche and Positive Mental Health and Happiness

Many a Hindu scriptures provide stories or by description of the descriptions of how human mind works or how to have conflict resolutions, we gain our knowledge through these stories to build our emotional strength both in normal life issues and during the times of crisis. In the *Katha Upanishad*, about 5th century BC, and possibly prior to the *Gita*, a description of our senses and how they function was detailed. The hierarchy of intellect called *Buddhi*, and mind *Manus*, and the ultimate control is in *manas* was well delineated the senses. The intellect is the reins held by the spirit, the charioteer. We find a non-dualistic view, which is so much unique that the body, the mind, and the spirit are seen as three legs of a stool. Implicit in this hierarchical organization is the principle that well-being of man is achieved by unattached action, regulation of the senses (cognition) and regulation of affect (emotion) by higher reasoning aspects of the psychic mind and a well appreciated by the self and its relation to others (cognition), are the integral learnings we understand from these valuable ancient scriptures.

How does Mind Work and Develop?

According to ancient Hindu scriptures and ayurveda the ancient medical systems during the times Hindu scriptures describe as the three different natures "tendencies, qualities, or temperaments":

The quality of balance, harmony, and goodness between three guans—rajas, tamas, and satva are well described. Each person is a combination of all the three and dominated by any one or two natures. Having lots of passion, high activity, large self-centeredness, strong egoism, self-centered individualization, high driven-ness, movement, and lots of dynamism consist of the qualities of Rajas. People with predominant Tamas which refers to high imbalance, very disorder, negativity, dullness or inactivity, sort of depressive tendencies apathy, inertia or lethargy, violence, viciousness, and ignorance.

These qualities are not either-or categories; everyone has all three, only in different proportions and in different contexts. The individual's personality and character are viewed as the composite effect of these three qualities.

Hinduism allows and encourages moving from the primitive tamasic traits toward Rajasic traits and eventually developing more and more Sattvic traits, both within the current life and from one life to another. The former is somewhat similar to the goals of modern psychotherapy where the therapist assists the individual to replace primitive in psychological assessment. In the Hinduism path we look for personality attributes identification and makes them aware through therapeutic process.[17]

RELEVANCE OF THE GITA FOR THE PSYCHOTHERAPY

Mittal and Prusty in a study conducted across India have observed in their findings revealed that the content of *Bhagavad Gita* gives insight about the determinants of our actions, motives behind our choices and the foundation of our belief system which has a positive impact on the mental health of the Indian population. This essentially, hence, helps the therapeutic benefits of using the cultural ethos in psychotherapy.

Teachings of the *Gita* as communicated by Lord Krishna provides resolution of conflicts in many ways which is quite similar to the task of a therapist, who while addressing conflicts and anxiety of the patients, paves the path to long-term recovery and healing while helping them with the symptom resolution. Henceforth, psychotherapy in India often incorporates therapeutic pearls from teachings of the *Bhagavad Gita.*

The concept of *Guru-Chela* has been publicized by Dr Neki, as a psychotherapy model, which has been discussed widely in the Indian scenario. Renowned psychiatrists and psychologists in India [11-13,18-23,32] debated and suggested *Bhagavad Gita* as a model and source to create concepts of psychotherapy suitable and appropriate in the Indian circumstances. Indian psychotherapy usually subsumes gem of therapy from the *Bhagavad Gita.*[12,18,25,26] Modern Indian psychiatry further contemplates spirituality as an integral component of mental health.[27] *Bhagavad Gita* stipulates several roads to comprehend and be aware about a deity/God. The teachings and knowledge of *Bhagavad Gita* are for all individuals with varied nature and characters. Some lessons are focused on action for pursuing the path of action (Karma Yoga), some are mainly emotional and direct the person toward devotion (Bhakti Yoga), and some are intellectual in nature to help the person to pursue knowledge (Gyana Yoga). *Bhagavad Gita* guides how action, devotion, and knowledge advance to unification with God/supreme power. Karma Yoga guides to achieve salvation through action. The ultimate state of consciousness is salvation that is desired by everyone. Working is the fundamental aspect of life. Work is motivated by intrinsic value, extrinsic value, or both. *Bhagavad Gita* preaches to do work with intrinsic value (that is, without thinking about what the result may be), as pondering over the outcome gives rise to stress, aggression, and competitiveness. Further, this state can lead to ailments or diseases, depression and even suicide.

GITA AND PSYCHOTHERAPY

Key Themes and Parallels

- *Mind-body connection:* Both the *Gita* and psychiatry emphasize the interconnectedness of the mind and body. The *Gita* speaks of the importance of yoga and meditation for achieving balance and harmony, while psychiatry recognizes the impact of physical health on mental well-being.
- *Emotional regulation:* The *Gita* delves into the nature of emotions and offers guidance on managing them. It encourages the cultivation of equanimity and detachment, concepts that are central to many therapeutic approaches.
- *Purpose and meaning:* The *Gita* provides a framework for understanding life's purpose and meaning. This can be particularly helpful for individuals struggling with existential questions or a sense of lost direction.
- *The self and identity:* The *Gita* explores the nature of the self and its relationship to the world. This can be relevant to individuals grappling with issues of self-esteem, identity, or purpose.
- *Duty and responsibility:* The *Gita* emphasizes the importance of fulfilling one's duty (dharma). This can be interpreted as a sense of purpose and responsibility that can contribute to mental health.

PRACTICAL UTILITY OF THE GITA IN PSYCHOTHERAPY

Concept of Happiness and the Stable Mind

There are a variety of 18 chapters in *Gita*. In the treatment of psychologically disturbed individuals we should be able to utilize the principles by elaborating many day-to-day examples. In the early stage of psychotherapy, we possibly would use the first three chapters to make the individual who is in distress the symptoms they have are uniquely similar to the descriptions in *Gita* and making cognitively aware.

Lord Krishna in his process of therapy in a step wise fashion followed by making the knowledge available of uncertainties and certainties in life, how they are governed, how the superior power. He will take care of the disciples when in need they approach him in a way here therapist is giving the direction of positivity and making the suffering individual aware of his or her strength is practiced many a psychotherapeutics techniques

In the further chapters the descriptions of ideal personality Sthitha Pragna and qualities are described. These can be mentioned as suggested by Maslow in strengthening the personality, and to help maintain the relation in therapy to show the positivity in the therapy as practicing *Gita* principles.

Pathways to Happiness: The Approach can be Used in Psychotherapy

The *Gita* and the earlier Hindu scriptures indicate three ways to achieve lasting happiness—the path of action (*Karma Yoga),* the path of knowledge (Jnana Yoga) and the path of contemplative meditation (*Dhyana Yoga*). Girding these pathways is faith (*Bhakti*).

The Karma path entails action that is not contingent on reward but is focused on the process. As detailed in this chapter the principles talk about duties responsibilities and how all should be aware in knowing and doing the respected duties. In psychotherapies, we can use this principle during the process to gradually in systematic manner to make aware to the client, reduce the anxiety generated by detailed insight-oriented therapy process and once again refocused of their duties and make the awareness help to reach the goal of their life at that point and beyond.

We can also make them aware of reaching perfection by practice not only for reward but their bounden duties.

Learning and practicing Karma yoga has a similar influence in leading the individual toward our work and living a satisfied life. This yoga might uniquely play a part in practicing positive psychology and helping in treating stress-related disorders. Bhakti yoga teaches us to practice devotion to achieve our goals in life. It is also known as "yoga of devotion". Bhakti yoga is usually considered as the highest form of yoga in Sanatana dharma.

It consists of rituals and practices that when followed by an individual fills them with pleasure and joy as it is more lively than other practices such as pranayama. Debra Trampe et al. (2015)[28] in their study indicated that our behaviors and thoughts are associated with our emotional experiences. Thus, it means that healthy and pure emotions lead toward healthy behavior and thoughts, which shows wellness in physical and mental wellbeing. In psychotherapy, *channeling negative emotions* is an essential part, in a way it is cognitive psychotherapy.

Practicing Bhakti yoga can aid the process of dealing with negative emotions such as anger, anxiety, disgust, guilt, contempt, fear, sadness, etc. Research evidence suggests that practices of Bhakti yoga (like A-U-M chanting, meditation, and singing devotional songs), can help in reducing the levels of *anxiety and depression* in patients, in fact we can see the practice of yoga principles, the Ashtangas as enunciated in the *Gita.*

Concept of the Self and Improving the Confidence

In the *Gita,* "What is taught" is to be selfless and move forward for the larger ideal goals, simultaneously not being worried to do the responsibilities selflessly. In therapy we should guide using *Gita* principles to make autonomy simultaneously being reminded of uncertainties and stresses of life.

The Upanishads were among the earliest to explain by various stories and making us aware of consciousness, self-concept, how we differ from each other, how to focus on things in hand to reach and impart our understandings on perceptions and their meanings, how to reach logical deductions by asking like "who am I", "who or the self we all know", it is a collection of our physical, mental, and social attributes that we create for ourselves with input from our perceptions, it is also very important to appreciate the social learnings, our own commitment to society and input by our families and society. In reality, the "self" may well be a collection of many emotional factors combined with social learnings.

Applications in Psychiatry

- *Psychotherapy:* The teachings of the *Gita* can be incorporated into psychotherapy, providing a spiritual framework for understanding and addressing mental health issues.
- *Mindfulness and meditation:* Practices inspired by the *Gita*, such as mindfulness and meditation, can be helpful for managing stress, anxiety, and depression.
- *Cognitive behavior therapies (CBT):* These are by far the large group of therapies and *Gita* as we see in practice of uses essentially the principles already available as source of knowledge and the elucidation of *Gita* in a methodical approach of first awareness and pushing the student Arjuna "*To Change his Cognitions*".
- *Existential therapy:* The Gita's exploration of life's meaning and purpose can be relevant to existential therapy, which helps individuals find meaning and purpose in life.
- *Metacognitive therapies:* Today most modern cognitive behavior therapies and the new wave mindfulness cognitive behavior therapies are more like to be revisiting the *Gita* principles.
- *These* called the cognitive attentional syndrome (CAS) where the important syndrome surrounding the individuals psyche and seems to be unnecessarily worrying all the time consisting and faulty self-regulatory strategies. The problem is not really negative thoughts but it is of negative thoughts, how the person reacts to them. *GITA* principles could be used in therapies.[29-31]

CONCLUSION

In conclusion, the *Bhagavad Gita* and psychotherapy, though originating from different traditions, share common principles in promoting mental and emotional well-being. The *Bhagavad Gita* offers profound insights into self-awareness, inner peace, and the resolution of inner conflicts—principles that align closely with therapeutic practices. It emphasizes detachment, mindfulness, and the importance of understanding one's true self, which are also key elements in psychotherapy. Integrating the wisdom of the *Bhagavad Gita* with modern therapeutic approaches can provide a holistic framework for healing, blending spiritual insights with psychological techniques to foster emotional balance, self-realization, and overall well-being.[32,33]

While the *Bhagavad Gita* and psychiatry offer different perspectives, they both seek to promote human well-being and understanding and also can be of therapeutic help. Both paths encourage individuals to confront their struggles, recognize their emotional patterns, and find ways to cultivate resilience and growth. By exploring the connections between these two disciplines, we can gain a deeper appreciation for the complex interplay of spiritual and psychological factors in mental health. By bridging these two realms, individuals gain a deeper sense of meaning, purpose, and inner peace, and learn to cope with life's challenges. This brief detail we have presented a capsule of the benefits of deriving the immense knowledge from *Bhagavad Gita*. Guess you can practice these principles without being spiritual too.

REFERENCES

1. Atwal S. Indian psychology: The connection between mind, body, and the universe. Pepperdine University; 2010.
2. Bhatia SC, Madabushi J, Kolli V, Bhatia SK, Madaan V. (2013). The Bhagavad Gita and

contemporary psychotherapies. Indian J Psychiatry 2013;55(Suppl 2):S315.

3. Burgin T. (2020). Jnana Yoga: The Yoga of Wisdom. [online] Available from https://www.yogabasics.com/learn/jnana-yoga-the-yoga-of-wisdom/ [Last accessed December, 2024].
4. Gayathri N, Meenakshi K. Emotional intelligence through the Bhagavad Gita. Int J Res Studies Psychol. 2012;1(2):73-80.
5. Shrimadbhagvadgita. Gorakhpur: Geeta Press; 1982.
6. Kumar A, Kumar S. Karma yoga: A path towards work in positive psychology. Indian J Psychiatry. 2013;55(Suppl 2):S150.
7. Manickam LSS. Psychotherapy in India. Indian J Psychiatry. 2010;52(Suppl1):S366.
8. Maurya K, Mishra GP, Gowda P. A comparative study of bhakti yoga practices used to reduce anxiety and depression levels in patients. 2018.
9. Montepare JM. Body consciousness across the adult years: Variations with actual and subjective age. J Adult Develop. 2006; 13: 102-7.
10. Mukherjee S. Bhagavad Gita: The key source of modern management. Asian J. Management. 2017;8(1).
11. Govindaswamy MV. Surrender-not to self-surrender. Trans. 1959;2. p. 1198.
12. Jeste DV, Vahia IV. Comparison of the conceptualization of wisdom in ancient Indian literature with modern views: Focus on the Bhagavad Gita. Psychiatry. 2008;71(3):197-209.
13. Neki JS. Psychotherapy in India: Past, present, and future. Am J Psychother. 1975; 29(1):92-100.
14. Pandurangi AK, Shenoy S, Keshavan MS. Psychotherapy in the Bhagavad Gita, the Hindu scriptural text. Am J Psychiatry. 2014; 171(8):827-8.
15. Phogat P, Sharma R, Grewal S, Malik A. The overlapping principles of Bhagavat Gita and contemporary psychotherapies. Intern J Indian Psychol. 2020;8:1902-8.
16. Rama S. Perennial psychology of the Bhagavad Gita. Himalayan Institute Press; 2000.
17. Rao KR, Paranjpe AC. Psychology in the Indian tradition. New Delhi: Springer India; 2016.
18. Balodhi JP, Keshavan MS. Bhagavad Gita and psychotherapy. Asian J Psychiatry. 2011; 4(4):300-02.
19. Balodhi JP. Relationship of Itihas and puranas to Vedas: Our Vedic Heritage. Bangalore: Chinmayananda Mission; 1984. pp. 64-8.
20. Gangadhar BN. Bhagavadgeeta: The Indian treatise on mental health care and promotion. Asian J Psychiatry. 2011;4(4):303.
21. Ramachandrarao SK. The conception of stress in Indian thought (the practical involvement in Gita and ayurveda. NIMHANS J. 1983;1:123-31.
22. Rao AV. Mind in Indian Philosophy. Indian J Psychiatry. 2002;44(4):315.
23. Satyananda D. Psychology of the Gita of Hinduism. London: Oxford and IBH; 1972.
24. Venkoba RA, Parvathi DS. The Bhagvad Gita treats body and mind. Ind J Hist Med. 1974;19:35-44.
25. Rao AV. Bhagavad Gita and psychotherapy. Bhavan's Journal. 1978;19-23, 35-8.
26. Reddy MS. Psychotherapy-insights from Bhagavad Gita. Indian J Psychol Med. 2012; 34(1):100-4.
27. Sharma A. Spirituality and mental health-Reflections of the past, applications in the present and projections for the future. Indian Psychiatry Society; 2009.
28. Trampe D, Quoidbach J, Taquet M. Emotions in everyday life. PloS One. 2015; 10(12):e0145450.
29. Sharma B, Ramachandran M. Need for Bhagavad Gita concepts in the present scenario of professional education. Intern J Appl Eng Res. 20115;10(11):10570-4.
30. Sharma T, Kumari P, Kumar V. Yoga and mental health: a review. J Indian Acad Appl Psychol. 2017;43(1):128.
31. Surya NC, Jayaram SS. Some Basic Considerations in the practice of Psychotherapy in the Indian Setting. Indian J Psychiatry. 1964;6(3):153-6.
32. Varma VK, Ghosh A. Psychotherapy as practised by the Indian psychiatrists. Indian J Psychiatry. 1976;18(3):177-86.
33. Virdi A. Invoking the Organizational Consciousness: Insights from Bhagvad Gita. SAMVAD. 2012;4:84-6.

3 SECTION

Beyond Clinical Practice

1

CHAPTER

Spirituality and Mental Health: From Evidence to Action

R Srinivasa Murthy

INTRODUCTION

Religion, spirituality, medicine, and health care have been related in all population groups throughout human history. Only in recent times, these systems of healing have been separated, and this separation has occurred largely in developed nations; in many developing countries, such as India, there is little or no such separation.[1-7] In fact, in India, spirituality forms an essential aspect of day-to-day life of the total population.[8] This existence of spirituality throughout human history and in all the communities that calls for serious examination of its value for the health of the population in general and mental health in particular. The link between spirituality and mental health has been effectively recognized by Indian mental health professionals, especially from the time of Independence.[9-24] Now is the time to convert evidence to action.

A recent milestone in this field is the publication of the third edition of "Handbook of Religion and Health".[4] This is over 1,000 pages, of which 200 pages are "studies of religion and health" and over 150 pages are references. Section 2, of nearly 200 pages, relates to "mental health". Koenig has recently published a book, "Spiritual Readiness: A Survival Guide for the Hindu Believer in an Age of Disbelief".[25] In the recent issues of Indian journals and books, there are several papers on spirituality,[26-28] social work,[29] "Advaita,"[30] meditation,[30,31] counseling,[32,33] and yoga.[34]

The current publication, the 2nd edition of the "Spirituality and Mental Health" with over 20+ chapters is a reflection of the importance of spirituality and mental health in the world.

Box 1 presents some of the recent "voices" reflecting the wide range of views.

The current chapters present the subject along: (i) Changing nature of understanding of mental disorders and therapy; (ii) Indian mental health professionals' contributions to spirituality and mental health; (iii) evidence for the linkages with spirituality and mental health; (iv) challenges to integrating spirituality in mental health care; and (v) road ahead to move from evidence to action to make spirituality an integral part of mental health in India. The chapter has a limitation of being largely based on Hinduism, because of my limitation of understanding other religions.

CHANGING NATURE OF UNDERSTANDING OF MENTAL DISORDERS AND THERAPY

Understanding of mental disorders, mental health, and well-being is at a crucial point in human history, due to a number of

BOX 1: Different professional voices.

- A tactful consideration of patients' religious beliefs and practices as well as their spirituality should routinely be considered and will sometimes be an essential component of psychiatric history taking[35]
- The power of myths and stories to cross-civilizations and their boundaries over time while maintaining an affinity with the whole experience of life can be utilized at a deep level of the world of the unconscious, through dreams and symbols, to provide a meaning of being sand belonging. Or, at a more practical and fundamental level, they can be used to facilitate a model, outside to be taken, to encourage insight and ultimate acceptance of those unacknowledged, unseen, and possibly rejected parts of oneself[36]
- *About Gita in psychotherapy:* "Why cannot we strive to become able to transform our patients in a similar fashion, even though to a tiniest extent?"[37]
- Social psychiatry pays special attention to the interpersonal and cultural context of mental disorders and mental well-being, and religion and spiritual beliefs are an important component of health. Therefore health professionals in general, but especially psychiatrists, psychologists, and other mental health professionals, need to be trained and pay attention to religious and spiritual beliefs[38]
- Meditation has been with humanity for thousands of years and has stood the test of time is still relevant and useful for myriad illnesses as well as states of consciousness. The challenge in future would be to see how it (meditation) could be used instead of, with, before or after medication (assuming medications care chemicals)[39]
- The ancient Indian wisdom has a lot to teach us. It has vastly elaborate systems of functioning of body, mind, and consciousness (soul) in health and disease as applicable to the individual and the society he/she inhabits[40]
- Clinicians who treat these conditions (mental disorders) should understand the foundational tenets of self-transcendence and nonduality, and the role these experiences may play in helping to alleviate their patients" experiences of suffering. If the many benefits of meditation practice, the one that has received the least attention from psychotherapists is perhaps the most important: *Transforming our sense of self*[41]
- *IPS group member responses:* (anonymous, to protect identity) (i)"Religion is poisoning the air all over the world. Religion, which should be a personal matter, has become a divisive force. I wish that the IPS would keep out of it instead of fanning the flames". (ii) "Adding spirituality to psychiatry treatment adds more confusion". (iii) "I strongly believe not only psychiatric patients everyone requires spirituality"

Q: Does yoga, spirituality or willpower cure people of mental disorders?

Dr Thara: For yoga, there is some evidence that yoga helps in depression, anxiety and dealing with stress. We need a little more literature as far as yoga in severe mental disorders is concerned but it is gathering steam.... Spirituality is a huge world by itself. You know people who are spiritual do go to seek support, but we do not have data as a researcher. I would only say that we have not studied it very effectively but we have seen it help others. (FAVMI—Unfolding mental Illness, March 6 YouTube, https://youtu.be/2TbT6tURNLw?si=PkSOaNEsVpBYvc-F)

developments in the last century and more specifically during the last few decades. Currently, there is a better understanding of the origins of mental disorders, mental health, and well-being from both biopsychosocio-spiritual dimensions as well as the climate and environment.[42,28] There is a shift from considering persons diagnosed with mental disorders as "bad", "mad", or "sad" toward being perceived as "individuals" and as "equal" members of the society. The place of care has shifted totally from custodial institutions to the community viz., "asylums as community to community as asylum".[43] The last 3 years of the COVID-19 epidemic has brought to the forefront, the importance of the health of the total population, and social determinants of health in general and mental health in particular.[44] The recognition of the health impact of chronic stresses such as discrimination and marginalization referred to as "weathering"[45] requires societal level interventions. Along with the new understanding, there is a bigger picture of biological aspects of mental health, from thinking of a single molecule such as "dopamine" to "psychoneuroimmunology."[46] There have also been several important recent international publications namely The Lancet Commission on Mental Health and Sustainable Development,[47] Lancet-World Psychiatric Association Commission: Time for united action on depression,[48] the World Mental Health Report 2022 by the World Health Organisation in June 2022,[49] the Lancet Commission on Stigma and Discrimination in October 2022,[50] the Mental State of the World in 2022,[51] the Countdown initiative of Global Mental Health Network (GMHN) to monitor the mental health of nations and the Surgeon General Report on "Our Epidemic of Loneliness and Isolation" released in May 2023.[52] At the therapeutic level, there is growing number of interventions that focus on empowering of the individuals by their own resources such as cognitive behavior therapy, Avtar therapy, meditation, and journaling, and lifestyle changes focusing on exercise, sleep, nutrition, etc.[28,42]

Recent review of "social determinants of mental health and mental disorder" with over 460 references concludes, "people exposed to more unfavorable social circumstances are more vulnerable to poor mental health over their life course, ...(and) addressing these challenges is an imperative matter of social justice".[53] Similar is the call for population salutogenesis as the future of psychiatry.[54] There is strong call for "decolonising global mental health"(GMNH, 2024 and utilize the "local knowledge and resources" for mental health.[55,56]

To summarize, aspects to relevant to the current topic of spirituality and mental health are the shifting of care from institutional care to care in the community, focus from mental illness to mental health, widening range of interventions, from control and medications to individual efforts, empowerment, social determinants, emphasis on culture specific interventions, and greater use of spirituality. There is also recognition of newer needs for mental health related to addictions, aging, loneliness, caregiving, people living with chronic illnesses, menopause, trauma survivors, moral injury, burn-out of health work force, etc. The overall shift in focus is on "All these actions are achievable, relying—for the most part—on resources already available to every community and country. What they do require is the acceptance that business as usual will fail and the solutions to transforming mental healthcare systems are already present within existing resources."[56]

Indian Mental Health Professionals and Spirituality

Spirituality is the essence of Indian culture. Indian psychiatrists have always recognized the value of spiritual ideas and practices in mental health practices. They have examined and written about a wide range of subjects; Nanda;[8] Deb Sikdar,[57] Surya and Jayaram,[10] Varma,[9] Vahia,[11-13] Neki,[13,15] Hoch,[58-59] Dube,[60,61] Rao,[16,17] Reddy et al.,[62] Wig,[63-66] Bhaskaran,[22] Grover et al.,[67-70] Varma,[71,72] Prabhakar et al.,[73] Shamsundar,[18,19] Gautam.[74] In more recent times, Janakiramaiah et al.,[75] Kohli,[76] Varma and Gupta,[72] Nayar et al.,[77], Vedamurthachar,[78,79] Verghese,[23] Sharma,[39,40]

Varma,[80] Srinivasa Murthy,[2,81-84] Behere et al.,[85] Khandelwal,[86] Manickam,[87] Chaturvedi,[88-89] Srinivasa Murthy and Banerjee,[90] Dhawan and Mongia,[91] and Rajagopal.[30] The writings of the above professionals cover a wide range of subjects related to mental health, from Indian philosophy, Ayurveda, yoga, meditation, psychotherapy, rehabilitation, and cancer care.

Research Evidence of Spirituality and Health/Mental Health

The Duke University, USA, under the leadership of Prof. Harold Koenig, has been working in the field of spirituality, health, and mental health from a number of perspectives. Koenig et al. have reviewed world-wide evidence and the clinical implications of religion, spirituality, and health **(Box 2)**.[4]

Koenig has outlined the clinical implications in terms of the rationale for integrating spirituality in health care in general and mental health care in particular and the ways to integrate spirituality in patient care.[92] He recognizes that many patients have spiritual needs in relation to their medical and psychiatric illnesses. R/S beliefs affect patients' medical decisions. Physicians' belief of R/S often influences medical care. R/S influences the kind of support and

BOX 2: Religion, spirituality and health.[4]

- Approximately 80% of research on religion/spirituality (R/S) and health involves studies on mental health
- Majority of studies show R/S to be helpful in coping with adversities such as living with medical illnesses, pain, caregiver burden, end-of-life issues, bereavement, natural disasters, and adverse life situations
- Positive association between R/S and well-being
- Hope, optimism, meaning and purpose, self-esteem, and sense of control are positively associated with health and mental health
- Greater R/S predicted lower levels of depression or faster remission of depression
- Inverse relationship between R/S and suicide
- R/S predicted lower level of anxiety and R/S reduced anxiety more than standard interventions.
- R/S predicts better outcomes in psychotic disorders
- R/S has inverse relationship with substance abuse
- R/S has inverse relationship with delinquency/crime
- R/S is related to greater marital stability
- R/S is associated with greater social support
- R/S is related to greater social capital. Health behaviors and R/S
- Positive correlation with exercise and physical activity
- Inverse relationship with cigarette smoking
- Healthier and better diet
- Inverse relationship with risky sexual behaviors. Physical health and R/S
- Inverse relationship with coronary heart disease
- Lower blood pressure
- Lower risk for stroke
- Better cognitive functioning
- Lower infection rates and viral loads
- Better immunity
- Lower risk of cancer and better prognosis
- Better self-rated health
- Lower levels of pain and better response to interventions
- Longer life-span

care received on returning home. Failure to address patients' spiritual needs can increase health costs, especially toward the end of life.

RESEARCH ON SPIRITUALITY AND SERIOUS MEDICAL ILLNESSES

2022 review of 371 articles[93] presents evidence concerning spirituality in serious illness and health and to identify implications for patient care and health outcomes. The Delphi panel review yielded 8 evidence statements supported by evidence categorized as strong and proposed three top-ranked implications of this evidence for serious illness, namely: (i) Incorporate spiritual care into care for patients with serious illness; (ii) incorporate spiritual care education into training of interdisciplinary teams caring for persons with serious illness; and (iii) include specialty practitioners of spiritual care in the care of patients with serious illness. Further, the Delphi panel review yielded 8 evidence statements supported by evidence categorized as strong and proposed three top-ranked implications of this evidence for health outcomes: (i) Incorporate patient-centered and evidence-based approaches regarding associations of spiritual community with improved patient and population health outcomes; (ii) increase awareness among health professionals of evidence for protective health associations of spiritual community; (iii) recognize spirituality as a social factor associated with health in research, community assessments, and program implementation.

Spirituality and Suicide

Social and spiritual roots of suicide have been well recognized following the pathbreaking research of Emily Durkheim during the 19th century (1897) "Suicide is individual action based on social factors". Koenig reviewing 141 studies examining the relationship between R/S and suicide variables found that 75% of studies reported inverse relationships and 3% positive relationships.[4] Of the 49 studies with the highest methodological rigor, 80% reported less suicide, fewer suicide attempts, and more negative attitudes toward suicide among the more spiritual individuals. The second edition of the "Oxford Textbook of Suicidology and Suicide Prevention" containing 96 chapters and 15 sections, the first section is on "Religion and Suicide" having 11 chapters.[94] Interestingly, April 8, 2024 article of youth suicide in The Hindu by Vijayakumar does not refer to spirituality![95]

Spirituality and HIV/AIDS

Persons living with AIDS (PLWAIDS) face many challenges from the time of diagnosis and throughout their life, stigmatization from the community, need for lifelong treatment, restrictions in personal, family, and community life. These relate to the questions relating to, why me? Dalmida et al. report negative religious coping, religious attendance, religiousness, and social support satisfaction significantly predicted quality of life.[96] Depressive symptoms, positive religious coping, and social support satisfaction significantly predicted quality of life. Participants who were females prayed less than daily, attended religious services less than weekly, or who were non/less religious had significantly poorer quality of life. Authors conclude that their findings confirm the importance of religion, mental health, medication adherence, and social support in the quality of life of PLWAIDS and further suggest that spirituality should all be routinely assessed by clinicians.

Spirituality and Loneliness/Aging

On May 3, 2023, Dr Vivek Murthy, Surgeon General of the United States of America, releasing the Report "Our Epidemic of Loneliness and Isolation 2023" observed "Loneliness and isolation represent profound threats to our health and well-being. But we have the power to respond by taking small steps every day to strengthen our relationships, and by supporting community efforts to rebuild social connection, we can rise to meet this moment together".[52] During the recent COVID-19 pandemic, the importance of social determinants has come to the forefront.[97] Researchers found about a 5% increase in loneliness during the pandemic.[98] There is a need for thinking the issue of loneliness in innovative ways. For example, the traditional practices of India have a special relevance to address the loneliness issues relating to old age. The view of focusing on "continued normalcy" misses the complimentary view of considering aging not as "loss" but as a "transition" in life. This is the essence of the spiritual approach to aging as reflected in the "Ashrama" system of India.[21,64] The focus is to move from loneliness to solitude that is filled with tranquility and peace. Instead of considering it as a "separate pathological entity" that deserves a "special treatment", to deal with it as part of aging by "letting go when it is time". The above approach forms the very foundation of the Hindu philosophy. Wig has written about the applicability of Vaanaprastha in modern society.[64] Manusmriti also describes how Eastern traditions aim for being with oneself (solitude/oneliness instead of loneliness), optimism, and hope which are associated with letting go of one's abilities in a graded yet respectful manner rather than lamenting for the loss. Wig has synthesized it as follows: (i) Voluntary withdrawal from the routine hustle of life and trying to unify emotionally with nature, (ii) deliberately attempting to reduce one's needs to maintain a balance with the available resources, (iii) acceptance of aging and associated limitations, enjoying the positive constructs and wisdom of age, reduced need to be in control, (iv) contribution to the society and focusing on social welfare to the extent possible, and (v) pursuit of spirituality.[64]

Spirituality in Cancer Care and Caregivers' Support

The following two experiences of the author illustrates the importance of spirituality in two medical situations, namely, cancer care and caregiver support.

Cancer Care and Spirituality[82]

The diagnosis of cancer is a life-changing experience for the affected individual and their families. A wide range of supports are needed by the patient and the family. There are two challenges in receiving/providing emotional support to persons living with a diagnosis of cancer. There is an urgent need to not only think of services and supports but also strengthening the individuals living with a diagnosis of cancer and their caregivers, by harnessing the resources within. There are difficulties in providing the needed emotional care by professional interventions. It is here the need through "self-care" becomes urgent. In India, one of the preexisting sources of support, to understand and master suffering, is the spiritual resource. Spirituality in all religions addresses the problems faced by a person experiencing pain, suffering, fear of death, and to find the meaning of life during adverse life situations.

Koenig reports 29 studies relating to cancer and spirituality to the relationship between religion/spirituality (R/S) and either the onset or outcome of cancer, including cancer mortality.[4] Of those, 16 studies (55%) found that those who are more R/S had a lower risk of cancer or a better prognosis, although two studies (7%) reported a significantly worse prognosis. Of the 20 studies, 12 (60%) found an association between R/S and lower risk or better outcomes and none reported worse risks or outcomes.

Epidemiological studies have shown that persons living with a diagnosis of cancer have higher rates of emotional disorders in all countries.[99] Indian research in the area of psycho-oncology has addressed the prevalence of emotional health problems,[100-103] needs for assessment of needs,[104,105] importance of family[106] issue of suicide,[107] need for emotional support,[108] and the importance of communication in cancer care.[109] A special area of studies has been in spirituality. Gielin et al. report that more than half of the Indian cancer patients need spiritual care.[110,111] An Indian measurement has been developed to measure spirituality and its utility has been evaluated.[112] Value of yoga too has been reported. Another area of recent interest is the scope for post-traumatic growth in cancer experiences.[113,114]

Following my life journey with cancer, I wanted to utilize the personal/family experiences and mental health professional expertise to assist people living with cancer. During the last few years, I am coordinating a WhatsApp group of persons living with a diagnosis of cancer and their caregivers. Group members have been sharing the value of the four "pillars" of cancer care, namely, medical care, psychological support, social support, and spirituality. There is growing literature on post-traumatic experiences in cancer survivors. Christodoulou et al., in a recent review of caregiving, identifies interventions for (i) life satisfaction; (ii) post-traumatic growth; (iii) targeting hope; (iv) self-compassion; (v) resilience; (vi) self-empowerment; (vii) optimism, positivity; and (viii) gratitude.[115]

Caregiving of Children with Special Needs and Spirituality

Throughout history of India, caregiving is a commitment that the family members of persons with special needs take up by choice.[116] Caregiving for a family member with special needs challenges the economic, physical, emotional, interpersonal, and intrapersonal relationship, and spiritual aspects of the caregivers. In the Indian context and culture, mothers are more involved in the caregiving rearing, and educating the child with special needs along with taking care of the needs of other family members and the responsibilities of running the home. In more than two dozen studies from India, these added efforts and responsibilities and associated increased emotional distress have been documented.[117] Spirituality is one resource that helps to meet the challenges of caregiving. The Association for Mentally Challenged (AMC), Bangalore, under project ENRICH (Empowering families to fulfill their Needs and Rebuild families through Information, and Skills of Caregiving towards Holistic development of the families), one of the areas explored with the caregivers of children with special needs has been the place of spirituality in their lives. The study identified seven themes **(Box 3)**.[118]

Spirituality is considered the master key of the Indian mind.[2,7] This was succinctly expressed by one caregiver, "caregiving has strengthened my faith and I have become stronger". The above two examples from

BOX 3: Spiritual themes as part of caregiving.[118]

- Meaning and relationship with God
- Spirituality as a coping tool
- Rituals to connect with God
- God's connection with self
- Spiritual practices
- Understanding the special child through spirituality
- Finding meaning through spirituality

clinical situations illustrate scope to integrate spirituality in clinical situations in India.

SPIRITUALITY AND TRAUMA CARE

Disasters challenge individuals, families, and communities with existential questions. There is a need to mobilize both internal and external resources to rebuild lives.[119,120] Spiritual understanding of the life changing event is an important part of recovery. Interestingly one of the recent developments in disaster care is the scope for post-traumatic growth.

Psychotherapy

The importance of spirituality has been extensively examined in the practice of psychotherapy. Shamsundar has this important observation:[121]

"In this context, let me recount an earlier incident I remembered when, in the 1970s our seniors like Prof. Neki and late Prof. Venkoba Rao proposed Bhagavadgita as a psychotherapeutic paradigm. The incident happened in early 1940s in my home-town on the last day of a fortnight, two-hours-a-day discourse on Bhagavadgita by a well-known local Sanskrit scholar, Sri Chakravarti Iyengar. During the question–answer session, I had a question, "Did the two armies on the battle field wait for so many hours for Lord Krishna to complete His sermon to Arjuna?" Sri Iyengar's answer was simple and revealing, "No, Lord Krishna just touched Arjuna and brought about the required transformation in the latter's knowledge by His spiritual power. Bhagavadgita is only an explanation and commentary on the 'content" of the transformation that took place in Arjuna's "living-knowledge". A question I like to pose for those who take this issue seriously is, "Why cannot we strive to become able to transform our patients in a similar fashion, even though to a tiniest extent?"

To summarize, there is a growing evidence to support the following observations:

- Firstly, people with spiritual practices are known to live longer and have better quality of life.
- Secondly, in the face of adverse life situations like exposure to conflicts/disasters, living with life-threatening illnesses like cancer, chronic illnesses, ageing, loneliness, refugee status, people with spiritual orientation respond with greater resilience.
- Thirdly, caregiving, a growing need all over the world, benefits from spirituality.
- Fourthly, in mental disorders treatment spirituality has importance understanding of clients, as part of the treatment and associated with better treatment acceptance and outcomes.

Challenges to Integration of Spirituality into Care Programs

Historically, especially in the Western countries, there is separation of the body-mind. The philosopher, Descartes, is a significant personality in this story.[122] Even now, in the Western countries, there are strict boundaries in dealing with the spiritual matters even in medical settings. This is not

BOX 4: Spiritual assessment.[26,27]

- *Step 1:* Elicit spiritual history, including information about spiritual practices and beliefs that exist within the patient's family
- *Step 2:* Elicit spiritual concerns, problems, and challenges
- *Step 3:* Assess Spiritual pain (meaning, believing in God and practicing religious activity, purpose, hope, legacy, values, attachment and detachment, faith, acceptance of reality, transcendence, relationships, forgiveness, losses, etc.)
- *Step 4:* Spiritual distress
- *Step 5:* Assessment of spiritual strength and weaknesses
- *Step 6:* Spiritual quotient
- *Step 7:* Spiritual sensitivity

so in the Eastern cultures, where there is greater openness to utilize spiritual resources by a wide range of community members. The second aspect is the politicization of the religion in many ways. Issues of abortion rights, food habits, same sex marriage, and personal laws are becoming the battle ground between opposing political groups, and this makes looking at spirituality in a neutral and personal manner difficult. Thirdly, religious/spiritual practices have been largely rooted in the local communities and thus there are no standardised ways of applying the interventions. The evidence for effectiveness is limited.[90]

FROM EVIDENCE TO ACTION

The evidence to support R/S is strong. What is needed is to convert evidence to action. There are challenges as this translation has to occur "locally", from assessment, interventions, and outcome evaluations. There are no universal solutions.

Chaturvedi has outlined a seven-step process of spiritual assessment in clinical settings **(Box 4)**.[26,27]

BOX 5: Approaches to develop practice of spirituality and evaluate its impact.

- Examination of the concepts and practices in different religions
- Adaptation of the concepts/practices to modern societal realities living in rural, urban, and other settings and different population groups
- The development of case studies of persons utilizing these measures and finding meaning of life

Preparing people, as they age (from 50 years on), to include this looking ahead their overall life plans

- Case control studies of people in society with varying degrees of spirituality
- Longitudinal studies in the specific population groups (elderly, adolescents, persons with chronic illnesses, disabilities, etc.), to understand the value of spirituality in promoting QOL, mental wellness, preventing depression, dementia, etc., and coping better with adverse life situations of disease, grief, etc.
- Standardization of spiritual practices as applicable to all groups, for wider dissemination in the society QOL (Quality of life)

He has outlined the need to create a suitable atmosphere in care settings, as follows: "All health care settings must have a cordial and welcoming spiritual atmosphere. It should comprise of an environment that encourages listening to each other, and people with similar spiritual wavelengths working together in an atmosphere of warmth, caring and kindness." Further, spiritual intervention should focus on strengthening the faith and reducing the feelings of hopelessness and abandonment.[26,27]

There is need to understand and identify the concepts and practises of R/S in different communities, religions, different health situations, and countries **(Box 5)**.

LOOKING AHEAD

India is the spiritual capital of the world. Sri Aurobindo in his essay "The Renaissance in India" described the Indian mind as "Spirituality is indeed the master key of the Indian mind; the sense of the infinite is native to it".[7] Indian spiritual contributions have influenced the world through leaders such as Sri Adi Shankaracharya of the 8th century, Swami Ramakrishna and Swami Vivekananda of the 19th century, Sri Aurobindo and Swami Chinmaya of the 20th century. In the current times, leaders such as Sri Sri Ravi Shankar, Guru Jaggi Vasudev, and others are spreading the spiritual wisdom of India, as it is applicable to the current times of the world. In addition, in the 21st century, yoga, meditation, and other spiritual practices in a wide range of forms have been accepted as an important part of life all over the world.[32-34,123,124] All over the world, there is recognition of "mental health epidemic" and the need to move from mental illness to mental health.[28,42] Further, many of the mental health issues that the current population is facing are migration, urbanization and disasters, child trauma and its mental health consequences, domestic violence, addiction, loneliness and living with chronic illnesses such as heart, kidney disease, and cancer do not have pure medical solutions. At the international level issues of "addiction epidemic",[125-127] adolescent suicides,[128] "loneliness epidemic",[98] "gun violence" "conflicts", and other societal issues need solutions beyond modern medicine. There is a need for rethink as noted by Klineman "The moral failure of humanity in the past does not mean we must tolerate this failure any longer".[129]

It is important to recall the choice of motto of the All India Institute of Mental Health, Bangalore, at the time of its establishment in 1954, "Samatvam Yoga Ucchayate-Equanimity is the goal of all existence". This focus at the start of the Institute, even at a time when the first medicines for mental health care were being introduced, on mental health is significant. The currently widely accepted method" cognitive behavior therapy" in different forms provides a model for empowering individuals to master their emotional health. There is need not only to glorify the past wisdom, but bring the knowledge and practices to address the current mental health challenges. The acceptance of yoga/meditation/mindfulness shows the way.

BOX 6: Priority areas for action to integrate spirituality in mental health care.

- Define the boundaries between religion and spirituality
- Development and standardization of measurement tools for spirituality
- Development of specific interventions, along with measurement of outcomes
- Models for collaboration with spiritual leaders
- Need for spiritual skills training of all mental health professionals at different levels
- Addressing the negative effects of some of the interventions
- Bringing about a larger consensus on spirituality in individual and public lives at the societal and political levels

The challenge is to convert evidence to action by systematic efforts **(Box 6)**.

CONCLUSION

It is appropriate to conclude the chapter, with a quotation from Rao which illustrates both the relevance of Hinduism to modern life as well as the need for modern examination of the concepts and practices to meet the modern world.[17] "India is an ancient and great cultural, spiritual and an anthropological laboratory. She has been the nursery of saints and sages, scientists and founders of world's major religions and promulgators of profound philosophy. Nevertheless, to be satisfied with the glory of the past is to turn into a fossil; but to interpret the old from a new point of view is to revitalize the past and bring in a current of fresh air into the monotonous present".

These are the challenges and opportunities for the mental health professionals of India and the world. Integrating spirituality in mental health care could be the greatest contribution of India to humanity.

REFERENCES

1. Harrington A. The Cure Within—A History of Mind-Body Medicine. New York: Norton; 2008.
2. Srinivasa Murthy R. Hinduism and Mental Health. In: Verhagen P, Van Pragg HM, Lopez-Ibor JJ, Cox J, Moussavi D. Religion and Psychiatry: Beyond Boundaries. New York: World Psychiatric Association. Wiley; 2010.
3. Koenig HG. Religion, spirituality and health: the research and clinical implications. ISRN Psychiatry. 2012;2012:278730.
4. Koenig HG, VanderWeele TJ, Peteet JR. Handbook of Religion and Health, 3rd edition. New York: Oxford; 2024.
5. Verhagen P, Van Pragg HM, Lopez-Ibor JJ, Cox JL, Moussavi D. Psychiatry and Religion: World Psychiatric Association Beyond Boundaries. New York: Wiley; 2009.
6. Pulla V, Salagame KKK. Wellbeing: Through the Lens of Indian Traditional Conceptualisations. Int J Soc Work Human Serv Pract. 2018;6:94-100.
7. Mehra B. The thinking Indian: Essays on Indian Socio-Cultural matters in the light of Sri Aurobindo. Mantriwords: Pondicherry; 2015.
8. Nand S. Positive Mental Health. New Delhi: Indian Council of Medical Research; 1961.
9. Varma LP. Psychiatry in Ayurveda. Indian J Psychiatry. 1965;7:292-312.
10. Surya NC, Jayaram SS. Some basic considerations in the practice of psychotherapy in the Indian setting. Indian J Psychiatry. 1968;4:153-6.
11. Vahia NS, Vinekar SL, Doongaji DR. Some ancient Indian concepts in the treatment of psychiatric disorders. Br J Psychiatry. 1966;112:1089.
12. Vahia NS, Doongaji DR, Jeste DV, Kapoor SN, Indubala A, Nath SR. Further experience with therapy based on the concepts of Patanjali in the treatment of psychiatric disorders. Indian J Psychiatry. 1973;15:32-8.
13. Vahia NS, Doongaji DR, Jeste DV. Value of Patanjali's concepts in the treatment of psychoneurosis. In: Arieti S, Chrzanowski G (Eds). New Dimensions of Psychiatry. New York: John Wiley; 1975.
14. Neki JS. Guru-Chela relationship: the possibility of a therapeutic paradigm. Am J Orthopsychiatry. 1973;3:755-66.
15. Neki JS. Psychotherapy in India. Indian J Psychiatry. 1977;19:1-10.
16. Rao AV. Psychiatric thought in ancient India. Indian J Psychiatry. 1978;20.
17. Rao AV. Culture, philosophy, mental health. Mumbai: Bharatiya Vidya Bhavan; 1997.
18. Shamasunder C. What kind of psychotherapy in the Indian setting? Indian J Psychiatry. 1979;21:34-8.
19. Shamsundar C. Psychotherapeutic paradigms from Indian mythology. In: Dwivedi KN (Ed). The Therapeutic Use of Stories. London: Routledge; 1997. pp. 64-82.
20. Dwivedi KN. The Therapeutic Use of Stories. London: Routledge; 1997.
21. Wig NN. Indian concepts of mental health and their impact on care of the mentally ill. Int J Mental Health. 1990;18:71-80.
22. Bhaskaran K. Meditation from a mental health prospective. Indian J Psychiatry. 1991; 33:87-94.
23. Verghese A. Spirituality and Mental health. Indian J Psychiatry. 2008;50:233-7.
24. Kapur RL. Another Way to Live—A Psychiatrist among Indian Ascetics. New Delhi: Penguin; 2009.
25. Koenig HG. Spiritual Readiness—A Survival Guide for the Hindu Believer in an Age of Disbelief; 2024.
26. Chaturvedi SK The spiritual satisfaction. J Psychosoc Rehabil Ment Health. 2022a;9: 125-6.

27. Chaturvedi S. Spirituality in the air. J Psychosoc Rehabil Ment Health. 2022b;9: 347-50.
28. Srinivasa Murthy R. Concept of Mental disorders, mental health and Well-being. In: Anand M (Ed). Mental Health Care Resource Book: Concept and Praxis for Social Workers and Mental Health Professionals. Singapore: Springer; 2024a.
29. Srinivasa Murthy R. Integrating 'spirituality' in social work-challenges and opportunities. In: Anand M (Ed). Mental Health Care Resource Book. Singapore: Springer Nature; 2024b.
30. Rajagopalan S. The spiritual philosophy of Advaita: Basic concepts and relevance to psychiatry. Indian J Psychiatry. 2024;66: 202-7.
31. Singhal PP, Sarkar V, Aggarwal T. Mental Health, SDGs, and Spiritual Care: A Call for Legal Advocacy. In: Kanojia S (Ed). Bridging Health, Environment, and Legalities: A Holistic Approach. IGI Global; 2024. pp. 182-204.
32. Kapur M, Shamasundar C, Bhatti RS. Psychotherapy training in India. Bangalore: NIMHANS Publications; 1996. Issue No. 36
33. Kapur M. It OK to ask for help. New Delhi: Vitasta; 2020.
34. Gangadhar BN, Verambally S. Integrating yoga in mental health services. Indian J Med Res. 141:741-2.
35. Moreira A, Sharma A, Cook A. WPA position statement on spirituality and religion in psychiatry. World Psychiatry. 2016;15:87-8.
36. Bhattacharyya A. Historical backdrop. In: Dwivedi KN. The Therapeutic Use of Stories. London: Routledge; 1997. pp. 1-18.
37. Shamsunder C. Relevance of ancient Indian wisdom to modern mental health—a few examples. Indian J Psychiatry. 2008a; 50:138-43.
38. Lopez-Ibor MI, Carrasco MM. Religion and Social Psychiatry. In: Gogineni RR, Pumariega AJ, Kallivayalil RA, Kastrup M, Rothe EM (Ed). The WASP Textbook on Social Psychiatry: Historical, Developmental, Cultural and Clinical Perspectives. New York: Oxford University Press; 2023. pp. 185-92.
39. Sharma A, Sharma S. Meditation: The future of medication. In: Sharma A (Ed). Spirituality and Mental Health-Reflections of the Past, Application in the Present, Projections for the Future. New Delhi: Indian Psychiatric Society; 2009. pp. 569-84.
40. Sharma A. Spirituality and Mental Health-reflections of the Past, Application in the Present, Projections for the Future. New Delhi: Indian Psychiatric Society; 2009.
41. https://www.hds.harvard.edu/2024-conference-alternative-spiritualities-celebration-resistance-and-accountability
42. Insel. Healing: Our Path from Mental Illness to Mental Health. New York: Penguin Press; 2022.
43. Scull A. Social order/mental disorder: Anglo American Psychiatry in Historical Perspective. London: Routledge; 1990.
44. Srinivasa Murthy R. COVID-19 Pandemic and Emotional Health-Social Psychiatry Perspective. Indian J Soc Psychiatry. 2020; 36:S24-42.
45. Geronimus AT. Weathering: The Extraordinary Stress of Ordinary Life in an Unjust Society. Blackstone; 2023.
46. Littrell JL. The Importance of Psychoneuroimmunology for Social Workers. Fam Soc. 2019;100:17-33
47. Patel P, Saxena S, Lund C, Thornicroft G, Baingana F, Bolton P, et al. The Lancet Commission on global mental health and sustainable development. Lancet 2018;392:1553-98.
48. Herrman H, Patel V, Kieling C, Berk M, Buchweitz C, Cuijpers P, et al. Time for united action on depression: a Lancet–World Psychiatric Association Commission. Lancet. 2022;399:957-1022.
49. World Health Organization. World Mental Health Report: Transforming Mental Health for All. Geneva: World Health Organisation; 2022.
50. Thornicroft G, Sunkel C, Aliev AA, Baker S, Brohan E, El Chammay R, et al. The Lancet commission on ending stigma and

discrimination in mental health. Lancet. 2022; 400:1438-80.
51. Thiagarajan T, Newson J. The Mental State of the World in 2022. A Publication of the Mental Health Million Project. Sapiens Lab; 2023.
52. Office of the Surgeon General. Our Epidemic of Loneliness and Isolation: The U.S. Surgeon General's Advisory on the Healing Effects of Social Connection and Community. Washington: Government of USA; 2023.
53. Kirkbride JB, Anglin DM, Colman I, Dykxhoorn J, Jones PB, Patalay P, et al. The social determinants of mental health and disorder: evidence, prevention and recommendations. World Psychiatry. 2024; 23:58-98.
54. Van Os, Guloksuz S. Population saluto-genesis—the future of psychiatry? JAMA Psychiatry. 2023;81:115-6.
55. Patel V. The right to mental health. Lancet. 2023;402(10411):1412-1413. doi: 10.1016/S0140-6736(23)02241-9. Epub 2023 Oct 6. PMID: 37813116.
56. Patel V, Saxena S, Lund C, Kohrt B, Kieling C, Sunkel C, et al. Transforming mental health systems globally: principles and policy recommendations. Lancet. 2023;402: 656-66.
57. Deb Sikdar BM. Glimpses of medico-psychological practices in ancient India. Indian J Psychiatry. 1961;11:250-9.
58. Hoch EM. Pir, faquir and psychotherapists. Human Context. 1974;6:668-76.
59. Hoch EM. Sources and resources—a western psychiatrist's search for meaning in the ancient Indian scriptures. Delhi: Bokk Faith India; 1993.
60. Dube KC. Nosology and therapy of mental illness in Ayurveda. Comparative Medicine-East West. 1978;6:209-28.
61. Dube KC, Kumar A, Dube S. Personality types in Ayurveda. Am J Chin Med. 1983;11: 25-34.
62. Narayana Reddy GN, Ramu MG, Venkataram BS Concept of manas(psyche) in Ayurveda. NIMHANS J. 1987;5:125-31.
63. Wig NN. Mental health and spiritual values. A view from the East. Int Rev Psychiatry. 1999;11:92-6.
64. Wig NN. The Joy of Mental Health. Chandigarh: Servants of the People Society; 2006.
65. Wig NN. Mental Health and Spiritual Values. In: Sharma A (Ed). Spirituality and Mental Health - Reflections of the Past, Application in the Present, Projections for the Future. New Delhi: Indian Psychiatric Society; 2009. pp. 3-21.
66. Wig NN. The relevance of Vanaprashtha Ashram in modern times. In: Chatrath, KJS (Ed). Joy of Mental Health, 2nd edition. Chandigarh: Servants of the People Society; 2010. pp. 151-7.
67. Grover P, Varma VK, Verma SK, Pershad D. Relationship between the patient's attitude towards yoga and the treatment outcome. Indian J Psychiatry. 1987;29:253-8.
68. Grover P, Varma VK, Pershad D, Verma SK. Role of yoga in the treatment of psychoneurosis. Bulletin PGI. 1988;22:68-77.
69. Grover P, Varma VK, Pershad D, Verma SK. Role of yoga in the treatment of neurotic disorders: current status and future directions. Indian J Psychiatry. 1994;36: 153-62.
70. Grover P, Varma VK, Verma SK. Drug addiction-can yoga help? Disabilities and Impairments. 1990;3:89-97.
71. Dhawan BN, Koslow SH, Murthy RS, Coelho GV. Decade of the Brain: India/USA Research in Mental Health and Neurosciences. Rockville: National Institute of Mental Health. 1995:197-202.
72. Varma VK, Gupta N (Eds). Psychotherapy in a Traditional Society: Context, Concept and Practice. New Delhi: Jaypee Brothers Medical Publishers Private Limited; 2008.
73. Prabhakar S, Grover P, Berma SK, Chopra JS. Role of yoga in the treatment of psychogenic headache. Neurol India. 1991;39:11-8.
74. Gautam S. Mental health in ancient India and its relevance to modern psychiatry. Indian J Psychiatry. 1999;41(1):5-18.
75. Janakiramaiah N, Gangadhar BN, Murthy PJNV, Harish MG, Subbakrishna DK,

Vedamurthachar A. Antidepressant efficacy of Sudarshan Kriya Yoga (SKY) in melancholia: a randomised comparison with electroconvulsive therapy and imipramine. J Affect Disord. 2000;57:255-9.
76. Kohli A, Varma VK, Nehra R. Comparison of the efficacy of psychorelaxation and pharmacotherapy in generalised anxiety disorder. JPCS. 2001;16:43-8.
77. Nayar P. Yoga. In: Varma VK, Gupta N. (Eds). Psychotherapy in a Traditional Society: Context, Concept and Practice. New Delhi: Jaypee; 2008. pp. 165-78.
78. Vedamurthachar A, Janakiramiah N, Hegde JM, Shetty TK, Subbakrishna DK, Sureshbabu SV, et al. Antidepressant efficacy and hormonal effects of Sudarshana Kriya Yoga (SKY) in alcohol dependent individuals. J Affect Disord. 2006;94:249-53.
79. Murthy PJNV, Gangadhar BN, Janakiramaiah N, Subbakrishna DK. P300 amplitude and antidepressant response to Sudarshan Kriya Yoga (SKY). J Affect Disord. 1998;50:45-8.
80. Varma. Ancient Indian concepts of reality, causality and cosmology. In: Varma VK, Kala AK, Gupta N (Eds). Culture, Personality and Mental Illness - A Perspective on Traditional Societies. New Delhi: Jaypee Publications; 2008.
81. Srinivasa Murthy R. Contemporary relevance of Hinduism to mental health. In: Sharma A (Ed). Spirituality and Mental Health-reflections of the past, application in the present, projections for the future. New Delhi: Indian Psychiatric Society; 2009. pp. 111-35.
82. Srinivasa Murthy R. Cancer and spirituality: Underutilised resource for cancer care in India. Indian J Med Paediatr Oncol. 2024; 45:271-5.
83. Srinivasa Murthy R, Gupta N. Leadership in Indian Psychiatry. Chandigarh: Department of Psychiatry, Chandigarh Medical College; 2023.
84. Srinivasa Murthy R. Rethinking public mental health – Personal reflections. World Soc Psychiatry. 2023;5:106-11.
85. Behere PB, Das A, Yadav R, Behere AP. Religion and Mental Health. Indian J Psychiatry. 2013;55:187-94.
86. Khandelwal S, Deb KS. Transcendental meditation: current status. In: Varma VK, Gupta N (Eds). Psychotherapy in a Traditional Society: Context, Concept and Practice. New Delhi: Jaypee; 2008. pp. 190-205.
87. Manickam LSS. Psychotherapy in India. Indian J Psychiatry. 2010;52:S366-70.
88. Chaturvedi S. What is important to Indians when they have cancer? Soc Sci Med. 1991; 33:91-4.
89. Chaturvedi SK, Strohschein FJ, Saraf G, Loisell ECG. Communication in cancer care: Psycho-social, interactional, and cultural issues. A general overview and the example of India. Front Psychol. 2014;5:1332.
90. Srinivasa Murthy R, Banerjee D. Loneliness in older people: from analysis to action. World Soc Psychiatry. 2021;3:120-2.
91. Dhawan A, Mongia M. Spirituality and Mental Health. In: Chaddha RK, Kumar V, Sarkar S (Eds). Social Psychiatry: Principles and Clinical Perspectives. New Delhi: Jaypee Brothers; 2024. pp. 153-60.
92. Koenig HG. Spirituality in Patient Care, 3rd edition. Conshohocken: Templeton; 2013.
93. Balboni TA, VanderWeele TJ, Doan-Soares SD, Long KNG, Ferrell BR, Fitchett G, et al. Spirituality in Serious Illness and Health. JAMA. 2022;328(2):184-97.
94. Wasserman D. Oxford Textbook of Suicidology and Suicide Prevention, 2nd edition. Oxford: Oxford University Press; 2021.
95. Vijayakumar L. Gone too soon-the subject of youth suicide in India. The Hindu, Apr 8, 2024.
96. Dalmida SG, Koenig HG, Holstad MM, Thomas TL. Religious and Psychosocial Covariates of Health-Related Quality of Life in People Living with HIV/AIDS. HIV/AIDS Res Treatment. 2015;1(1):1000HARTOJ1101.
97. Srinivasa Murthy R. COVID-19 Pandemic and Emotional Health - Social Psychiatry Perspective. Indian J Soc Psychiatry. 2020; 36:S24-42.

98. Law T. Loneliness is a public health emergency. The Time, June 1, 2022.
99. Srinivasa Murthy R, Alexander A. Progress in psycho-oncology with special reference to developing countries. Curr Opin Psychiatry. 2019;32:442-50.
100. Mehrotra S. Psycho-oncology research in India: Current status and future directions. J Indian Acad Appl Psychol. 2008;34:7-18.
101. Chaturvedi S. Hand of God in psychosocial rehabilitation. Psychosoc Rehabil. J Psychosoc Rehabil Ment Health. 2018;5:1-3.
102. Alexander A, Sreenath K, Murthy RS. Beyond numbers - Recent understanding of emotional needs of persons diagnosed with cancer 2007–2018. Indian J Palliative Care. 2020;26:120-8.
103. Alexander A, Murthy RS. Living with cancer: Urgent need for emotional health support. Indian J Can. 2020;57:360-2.
104. Saxena PPU, Kulkarni V, Thapar R, Pai K, Gupta A, Kotian H. Assessment of spectrum of mental disorders in cancer patients. J Cancer Res Ther. 2018; 14:1312-5.
105. Chittem M, Norman P, Harris PR. Relationships between perceived diagnostic disclosure, patient characteristics, psychological distress and illness perceptions in Indian cancer patients. Psychooncology. 2012;22:1375-80.
106. Alexander A, Kaluve R, Prabhu JS, Korlimarla A, Srinath BS, Manjunath S, et al. The impact of breast cancer on the patient and the family in Indian perspective. Indian J Palliative Care. 2019;25:66-72.
107. Mohandoss AA, Thavarajah R. A study on suicide among Indians living with cancer during 2001-2014. Indian J Cancer. 2016;53: 435-40.
108. Kandasamy A, Chaturvedi SK, Desai G. Spirituality, distress, depression, anxiety, and quality of life in patients with advanced cancer. Indian J Cancer. 2011;48:55-9.
109. Shukla P, Rishi PA. Correlational study of psychosocial and spiritual well being and death anxiety among advanced stage cancer patients. Am J Appl Psychol. 2014;2:59-65.
110. Gielen J, Bhatnagar B, Chaturvedi SK. Prevalence and Nature of Spiritual Distress among Palliative Care Patients in India. J Religion and Health. 2017;56:530-44.
111. Gielen J, Kashyap K, Singh SP, Bhatnagar S, Chaturvedi SK. Psychometric Assessment of SpiDiscI: Spiritual Distress Scale for Palliative Care Patients in India. Indian J Palliative Care. 2022;28:13-20.
112. Bhatnagar B, Noble S, Chaturvedi SK, Gielen J. Development and Psychometric Assessment of a Spirituality Questionnaire for Indian Palliative Care Patients. Indian J Palliative Care. 2016;22:9-18.
113. Tandon S, Mehrotra S. Posttraumatic growth and its correlates in an indian setting. Inter J Indian Psychol. 2016; 4(1):101-119.
114. Parker-Pope T. Interrupted, Again: Suleika Jaouad on Cancer and Healing the Second Time Around. New York Times, Mar 29, 2022.
115. Christodoulou L, Parpottas P, Petkari E. Psychological interventions to enhance positive outcomes in adult cancer caregivers: A systematic review. J Health Psychol. 2024; 1-23.
116. Srinivasa Murthy R. Overview (of Disability in India) in Comprehensive Textbook on Disability. In: Chavan BS, Ahmad W, Gupta RK (Eds). New Delhi: Jaypee; 2021. pp. XXVII-XXXI.
117. Nischitha S, Divya B, Murthy, RS. Caregivers emotional health: a priority. In: Srinivasa Murthy R, Gupta N (Eds.) Leadership in Indian Psychiatry. Chandigarh: Department of Psychiatry, Chandigarh Medical College; 2023.
118. Divya B, Nischitha S, Murthy RS. Caregivers and Spirituality. In: Srinivasa Murthy R, Gupta N (Eds.) Leadership in Indian Psychiatry. Chandigarh: Department of Psychiatry, Chandigarh Medical College; 2023.
119. Srinivasa Murthy R. Psychosocial and behavioral aspects of populations affected by humanitarian emergencies: Recent developments. Curr Opin Psychiatry. 2016; 29(5):280-5.

120. Srinivasa Murthy R. Mental health of survivors of 1984 Bhopal disaster: A continuing challenge. Ind Psychiatry J. 2014;23:86-93.
121. Shamsunder C. Burden of Being a Psychiatrist - Professional Stress. Indian J Psychol Med. 2008b;30:70-4.
122. Thomas KQ. (1997). The Mind-BODY Connection: Granny was Right, after All. [online] Available from https://www.rochester.edu/pr/Review/V59N3/feature2.html [Last accessed December, 2024].
123. McCall T. Yoga as Medicine: The Yogic prescription for health and healing. New York: Bantam; 2007.
124. Chopra D, Chopra S. Brotherhood: Dharma, Destiny, and the American Dream. Publisher Houghton Mifflin Harcourt, 2013.
125. Smith E. The opioid epidemic and the addiction crisis. Lerner Publications™; 2021 Aug 1.
126. Westoff B. Fentanyl Inc. London: Scribe; 2019.
127. Kala A. Most of what you want to knout addiction. New Delhi: Speaking Tiger; 2023.
128. Twenge JM. Generations. New York; Atria; 2023.
129. Klineman A. Global mental health: a failure of humanity. Lancet. 2009;374:603-4.

2 CHAPTER

Creativity and Spirituality

Astha, Vinay Kumar

INTRODUCTION

Creativity and spirituality appear distinct from a distance. However, a closer perspective reveals that they are both a process, sharing a common origin called the mind. There is a need to assess their neurobiological correlates to understand their connection along with an emphasis on their psychoanalytical explanations. Creativity is present in our day-to-day lives and continues to enrich our experiences. Preparing an exquisite meal from scratch, painting a beautiful landscape when one does not know how to paint or picking up a new skill after the loss of a loved one. Extraordinary creativity or the making of a creative genius is often attributed as a product of the non-rational unconsciousness from where spirituality originates and transcends.[1] The link between creativity and spirituality is fascinating. They are in essence complementary to one another and have the power to significantly inspire one another. Unlocking new levels of creativity, meaning, and imagination can be facilitated by investigating the junction of these two entities.

Surrendering of the ego, absorption and *flow* are some of the common components in both mystical experience and artistic expression. However, the different connotations of mysticism become significant when assessing the degree of similarity between creativity and spirituality. Examining the creations of musicians, scientists and artists advances the study of the connection between spirituality, wellbeing, and the arts.[2]

Can creativity be a type of "spiritual seeing"? Can creative pursuits be an alternative for spiritual pursuits? In this chapter, we will explore:

- *Creativity:* Its definitions, stages, and processes.
- *The role of the unconscious mind:* How unconscious processes nurture creativity.
- *Neurobiological theories:* Examining the brain's role in creativity and spirituality.
- *Mental health benefits:* The dividends of engaging in creative and spiritual pursuits for emotional and psychological well-being.

By investigating the interplay between creativity and spirituality, we aim to illuminate how these forces enhance the human experience, providing profound opportunities for growth, healing, and transformation.

WHAT IS CREATIVITY?

Human creativity is defined in many ways. The most widely used definition states that *"a creative act represents something that is different or new and appropriate to the task at hand*".[3] It is the ability to discover innovative and original ideas. However, it takes more than just originality to qualify as creative thinking or an act; it also needs to meet the requirements of *societal usefulness* or *adaptability*.[4] Nancy Andreasen simplifies creativity in three steps. A person seeks out a problem, perceives it using a cognitive process and creates a product.[1]

M Csikszentmihalyi divides it into domain, field and person. He said, "*Creativity occurs at the interface of three subsystems: An Individual who absorbs information form the culture and changes it in a way that will be selected by the relevant Field of gatekeepers for inclusion into the Domain, from whence the novelty will be accessible to the next generation.*"[5]

Kaufman and Beghetto[6] grouped the various types into four Cs and named it the "four-C model of creativity". The various groups are as follows:

- Big-C (eminent accomplishments)
- Little-c approaches (everyday innovations)
- Mini-c creativity (transformative learning)
- Pro-c creativity (professional expertise)

TAPPING INTO THE UNCONSCIOUS

"*Brain is the organ of mind and mind is the house of soul.*"

The journey of self-exploration usually begins with a question, for instance "where am I?" The question is followed by another set of questions such as where am I in this whole universe? What is the purpose of existence? Is my existence being driven by a mystical force/God/? In the quest of finding such answers one also tries to draw inspiration from religion or mythological figures. The emptiness is filled with spiritual practices such as meditation, prayers, or connecting to nature. Spirituality begins with a quest and the unconscious breeds and facilitates it. Viktor Frankl stressed the idea of *spiritual unconsciousness*. He thought that the incorporation of the indispensable spirit that resides within our mortal shell is necessary for the integration of the human personality "thus the spiritual core, and only the spiritual core, warrants and constitutes oneness and wholeness in man".[7]

Creativity is a process that goes through different stages (as illustrated in **Fig. 1**).[8] There is period of "*incubation*" where the mind assimilates the gathered information while being at rest. During this period *the creative unconscious* comes into action. Repressed memories resurface, ideas collide and imagination links them to create something that is a pure novelty, an art, or a masterpiece.

Similarly, a spiritual practice like meditation can be divided into four phases "*pratyāharā* i.e., withdrawal of external senses, *dhāranā* (concentration), *dhyāna* (uninterrupted concentration), *samādhi* (absorption). To reach a state of pure consciousness during meditation, a conscious purpose must be formed and then carried into the unconscious through absorption.

Thus, it can be said that both the processes of creativity and spirituality lead to the path of awakening. It has been cited in ancient literature that the awakened sapiens are capable of creative explorations (*Navonmesh Shalini Pragya*). The *awakening* precedes before a man turns into a monk or a writer begins to write.

NEUROBIOLOGY OF CREATIVITY AND SPIRITUALITY

"*That the brain is spontaneously reorganizing and acting as a self-organizing system*"

– Nancy Andreasen, *The Creative Brain*

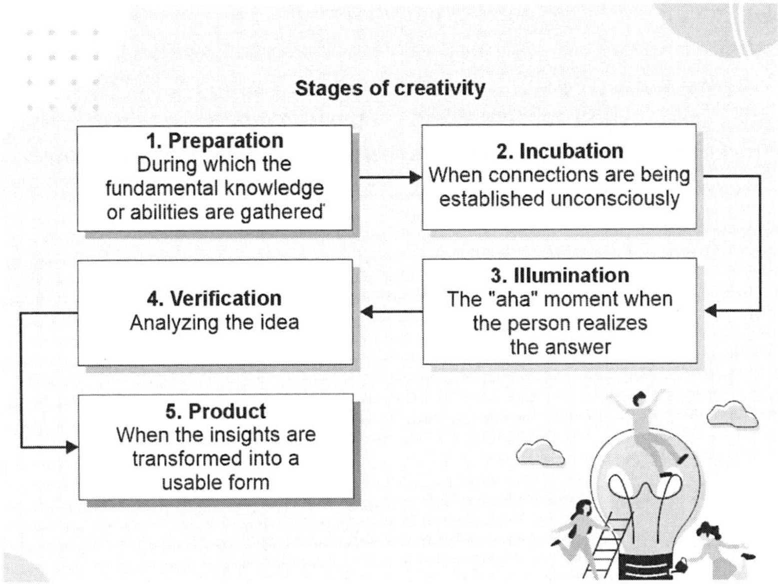

Fig. 1: The stages of creativity as proposed by Wallas.

A creative performance is shaped by the interaction between cognition, emotion, mood-state, and the three neuromodulators, i.e., dopamine, norepinephrine, and 5-HT. A metanalysis of 45 functional magnetic resonance imaging (MRI) studies have suggested that the creative cognition depends on multicomponent neural networks.[9]

According to *the Dual Pathway model,*[10] the nigrostriatal and mesocortical pathways influence creative drive and creative cognition through an optimal balance of resistance and cognitive flexibility. Executive functions (i.e., shifting, inhibition, and working memory) that predict creativity need to strike the ideal balance between purposeful (controlled) and spontaneous processing. There is also a connection between reward (i.e., training, intrinsic interest, and promises) and creativity. The moderating influence of cognitive resources along with competitive mentality on creative urges (i.e., mood, motivation, and emotion) is also responsible. However, reduced brain norepinephrine levels are frequently connected with the most creative mental states in humans, which may improve communication between dispersed networks.

DEFAULT MODE NETWORK

Studies using functional imaging provide an objective means of examining these intricate aspects of the human mind. When people close their eyes and begin to form internal ideas and images, the default network comes into action. One of the most important processes of creativity is the creation of *internal ideas* and *imagery*.[11]

Studies done on highly creativity individuals suggest that at the neural level the unconscious plays a major role in nurturing the moments of creativity. During the random episodic silent thought (REST) (currently renamed as the default state) the multiple regions of association cortex, including the frontal, temporal, and parietal, as well as the retro-splenial cingulate are in an active mode.[11] Further studies have elaborated that highly creative individuals have more intense activity in association cortices when performing tasks that challenge them to "*make associations*."[11] Jung and colleagues measured creativity and performed structural magnetic resonance imaging, analyzing cortical volume. These investigators found that the right posterior cingulate correlated positively with the participants' scores on the composite creativity index.[12]

INTERHEMISPHERIC COMMUNICATION

Associative and convergent thinking, which depend on the integration of widely scattered networks, are necessary for creativity. The right and left hemisphere store many different forms of information and many creative works require interhemispheric communication. The left hemisphere mediates language and mathematical calculations, and the right mediates spatial reasoning and imagery. So, in developing a theory a physicist needs to use both of his hemispheres.[13]

Interhemispheric integration is necessary even when playing music because the left hemisphere controls rhythm and the right hemisphere is crucial for processing melody. It has been demonstrated that whereas the left hemisphere mediates focused attention, the right mediates global attention and thus, creation of great painting requires the coordination of both hemispheres[14] **(Table 1)**.

THROUGH THE PSYCHOANALYTIC LENS

Marion Milner (1900–1998): A Psychoanalyst, Writer Who Doodled to Unlock Mysticism[2]

"It is unusual to combine mysticism and psychoanalysis. Marion Milner, however, precisely achieved this. Through her self-analysis and analytic work with children and adults and using as an illustration her own and others' imaginative ideas, paintings, doodles, drawings, and pictures drew attention to the potential for health and creativity of undoing the obstacles to mystical experience of oneness with what is beyond or other than the self, which she sometimes called God, the unconscious, or the Id."

According to *Freud,* the unconscious plays a significant part in creativity and is facilitated by the sublimation process and libidinal energy. The creative process elevates the sexual desire into a cultural manifestation, which improves the acceptability, productivity, and pleasure of unconscious thoughts. He also suggests the fact that the creative process serves as a safeguard against neurosis.[18]

Moreno proposed for *a more flexible capacity for creative thinking to* manage habitual thinking, the major source of psychopathology. According to him creativity is best promoted through *an interactive process of improvisation,* involving both the mind and body that induces spontaneity.[18] Moreno said, *"Spontaneity operates in the present, here and now; it induces the individual to respond adequately to a novel situation or to respond in a novel way to an old situation."*[19]

COPING THROUGH THE PATH OF CREATIVE AND SPIRITUAL PURSUITS

Since ancient times people have been using creativity and spirituality to cope with stressors of external reality. The Natyashastra created by Bharat Muni to calm the mind is one such example. The narration of folklore by the wise and old of the village preceded much before bibliotherapy came into scientific

TABLE 1: Brain structures involved in creativity and spirituality.

Structures	*Creativity*	*Spirituality*	*Remarks*
Frontal: • Dorsolateral prefrontal cortex (right) • Orbitofrontal cortex • Left medial prefrontal cortex • Bilateral medial frontal gyrus • Left medial frontal	• Divergent creative cognition • Music • Music and verbal creativity	• Gratitude and its neural circuits • Moral cognition	• Observational learning might critically depend on the cerebellum and the prefrontal cortex.[15] • *Prefrontal cortex is linked with innovative behavior*
Temporal:		***Hyper-religiosity***	
• Cuneus • Pre-cuneus • Cingulate	*Default Mode Network*	Empathy, forgiveness	"The default network activates when people close their eyes and generate internal thoughts." Takeuchi et al. (2011) reported a significant positive correlation between individual creativity and brain activity in the precuneus and images[16]
• Ventral tegmental area (VTA) • Nucleus accumbens • Amygdala • Hippocampus • Orbitofrontal cortex (OFC)	• *Neural and reward circuits* (training, intrinsic interest, and promises) • Novelty recognition		Bittner et al. (2016) pointed out that positive-activating moods with an approach motivation and promotion focus (e.g., happiness) activated creativity. On the contrary, negative-activating moods with avoidance motivation and a prevention focus (e.g., fear, anxiety, or even relaxation) correlated with lower creativity[17]

practice. The stories written by oppressed women stirred up a revolution.

Gradually such works started being documented and today we have established grounds to say that various creative and spiritual pursuits **(Table 2)** are a survival mechanism in the progress of civilization.

"Creativity is an adaptive interface with the world". Responding to a stressful situation requires knowledge and abilities that are driven by a person's unique genetic foundation. Some people are born with more resilient personalities than others. Because optimism mitigates the deleterious effects of stress on the brain, resilient people experience stress in different ways than others and escape some of its consequences. This process is directly impacted by creativity. Creative coping is the use of creativity as a positive coping strategy when facing stress.[20] Its adaptive shell fosters resilience and favorably alters perception. Aside from producing something external,

TABLE 2: The different creative and spiritual pursuits.

Performing arts (music, dance, theater, singing, and film)	Mindfulness meditation/ transcendental meditation/ concentrative meditation *(sadhana)*
Visual arts (painting, photography, and sculpture), design, and craft	*Rituals:* Chanting *(prayers/mantras/ spiritual fasting)*
Literature (writing and reading)	Spiritual company *(Satsang)*
Culture (museums, galleries, art exhibitions, concerts, theater, community events, cultural festivals, and fairs)	Selfless services (serving the homeless and poor, helping the ill) *(Seva)*
Online, digital, and electronic arts (animations, filmmaking, and computer graphics)	Naturalists

creativity continues to have an impact on the self, increasing one's sense of self and inner resilience, providing comfort, and finding meaning in the suffering.[18]

Patients who have serious and chronic ailments frequently exhibit signs of low hope which is crucial for healing. Hope relies on the capacity to imagine a better future. Spirituality helps in restoring it through stories, symbols, or metaphors through the power of imagination which is basically derivative of creativity. Narrative is an expression of imagination and religion that can serve as a warehouse for stories. The *scriptures* can be utilized to help patients with the effort of rewriting their life stories; this is explained via *narrative therapy*. For instance, Lord Krishna can be seen as either a chariot climber, a romantic lover, or a victor.

Spirituality and creativity can work in sync to recover a person from mental illness. Bipolar mood disorder has often been associated with heightened states of both religiousness and creativity. Spiritual strategies can be used alongside other treatment modalities to treat anxiety. For example, mindfulness meditation or religious cognitive therapy can be used for patients with similar belief. A spiritual approach also needs to consider "existential anxiety," or the anxiety that comes with being human. Given the certainty of death, existentialist viewpoints must be applied to modern anxiety, religious narratives, and creativity that helps one to hope.[2]

MENTAL HEALTH DIVIDENDS OF CREATIVE AND SPIRITUAL PURSUITS (FIG. 2)

Mental Health Promotion

There is enough scientific background to say that indulging in creative pursuits prevents mental illnesses. Its transformational effects and association with positive mental health also signifies its role in mental health promotion as mentioned in the World Health Organization (WHO) report.[20] The process of creativity encourages *the authentic self* to express while it enhances *positive focus* and helps in attaining the state of flow. *The psychological components are focused on aesthetic engagement, imagination, sensory, and cognitive stimulation.*

Developmental Effects

Research has demonstrated that a mother's lullaby increases attachment and strengthens the mother-child *bonding* as it lowers stress hormones in nursing mothers. Arts help people with neurodevelopmental and including autistic spectrum disorder.

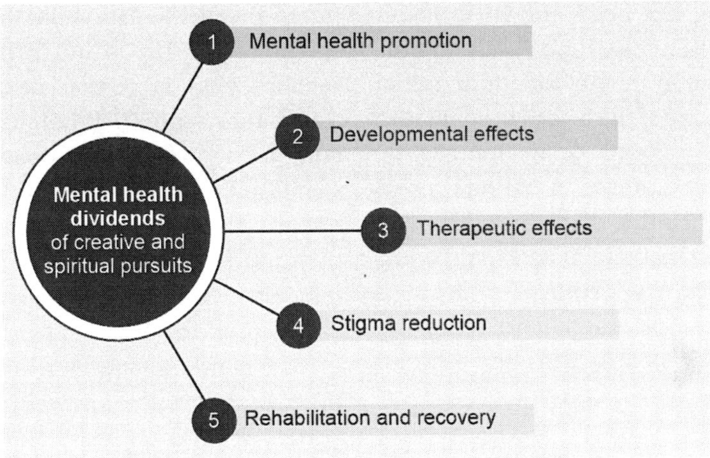

Fig. 2: The mental health dividends of creativity.

Music also plays a crucial role in language acquisition and learning in children with hearing impairment,[21] dyslexic,[22] struggle with communicating[23] have developmental impairments[24] or young poor readers.[25] Engaging in artistic pursuits can mitigate the psychological effects of speech impairments, resulting in decreased levels of anxiety.

Therapeutic Effects

Participating in cultural events, such as attending plays, concerts, museums, or exhibitions, promotes cognitive reserve.[26] Studies have shown that those who have trained in music for 10 or more years have much improved memory, executive functioning, and visual-spatial abilities as they age.[27] These effects have been linked to distinct neural pathways, which have been identified. It has also been discovered that these people are less likely to experience dementia or cognitive impairment. Dancing has been associated with improved learning and memory over the lifespan.[28] Dance has been demonstrated to enhance functional improvements in balance and attention by increasing hippocampus volume, white matter integrity, and levels of neurotrophic factors. In a method of psychotherapy called SACBT (spiritually augmented cognitive behavior therapy), developed in Australia, a patient is guided through different phases. It begins by examining the concept of birth and death, followed by the next stage of letting go of anxiety and desensitizing to mortality. Then the client's lifestyle choices are reflected upon that keep them from facing death and feed their anxiety. The last stage asks one to examine and accept their life's journey, by focusing on pursuing a divine purpose.

Stigma Reduction

The stigma attached to specific medical illnesses has been lessened via the use of the arts. Empathy, inclusivity, and mental health literacy have all been enhanced by arts initiatives in schools.[29] It has been discovered that arts festivals foster a more favorable perception of mental health, as well as a greater understanding of the skills and creativity of those who suffer from mental illness.

Songwriting has been shown to lower levels of experienced stigma, self-stigma, and total stigma in mental health inpatient facilities.[30] The use of the arts to destigmatize mental illness appears to be increasing, as evidenced by patterns in national press articles. This includes dispelling the myth that people with mental illness cannot work, highlighting the importance of the arts in promoting employment and removing barriers between people with and without mental illness.

Rehabilitation and Recovery

The arts can offer additional support to conventional psychological and pharmaceutical therapies. In the aftermath of invasive and surgical treatments, the arts can facilitate recovery. Following a knee replacement, listening to music during physiotherapy lead to improved flexibility, as well as a decrease in perceived exertion and weariness.[31]

In a multicentric study at the psychiatry department of Vellore, Chennai, and Lucknow the variables influencing the course and outcome of schizophrenia were studied. A 2- and 5-year follow-up revealed that patients with higher rates of religious participation also generally had better prognoses.[32] A spiritual caregiver is an integral part of the interdisciplinary team in most hospitals, particularly in palliative care.

CONCLUSION

Among the various definitions and theories of creativity discussed in this chapter the four-C model proposed by Kauffman is critical to understand as it discusses the self-transformative effects of creativity (mini c). Creativity focusses on an individual's growth and helps one to utilize their potential to create something tangible, useful and productive for the society. Although the concept of spirituality is broad but it is not entirely secular. There is a component of religiosity associated with it. Whereas creativity is completely a secular endeavor that has a significant role in promoting positive mental health. The available literature highlights the fact that more research is required to understand the socio-cultural dimensions of creativity and their role in psychiatry.

The neurobiology of creativity highlights the role of default mode network, prefrontal cortex, reward pathway along with other structures and neurotransmitters in the process of creativity which overlaps to some extent with neurobiology of spirituality too. In the light of the proposed mental health dividends, it can be said that creative pursuits can be explored as an alternative to spiritual pursuits.

REFERENCES

1. Nancy A. The Creative Brain. New York: Plume, Penguin Group, USA Inc.; 2006.
2. Mayo KR. Creativity, Spirituality, and Mental Health: Exploring Connections. 1st edition. London: Routledge; 2009.
3. Plucker J, Beghetto RA, Dow G. Why isn't creativity more important to educational psychologists? Potential, pitfalls, and future directions in creativity research. Educational Psychologist. 2004;39:83-96.
4. Kaufman AB, Butt AE, Kaufman JC, Colbert-White EN. Towards a neurobiology of creativity in nonhuman animals. J Comp Psychol. 2011;125(3):255-72.
5. Csikszentmihályi M. The domain of creativity. In: Runco MA, Albert RS (Eds). Theories of creativity. Sage Publications, Inc.; 1990. pp. 190-212.
6. Kaufman JC, Beghetto RA. Beyond big and little: The four C model of creativity. Rev General Psychol. 2009;13:1-12.
7. Frankl VE. Man's search for ultimate meaning. Random House; 2011. p. 34.

8. Wallas G. Art of Thought. New York, NY: Harcourt, Brace and Company; 1926.
9. Boccia M, Piccardi L, Palermo L, Nori R, Palmiero M. Where do bright ideas occur in our brain? Meta-analytic evidence from neuroimaging studies of domain-specific creativity. Front Psychol. 2015;6:1195.
10. Nijstad BA, De Dreu CKW, Rietzschel EF, Baas M. The dual pathway to creativity model: creative ideation as a function of flexibility and persistence. Eur Rev Soc Psychol. 2010;21:34-77.
11. Andreasen NC. A journey into chaos: creativity and the unconscious. Mens Sana Monogr. 2011;9(1):42-53.
12. Jung RE, Segall JM, Jeremy Bockholt H, Flores RA, Smith SM, Chavez RS, et al. Neuroanatomy of creativity. Human Brain Map. 2010;31:398-409.
13. Heilman KM. Possible Brain Mechanisms of Creativity. Arch Clin Neuropsychol. 2016; 31(4):285-96.
14. Barrett AM, Beversdorf DQ, Crucian GP, Heilman KM. Neglect after right hemisphere stroke: A smaller floodlight for distributed attention. Neurology. 1998;51:972-8.
15. Khalil R, Godde B, Karim AA. The Link Between Creativity, Cognition, and Creative Drives and Underlying Neural Mechanisms. Front Neural Circuits. 2019;22:13:18.
16. Takeuchi H, Taki Y, Hashizume H, Sassa Y, Nagase T, Nouchi R, et al. The association between resting functional connectivity and creativity. Cereb Cortex. 2012;22:2921-9.
17. Bittner JV, Bruena M, Rietzschel EF. Cooperation goals, regulatory focus, and their combined effects on creativity. Think. Ski. Creat. 2016;19:260-8.
18. Kumar V. Mental health dividends of creative pursuits. Indian J Psychiatry. 2023; 65(11):1087-95.
19. Moreno JL. Theory of spontaneity-creativity. Sociometry. 1955;18(4):105-18.
20. Fancourt D, Finn S. What is the Evidence on the Role of the Arts in Improving Health and Well-Being? A Scoping Review. Copenhagen: WHO Regional Office for Europe; 2019.
21. Rochette F, Moussard A, Bigand E. Music lessons improve auditory perceptual and cognitive performance in deaf children Front Hum Neurosci. 2014;8:488.
22. Flaugnacco E, Lopez L, Terribili C, Montico M, Zoia S, Schön D. Music training increases phonological awareness and reading skills in developmental dyslexia: a randomized control trial PLOS One. 2015;10(9):e0138715.
23. Barnes J. Drama to promote social and personal well-being in six- and seven-year-olds with communication difficulties: the speech bubbles project. Perspect Public Health. 2014;134(2):101-9.
24. Mendelson J, White Y, Hans L, Adebari R. A preliminary investigation of a specialized music therapy model for children with disabilities delivered in a classroom setting. Autism Res Treat. 2016;2016:1284790.
25. Cogo-Moreira H, Brandão de Ávila CR, Ploubidis GB, Mari Jde J. Effectiveness of music education for the improvement of reading skills and academic achievement in young poor readers: a pragmatic cluster-randomized, controlled clinical trial. PLOS One. 20138(3)e59984.
26. Strong JV, Mast BT. The cognitive functioning of older adult instrumental musicians and non-musicians. Neuropsychol Dev Cogn B Aging Neuropsychol Cogn. 2018;26(3): 367-86.
27. Stern Y. What is cognitive reserve? Theory and research application of the reserve concept. J Int Neuropsychol Soc. 2002;8(3):448-60.
28. Porat S, Goukasian N, Hwang KS, Zanto T, Do T, Pierce J, et al. Dance experience and associations with cortical gray matter thickness in the aging population Dement Geriatr Cogn Dis Extra. 20166(3):508-17.
29. Campos L, Dias P, Duarte A, Veiga E, Dias CC, Palha F. Is it possible to "find space for mental health" in young people? Effectiveness of a school-based mental health literacy promotion program. Int J Environ Res Public Health. 201815(7):1426.
30. Silverman MJ. Effects of music therapy on self- and experienced stigma in patients on an acute care psychiatric unit: a randomized three group effectiveness study. Arch Psychiatr Nurs. 2013;27(5):223-30.

31. Hsu CC, Chen WM, Chen SR, Tseng YT, Lin PC. Effectiveness of music listening in patients with total knee replacement during CPM rehabilitation Biol Res Nurs. 2016;18(1):68-75.
32. Verghese A, John JK, Rajkumar S, Richard J, Sethi BB, Trivedi JK. Factors associated with the course and outcome of schizophrenia: results of a five year follow up study. Br J Psychiatry. 1990;32:211-16.

3 CHAPTER

Spirituality and Sexuality: Some Insights

Pooja Vora, Sathyanarayana Rao TS, Avinash De Sousa

INTRODUCTION

Sexuality and spirituality are two deeply personal and complex aspects of human experience that often intersect and influence each other in various ways. Spirituality, broadly defined, refers to the search for meaning, purpose, and connection to something greater than oneself. It can involve religious beliefs and practices, but it can also encompass a sense of awe, wonder, and transcendence that may not be tied to any specific religious tradition. Sexuality, on the other hand, encompasses a person's sexual orientation, desires, behaviors, and identity. It is a fundamental aspect of human nature that influences relationships, intimacy, and personal fulfillment. The intersection of sexuality and spirituality can take many forms, viz., like different religious traditions have various perspectives on sexuality. Some may view sexuality as sacred and emphasize the importance of sexual expression within the bounds of marriage or committed relationships, while others may impose strict rules and taboos regarding sexual behavior.

SPIRITUALITY

Some people may discover that their spiritual life is inextricably related to their involvement with a church, temple, mosque, or synagogue. People may pray or seek consolation in a personal connection with God or a higher force while others seek meaning via their ties with nature or art. A person's own concept of spirituality, like your sense of purpose, may evolve over time to reflect your unique experiences and connections.[1]

There is a broad definition of spirituality, stating that it is a vast concept with many different interpretations. The definition encompasses a sense of belonging to something greater than ourselves, as well as a desire for purpose in life. People may characterize a spiritual encounter as sacred, sublime, or just a profound sense of aliveness and connectivity.[2]

Some academics describe spirituality in a different way where "Spirituality is the aspect of humanity that refers to the way individuals seek and express meaning and purpose, as well as the way they experience their connectedness to the moment, to self, to others, to nature, and to the significant or sacred."[3] It is also defined as "any experience that is thought to bring the experiencer into contact with the divine" (rather than merely any experience that feels important).[4] Yet another definition mentions that "the spiritual dimension aspires to be in harmony with the cosmos, and looks for answers concerning the infinite, and comes into focus when the individual experiences emotional stress, physical disease, or death."[5]

In psychology, the theory of spirituality encompasses various perspectives and approaches. Some psychologists view spirituality as a fundamental aspect of human experience that contributes to psychological well-being and fulfillment. Others study spirituality in the context of its influence on mental health, coping mechanisms, and resilience in the face of adversity.[6]

One prominent theory in psychology is the concept of "spiritual well-being," which emphasizes the importance of spirituality in promoting holistic health and functioning. According to this theory, spiritual well-being consists of several dimensions, including a sense of meaning and purpose in life, a connection to something greater than oneself, inner peace, and the ability to transcend personal challenges.[7]

Psychologists may also explore the role of spirituality in coping with stress, trauma, and grief, as well as its relationship to positive psychological traits such as compassion, gratitude, and forgiveness. Additionally, research in this area may examine the psychological benefits of spiritual practices such as meditation, prayer, and mindfulness. Overall, the theory of spirituality in psychology recognizes the significance of spiritual beliefs and experiences in shaping human behavior, emotions, and relationships, and seeks to understand their impact on mental health and well-being.[8]

SEXUALITY

According to the American Psychological Association (APA), sex is commonly used to describe the features and attributes of biological sex. Sex specifically refers to anatomical and biological characteristics, whereas gender relates to social or cultural characteristics. Sex may also refer to the physiological and psychological processes associated with reproduction and sexual pleasure.[9]

Sexuality refers to all elements of sexual behavior, including gender identity, orientation, attitudes, and actions. APA defines sexuality as:[10]

- The capacity to derive pleasure from various forms of sexual activity and behavior, particularly from sexual intercourse.
- All aspects of sexual behavior, including gender identity, orientation, attitudes, and activity.
- In classical psychoanalytic theory, the "organ pleasure" derived from all erogenous zones and processes of the body, including the mouth, anus, urethra, breasts, skin, muscles, and genital organs, as well as such functions as sucking, biting, eating, defecating, urinating, masturbating, and having intercourse.

Sexuality may be seen from a variety of viewpoints, including historical, biological, cross-species, cross-cultural, psychological, and sociological. History contextualizes sexual activity, and there is scant evidence of universal sexual tendencies across the ages. Prehistoric evidence suggests that female idols and the penis were worshipped as symbols of fertility and reproductive power. Jews and Christians have highlighted the function of sex in procreation, followed by the setting of family life (marriage). Ancient Greek and Roman cultures were male-oriented, with women viewed as chattel.[11] In several Eastern civilizations, sexual outlets have been linked to religious experiences. They also developed sexual guides such as the Kama Sutra. Repressed Victorian sexual views gave way to the sexual revolution in the West throughout the 1960s and 1970s.[12]

Another approach, known as the biological perspective, states that biological processes such as genetic, hormonal, vascular, and neurological components are employed to explain human sexual behavior. Rapid strides have been made in the detailed neurobiology of sexual function but there is definitely an overlay of social and psychological factors.[13]

Psychological views examine elements such as perception, learning, motivation, emotion, and personality that impact an individual's sexual behavior. Sigmund Freud's psychoanalytic theory suggested that the biological sex urge conflicts with societal standards. Defense systems keep threatening ideas and impulses out of the conscious mind as the person progresses through the phases of psychosexual development. Learning theories explain sexual behavior via classical or operant conditioning, which includes the roles of reward, punishment, and modeling.[14]

Spiritual Practice in Sexuality

For many people, sexuality serves several objectives. On the surface, it provides physical pleasure and relief, but that is not all. It can also help people connect emotionally, resulting in greater closeness and trust. Some people go even further, believing that sex is not just a physical and emotional experience, but also a spiritual one.[15]

Spiritual sex has various definitions, just as spirituality does. Some individuals regard spiritual sex to be inextricably linked to their religious practices. Others regard it as a distinct set of spiritual practices, also known as Tantric sex. Others consider it simply as a method of having sex that leads to a deeper, more spiritually satisfying relationship with a partner.[16]

Some spiritual practices incorporate sexuality as a pathway to spiritual growth and enlightenment. Tantra, for example, is a spiritual tradition that embraces sexuality as a means of connecting with the divine. Individuals may integrate their sexuality and spirituality based on their personal beliefs and values. For some, sexuality may be seen as a natural and integral part of the human experience, while others may struggle with feelings of guilt or shame due to religious teachings. Some spiritual practices, such as mindfulness meditation or energy work, may be used to explore and heal issues related to sexuality.

Tantric sex and spiritual sex are both approaches to intimacy that emphasize a deeper connection between partners, but they have distinct differences in philosophy and practice. Spiritual sex is a broader concept that encompasses any approach to sexuality that is infused with spiritual meaning, intention, and connection. While it may draw inspiration from tantric principles, spiritual sex is not limited to any specific tradition or set of practices. It emphasizes emotional intimacy, trust, and mutual respect between partners, as well as a sense of reverence for the sacredness of the sexual experience. Spiritual sex can involve practices such as mindfulness, communication, and the cultivation of love and compassion.[17]

On the other hand, tantric sex originates from ancient Hindu and Buddhist traditions and is rooted in the belief that sexual energy is a powerful force that can be harnessed for spiritual growth and enlightenment.[18]

Spiritual practice in sexuality involves incorporating spiritual principles, mindfulness, and intention into sexual experiences to deepen connection, intimacy, and personal growth. It encompasses a wide range of practices and beliefs from various spiritual traditions, as well as individual interpretations and explorations of the sacred nature of sexuality.[19]

There are myths and misconceptions concerning spiritual sex. Spiritual sex, contrary to popular belief, is not associated with any one faith. While some types of spiritual sex are associated with various religious traditions, anybody can have spiritual sex. There are writings by intellectuals from a wide range of religions that promote spiritual sex as not just conceivable, but essential components of personal religious devotion. Spiritual sex is never obligatory, but it is a choice regardless of your beliefs. Indeed, research suggests that persons who identify as spiritual may be more inclined to engage in sexual activity on a regular basis.[20]

Sexuality and Religion

According to Hindu custom, a husband should only sexually contact his wife during her *ritu* (season), which lasts sixteen days throughout the menstrual cycle. However, intercourse is prohibited on 6 of these 16 days: The first four, as well as the eleventh and thirteenth.[21] Religion is a complex entity that includes individual and collective actions (e.g., prayer), cognition (e.g., theology and beliefs), emotions (e.g., joy and peace), and motives (e.g., intrinsic vs. extrinsic). Sexism is based on three beliefs: Paternalism (the ideology of male supremacy), binary gender differentiation (the view that men and women are fundamentally different), and heteronormativity (the norm of heterosexual love interactions). Sexism is a complex concept with both negative and positive aspects. Benevolent sexism includes a condescending attitude, the idealization of conventional gender norms, and women's reliance on male protection/nurturance. In contrast, hostile sexism is characterized by hostility and anger against women who are believed to be challenging male dominance or traditional gender norms. Sexism is often promoted by religious groups and theological systems, while such views can exist independently. Sexist views are typically linked to discrimination based on sexual orientation.[22]

The relationship between sexuality and religion is a topic of profound significance, reflecting the intricate interplay between cultural, moral, and spiritual dimensions of human experience. Throughout history, religions have exerted considerable influence on attitudes, beliefs, and practices related to sexuality, shaping societal norms and individual behaviors. This essay examines the diverse perspectives and approaches to sexuality within several major world religions, highlighting the complexity and richness of this intersection.[20]

Christianity has historically played a pivotal role in shaping Western attitudes toward sexuality. Traditional Christian teachings emphasize values such as chastity, monogamy, and marital fidelity, viewing sexual relations within the context of heterosexual marriage as morally permissible and sacred.[23]

In Islam, sexuality is regarded as a natural and integral aspect of human life, with guidelines provided in religious texts such as the Quran and Hadith. Islamic teachings emphasize the sanctity of marriage and advocate for modesty, fidelity, and mutual respect between spouses. Hinduism has a rich and diverse approach to sexuality, influenced by various texts, traditions, and cultural practices. The ancient texts known as the Vedas contain hymns celebrating the sacredness of sexuality and fertility.[20]

Buddhism teaches that desire and attachment are sources of suffering, including sexual desire. However, Buddhism does not inherently condemn sexuality, instead emphasizing ethical conduct, mindfulness, and moderation in all aspects of life, including sexuality.[24]

The intersection of sexuality and religion is characterized by diverse perspectives, beliefs, and practices that reflect the complexity of human sexuality and the diversity of religious traditions. While religious teachings often provide moral guidance and ethical frameworks for sexual conduct, individual and cultural factors play significant roles in shaping attitudes and behaviors related to sexuality within religious communities. Ultimately, the exploration of sexuality within the context of religions offers insights into the multifaceted nature of human experience and the ways in which spirituality intersects with intimate aspects of life.[25]

A growing body of research shows that religions have a significant impact on people's and families' economic, demographic, marital, and sexual behavior, spanning from work patterns to fertility and marriage stability. Religion has been recognized as a complementing attribute in the context of marriage, for which positive forceful mating is preferred. Religion has also been shown to influence one's choice of a marriage partner. Religion has been shown to influence sexual behavior patterns, views regarding pregnancy and premarital sex, desired fertility, and the division of work among partners throughout the life cycle. The current chapter examines the influence of various Indian religious notions on marriage and sexuality from an Indian perspective.[26]

Religion and Spirituality and Sexual Practice

Emerging adulthood can be a period of discernment and meaning-making, with many young people seeking to establish religious and/or spiritual identities and integrating these domains with other important aspects of identity and behavior, such as interpersonal relationships and sexuality. Religion and spirituality play significant roles in shaping attitudes, beliefs, and practices related to sexuality. While often intertwined, religion and spirituality can also diverge in their influence on sexual behavior, reflecting diverse interpretations of sacred texts, cultural norms, and individual experiences. There is a complex interplay between religion, spirituality, and sexual practice, highlighting both the converging and diverging perspectives within different religious and spiritual traditions.[27]

Religion, as an organized system of beliefs and practices, often provides moral frameworks and ethical guidelines regarding sexual behavior. Many religions prescribe norms and rules governing sexuality, such as prohibitions on premarital sex, adultery, and homosexuality, while also promoting ideals of chastity, fidelity, and procreation within the context of heterosexual marriage. For example, Christianity traditionally upholds monogamous heterosexual marriage as the ideal expression of sexuality, emphasizing values of purity and marital fidelity. Similarly, Islam emphasizes modesty, marital fidelity, and respect for one's spouse, with Sharia providing detailed regulations regarding sexual conduct.[28]

However, religious teachings on sexuality are not monolithic and can vary widely among different denominations, cultural contexts, and historical periods. Within Christianity, for instance, interpretations of biblical teachings on sexuality range from conservative to liberal perspectives, with some denominations affirming lesbian, gay, bisexual, and transgender (LGBTQ+) identities and relationships, while others maintain more traditional views. Likewise, within Islam, interpretations of Sharia can vary, with some advocating for more progressive understandings of sexuality, while others adhere to more conservative interpretations.[29]

Spirituality, on the other hand, encompasses a broader and more individualized approach to the search for meaning, purpose, and connection with the divine or transcendent aspects of existence. While spirituality may draw inspiration from religious traditions, it is not necessarily bound by organized religion or specific doctrines. In the realm of sexuality, spirituality emphasizes themes such as intimacy, mindfulness, and sacredness, viewing sexual experiences as opportunities for personal growth, healing, and spiritual connection.[17]

Spiritual practices related to sexuality often involve cultivating mindfulness and presence during sexual encounters, focusing on the connection between partners and the deeper dimensions of intimacy beyond physical pleasure.[30] Practices such as tantra, which originated from Hindu and Buddhist traditions, seek to harness sexual energy for spiritual awakening and transformation. Tantra emphasizes the integration of mind, body, and spirit in sexual experiences, with rituals, meditations, and breathwork designed to deepen intimacy and spiritual connection between partners.[18]

Moreover, spirituality encourages individuals to explore their own beliefs, values, and desires in relation to sexuality, without necessarily conforming to external religious norms or moral codes. It promotes self-awareness, self-acceptance, and authenticity in sexual expression, allowing individuals to cultivate healthy and fulfilling relationships based on mutual respect, consent, and love. In summary, the intersection of religion, spirituality, and sexual practice is complex and multifaceted, reflecting the diversity of human experiences and interpretations. While religion often provides moral guidance and ethical frameworks for sexual behavior, spirituality offers a more individualized and holistic approach, emphasizing personal growth, connection, and authenticity in sexual relationships. Both religion and spirituality contribute to the rich tapestry of human sexuality, shaping attitudes, beliefs, and practices in profound and nuanced ways.[31]

Mindfulness and Sexuality

Maintaining a fulfilling love relationship and sex life benefits both physical and mental health. Researchers have investigated the role of trait mindfulness in improving healthy sexual relationships by increasing intimacy[32,33] and decreasing cognitive distraction,[34] which may contribute to overall well-being.[35]

Despite previous studies on trait mindfulness and romantic and sexual relationships, less attention has been paid to sexual mindfulness, a subset of state mindfulness that may be more directly associated with partnerships. Practicing sexual mindfulness, or remaining mindful during sex in particular, a context that is frequently fraught with anxiety,[36] may necessitate a greater application of attention and nonjudgment than practicing mindfulness in other less stressful situations. For example, being aware while doing yoga differs from keeping mindfulness while having sex.

One of the key benefits of mindfulness in sexuality is its ability to counteract distractions and mental chatter that often interfere with sexual pleasure and connection. In our fast-paced world, individuals may find it challenging to be fully present during sexual encounters, as thoughts about work, relationships, or daily concerns intrude on the moment. Mindfulness helps individuals to redirect their attention to the sensations and experiences unfolding in the present, allowing for a more profound engagement with sexual experience.[37]

Moreover, mindfulness can help individuals to become more attuned to their own bodies and desires, facilitating a greater sense of self-awareness and self-acceptance in sexual expression. By tuning into bodily sensations and signals of pleasure, individuals can learn to honor their own needs and preferences, thereby enhancing their ability to communicate and advocate for their desires within intimate relationships.[38]

In addition to enhancing individual well-being, mindfulness in sexuality also promotes deeper connection and intimacy between partners. By fostering present-moment awareness and attunement to each other's needs and desires, mindfulness creates a supportive environment for open communication, trust, and vulnerability in sexual relationships. Partners who practice mindfulness together can experience a greater sense of connection and shared intimacy, leading to more fulfilling and satisfying sexual experiences.[39]

Several practices can help individuals incorporate mindfulness into their sexual experiences. Mindful breathing, for example, involves focusing on the breath as a way to anchor attention in the present moment during sexual encounters. By paying attention to the rhythm and sensation of the breath, individuals can cultivate a sense of calm and presence, enhancing their ability to connect with their bodies and their partners.[40]

Body scanning is another mindfulness practice that can be applied to sexuality, involving systematically bringing awareness to different parts of the body during sexual activity. By scanning the body for sensations of pleasure or tension, individuals can deepen their embodied awareness and enhance their capacity for sexual enjoyment.[41]

Additionally, mindfulness meditation can be a valuable tool for cultivating present-moment awareness and reducing distractions during sexual encounters. Regular meditation practice can help individuals develop the skills needed to stay grounded and focused amidst the sensory stimulation of sexual activity, leading to more fulfilling and satisfying experiences.[42]

Mindfulness offers a transformative approach to sexuality that fosters deeper connection, intimacy, and satisfaction in sexual relationships. By cultivating present-moment awareness and attunement to bodily sensations, thoughts, and emotions, individuals can enhance their capacity for pleasure, communication, and intimacy in sexual encounters. Through mindfulness practices such as mindful breathing, body scanning, and meditation, individuals can develop the skills needed to fully engage with their sexuality and cultivate more fulfilling sexual experiences.[42]

CONCLUSION

The relationship between sexuality and spirituality is deeply personal and varies significantly from individual to individual. For some, sexuality enriches their spiritual practice, fostering a deeper connection with themselves and the divine. For others, reconciling the two can be challenging, reflecting the complexity of personal beliefs and experiences. It is crucial for individuals to explore their own values, beliefs, and experiences to cultivate a balanced and authentic relationship with both their sexuality and spirituality.

Integrating spirituality and sexuality involves recognizing both as interconnected aspects of the human experience, emphasizing personal growth, connection, and transcendence. This approach views sexuality as a sacred and profound dimension of life—a potential pathway to spiritual enlightenment and deeper intimacy with oneself, others, and the divine.

Clinicians often encourage mindfulness and presènce during sexual experiences, highlighting how such practices can deepen intimacy and foster a stronger emotional and spiritual connection with a partner. Spirituality, in this context, aims to unify the physical, emotional, mental, and spiritual facets of life, acknowledging that sexuality is not separate from spirituality but an integral part of it.

While some individuals may find spiritual fulfillment through traditional religious teachings, others may be drawn to more esoteric or alternative pathways. Ultimately, integrating sexuality and spirituality is about honoring the sacredness of sexuality and embracing its potential as a catalyst for personal and spiritual growth. This holistic approach underscores the transformative power of embracing one's full humanity.

REFERENCES

1. Chiu L, Emblen JD, Van Hofwegen L, Sawatzky R, Meyerhoff H. An integrative review of the concept of spirituality in the health sciences. West J Nurs Res. 2004;26(4):405-28.
2. McBrien B. A concept analysis of spirituality. Br J Nursing. 2006;15(1):42-5.
3. Puchalski C. Spirituality in health: the role of spirituality in critical care. Critical care clinics. 2004;20(3):487-504.
4. Beauregard M, O'Leary D. The spiritual brain: A neuroscientist's case for the existence of the soul. HarperOne/HarperCollins.
5. Lepherd L. Spirituality: Everyone has it, but what is it? Int J Nurs Pract. 2015;21(5):566-74.
6. Gottlieb RS. Spirituality: What it is and why it matters. Oxford: Oxford University Press; 2013.
7. Gomez R, Fisher JW. Domains of spiritual well-being and development and validation of the spiritual well-being questionnaire. Personality and individual differences. 2003; 35(8):1975-991.
8. Rowold J. Effects of spiritual well-being on subsequent happiness, psychological well-being, and stress. J Relig Health. 2011;50(4): 950-63.
9. Ader DN, Johnson SB. Sample description, reporting, an analysis of sex in psychological research: A look at APA and APA division journals in 1990. Am Psychol. 1994;49(3):216.
10. Weeks J (Ed). Sexuality. New York: Routledge; 2022.
11. Okechi OS. The indigenous concept of sexuality in African tradition and globalization. Global J Reprod Med. 2018;6(1):1-5.
12. Das K, Rao TSS. A chronicle of sexuality in the Indian subcontinent. J Psychosexual Health. 2019;1(1):20-5.
13. Rowland DL. Neurobiology of sexual response in men and women. CNS Spectrums. 2006;11(S9):6-12.
14. Lehmiller JJ. Cognitive-behavioral and learning theories. The Psychology of Human Sexuality, 2nd edition. Wiley-Blackwell, 2017; p. 472.
15. MacKnee CM. Peak sexual and spiritual experience: Exploring the mystical relationship. Theol Sexual. 1996;3(5):97-115.
16. Wilber K. Sex, ecology, spirituality: The spirit of evolution. Shambhala Publications; 2001.
17. Luquis RR, Brelsford GM, Rojas-Guyler L. Religiosity, spirituality, sexual attitudes, and sexual behaviours among college students. J Relig Health. 2012;51(3):601-4.
18. In: White DG (Ed). Kiss of the yogini: "Tantric sex" in its South Asian contexts. University of Chicago Press; 2003.
19. Horn MJ, Piedmont RL, Fialkowski GM, Wicks RJ, Hunt ME. Sexuality and spirituality: The embodied spirituality scale. Theol Sexual. 2005;12(1):81-101.
20. Mahajan PT, Pimple P, Palsetia D, Dave N, De Sousa A. Indian religious concepts on sexuality and marriage. Indian J Psychiatr. 2013;55(Suppl 2):S256-62.
21. Chakraborty K, Thakurata RG. Indian concepts on sexuality. Indian J Psychiatr. 2013;55(Suppl 2):S250-5.

22. Thomas L. Sexism and racism: Some conceptual differences. Ethics. 1980;90(2): 239-50.
23. Newheiser, D. Sexuality and Christian tradition: Innovation and fidelity, ancient and modern. J Relig Ethics. 2015;43(1):122-45.
24. In: Faure B (Ed). The red thread: Buddhist approaches to sexuality. New Jersey: Princeton University Press; 1998.
25. Turner Y, Stayton W. The twenty-first century challenges to sexuality and religion. J Relig Health. 2014;53(2):483-97.
26. Marks L. How does religion influence marriage? Christian, Jewish, Mormon, and Muslim perspectives. Marriage Family Rev. 2005;38(1):85-111.
27. Allen KR, Brooks JE. At the intersection of sexuality, spirituality, and gender: Young adults' perceptions of religious beliefs in the context of sexuality education. American J Sexual Educat. 2012;7(4):285-308.
28. Tuttle JD, Davis SN. Religion, infidelity, and divorce: Re-examining the effect of religious behavior on divorce among long-married couples. J Divorce Remarriage. 2015; 56(6):475-89.
29. Beagan BL, Hattie B. Religion, spirituality, and LGBTQ identity integration. Journal of LGBT Issues in Counseling. 2015;9(2):92-117.
30. Das K, Rao TSS. A chronicle of sexuality in the Indian subcontinent. J Psychosexual Health. 2019;1(1):20-5.
31. Cranney S. The influence of religiosity/ spirituality on sex life satisfaction and sexual frequency: Insights from the Baylor religion survey. Rev Relig Res. 2020;62(2):289-314.
32. Lucas M. Rewire your brain for love: Creating vibrant relationships using the science of mindfulness. United Kingdom: Hay House.
33. Metz ME, McCarthy BW. The "Good-Enough Sex" model for couple sexual satisfaction. Sexual and Relationship Therapy. 2007; 22(3):351-62.
34. Newcombe BC, Weaver AD. Mindfulness, cognitive distraction, and sexual well-being in women. Can J Hum Sex. 2016;25(2):99-108.
35. Chang YC, Lin GM, Yeh TL, Chang YM, Yang CH, Lo C, et al. Impact of mindfulness-based stress reduction on female sexual function and mental health in patients with breast cancer. Supportive Care in Cancer. 2022; 30(5):4315-25.
36. Barnes S, Brown KW, Krusemark E, Campbell WK, Rogge RD. The role of mindfulness in romantic relationship satisfaction and responses to relationship stress. J Marit Fam Ther. 2007;33(4):482-500.
37. Lazaridou A, Kalogianni C. Mindfulness and sexuality. Sex Relationsh Ther. 2013;28(1-2): 29-38.
38. Pepping CA, Cronin TJ, Lyons A, Caldwell JG. The effects of mindfulness on sexual outcomes: The role of emotion regulation. Arch Sex Behav. 2018;47(6):1601-12.
39. Vilarinho S. Management of sexual problems: the approach of mindfulness. Curr Opin Psychiatry. 2017;30(6):402-8.
40. Mize SJ. A review of mindfulness-based sex therapy interventions for sexual desire and arousal difficulties: From research to practice. Current Sexual Health Reports. 2015;7(2):89-97.
41. Jaderek I, Lew-Starowicz M. A systematic review on mindfulness meditation-based interventions for sexual dysfunctions. J Sex Med. 2019;16(10):1581-96.
42. Brotto LA. Mindful sex. The Canadian Journal of Human Sexuality. 2013;22(2):63-8.

4 CHAPTER

Religion, Spirituality, and Crime

Afzal Javed, Kaustav Chakraborty, Debanjan Banerjee

INTRODUCTION

The relationship between religion and crime is a multifaceted and intricate subject that has captivated the attention of scholars, theologians, and sociologists for centuries. While some argue that religion serves as a moral compass, guiding individuals away from criminal behavior, others contend that it can be a source of conflict, intolerance, and even a justification for illicit activities. In this exploration, we delve into the complex interplay between religion and crime, acknowledging the diverse perspectives that shape this relationship.

RELIGION AS A MORAL COMPASS

One perspective posits that religion acts as a moral compass, instilling a sense of ethics and morality in individuals that discourages criminal behavior. Many religions emphasize principles such as love, compassion, and justice, providing adherents with a framework for ethical decision-making. The teachings of various faiths often promote virtues that contribute to a harmonious and law-abiding society.[1]

For example, the Ten Commandments in Christianity and similar moral codes in other religions explicitly prohibit actions such as theft, murder, and adultery. These moral guidelines are believed to serve as a deterrent against criminal conduct, as individuals are encouraged to live in accordance with their religious teachings.

RELIGIOUS COMMUNITIES AND SOCIAL BONDS

Religious communities can also foster social bonds and support networks that discourage criminal behavior. Participation in religious congregations often provides individuals with a sense of belonging, purpose, and accountability. The community's shared values and collective moral standards create an environment that reinforces positive behavior and discourages criminal tendencies.

Studies have shown that religious involvement is associated with lower rates of crime, with religious communities acting as protective factors against delinquency. The strong social ties within religious groups may create a sense of responsibility and accountability, reducing the likelihood of individuals engaging in criminal activities.

RELIGIOUS CONFLICT AND CRIME

Religion has been a catalyst for conflict throughout history, and in some cases, it has been invoked to justify criminal acts. Religious extremism, fueled by radical interpretations of sacred texts, has led to violence and terrorism in various parts of the world. The intertwining of religious fervor with political ideologies can create a volatile mix, resulting in criminal behavior such as hate crimes, discrimination, and even mass violence.[1]

Rigid religious doctrines that condemn certain lifestyles or beliefs can contribute to the stigmatization of individuals, potentially leading to discrimination and marginalization. In extreme cases, this exclusion may drive individuals toward criminal subcultures in search of acceptance or identity.

Thus, the relationship between religion and crime is complex, influenced by a range of factors that vary across cultures and individuals. While religion can provide a moral compass and foster positive social bonds, it can also act as a divisive force, contributing to conflict and criminal behavior. Recognizing this complexity is crucial for developing a nuanced understanding of the role religion plays in shaping societal attitudes toward crime and morality. Ultimately, the interplay between religion and crime is a dynamic and evolving aspect of human society that warrants ongoing exploration and scholarly inquiry.

Christianity, Islam, Atheism/Secularism, and Hinduism being the four most dominant religions on this planet, we will restrict our discussion to those only. Whatever has been written in this scientific chapter in no way intends to offend any religious community.

RELIGION AND CRIME IN CHRISTIANITY

The relationship between religion and crime within the context of Christianity is a rich and nuanced subject that has been debated throughout history. Christianity, with its diverse denominations and interpretations, presents a complex interplay between faith, morality, and criminal behavior. In this exploration, we delve into the multifaceted dynamics of how Christianity influences attitudes toward crime, examining both the positive aspects, where it serves as a moral guide, and the challenges, where it can be associated with conflicts and justifications for wrongdoing.

Christianity as a Moral Foundation

Christianity, at its core, espouses a set of moral principles and ethical guidelines that are believed to guide adherents away from criminal behavior. Central to this moral foundation are the teachings found in the Bible, particularly in the Old and New Testaments. The Ten Commandments, given to Moses in the Old Testament, outline fundamental moral imperatives such as not committing murder, theft, or adultery. The Sermon on the Mount, as articulated by Jesus in the New Testament, further emphasizes virtues such as humility, compassion, and forgiveness.[2]

Christianity's moral teachings provide a framework for ethical decision-making and encourage believers to lead virtuous lives. The Christian emphasis on love for one's neighbor, charity, and justice creates a foundation that aims to deter individuals from engaging in criminal conduct.

Forgiveness and Rehabilitation

One unique aspect of Christianity's approach to crime is its emphasis on forgiveness and the possibility of rehabilitation. The Christian faith teaches that individuals can seek redemption and forgiveness through repentance and a sincere commitment to change. This perspective encourages a more compassionate view of individuals who have committed crimes, promoting the idea that redemption is achievable.

The parable of the Prodigal Son, for instance, illustrates the theme of forgiveness and reconciliation. This narrative suggests that even those who have strayed from the moral path can find forgiveness and acceptance upon their return. Such teachings may influence Christian communities to support rehabilitation efforts and advocate for a criminal justice system that emphasizes restoration over retribution.

Social Justice and Christian Activism

Many Christian denominations emphasize the call to social justice as an integral part of living out one's faith. The Christian commitment to addressing societal inequities and championing the cause of the marginalized can be a powerful force in reducing crime. Christian activism often involves efforts to address root causes of criminal behavior, such as poverty, inequality, and lack of education.

Historically, Christian leaders like Martin Luther King Jr. have played key roles in advocating for civil rights and challenging systemic injustices. Christian communities that actively engage in social justice initiatives may contribute to creating environments where crime is less likely to flourish.

Challenges and Conflicts within Christianity

Despite its moral teachings, Christianity has also been associated with challenges and conflicts that intersect with criminal behavior. Religious extremism, fueled by radical interpretations of Christian doctrine, has led to instances of violence and terrorism throughout history. The Crusades, for example, represent a dark chapter where religious fervor was harnessed to justify acts of aggression.[2]

Additionally, certain historical periods saw the church wield significant political power, leading to the use of religious doctrine to legitimize actions that would be considered criminal by contemporary standards. The Inquisition and witch trials are examples where religious institutions were directly involved in persecuting individuals, often resulting in harm, torture, or death.

Contemporary Issues and Moral Dilemmas

In the modern context, Christianity grapples with moral dilemmas related to evolving societal norms. Debates around issues such as LGBTQ+ rights, reproductive rights, and capital punishment highlight the tensions between traditional Christian teachings and changing cultural attitudes.

While some Christian denominations advocate for a more inclusive and progressive interpretation of Christian values, others adhere to more conservative views, potentially contributing to societal divisions and conflicts. These tensions can influence attitudes toward certain behaviors and may impact how the church addresses contemporary moral challenges.

In conclusion, the relationship between Christianity and crime is complex, encompassing a spectrum of influences that range from moral guidance to historical conflicts. Christianity's teachings provide a moral foundation that, at its best, encourages virtuous living, forgiveness, and social justice. However, challenges arise when the faith is exploited to justify violence or when its doctrines clash with evolving societal norms.

Understanding the dynamic interplay between Christianity and crime requires a nuanced examination of historical contexts, theological interpretations, and the diverse ways in which Christian communities engage with their faith. By acknowledging both the positive and the challenging aspects of this relationship, we can foster a more comprehensive understanding of how Christianity shapes attitudes toward crime and morality in the contemporary world.

RELIGION AND CRIME IN ISLAM

Islam, as a major world religion, has a profound impact on the moral and ethical framework of its followers. The relationship between Islam and crime is a complex and multifaceted subject that encompasses a wide range of perspectives. In this exploration, we delve into the intricate dynamics of how Islam influences attitudes toward crime, examining the role of Islamic teachings, cultural contexts, and historical influences in shaping the relationship between the religion and criminal behavior.

Islamic Teachings on Morality and Ethics

At the core of Islam are the teachings found in the Quran, the holy book, and the Hadith, the sayings and actions of Prophet Muhammad. These scriptures provide a comprehensive guide to ethical behavior and morality, outlining principles that govern both personal conduct and interactions within society. The Quran emphasizes virtues such as justice, compassion, and honesty, setting a moral standard that aims to guide Muslims away from criminal behavior.[2]

The concept of Ma'ruf (that which is known to be good) and Munkar (that which is known to be evil) plays a central role in Islamic ethics. Muslims are encouraged to enjoin the good and forbid the evil, creating a sense of collective responsibility for upholding moral standards within the community.

Islamic Criminal Law

Islamic criminal law, known as Hudud, is derived from Quranic principles and covers offenses such as theft, adultery, and apostasy. The severity of punishments prescribed in Hudud, such as amputation for theft or stoning for adultery, has been a subject of controversy and debate within and outside the Muslim world. It is important to note that the implementation of Hudud varies widely among Muslim-majority countries, and interpretations may differ among different Islamic legal traditions.

Islamic criminal law also incorporates the concept of Qisas, which allows for retaliation in cases of intentional bodily harm. However, Islam encourages forgiveness, and compensation (*Diyya*) is often considered a more merciful alternative to retaliation.

Forgiveness and Repentance in Islam

One distinctive aspect of Islam is the emphasis on forgiveness and the potential for redemption. The Quran frequently underscores the concept of Taubah (repentance), stating that Allah is oft-forgiving and merciful. The idea that individuals can seek forgiveness for their sins and crimes through sincere repentance aligns with the belief in a compassionate and benevolent deity.

Islamic teachings promote the notion that individuals, regardless of their past actions, can transform their lives through repentance and commitment to righteous conduct. This perspective may influence both the personal attitudes of Muslims toward those who have committed crimes and the approach of Islamic societies to rehabilitation and reintegration.

Islamic Social Justice

Islam places a significant emphasis on social justice and equity. Zakat, one of the Five Pillars of Islam, involves giving a portion of one's wealth to those in need. The concept of Zakat is rooted in the idea of wealth distribution, poverty alleviation, and creating a just society. The pursuit of social justice within an Islamic framework aims to address societal issues that may contribute to criminal behavior, such as poverty and inequality.

Historically, Islamic civilizations have been centers of learning and culture, fostering environments where arts, sciences, and philosophy thrived. The Islamic emphasis on knowledge and wisdom contributes to the development of societies that may be less susceptible to crime due to improved education and opportunities.

Challenges and Extremism

While Islam, as a religion, promotes peace and justice, it has faced challenges with extremism. Radical interpretations of Islamic teachings have been used to justify acts of terrorism and violence. Groups such as Al-Qaeda and ISIS have exploited religious rhetoric to recruit followers and carry out criminal acts in the name of Islam.[2]

It is crucial to recognize that such extremist ideologies are not representative of Islam as a whole, and the majority of Muslims vehemently reject acts of terrorism. However, the association between Islam and violent extremism has created stereotypes and prejudices that can contribute to discrimination against Muslims and exacerbate social tensions.

Cultural Context and Interpretations

The relationship between Islam and crime is also influenced by cultural contexts and diverse interpretations of religious texts. Different Muslim-majority regions may have varying cultural norms and practices that shape the way Islam is understood and applied in daily life. Additionally, the interpretation of Islamic teachings can vary among Sunni and Shia traditions, leading to differences in legal and ethical perspectives.

Muslim scholars and jurists play a crucial role in interpreting Islamic law (Fiqh), adapting it to contemporary contexts, and addressing the evolving challenges faced by Muslim communities globally. The diversity within the Muslim world highlights the importance of understanding the cultural and contextual nuances that shape the relationship between Islam and crime.

Contemporary Challenges and Opportunities

In the contemporary world, Islam faces challenges related to globalization, modernity, and cultural diversity. Issues such as women's rights, freedom of expression, and LGBTQ+ rights can create tensions between traditional Islamic teachings and evolving societal norms.

However, many Muslim scholars and intellectuals engage in ongoing dialogues to reconcile Islamic principles with contemporary values. Progressive interpretations of Islam seek to emphasize its underlying principles of justice, compassion, and equality, aligning them with the aspirations of a globalized and interconnected world.

In conclusion, the relationship between Islam and crime is a complex interplay of religious teachings, cultural influences, historical contexts, and individual interpretations. Islam provides a moral framework that aims to guide Muslims toward virtuous conduct, emphasizing justice, compassion, and forgiveness. However, challenges arise when religious teachings are misinterpreted, leading to extremism and violence.

Understanding the intricate dynamics of Islam and crime requires a nuanced examination of both the foundational principles of the faith and the diverse ways in which these principles are interpreted and applied across different cultures and communities. By acknowledging the complexities within Islam and fostering informed discussions, we can contribute to a more comprehensive understanding of how the religion shapes attitudes toward crime in the contemporary world.

RELIGION AND CRIME IN HINDUISM

Hinduism, one of the world's oldest religions, is a complex tapestry of beliefs, practices, and cultural diversity. The relationship between Hinduism and crime is influenced by a rich blend of religious scriptures, philosophical traditions, and cultural nuances. In this exploration, we delve into the multifaceted dynamics of how Hinduism shapes attitudes toward crime, examining the role of religious teachings, ethical principles, and sociocultural context in defining this relationship.

Dharma and Moral Guidance

At the heart of Hinduism lies the concept of Dharma, a multifaceted term that encompasses duty, righteousness, and moral order. The Hindu scriptures, including the Vedas, Upanishads, and epics like the Mahabharata and Ramayana, provide a guide to righteous living and moral conduct. Dharma serves as a moral compass, guiding individuals toward virtuous behavior and discouraging actions that may be deemed criminal or unethical.[2]

The Bhagavad Gita, a revered scripture in Hinduism, presents a dialogue between Lord Krishna and the warrior Arjuna, exploring themes of duty, righteousness, and the nature of existence. The teachings of the Gita emphasize the pursuit of one's duty (*Svadharma*) with detachment and a focus on righteousness.

Ahimsa and Nonviolence

Ahimsa, the principle of nonviolence, is a cornerstone of Hindu ethics. Rooted in the teachings of Mahatma Gandhi, who drew inspiration from Hindu philosophy, Ahimsa advocates for refraining from causing harm to any living being. The ethical imperative of nonviolence extends beyond physical harm to encompass mental, verbal, and emotional harm.[3]

Ahimsa influences attitudes toward crime by promoting a culture of compassion, empathy, and conflict resolution. The belief in Karma, the law of cause and effect, further reinforces the idea that one's actions have consequences, fostering a sense of responsibility and accountability.

Karma and Consequences

The concept of Karma, central to Hindu philosophy, underscores the idea that individuals reap the consequences of their actions. Positive actions lead to positive outcomes (*Punya*), while negative actions result in negative consequences (*Papa*). This understanding of cause and effect influences Hindu perspectives on crime by emphasizing personal responsibility and the interconnectedness of all beings.

The concept of rebirth and reincarnation in Hinduism adds another layer to the understanding of Karma. Individuals carry forward the consequences of their actions from one life to the next, providing an ethical framework that extends beyond the immediate consequences of criminal behavior.[2]

Legal Frameworks in Hindu Societies

Hinduism, as a religion, does not prescribe a unified legal code. However, legal traditions in Hindu-majority regions have historically been influenced by Dharmashastra, ancient Hindu legal texts that provide guidelines for social and legal conduct. These texts address issues related to marriage, inheritance, and social responsibilities, contributing to the development of legal frameworks within Hindu societies.

In contemporary times, Hindu-majority countries like India have legal systems that draw from a mix of colonial-era laws, modern statutes, and constitutional principles. The legal landscape reflects a diverse society where individuals from various religious and cultural backgrounds coexist, shaping laws that attempt to balance religious values with the principles of justice and equality.

Cultural Context and Caste Dynamics

The relationship between Hinduism and crime is also influenced by cultural contexts and societal structures, including the historical caste system. While Hindu scriptures emphasize the spiritual equality of all individuals, the caste system has, at times, been associated with social inequalities and discrimination. Crime rates and attitudes toward crime may be influenced by socio-economic factors, with marginalized communities facing greater challenges.

Efforts to address social inequalities and uplift marginalized communities are often framed within the broader principles of Dharma and social justice. Hindu reformers and social activists advocate for a more inclusive interpretation of Hindu values to promote social harmony and equity.

Ascetic Traditions and Spiritual Discipline

Hinduism encompasses diverse spiritual traditions, including asceticism and the pursuit of moksha (liberation from the cycle of birth and death). Ascetics, known as sadhus or sannyasis, renounce worldly possessions and live a life of spiritual discipline. While not representative of all Hindus, ascetic traditions contribute to the religious landscape by embodying ideals of simplicity, detachment, and self-discipline.

Asceticism may influence attitudes toward crime by emphasizing the importance of self-control, moderation, and detachment from material desires. The ascetic's commitment to a life of virtue serves as a model for ethical living and may inspire individuals to re-evaluate their own choices and behaviors.

Challenges and Contemporary Dynamics

Hinduism, like any religion, faces challenges in the contemporary world, particularly in the context of globalization, cultural diversity, and changing social norms. Debates around issues such as caste-based discrimination, women's rights, and environmental stewardship require a nuanced examination of Hindu teachings and their relevance in addressing modern challenges.

Interactions between Hinduism and crime may also be influenced by socio-economic disparities, urbanization, and the impact of technology on social behavior. While the foundational principles of Hindu ethics remain relevant, adapting them to address emerging issues is an ongoing process that involves dialogue, reflection, and reinterpretation.

In conclusion, the relationship between Hinduism and crime is shaped by a complex interplay of religious teachings, cultural dynamics, and ethical principles. Hinduism provides a moral framework rooted in concepts such as Dharma, Ahimsa, and Karma, guiding individuals toward virtuous conduct and social responsibility. The diverse cultural contexts within Hindu-majority regions, coupled with ongoing efforts to address social inequalities, contribute to the evolving dynamics of this relationship.

Understanding Hinduism's influence on attitudes toward crime requires a nuanced exploration that considers the diversity of beliefs within the religion, the impact of cultural and historical factors, and the ongoing dialogue within Hindu communities. By navigating this intricate landscape, we can gain insights into how Hindu values contribute to the moral fabric of societies and shape individuals' perspectives on crime in the contemporary world.

ATHEISM AND CRIME

Atheism, the lack of belief in a deity or deities, is a diverse and often misunderstood worldview that encompasses a wide range of perspectives. The relationship between atheism and crime is a complex and nuanced subject that requires careful examination. Unlike religious traditions that often provide explicit moral frameworks, atheism does not inherently prescribe a set of moral guidelines. In this exploration, we delve into the multifaceted dynamics of how atheism intersects with crime, examining the role of individual ethics, societal factors, and the broader cultural context.[4,5]

Individual Ethics and Morality

Atheism, by definition, does not dictate a specific moral code or set of commandments. Instead, atheists derive their ethical principles from a variety of sources, including philosophy, humanism, and personal experiences. The absence of religious doctrine does not imply a lack of moral values among atheists; rather, it highlights the diverse and individualistic nature of ethical frameworks within the atheist community.

Many atheists adhere to secular humanism, a philosophical and ethical stance that prioritizes human well-being, reason, and compassion. Within this framework, ethical decision-making is guided by principles such as empathy, rationality, and a commitment to social justice. Atheists who embrace humanistic values may view criminal behavior as contrary to the well-being of individuals and society at large.

Secular Legal Systems

Countries with a high percentages of atheists or secular populations often have legal systems founded on principles of secularism and equality. Secular legal frameworks aim to provide justice and protect individual rights without reliance on religious doctrine. These systems typically base laws on principles of reason, societal well-being, and the protection of individual liberties.[2]

Secular legal systems do not necessarily imply a higher or lower prevalence of crime; rather, they reflect a commitment to ensuring justice without religious bias. Atheists, like anyone else, are subject to and protected by the laws of their respective secular societies.

Social Factors and Atheist Communities

Atheists, as a diverse group, form communities that vary widely in their values, norms, and social dynamics. Atheist organizations and communities often emphasize critical thinking, scientific inquiry, and free thought. While these principles contribute to a shared identity, they do not necessarily provide a unified moral code, as atheists may differ in their ethical perspectives.

Social factors within atheist communities, such as education, socioeconomic status, and cultural background, can influence criminal behavior. Factors like poverty, lack of access to education, and social inequality may correlate with higher crime rates in some atheist-majority or secular societies. It is important to recognize that these social challenges are not exclusive to atheistic communities but are shared across diverse religious and nonreligious populations.

Philosophical Foundations of Atheism

Atheism, as a philosophical stance, is often associated with critical thinking, skepticism, and a reliance on empirical evidence. Philosophical discussions within atheist circles may explore questions related to morality, ethics, and the nature of right and wrong without relying on divine authority. Atheistic philosophies, such as existentialism or secular ethics, can provide frameworks for individuals to derive their moral principles from human experience and reason.[2]

While atheism itself does not prescribe a particular ethical system, atheists may draw from various philosophical traditions to form their moral perspectives. These philosophical foundations contribute to the diversity of ethical viewpoints within the atheist community.

Cultural Context and Atheism

The relationship between atheism and crime is also influenced by the broader cultural context in which atheism exists. In some societies, atheism may be met with acceptance and tolerance, while in others, it may face social stigma or discrimination. Cultural attitudes toward atheism can shape the experiences and perspectives of atheists within their communities.

In regions where atheism is met with hostility, atheists may face challenges in openly expressing their beliefs, potentially leading to social isolation or stress. It is essential to consider how cultural dynamics and societal attitudes toward atheism may impact individuals' well-being and, by extension, their engagement with criminal behavior.

Moral Development and Atheist Perspectives

Moral development, influenced by factors such as education, upbringing, and personal experiences, plays a significant role in shaping individuals' ethical perspectives, regardless of religious or nonreligious beliefs. Atheists, like religious individuals, undergo processes of moral development that guide their decisions and behaviors.

Psychological studies suggest that moral development is a complex interplay of cognitive, emotional, and social factors. Atheists, influenced by their unique set of experiences, may develop moral principles based on empathy, reciprocity, and societal well-being, contributing to their ethical decision-making.

Atheism and Secular Humanism

Secular humanism, a worldview aligned with atheistic principles, emphasizes human dignity, reason, and ethical values without invoking the divine. Atheists who identify with secular humanism often prioritize the well-being of humanity, equality, and the pursuit of knowledge. Within this framework, criminal behavior may be viewed as a threat to the flourishing of individuals and society.

Secular humanism's emphasis on reason and evidence-based decision-making can contribute to ethical conduct by promoting critical thinking and informed choices. However, it is essential to recognize that adherence to secular humanism is not universal among atheists, and individual perspectives on morality may vary.

Contemporary Challenges and Opportunities

Atheists, like any other group, face contemporary challenges related to societal expectations, discrimination, and the negotiation of ethical values in an interconnected world. Debates around issues such as ethics in technology, bioethics, and environmental stewardship require thoughtful consideration and dialogue within the atheist community.

Efforts to promote secular ethics, human rights, and social justice underscore the potential for atheists to contribute positively to ethical discussions and societal well-being. Engaging in conversations that transcend religious divides can foster understanding and collaboration in addressing common challenges faced by diverse communities.

In conclusion, the relationship between atheism and crime is intricate, influenced by a variety of factors, including individual ethics, societal dynamics, cultural contexts, and philosophical perspectives. Atheism, as a lack of belief in deities, does not inherently prescribe a specific moral code, leading atheists to derive their ethical principles from diverse sources.

Understanding the complexities of the relationship between atheism and crime requires a nuanced exploration that recognizes the diversity within atheist communities and the impact of societal factors on individual behavior. By acknowledging the multifaceted nature of this relationship, we can contribute to informed discussions that promote dialogue, empathy, and a shared commitment to ethical conduct within diverse societies.

SPIRITUALITY AND CRIME

The relationship between spirituality and crime is a multifaceted and dynamic aspect of human behavior that has captivated the attention of scholars, theologians, and criminologists alike. Spirituality, often distinct from organized religion, encompasses a diverse range of beliefs, practices, and experiences that connect individuals to a sense of the transcendent or higher purpose. In this exploration, we delve into the intricate dynamics of how spirituality intersects with criminal behavior, examining both the potential mitigating influences and the challenges that may arise within this complex relationship.

Spirituality as a Moral Compass

One perspective suggests that spirituality can serve as a moral compass, guiding individuals away from criminal behavior. Many spiritual traditions emphasize virtues such as compassion, empathy, and love, fostering a sense of interconnectedness with others. Individuals who cultivate a strong spiritual connection may derive a sense of purpose and meaning that encourages ethical decision-making and discourages actions deemed criminal.

For example, contemplative practices like meditation and mindfulness, often associated with spirituality, aim to cultivate inner peace and a heightened awareness of one's actions. Such practices may contribute to self-reflection and the development of empathy, potentially reducing the likelihood of engaging in criminal conduct.

Restorative Justice and Spirituality

Some spiritual traditions advocate for restorative justice principles, emphasizing the importance of healing and reconciliation over punitive measures. Restorative justice seeks to address the harm caused by criminal behavior by involving offenders, victims, and the community in a collaborative process of repair. Restorative practices align with spiritual values of forgiveness, redemption, and the potential for personal transformation.

Certain indigenous spiritual practices, such as the Maori concept of "whakapapa" in New Zealand, underscore the interconnectedness of individuals and the importance of restoring balance within the community. Embracing restorative justice principles may reflect a spiritual worldview that values healing and reconciliation as essential components of the justice process.

Challenges of Spiritual Bypassing

While spirituality can be a source of moral guidance, it is essential to acknowledge the phenomenon of "spiritual bypassing", where individuals use spiritual beliefs as a defense mechanism to avoid confronting personal issues. In some cases, individuals may use spirituality to rationalize or justify criminal behavior, distorting spiritual principles to serve their own interests.

For example, charismatic leaders within certain spiritual movements may exploit their followers, engaging in criminal activities under the guise of spiritual teachings. This misuse of spirituality highlights the importance of critical discernment and ethical integrity within spiritual communities.

Eastern Spiritual Traditions and Mindfulness

Eastern spiritual traditions, such as Buddhism and Hinduism, have introduced mindfulness practices that focus on cultivating present-moment awareness and inner clarity. Mindfulness has gained popularity in various contexts, including criminal justice settings, as a tool for promoting self-awareness and reducing impulsive behavior.

Mindfulness-based interventions in correctional facilities aim to address issues such as anger management, substance abuse, and violence. By incorporating elements of spirituality, these programs seek to instill a sense of personal responsibility and encourage positive behavioral change among individuals within the criminal justice system.

Community and Social Support

Spirituality often involves a sense of community and interconnectedness. Spiritual communities may offer social support, a sense of belonging, and opportunities for individuals to find purpose and meaning. The presence of a supportive community can act as a protective factor against criminal behavior, providing individuals with a network of relationships that encourage prosocial activities.

Research suggests that individuals who are connected to supportive spiritual or religious communities may be less likely to engage in criminal conduct. The social bonds within these communities may contribute to the development of a strong moral foundation and a sense of accountability.

Existential Perspectives and Crime

Certain spiritual and existential perspectives delve into questions of purpose, meaning, and the human condition. Individuals grappling with existential concerns may experience a sense of nihilism or despair, potentially contributing to engagement in criminal behavior as a way to cope with or escape from existential distress.[3]

Conversely, some spiritual traditions offer frameworks for addressing existential questions, emphasizing the search for purpose and the cultivation of a meaningful life. Existential exploration within a spiritual context may act as a protective factor against criminal behavior by providing individuals with a sense of purpose and a framework for navigating life's challenges.[5]

Religious and Spiritual Rehabilitation Programs

Within criminal justice systems, rehabilitation programs that incorporate religious or spiritual components aim to address the underlying factors contributing to criminal behavior. These programs recognize the potential transformative power of spirituality in the process of rehabilitation and reintegration into society.

For example, faith-based programs may offer counseling, mentorship, and community support to individuals seeking to break free from cycles of criminality. The emphasis on spiritual growth and personal transformation aligns with the idea that individuals can overcome past mistakes and contribute positively to their communities.

Cultural Variations and Indigenous Spirituality

The relationship between spirituality and crime is also influenced by cultural variations and the diversity of spiritual traditions around the world. Indigenous spirituality, rooted in the connection to the land, community, and ancestral wisdom, often approaches justice and crime within a holistic framework.

Indigenous justice practices, such as circle sentencing, involve community members in the resolution of conflicts and crimes. The spiritual and cultural context within which these practices operate reflects a worldview that seeks to restore harmony and balance rather than solely focusing on punishment.

Crisis of Meaning and Criminal Behavior

In some cases, individuals experiencing a crisis of meaning or a lack of purpose in life may turn to criminal activities as a way to fill a perceived void. Spirituality, with its emphasis on finding meaning and purpose, can play a role in addressing these existential concerns and offering individuals an alternative path toward personal fulfillment.[5,6]

Reconnecting individuals with a sense of purpose through spiritual exploration may contribute to reducing the risk of criminal behavior associated with a lack of meaning or a sense of hopelessness.

In conclusion, the relationship between spirituality and crime is a complex interplay of moral guidance, community support, and existential perspectives. While spirituality can serve as a source of positive influence, offering individuals a moral compass and a sense of purpose, challenges such as spiritual bypassing and the misuse of spiritual teachings highlight the need for critical discernment.

Recognizing the diversity of spiritual traditions and their impact on criminal behavior requires an interdisciplinary approach that considers individual experiences, cultural variations, and the dynamic nature of spiritual beliefs. By exploring the complexities within the relationship between spirituality and crime, we can gain insights into how spiritual perspectives influence individuals' ethical choices and contribute to broader discussions within the fields of criminology and criminal justice.

RESEARCH EVIDENCE

Lot of research has been done in this field. A detailed discussion of those is beyond the scope of this chapter. However, we would like to highlight a very few recent findings from systematic review and meta-analysis.

A systematic review was done by Adamczyk et al. in 2017. The authors conducted a systematic review of empirically based journal articles published between 2004 and 2014. The findings highlight the most popular theoretical perspectives, which include religious contextual effects, social control, and social learning. The authors commented, "one key theoretical issue is that crime and religion could have a reciprocal relationship. The literature until now, has perhaps surprisingly, almost completely ignored this possibility".[2]

Another systematic review and meta-analysis published in 2023 attempted to find out the relationship between religiosity/spirituality and interpersonal violence. After screening about 16,599 articles from the scientific database, the authors included 67 articles for systematic review and 43 articles for meta-analysis. The authors found that higher levels of religiosity and spirituality were significantly associated with decreased sexual and physical aggression but not with domestic violence.[3]

A study from Asia by Chui et al. in 2013 explored the attitudes of Christians, Buddhists, and those identifying themselves as nonreligious toward crime. Surprisingly, the authors found that although the Buddhists were more spiritual, they attributed crime to individual and environmental causes and advocated for both coercive and social intervention measures. When compared to the Buddhists, Christians and the nonreligious are more supportive of assistance toward the treatment of offenders in this study.[4]

CONCLUSION

The relationship between religiosity, spirituality, and crime is a complex and multidimensional one. Religion has many components, and which components specifically protect against committing crime and which do not make it difficult to tell at this juncture. In principle, all religions teach us to be tolerant and benevolent and encourage us to self-introspect and do good to others. In general, high religiosity and spirituality protect from criminal behavior. But like every law has a loophole, every religion has some loophole and/or some religious sanctions in place that have been misutilized and contributed to behavior that was uncalled for. Fanatics have misinterpreted religion from time to time and have taken the upper hand over political and legal justice systems. History is abundant with examples that whenever emperors became weak, religious leaders dominated them and wielded their power over the masses and often committed heinous crimes. Moreover, it would be a wishful thinking that in a fast-changing society that is grappling with the issues of poverty, unemployment, climate change, migration, and rapid urbanization, only religion will protect from crime. Nevertheless, religious teachings and accurately understanding the essence of it would soothe the wrecked souls.

At the end, all we can say—

"Yada yada hi dharmasya glanirbhavati
bharata |
Abhythanamadharmasya tadatmanam
srijamyaham ||
Paritranaya sadhunang vinashay cha
dushkritam |
Dharmasangsthapanarthay sambhabami
yuge yuge ||"

[Verses 7 and 8 of Chapter 4 of
The Bhagavat Gita]

(The meaning of this verse is—I incarnate. I appear. Whenever there is a loss of religion, then I come. Whenever unrighteousness increases, I personally appear before people, I come to protect the noble people, I come to destroy the wicked, I come to establish righteousness and in every age I take birth.)

REFERENCES

1. Kerley KR. (2018). Religion and Crime: Theory, Research, and Practice. [online] Available from https://www.mdpi.com/journal/religions/special_issues/crime. [Last accessed December, 2024].
2. Adamczyk A, Freilich JD, Kim C. Religion and Crime: A Systematic Review and Assessment of Next Steps. Sociology of Religion: A Quarterly Review. 2017;1-34.
3. Gonsalves JPB, Lucchetti G, Maraldi EO, Fernandez PEL, Menezes PR, Vallada H. The role of religiosity and spirituality in interpersonal violence: a systematic review and meta-analysis. Braz J Psychiatry. 2023; 45(2):162-81.
4. Chui WH, Cheng KK, Wong LP. Spirituality and punitiveness: An exploration of Christian, Buddhist, and non-religious attitudes towards crime. Int J Law Crim Justice. 2013;41:1-15.
5. Conover-Williams M, Chang J. Pray away the criminal? Crime, religiosity, gender and sexuality over the life course. Humboldt J Soc Relat. 2016;38:28-45.
6. Dilulio J. More religion, less crime? Science, felonies, and the three faith factors. Annu Rev Law Soc Sci. 2009;5:115-33.

5 CHAPTER

Religion, Spirituality, and Global Mental Health: Challenges and Opportunities

Natália Macedo Cavagnoli, Bruno Paz Mosqueiro

INTRODUCTION

Religiosity and spirituality (R/S) represent important conditions for most people's lives worldwide.[1] Global surveys indicate that over 83% of individuals identify with a religious group, and for those not affiliated, many still hold spiritual beliefs.[2] Additionally, in high-quality scientific research, R/S have been generally associated with protective effects for mental health and psychological well-being.[3] Religious or spiritual beliefs serve as crucial sources of social integration and support and are capable of providing meaning, purpose and resilience to many people, especially during times of adversity and disease.[4]

Despite the large number of studies evaluating the clinical effect of R/S to different health conditions, a current point in the literature is to comprehend the global implications of religious, spiritual, and cultural factors on communities' mental health and public health care. Particularly in highly religious communities or in low-income settings, religious communities sometimes represent a first resource to people when facing mental health conditions.[5] It is also important to recognize the potential association between religiosity and negative mental health outcomes in some specific conditions.[6] Religious beliefs or groups might eventually be a source of stigma and might create barriers to healthcare access and treatments.[7]

The objectives of this chapter are to evaluate the main evidence regarding the relationship between religion, spirituality, and mental health, discuss the definitions and implications of recent global mental health (GMH) research, and understand how R/S could contribute to the GMH agenda.

DEFINITIONS OF RELIGION AND SPIRITUALITY

There are many definitions of religion or spirituality. Usually, the term religiosity/spirituality (R/S) represents a more general expression encompassing both constructs.[8] One of the most agreed definitions states that the distinctive aspect of spirituality *"is the relationship or contact with a transcendent realm of reality that is considered sacred, the ultimate truth or reality"*. Religion would be defined as *"the institutional or communal aspect of spirituality, a shared set of beliefs, experiences and practices related to the transcendent and the sacred"*.[1]

Another important and more comprehensive definition, especially useful for clinical practice, understands that: *"Spirituality is the aspect of humanity that refers to the way individuals seek and express meaning and purpose and the way they experience their connectedness to the moment, to self, to others, to nature, and to the significant or sacred"*.[9] Both definitions highlight the complexity and importance of various dimensions and aspects of R/S in people's lives.

SCIENTIFIC EVIDENCE REGARDING RELIGIOSITY AND SPIRITUALITY AND MENTAL HEALTH

The increase in the number of scientific publications in recent decades on the relationships between religiosity/spirituality (R/S) and health demonstrates the growing interest in the subject. In general, scientific research identifies a general protective factor of R/S for health, especially for mental health. Individuals with higher R/S have a lower risk of depression,[10] suicide,[11] alcohol, tobacco, and substances abuse,[12] in addition to reporting greater psychological well-being and quality of life.[12] General health measures such as immunity, blood pressure control, longevity, and lower mortality have been studied and associated with R/S throughout life.[13]

On the other hand, some forms of R/S involvement may be associated with negative effects, with worsening mental health, lower adherence, and overall worse treatment outcomes.[7] Therefore, understanding and approaching the subject appropriately is of great importance for healthcare professionals. The presence of religious struggles or nonadaptive R/S coping strategies, for instance, have been associated with poor quality of life in bipolar disorder patients[14] and worse outcomes among depressive patients in prospective studies.[10]

Nevertheless, the overall literature consistently reinforces the main protective effect of R/S on healthcare and mental health. A recent comprehensive review published in JAMA, for instance, yielded strong evidence-based statements reinforcing the implications of R/S for health care, including three main statements particularly relevant for GMH, including the importance of incorporating *"patient-centered and evidence-based approaches regarding associations of spiritual community with improved patient and population health outcomes"*, increasing *"awareness among health professionals of evidence for protective health associations of spiritual community"*, and recognizing *"spirituality as a social factor associated with health in research, community assessments, and program implementation"*.[4]

RELIGION, SPIRITUALITY, AND MENTAL HEALTH CARE

Different international associations provide recommendations about the importance of integrating R/S into mental health care, including the World Psychiatric Association, the American Psychiatric Association, the Royal College of Psychiatrists or the Brazilian Psychiatric Association.[8,15]

Most patients would like to talk about their R/S in healthcare settings but, most of them have never been asked about these topics in their healthcare consultations.[16] Interestingly, most physicians also agreed about the importance of integrating R/S issues in clinical practice, but report barriers such as lack of time, training, and ethical concerns to integrate R/S issues in clinical care.[17] A recent Brazilian Psychiatric Association Guideline provided useful and evidence-based practical recommendations based on the best evidence available regarding R/S in mental health clinical practice, including for instance how to take a spiritual history and how to make a differential diagnosis between R/S experiences and psychopathology.[8]

Different studies emphasize the relevance of therapeutic strategies that integrate religious-spiritual aspects in a complementary way to conventional mental health treatments. The so-called *Spiritually Integrated Psychotherapies* can be valuable resources, integrating therapeutic aspects with the R/S beliefs of individuals, addressing dysfunctional aspects, and reinforcing resources, strengths, and positive aspects.[18]

GLOBAL MENTAL HEALTH

Global mental health is a field of knowledge that encompasses the study, research, and practice of improving mental health globally, focusing on equity among people around the world.[19] Recognizing the importance of mental health around the world and the evident inequality between countries or communities, the Lancet Global Burden of Disease Report in 2008 made clear the magnitude of mental illness as a cause of illness, disability, and death.[20] The term GMH, since then, became widespread. The challenges and difficulties in achieving the proposed GMH goals to improve mental health were evident in a 2018 follow-up, given the substantial increase in mental illnesses and their worldwide consequences.[21]

EPIDEMIOLOGY AND PUBLIC MENTAL HEALTH

In the 2022 World Mental Health Report, the World Health Organization showed that 13% of the global population was living with mental disorders, a prevalence that remained steady between 2000 and 2019.[22] The most prevalent mental disorders, in both males and females, were anxiety and depressive disorders. In 2019, their prevalences were, respectively, 4% and 3.8%. In the same year, 36 million people had a diagnosis of substance use disorders and 55 million people had dementia.

In 2020, as a result of the COVID-19 pandemic, there was a significant increase in these numbers and mental health challenges.[22] It is estimated that there was an increase of 28% in reports of depressive and 26% in anxiety symptomatology in just 1 year. Women were more affected, precisely because they are more affected by the socioeconomic issues of the pandemic. Among age groups, young people were more diagnosed with anxiety and depression, which reflects the impact of social restrictions in this population. Serious mental health condition, such as schizophrenia, affects 24 million people in the world and is the most impairing of all health conditions. Bipolar disorder occurs in 40 million people. Both disorders directly affect working-age populations.[22]

Mortality

Estimating mortality from mental disorders is complex. However, premature mortality, particularly in bipolar disorder and schizophrenia, leads to a life expectancy 10–20 years earlier than in the general population.[22] Most of the causes of death in this group are preventable diseases: cardiovascular, respiratory, and infectious. People living with mental disorders are more vulnerable to risk factors for chronic diseases, and the adverse effects of medications also favor obesity, glucose intolerance, and dyslipidemia. Overall, the lack of integration of physical and mental care exacerbates the problem. Often, when linked to a mental health service, the individual is neglected in other health services.

Suicide

For every 100 deaths in the world, one is a suicide. There are 20 attempts for each completed suicide. In 2019, for instance, 703 million people died by suicide in the world.

Around 77% of all suicide occur in low- and middle-income countries, but high-income countries grouped together have the highest suicide rates. Despite that, since 2000, the suicide rate has dropped by 36%, globally.[22]

Disability

Among all causes of years lived with disability, those attributed to mental illness are the most significant: one year in six. According to the Global Burden of Disease Study, mental disorders were, in 2019, the second leading cause of years living with disability.[23]

CHALLENGES AND OPPORTUNITIES FOR ACTION

The concept of GMH aligns with the recognition that there are significant disparities between countries in the promotion of mental health. Moreover, it underscores the necessity of integrating mental health services in primary care and community settings and making them more accessible to the people.[20]

Wainberg et al. (2017), reviewing a series of publications and key challenges and advances in different regions of the world, reinforce the belief that community mental health care is an essential way to expand mental health coverage.[24] It is understood that it is possible to associate mental health with the community, training mental health workers, and also lay people who can play an important role in improving access to the service.

Strengthening Mental Health in Primary Care

Several challenging factors for the implementation of a more capable mental health service in primary care include insufficient training of the multidisciplinary healthcare team, the need of more professionals and funding, and the lack of specialists to support teams and help in treatment decisions.[25]

Very often, patients with mental health issues commonly have multiple clinical comorbidities, seek more consultations, or require longer consultations, factors that can overload the services. Such patients typically have greater social vulnerability, requiring a multidisciplinary team approach to optimize care.[25]

Prince (2007), reinforcing the World Health Organization slogan that there is "*no health without mental health*", recalls the different pathways to understanding the relationship between mental health and different health conditions. Cardiovascular disease and cancer are major contributors to disability and mortality, as are mental illnesses. The comorbidity between them is evident, since both depressive disorders and anxiety disorders commonly develop after such diagnoses. Among the communicable diseases, there are several psychiatric symptoms that can develop in HIV infection, especially in individuals without treatment or with ineffective treatment. The stigma of the disease also favors the appearance of mood and anxiety symptoms. Tuberculosis, which is linked to substance use disorders and incarcerated populations, also joins the group of diseases that require a mental health approach.[26]

Mental Health in Conflict Areas and Migrant Populations

Countries or communities facing violence, war, or territorial disputes are faced with serious mental health damage over time. Mental health is affected by the precariousness of services and instability of care, and is jeopardized by personal and community traumatic experiences.[27]

Forced migrations produce severe mental suffering and impose early adaptations to new cultures. The role of religious, spiritual, and cultural issues is certainly especially relevant in these situations. Within the field of GMH, it is understood that, in addition to the search for equity in access to health, it is necessary to consider cultural differences and adapt methods to serve these individuals ethically and satisfactorily.[28]

Treatment Gap

The treatment gap is understood as the absolute difference between the prevalence of a disorder and the proportion of people treated for this disorder. In other words, it represents the percentage of individuals with a disorder who are not receiving treatment.[29] It is determined at both individual and public health levels. Therefore, it underscores the need for educational and health promotion efforts among healthcare professionals, as well as global investments in healthcare policies and programs.

A recent study reported that 75% of cases of major depressive disorder occur in low- and middle-income countries, reinforcing the mental health burden and treatment gap, since such locations lack centers for mental health care and multidisciplinary treatments.[30] Among the globally experienced difficulties, younger populations and men tend to utilize services less frequently. Additionally, subjective factors such as stigma and acceptance of treatment play a role in the treatment gap.

The approach to substance use disorders illustrates the difficulties in solving problems related to the treatment gap, but also points to new ways of understanding mental health. Substance consumption is seen, globally, from different points of view that do not always put the individual's health in the foreground. In some countries, the rigid drug policy does not allow for a reliable epidemiological profile and ignores the need for treatment for addicts. On the other hand, there are care models for this population that invest only in pharmacological treatments or statically controlled by long-term hospitalization, which ignores the place of the individual in their social environment. Based on this finding, it is important that treatment gaps are addressed not only from a medical point of view, but also taking into account the social, political, and community environment.[31]

The gap in treatment for psychotic episodes is an even more pressing concern. Both schizophrenia and the brief psychotic disorder greatly benefit from early intervention, which can define a favorable outcome for the individual.[32] Schizophrenia, due to its chronic nature, is generally disabling. However, shortening the duration of the psychotic episode may prevent disease progression. Mental health services closer to the patients help to maintain the treatment: treatment abandonment is common among schizophrenics. Access to the service should also include caregivers. The relationships between spiritual experiences and psychotic disorders present additional challenges to clinical and public health care, reinforcing the need for dialog and partnerships between R/S leaders, communities, and mental health professionals.[5,8]

Stigma

Goffman (1963) described stigma as a deeply discreditable or undesirable attribute that separates the individual from the group in which he lives.[33] The 2022 Lancet Commission on ending stigma and discrimination in mental health adds the term discrimination as it understands that stigma, in addition to evidencing the loss of status, provides important social exclusion of those labeled individuals.[34]

The stigmatization extends to groups in which, as a result of their stereotype or social labeling, a social apartment is built. People living with mental disorders are, therefore, susceptible to stigmatization. As characteristics of this group, the essential clinical diagnosis stands out, which cannot be proven by complementary examinations, and its legal and social outcome, since these individuals often become dysfunctional or dependent.

The involvement of religious or spiritual groups and communities plays a significant role in various aspects of stigma. When conceptualizing stigma in mental health, the Lancet Commission cited above presents four categories:

1. *Self-stigma:* It is defined as the internalization of the negative stereotype of others by the person suffering from a mental health condition. It interferes with individual self-esteem and carries several negative beliefs, which influence people's fear and dismay. On the other hand, the idea of stigma resilience has been emerging, in order to empower those who suffer from it, based on positive actions that insert individuals into society.
2. *Stigma by association:* It is the extent of stigma to family members and caregivers of people suffering from mental health conditions. They depend on the mental illness presented and can be loaded with moral judgments, in the case of substance use disorders, and guilt in diseases with a noticeable genetic inheritance. The concept also encompasses the stigma of mental health workers, which can be associated with negative and retrograde attitudes when compared to other health services.
3. *Public (or interpersonal) stigma:* It is the one presented within society, in the public sphere. It ratifies discrimination, stereotypes, and negative attitudes toward people living with mental disorders. It can manifest itself directly but also in a benevolent way, with paternalistic behaviors that exclude these individuals from society.
4. *Structural stigma:* It is one that, intentionally or not, occurs across institutions and is directly linked to issues of social well-being. People living with mental disorders have greater difficulty in accessing legal rights, such as marriage, divorce, voting, access to housing and employment, and, as they are at greater risk of becoming dysfunctional, they also suffer new stigmatization when they need to resort to social security services. This stigma is also favored by the deficit in resources destined to mental health.

HOW RELIGION AND SPIRITUALITY CAN CONTRIBUTE TO GLOBAL MENTAL HEALTH?

Religion can contribute to GMH in several significant ways. Firstly, it can serve as a source of social support and community integration for individuals experiencing mental health challenges. Religious communities often provide a sense of belonging and understanding, which can be crucial for those struggling with mental disorders. Religious beliefs and practices can offer valuable coping mechanisms and enhance resilience for people facing adversities, loss, disease, and mental health suffering. For many individuals with mental disorders and serious illness, faith provides a sense of purpose, meaning, and hope, which can be instrumental in the recovery process. The access to evidence-based strategies in community and primary care settings represents ways to improve training and access to scientific-based and culturally adapted interventions to support positive R/S resources in mental health.

Furthermore, partnerships between religious organizations and mental health professionals represent important pathways to create networks and collaboration that can lead to improved access to treatment. These collaborations can help bridge gaps in healthcare delivery, especially in underserved or remote areas where formal mental health services may be limited.

Religion also has the potential to reduce stigma surrounding mental health issues. Indeed, this is an important topic that warrants further research and understanding, in order to grasp how religiosity contributes to stigma and in which cultures and contexts. When religious leaders and communities openly address mental health concerns, it helps normalize conversations about mental well-being and encourages individuals to seek help without fear of judgment.

By fostering partnerships between religious institutions and mental health organizations, we can leverage these strengths to create a more inclusive, supportive, and accessible mental health ecosystem on a global scale. This collaborative approach holds the potential to not only enhance mental health treatment but also contribute to broader societal goals of well-being, recovery, and social integration. It helps people to understand and seek help for their health conditions, but also improves mental health professionals' awareness of relevant cultural and R/S resources to improve mental health treatments.

CONCLUSION

The GMH paradigm represents a relevant perspective for addressing public healthcare concerns and enhancing mental health awareness and care worldwide. Religion and spirituality are fundamental dimensions for most people globally, exhibiting significant associations with mental health conditions. Collaborative initiatives with R/S communities also represent an opportunity to tackle GMH challenges, including preventive efforts, mental health awareness, and stigma, with the aim of enhancing prevention, health promotion, and facilitating access to treatments.

REFERENCES

1. Moreira-Almeida A, Bhugra D. Religion, Spirituality and Mental Health: Setting the Scene. In: Moreira-Almeida A, Mosqueiro BP, Bhugra D (Eds). Spirituality and Mental Health Across Cultures. Oxford: Oxford Academic Books; 2021. pp. 11-25.
2. Pew Research Center. (2017). The Changing Global Religious Landscape. [online] Available from https://www.pewresearch.org/religion/2017/04/05/the-changing-global-religious-landscape/. [Last accessed December, 2024]
3. Rosmarin DH, Pargament KI, Koenig HG. Spirituality and mental health: challenges and opportunities. Lancet Psychiatry. 2021; 8(2):92-93.
4. Balboni TA, VanderWeele TJ, Doan-Soares SD, Long KNG, Ferrell BR, Fitchett G, et al. Spirituality in Serious Illness and Health. JAMA. 2022;328(2):184-97.
5. Gureje O, Appiah-Poku J, Bello T, Kola L, Araya R, Chisholm D, et al. Effect of collaborative care between traditional and faith healers and primary health-care workers on psychosis outcomes in Nigeria and Ghana (COSIMPO): a cluster randomised controlled trial. Lancet. 2020;396(10251):612-22.
6. Pargament KI, Zinnbauer BJ, Scott AB, Butter EM, Zerowin J, Stanik P. Red Flags and

Religious Coping: Identifying Some Religious Warning Signs Among People in Crisis. J Clin Psychol. 1998;54:77-89.

7. Pargament KI, Lomax JW. Understanding and addressing religion among people with mental illness. World Psychiatry. 2013; 12(1):26-32.
8. Mosqueiro BP, Costa MA, Caribé AC, de Oliveira FO, Pizutti L, Zimpel RR, et al. Brazilian Psychiatric Association Guidelines on the Integration of Spirituality into Mental Health Clinical Practice: Part 1. Spiritual History and Differential Diagnosis. Braz J Psychiatry. 2023;45(6):506-17.
9. Puchalski CM, Vitillo R, Hull SK, Reller N. Improving the spiritual dimension of whole person care: reaching national and international consensus. J Palliat Med. 2014;17(6):642-56.
10. Braam AW, Koenig HG. Religion, spirituality and depression in prospective studies: a systematic review. J Affect Disord. 2019;257: 428-38.
11. VanderWeele TJ, Li S, Tsai AC, Kawachi I. Association Between Religious Service Attendance and Lower Suicide Rates Among US Women. JAMA Psychiatry. 2016;73(8): 845-51.
12. Koenig H, Al-Zaben F, VanderWeele T. Religion and psychiatry: recent developments in research. BJPsych Advances. 2020; 26(5):262-72.
13. Koenig HG, King DE, Carson VB. Handbook of Religion and Health. New York, NY: Oxford University Press; 2012.
14. Stroppa A, Colugnati FA, Koenig HG, Moreira-Almeida A. Religiosity, depression, and quality of life in bipolar disorder: a two-year prospective study. Rev Bras Psiquiatr. 2018;40(3):238-43.
15. Moreira-Almeida A, Sharma A, van Rensburg BJ, Verhagen PJ, Cook CC. WPA Position Statement on Spirituality and Religion in Psychiatry. World Psychiatry. 2016;15(1):87-8.
16. Best M, Butow P, Olver I. Doctors discussing religion and spirituality: A systematic literature review. Palliat Med. 2016;30(4): 327-37.
17. Menegatti-Chequini MC, Gonçalves JPB, Leão FC, Peres MFP, Vallada H. A preliminary survey on the religious profile of Brazilian psychiatrists and their approach to patients' religiosity in clinical practice. BJPsych Open. 2016;2(6):346-52.
18. Captari LE, Hook JN, Hoyt W, Davis DE, McElroy-Heltzel SE, Worthington EL Jr. Integrating clients' religion and spirituality within psychotherapy: a comprehensive meta-analysis. J Clin Psychol. 2018;74(11): 1938-51.
19. Patel V, Prince M. Global mental health: a new global health field comes of age. JAMA. 2010;303(19):1976-7.
20. Horton R. Launching a new movement for mental health. Lancet. 2007;370(9590):806.
21. Patel V, Saxena S, Lund C, Thornicroft G, Baingana F, Bolton P, et al. The Lancet Commission on global mental health and sustainable development. Lancet. 2018;392(10157):1553-98.
22. World Health Organization. World mental health report: transforming mental health for all. Geneva: World Health Organization; 2022.
23. GBD 2019 Mental Disorders Collaborators. Global, regional, and national burden of 12 mental disorders in 204 countries and territories, 1990–2019: a systematic analysis for the Global Burden of Disease Study 2019. Lancet Psychiatry. 2022;9(2):137-50.
24. Wainberg ML, Scorza P, Shultz JM, Helpman L, Mootz JJ, Johnson KA, et al. Challenges and Opportunities in Global Mental Health: a Research-to-Practice Perspective. Curr Psychiatry Rep. 2017;19(5):28.
25. Esponda GM, Hartman S, Qureshi O, Sadler E, Cohen A, Kakuma R. Barriers and facilitators of mental health programmes in primary care in low-income and middle-income countries. Lancet Psychiatry. 2020;7(1): 78-92.
26. Prince M, Patel V, Saxena S, Maj M, Maselko J, Phillips MR, et al. No health without mental health. Lancet. 2007;370(9590):859-77.
27. Lu J, Jamani S, Benjamen J, Agbata E, Magwood O, Pottie K. Global Mental Health and Services for Migrants in Primary Care Settings in High-Income Countries:

a Scoping Review. Int J Environ Res Public Health. 2020;17(22):8627.
28. Frizi R, Lay B, Seifritz E, Kawohl W, Habermeyer B, Roser P. Sociodemographic and Clinical Predictors of the Length of Psychiatric Inpatient Stay of Immigrants in Switzerland. Front Psychiatry. 2020;11: 585798.
29. Kohn R, Saxena S, Levav I, Saraceno B. The treatment gap in mental health care. Bull World Health Organ. 2004;82(11):858-66.
30. Moitra M, Santomauro D, Collins PY, Vos T, Whiteford H, Saxena S, et al. The global gap in treatment coverage for major depressive disorder in 84 countries from 2000–2019: A systematic review and Bayesian meta-regression analysis. PLoS Med. 2022; 19(2): e1003901.
31. Bartlett N, Garriott W, Raikhel E. What's in the 'treatment gap'? Ethnographic perspectives on addiction and global mental health from China, Russia, and the United States. Med Anthropol. 2014;33(6):457-77.
32. Mohr P, Galderisi S, Boyer P, Wasserman D, Arteel P, Ieven A, et al. Value of schizophrenia treatment I: The patient journey. Eur Psychiatry. 2018;53:107-15.
33. Goffman E. Stigma: Notes on the Management of Spoiled Identity. New York, NY: Simon and Schuster Inc.; 1963.
34. Thornicroft G, Sunkel C, Alikhon Aliev A, Baker S, Brohan E, El Chammay R, et al. The Lancet Commission on Ending Stigma and Discrimination in Mental Health. Lancet. 2022;400(10361):1438-80.

6 CHAPTER

Integrating Spirituality in Medical Curriculum

Rajashree Ray, Gautam Saha

INTRODUCTION

India has made commendable progress in expanding medical education in the past decade. Medical colleges increased by 88% from 387 in 2013–14 to 731 in 2024–2025, while MBBS and PG seats increased by 118% and 133%, respectively, during the same period.[1] This trend will have a significant impact on healthcare delivery in India as it will help to bridge the current gap in providing quality healthcare services in the country. Its objective is to train Indian medical graduates who are ready to deal with real-life situations from day 1 of their internship.

It is universally agreed that students need to acquire competencies for practical applications in diagnosing, treating, and managing a wide range of medical conditions. The Competency-Based Medical Education (CBME) published by the National Medical Board is designed to create a new generation of Indian medical graduates (IMGs) with the knowledge, skills, and attitudes needed to work as primary healthcare providers in communities around the world, fulfilling the roles of a clinician, leader, communicator, lifelong learner, professional, critical thinker, and researcher.[2] A new module named "AETCOM" (Attitude, Ethics, and Communication) has been introduced which focuses on creating ethical values, communication skills, and professional abilities for future doctors aiming to instill the values of care, respect, and professional conduct that are important to patient care.[3]

This is a major leap forward in the training of medical professionals, reinforcing Theodore Roosevelt's statement, "To educate a person in the mind but not in morals is to educate a menace to society." Intellectual development (education of the mind) and moral development (moral education) need to be connected from childhood to ensure that knowledge and wisdom are not used to manipulate or exploit others. AETCOM has many specific modules on: What does it mean to be a doctor, What does it mean to be a patient, The doctor-patient relationship, The foundations of communication, The foundations of bioethics, Cadaver as our first teacher, and What does it mean to be family member of a sick patient, which are designed for learners to gain competencies in moral and ethical development. As the curriculum is now emphasizing on the key pillars of bioethics, such as autonomy, beneficence, nonmaleficence, and justice, it is perhaps time to integrate principles of spirituality into the medical curriculum to create doctors and practitioners who can make a difference in society.

UNDERSTANDING SPIRITUALITY IN MEDICINE

Before exploring how spirituality can be integrated into medical education, it is critical to understand what spirituality means in the context of health care. Puchalski (2001) defines spirituality as "the aspect of humanity that refers to the way individuals seek and express meaning and purpose and the way they experience their connectedness to the moment, to self, to others, to nature, and to the significant or sacred".[4]

In medical practice, spirituality influences the relationship, communication, and decision-making process between doctor and patient. One important aspect is distinguishing it from religion, as the two are often intertwined.

Religion generally involves organized beliefs and practices, whereas spirituality is more individualistic. It integrates a person's inner sense of meaning, purpose, and connection to the world. Medical professionals encounter patients at critical moments in their lives, such as during a terminal diagnosis or managing a chronic illness. For patients facing significant health challenges spirituality can provide comfort, hope, and meaning in suffering, having effects on both physical and mental well-being.[5] For healthcare providers, addressing spiritual well-being can help prevent burnout, promote flexibility, and increase empathy.[6]

SPIRITUALITY IN MEDICAL EDUCATION: THE TREND SO FAR

Over the decades, medical education has focused on developing technical expertise, clinical knowledge, and scientific rigor. Spirituality, on the other hand, was often overlooked or considered irrelevant in formal curricula. This approach has its origins in a former understanding of medicine that is rooted in the natural sciences, where objective evidence and empirical data are considered paramount. In many cases, health professionals are trained to separate their personal beliefs from clinical practice to maintain objectivity.[7] However historically, spirituality and medicine have been deeply intertwined, and early healers, shamans, and priests often combined spiritual rituals with physical therapy. Traditional medical systems such as Ayurveda and traditional Chinese medicine (TCM) have long incorporated spirituality into their practices, providing valuable insight into the connection between mind, body, and spirit, which has influenced modern integrative therapy. With the rise of modern biomedicine in the 19th and 20th centuries, metaphysical concepts declined and science prioritized empirical evidence and measurable outcomes.

The Role of Spirituality in Global Healthcare Trends

Over the past few decades, there is a resurgence of interest in spirituality as evidence has shown that by meeting the emotional and psychological needs of patients and healthcare providers it has growing impact on health outcomes and patient satisfaction. From literature review, we know that the first formal attempt to integrate spirituality into medical education in the United States was in the 1990s with the founding of the George Washington Institute for Spirituality and Health.[8] Additionally, several studies have shown the positive effects of spirituality-focused curricula on empathy, communication skills, and professional development of medical students.[9,10] To meet this need, the Association of American

Medical Colleges (AAMC), the World Health Organization (WHO), and the Joint Commission on Accreditation of Healthcare Organizations (JCAHO) recommend addressing spiritual issues in clinical care and health education. The relationship between spirituality and health is receiving increasing attention, and as a result, medical schools are beginning to question whether and how these issues should be addressed in medical education.[11]

In the United Kingdom, the National Health Service (NHS) emphasizes spiritual care as a key component of holistic health. Spirituality is also being embraced in the areas of mental health and chronic disease management. For example, community-based programs in low-resource settings often incorporate spiritual elements to build resilience and promote collaboration. A study in Iran highlighted the role of spirituality in medical education and the impact of COVID-19 on healthcare provider, emphasizing the importance of integrating spirituality into the medical curriculum as well as the cultural, ethical, and spiritual competence of healthcare providers.[12]

Medical schools around the world have begun to incorporate spirituality into their curricula in a variety of ways. For example, medical students at the University of Toronto engage in reflection that encourages them to explore personal values and roles. At the University of Michigan, spirituality is addressed through workshops, case studies, and role-playing activities.[13] The World Psychological Association (WPA) has included "religion and spirituality" in its "Core Training Curriculum for Psychiatry." The position statement comments that spirituality and religion are linked to human experiences and values, and its relevance to the treatment of psychosis and the patient's attitude toward illness should be central to clinical and academic psychiatry. Religious and spiritual approaches should be person-centered, respectful, and sensitive to the patient and family's spiritual beliefs and practices.[14]

Despite these advances, challenges remain in universally integrating spirituality in medical education, of which the most important is the lack of standardized guidelines in medical institutions. The diversity of spiritual beliefs and practices among students and the potential for personal bias to influence interactions with patients can complicate effective training efforts. Additionally, some medical professionals view it as incompatible with scientific inquiry. This leads to resistance when attempting to integrate spirituality into the curriculum.[15] According to a recent survey, 59% of British medical schools and 90% of US medical schools have a curriculum or content on spirituality and health (S/H).[16,17] This includes 50% compulsory teaching, 80% supplementary elements, and 88% complementary alternative medicine, but there is still room for improvement.

At Mount Sinai, the Icahn School of Medicine team has developed mandatory spirituality and health training for students. It is integrated into every undergraduate medical education curriculum. This initiative aims to improve the curriculum by linking learning to specific competencies and develop performance assessments and strengthen professional development efforts.[18]

There is some research on S/H education in medical schools in other countries such as Latin America, Asia, Australia, and Africa, where it is recommended to use a standard curriculum for spirituality.[19]

THE IMPORTANCE OF SPIRITUALITY IN MEDICAL EDUCATION AND HEALTHCARE DELIVERY

Holistic health care recognizes the interconnectedness of an individual's physical, emotional, mental, and spiritual well-being. This approach is especially important in treating chronic diseases, mental health conditions, and terminal illness where traditional medical intervention alone may not be enough to meet the needs of patients. Research suggests that addressing spiritual concerns can improve mental well-being, reduce feelings of depression and anxiety and help improve the quality of life of patients.[9] Additionally, combining spiritual care with medical care may strengthen patient adherence to medical recommendations and promote a more positive attitude toward treatment.

In oncology studies show that when spiritual care is integrated into cancer treatment, patients experience improved overall well-being and are more willing to pursue treatment options that are consistent with their values and beliefs.[20] Research shows that addressing spiritual concerns in healthcare can reduce symptoms of depression and anxiety, improve coping strategies, and help patients make more informed decisions about treatment plans.[21] In palliative care spiritual issues reduce suffering, improves emotional well-being, and helps patients and families make informed decisions about treatment plans[22] and care planning frameworks.[8]

Improve Patient Satisfaction and Confidence

One tangible benefit of integrating spirituality into health care is improving patient satisfaction and trust. Research shows that patients who feel their spiritual needs are accepted and addressed by their health care providers report higher levels of satisfaction with their care.[23,24] Patients who trust their healthcare providers feel more confident in sharing important personal medical information and comply with the treatment plan in their health care journey. On the other hand, providers who demonstrate compassion and spiritual sensitivity are more likely to build stronger and more effective relationships with their patients.

With funding from the John Templeton Spirituality and Medical Curriculum Award from the George Washington Institute for Spirituality and Health, faculty at Kansas City University of Medical Biology (KCUMB) developed a curriculum called "Spirituality in Medicine". It was seen that the majority of the 250 students trained in 2010–2011 were able to demonstrate the following abilities: (1) Be sensitive to the spiritual and cultural needs of patients; (2) assess the spiritual and cultural needs of patients; spirituality of the patient and one's own; (3) use chaplain services appropriately patient care; and (4) health ethics issues that are unequal to patients and ensuring that the impacts are understood.[25]

SPIRITUALITY AND COPING WITH ILLNESS

A patient's ability to cope with their illness is affected by a number of factors including mental and emotional flexibility, social support system, and spiritual beliefs. Spirituality is important to how patients perceive their illness, manage symptoms, and find meaning in their experiences when facing chronic or life-limiting illnesses. Their spiritual beliefs and practices such as prayer, meditation, or mindfulness reduce stress and give them hope, comfort, and control over their symptoms. A number of patients have benefitted in emotional well-being and physical healing.[21] More than 70% felt that spiritual practices were relevant to health and disease but were not integrated into health management strategies owing to lack of reliable scientific data.[26]

Spirituality and end-of-life care: Spirituality plays an important role in end-of-life care. Where patients often struggle with existential anxiety, fear of death and the meaning of life as a person approaches the end of his or her life they may seek meaning and comfort through their spiritual beliefs. Spiritual care is an important part of any approach to helping the terminally ill in palliative care focusing on relieving suffering. By combining spirituality with palliative care, health care providers can help patients deal with their fear of death, fix unfinished business, and find closure. This holistic approach helps make the end of life more peaceful and meaningful.[22]

Strengthen the Relationship between Doctors and Patients

"Medicine is an art whose magic and creative ability have long been recognized as residing in the interpersonal aspects of patient-physician relationship".[27] Studies have found that when healthcare providers engage with patients' spiritual concerns, will make the patient satisfied, trust doctors more, and improve health outcomes.[20] If doctors can communicate effectively with patients and relatives, the diagnostic ability of doctors will also be greatly increased, reducing the doctor's frustration with the patient or relative. Healthcare professionals can develop a deeper understanding of patients' values, beliefs, and sources of meaning, which can influence medical decisions. Spiritually competent healthcare providers can provide emotional support, give a feeling of hope, and help patients make difficult decisions, such as end-of-life care.

Reduce Fatigue by Improving Physician Health

Physician burnout is a growing concern in health care with many doctors feeling emotionally exhausted with a decreased sense of personal accomplishment. The multiple demands of medical practice—long hours and high stress—can lead to burnout, depression, and compassion. Students can develop coping strategies to manage stress, maintain emotional well-being, and be a source of emotional resilience. As doctors become more self-compassionate in their own lives, they are better equipped to offer authentic, empathetic care to their patients.[28] Mindfulness training has been shown to increase empathy and reduce burnout in healthcare providers.[29]

Develop Cultural Competence and Respect for Diversity

In today's diverse and multicultural society, healthcare providers must be sensitive to patients' diverse spiritual and religious beliefs. As spirituality varies from culture to culture, its meaningfulness varies from person to person. Cultural competence in health care includes awareness of the ways in which spirituality intersects with a patient's cultural identity and health practices. Teaching spirituality in medical education helps students develop cultural competence, allowing them to identify and respect the spiritual and religious practices of patients from different backgrounds and communicate more effectively with patients, guide them around and avoid imposing their personal beliefs on others. Additionally, being aware of a patient's spiritual beliefs can help guide medical decisions respectfully on sensitive issues and ensure that care is consistent with patient values and preferences.[13]

CHALLENGES IN TEACHING SPIRITUALITY IN MEDICAL EDUCATION

Although the arguments for teaching spirituality in medical education are compelling, there are challenges that need to be addressed. Most students and teachers believe that they must address spirituality in patients and carers, but the limiting factor becomes the consensus on availability of teaching methods and content.[30] First, there is no consensus on how spirituality should be defined and taught. Spirituality is a deeply personal and personal experience. And different students and patients may access it in different ways. Secondly, there is confusion with religion and a place for potential discomfort in a diverse classroom. Medical schools should develop curricula that respect this diversity and ensure that students are trained to handle spiritual issues compassionately and professionally. Additionally, some students and faculty may feel uncomfortable integrating spirituality into their medical education, especially if it feels inconsistent with the scientific foundations of medicine.[31]

Faculty resistance arises from lack of training in teaching spirituality and the notion that spirituality is less important than biomedical fields. Teaching spirituality does not require religious beliefs or practices. Instead, the focus is on strengthening communication, sympathy, and cultural competence which is necessary for effective patient care.[32] Finally, integrating spirituality into an already crowded medical curriculum can be logistically challenging due to time pressures. But these challenges can be overcome by integrating spirituality into existing curricula in communications, ethics, and patient care. This includes providing extracurricular opportunities for reflection and discussion.

To overcome this obstacle, medical education programs can provide training in spiritual care and emphasize the value of managing the emotional and psychological aspects of health. Spiritual care does not conflict with the scientific foundations of medicine. Additionally, healthcare systems can integrate spiritual care services into their organizational structures to provide resources for both healthcare providers and patients.[28]

Institutional and systematic barriers exist in healthcare system, especially in areas with limited resources. Efficiency is often prioritized over holistic care. Addressing spiritual concerns can feel impossible when patient consultations are often limited to 15 minutes or less. Additionally, many institutions lack clear policies or guidelines for integrating spirituality, as a result, service providers are uncertain about their role and limitations. The strong emphasis on evidence-based practice in the medical field can also act as a barrier.

The cultural sensitivity and diversity of spiritual and religious beliefs among patients present another important challenge. Healthcare providers need to be guided through the complexities of respecting different traditions while avoiding stereotyping or assuming patients' needs. For instance, a practitioner might inadvertently project their own beliefs onto a patient or fail to recognize nontraditional spiritual expressions. Striking the right balance between cultural competence and professional boundaries requires nuanced understanding, respecting patients' autonomy and preferences while maintaining a neutral stance.

Spiritual care also requires interdisciplinary collaboration between medical teams and specialized professionals such as chaplains. However, gaps in communication and collaboration hinder this process. Many hospitals either lack adequate spiritual care teams or their roles are not always well integrated into medical workflows. Interdisciplinary efforts are further complicated by differing priorities and approaches. While chaplains focus on spiritual well-being, medical teams prioritize physical health, leading to misalignment in patient care objectives.

Addressing spirituality in health care raises ethical and legal concerns and providers must tread carefully to avoid appearing biased or discriminatory when discussing spiritual matters. For example, initiating spiritual conversations without explicit patient consent might infringe on their privacy or autonomy. Moreover, ethical dilemmas arise when patients' spiritual beliefs conflict with medical recommendations. For instance, a patient refusing life-saving treatment due to religious convictions poses a challenge for providers striving to balance respect for autonomy with the duty to provide care.

POSSIBLE SOLUTIONS AND APPROACHES

Systematic, educational, and cultural reforms are needed to address the challenge of integrating spirituality into medicine.

The future of spirituality in medicine begins with medical education. Training health care professionals to address spiritual needs requires the following:

- *Specific Curriculum:* Medical schools should include courses on spirituality, ethics, and cultural competence. These courses may include case-based learning, reflective exercises, and learning spiritual history to equip providers with the skills to recognize and respond to spiritual needs. Cultural competence and communication courses can increase sensitivity to diverse beliefs.
- *Encourage reflective practice:* Reflective exercises, such as journaling and conversations with friends, help students to explore their own spiritual beliefs and increase the ability to provide patient-centered care.
- *Continuing education:* Workshops and certifications for practicing physicians can enhance their ability to integrate spirituality into patient care. The following key characteristics are frequently used: Shadowing. Communication skills training, self-reflection, checking for evidence and building relationships" for integration

A spiritual health education curriculum was developed according to Tyler's curriculum planning framework including four different components". (1) Case studies and role plays to practice spiritual conversations. (2) Reflective journaling to explore personal beliefs and values as it promotes empathy. Self awareness and critical thinking. (3) Faculty development and teacher training with workshops and resources to assist faculty in their spiritual studies. (4) Role modeling by faculty to show compassion and spiritually sensitive care. Such models can be adapted for training in medical curriculum.

The use of modern technology is encouraged with virtual reality (VR) and artificial intelligence (AI) devices, simulating spiritual conversations to help students practice navigating complex situations, such as dealing with spiritual suffering in a multicultural context.

Second, organizations should develop clear guidelines for spiritual care. This includes a detailed spiritual assessment. Tools such as the FICA (Faith, Important, Community, Address) model can help providers navigate spiritual discussions in a structured manner.[33]

Medical students must receive structured training in conducting spiritual assessments and addressing existing concerns and participate in the spiritual care of culturally sensitive people.

Third, it is important to promote inter-disciplinary cooperation by including chaplain services in the care team of hospitals. This is to ensure that spiritual care complements medical treatment. Regular communication between medical and spiritual providers can set goals and improve patient outcomes. Attention must be paid to how to influence individual learning, promote open attitudes, and develop clinical skills in learners to integrate religion and spirituality into patient care.[34] Specialized clinical environments such as cancer care, geriatric psychiatry, hospital or geriatric unit palliative care, pediatrics, and substance abuse clinics offer a rich environment for learning about spiritual issues in patient care.[34]

Finally, continued research on the impact of spirituality in health care is important. By creating an evidence-based framework, spirituality can be increasingly recognized as a valid aspect of holistic care. Expanding research on spirituality and health will strengthen credibility and guide evidence-based interventions and practices, gathering together integration with pastoral care services.

CONCLUSION

Integrating spirituality with medicine represents a transformative opportunity for the healthcare system. Several steps are important in moving forward to ensure that healthcare providers are prepared to meet spiritual needs competently and compassionately. By 2050, spirituality will be deeply integrated into medicine and change the way health services are delivered and experienced. Its role will extend beyond addressing existing concerns to preventive care models, improving patient outcomes and promoting resilience in the face of global health challenges. With advances in technology, education, research, and policy, spirituality will bridge the gap between science and humanity. To ensure that the healthcare system respects the full range of the human experience we pursue a vision of care that is compassionate, comprehensive, and deeply connected to the core of what it means to be the human spirit. And this can happen with active steps to include spirituality in the medical curriculum.

REFERENCES

1. Department of Health & Family Welfare, Ministry of Health & Family Welfare. Steps Taken to Increase Medical Colleges and MBBS Seats. [online] Available from https://mohfw.gov.in/?q=pressrelease-33 [Last accessed December, 2024].
2. Medical Council of India. (2018). Competency-based Undergraduate Curriculum for the Indian Medical Graduate. https://www.nmc.org.in/wp-content/uploads/2020/01/UG-Curriculum-Vol-III.pdf.
3. Medical Council of India. (2018). AETCOM. [online] Available from https://www.nmc.org.in/wp-content/uploads/2020/01/AETCOM_book.pdf [Last accessed December, 2024].
4. Puchalski CM. The role of spirituality in palliative care. J Palliative Med. 2001;4(4):423-7.
5. Koenig HG. Spirituality in Patient Care: Why, How, When, and What? Templeton Foundation Press; 2012.

6. Monroe MH, Bynum D, Susi B, Phifer N, Schultz L, Franco M, et al. Primary care physician preferences regarding spiritual behavior in medical practice. Arch Intern Med. 2003;163(22):2751.
7. Sulmasy DP. A biopsychosocial-spiritual model for the care of patients at the end of life. Gerontologist. 2002;42(Suppl_3):24-33.
8. Puchalski C, Romer AL. Taking a spiritual history allows clinicians to understand patients more fully. J Palliative Med. 2000; 3(1):129-37.
9. Puchalski CM, Ferrell B, Virani R, Otis-Green S, Baird P, Bull J, et al. Improving the quality of spiritual care as a dimension of palliative care: The report of the Consensus Conference. J Palliat Med. 2009;12(10):885-904.
10. Sokol D. Religion and spirituality in medicine: friend or foe? BMJ. 2020;368:m106.
11. Guck TP, Kavan MG. Medical student beliefs: spirituality's relationship to health and place in the medical school curriculum. Medical Teacher. 2006;28(8):702-7.
12. Adeli S, Heidari M, Heidari A. Spirituality in medical education and COVID-19. Clin Teacher. 2021;18(4):372-3.
13. Lavrič M, Flere S. The role of culture in the relationship between religiosity and psychological well-being. 2008; pp. 164-75.
14. Moreira-Almeida A, Sharma A, Van Rensburg BJ, Verhagen PJ, Cook CC. WPA Position Statement on Spirituality and Religion in Psychiatry. World Psychiatry. 2016;15(1): 87-8.
15. Koenig HG. Spirituality in patient care: Why, how, when, and what? J Religion Health; 2009;48(4):587-98.
16. Lucchetti G, Lucchetti ALG, Espinha DCM, De Oliveira LR, Leite JR, Koenig HG. Spirituality and health in the curricula of medical schools in Brazil. BMC Med Educ. 2012;12(1).
17. Lucchetti G, Lucchetti ALG, Puchalski CM. Spirituality in medical Education: global reality? J Religion Health. 2011;51(1):3-19.
18. Fleenor DW, Atkinson HG, Karani R, Lerner S, Leisman S, Marin D. An innovative approach for integrating mandatory, longitudinal spirituality training into the medical school curriculum. Acad Med. 2021;97(2):215-21.
19. Neely D, Minford EJ. Current status of teaching on spirituality in UK medical schools. Med Educ. 2008;42(2):176-82.
20. Balboni MJ, Sullivan A, Amobi A, Phelps AC, Gorman DP, Zollfrank A, et al. Why is spiritual care infrequent at the end of life? Spiritual Care Perceptions Among Patients, Nurses, and Physicians and the Role of Training. J Clin Oncol. 31(4). https://doi.org/10.1200/JCO.2012.44.6443
21. Miller WR, Thoresen CE. Spirituality, religion, and health. An emerging research field. Am Psychol. 2003;58(1):24-35.
22. Phelps AC, Lauderdale KE, Alcorn S, Dillinger J, Balboni MT, Wert MV, et al. Addressing spirituality within the care of patients at the end of life: perspectives of patients with advanced cancer, oncologists, and oncology nurses. J Clin Oncol. 30(20). https://doi.org/10.1200/JCO.2011.40.3766.
23. Koenig HG. Religion, spirituality, and health: The research and clinical implications. ISRN Psychiatry. 2012;2012:1-33.
24. Koenig HG, Hooten EG, Lindsay-Calkins E, Meador KG. Spirituality in Medical School Curricula: Findings from a National Survey. Intern J Psychiatry Med. 2010;40(4): 391-8.
25. Talley JA, Magie R. The integration of the "Spirituality in Medicine" curriculum into the Osteopathic Communication Curriculum at Kansas City University of Medicine and Biosciences. Acad Med. 2013;89(1):43-7.
26. Jain MM, Joshi A, Tayade NG, Jaiswar SR, Thakkar KB. Knowledge, attitude and practices regarding "the role of spirituality in current medical practice amongst medical professionals" in a tertiary care hospital. J Evolution Med Dent Sci. 2013;2(3):204-25.
27. Hall JA, Roter DL, Rand CS. Communication of Affect between Patient and Physician. J Health Soc Behav. 1981;22(1):18.
28. Raab K. Mindful medical practice: a call to action. J Am Med Assoc. 2014;311(7):703-4.
29. Epstein RM, Krasner MS. Physician resilience: What it means, why it matters, and how to promote it. Acad Med. 2013;88(3):301-3.

30. De Aguiar PRDC, Cazella SC, Da Costa MR. What do we know about the teaching of religiosity/spirituality in medical undergraduate curricula? An integrative review. Med Ed Publish. 2016;5:48.
31. Wenham J, Best M, Kissane DW. Systematic review of medical education on spirituality. Intern Med J. 2021;51(11):1781-90.
32. Nahardani SZ, Memaryan N, Keshavarzi MH, Hadi F, Koenig HG, Pashmdarfard M. Development of a Spiritual Health Curriculum: an applied study in Iran. Shiraz E-Med J. 2023;24(4):e130784.
33. Puchalski CM, Vitillo R, Hull SK, Reller N. Improving the spiritual dimension of whole person care: Reaching national and international consensus. J Palliat Med. 2014;17(6):642-56.
34. LoboPrabhu S, Lomax J. The role of spirituality in medical school and psychiatry residency education. Intern J Appl Psychoanalytic Studies. 2010;7(2):180-92.

7

CHAPTER

Recent Global Initiatives in the Interface between Spirituality/ Religion and Psychiatry

Alan Fung

THE WORLD PSYCHIATRIC ASSOCIATION AS THE GLOBAL VOICE FOR PSYCHIATRY

The World Psychiatric Association (WPA) is a global association representing more than 145 psychiatric societies in more than 120 countries, thus representing more than 250,000 psychiatrists of these member societies.[1] The WPA consists of around 65 scientific sections, representing different psychiatric subspecialties and/or areas of interest. With accumulating evidence base demonstrating the relevance of spirituality/religion (S/R) to mental health, the WPA established a Section on Religion, Spirituality, and Psychiatry (SRSP) in 2003.[2] The goals of the SRSP are to: (1) Encourage and accelerate research, theory, and practice in the area of religion, spirituality and psychiatry, and related areas; (2) facilitate the dissemination of data on religious and spiritual issues, in relation to psychiatry and allied domains; (3) develop and to stimulate educational and training programs and courses in order to improve knowledge, skills, and professional attitude regarding religion and spirituality in psychiatric practice.[2] The first major scholarly output by members of the SRSP was the book "Religion and Psychiatry: Beyond Boundaries,"[3] which has been widely considered as a leading text in the field of S/R and psychiatry internationally. Members of the SRSP also developed the WPA Position Statement on Spirituality and Religion in Psychiatry,[4,5] which will be discussed further in the next section.

The current (2023–2026) SRSP Executive Committee (EC) members are as follow: Chair: Dr Alan Fung (Canada); Co-Chair: Dr Bruno Paz Mosqueiro (Brazil); Secretary: Dr Rajashree Ray (India); other EC Members: Dr Farha Z Abbasi (USA), Dr Agatha Chong (Hong Kong SAR, China), Dr Sarah Eagger (UK), and Dr Anahy Fagundes Dias Fonseca (Brazil).

THE WORLD PSYCHIATRIC ASSOCIATION POSITION STATEMENT ON SPIRITUALITY AND RELIGION IN PSYCHIATRY

Probably one of the most important contributions of the SRSP to the WPA has been the development by SRSP members, the WPA Position Statement on Spirituality and Religion in Psychiatry, which provides recommendations to psychiatrists about how to appropriately address matters related to S/R and psychiatry. The Position Statement was approved by the WPA EC in 2015, and published in the journal World Psychiatry in 2016.[4] The Position Statement was subsequently revised by a Revision

Committee consisted of Dr Alan Fung (Chair), Dr Alexander Moreira-Almeida, Dr Peter Verhagen, Dr Christopher Cook, and the late Dr Avdesh Sharma. The revised version was approved by the WPA EC and General Assembly in 2023.[5]

As discussed in the Position Statement, spirituality and/or religion are concerned with the core beliefs, meaning making, values and experiences of human beings, and have been associated with hope and resilience for many.[6] Also, surveys have shown that S/R values, beliefs, and practices remain relevant to most of the world population and that patients would like to have their S/R concerns addressed in health care.[3,7,8] As such, a consideration of their relevance to the origins, understanding and treatment of psychiatric disorders and the patient's attitude toward illness should be central to clinical and academic psychiatry. Indeed, there is substantial research evidence that S/R has significant implications for prevalence (especially depressive and substance use disorders), diagnosis (e.g., differentiation between spiritual experiences and mental disorders), treatment (e.g., help seeking behavior, compliance, mindfulness, S/R-adapted psychotherapy, compassion-focused and forgiveness therapies, engaging in S/R community activities for patients who have self-identified with a S/R tradition, complementary therapies etc.), outcomes (e.g., recovering and suicide), prevention, as well as for quality of life and well-being.[9-14]

Of note, it has been emphasized in the Position Statement that while S/R is usually associated with better health outcomes, it may also cause harm (e.g., treatment refusal, intolerance, and negative religious coping).[5] As such, attention to S/R in clinical practice should show due attention to ethical and professional standards, should never be discriminatory on grounds of race, ethnicity, gender, sexuality, or religion, and should not in any way be allowed to detract from the usual biopsychosocial concerns of psychiatry.[15-17]

In spite of its relevance to clinical psychiatry, few medical schools or specialist curricula provide any formal training for psychiatrists to learn about the evidence available, or how to properly address R/S in research and clinical practice.[8,18] The sections or special interest groups on S/R and psychiatry of the WPA and several national psychiatric associations (e.g., Brazil, India, South Africa, UK, and USA) have partially addressed these educational needs, but more remain to be done.[5]

Another important aspect emphasized in the Position Statement is the value of increased collaborations between mental health professionals and faith communities for enhancing mental health outcomes.[6,19] Such collaborations would be facilitated by mutual respect and trust, and by recognition of the different languages and paradigms that psychiatry and faith communities use to address their common concerns about mental health and wellbeing.[19]

To provide concrete guidelines for psychiatrists in addressing S/R-related matters in their professional endeavors, the Position Statement has included eight specific recommendations:[5]

1. A tactful consideration of patients' religious beliefs and practices as well as their spirituality should routinely be considered and will sometimes be an essential component of psychiatric history taking.
2. Religion and spirituality may be relevant for treatment planning, and when they are, should be supportive of other (e.g., physical, psychological, and social) interventions. Psychiatrists should

facilitate the utilization of evidence-based treatments, including those with R/S elements.

3. An understanding of religion and spirituality and their relationship to the diagnosis, etiology, and treatment of psychiatric disorders across the lifespan should be considered as essential components of both psychiatric training and continuing professional development.
4. There is a need for more research on both religion and spirituality in psychiatry, especially on their clinical applications. These studies should cover a wide diversity of cultural and geographical backgrounds.
5. The approach to religion and spirituality should be person-centered. Psychiatrists should not use their professional position for proselytizing for spiritual or secular worldviews. Psychiatrists should be expected always to respect and be sensitive to the spiritual/religious beliefs and practices of their patients, and of the families and carers of their patients.
6. Psychiatrists, whatever their personal beliefs, should be willing to work with leaders/members of faith communities, chaplains and pastoral workers, and others in the community, in support of the well-being of their patients, and should encourage their multidisciplinary colleagues to do likewise.
7. Psychiatrists should demonstrate awareness, respect, and sensitivity to the important part that spirituality and religion play for many staff and volunteers in forming a vocation to work in the field of mental health care, as well as in promoting resilience.
8. Psychiatrists should be knowledgeable concerning the potential for both benefit and harm of religious, spiritual, and secular worldviews and practices and be willing to share this information in a critical but impartial way with the wider community in support of the promotion of health and well-being.

Full text of the Position Statement is available from the WPA website, under the "Position Statements" section: <https://www.wpanet.org/2023-position-statements>.

SOME OTHER KEY ENDEAVORS OF THE WORLD PSYCHIATRIC ASSOCIATION SECTION ON SPIRITUALITY, RELIGION, AND PSYCHIATRY

Global Meetings on Spirituality and Mental Health

To facilitate global discussions and collaborations on S/R and psychiatry, Dr Alexander Moreira-Almeida (Chair of the WPA SRSP, 2014–2020) and colleagues initiated the first Global Meeting on Spirituality and Mental Health, which was held in November 2015 in Brazil, in the form of a 2.5-day, special track on spirituality and mental health during the 2015 Brazilian Congress of Psychiatry. This global meeting was organized by the Committee of Studies and Research on Spirituality and Mental Health in the Brazilian Association of Psychiatry, and co-sponsored by the WPA SRSP. Seven international and 16 Brazilian psychiatrists and psychologists were involved in the program, consisting of a course on Spirituality in Clinical Practice, as well as three conferences, seven symposia, and two poster sessions covering research, educational, and clinical aspects of S/R and psychiatry. The international presenters included Drs Arjan Braam (Netherlands), Lionel Corbett (USA), John Cox (UK), Alan Fung (Canada), Bernard Janse van Rensburg (South Africa), Kenneth Pargament (USA), and John Peteet (USA). The sessions were very well-attended and the meeting received very positive reviews.

Following the success of this global meeting, the 2nd global meeting was held in November 2016, as a specialized track during the 2016 WPA International Congress in Cape Town, South Africa. Of note, to better address the issue of promoting collaborations between mental health professionals and faith leaders, a day-long Round Table discussion was held on November 20, 2016 among faith leaders from 12 organizations and 15 mental health professionals, with the goal of generating some principles of interprofessional collaborations between mental health and spiritual care professionals.[19] This important endeavor was organized by the SRSP (led by the late Dr Avdesh Sharma who served as a SRSP EC member then, and his wife Dr Sujatha Sharma), and co-organized by Brahma Kumaris. On the same day, public programs for interfaith leaders and mental health professionals were held at the Nelson Mandela Auditorium, Cape Town, organized by Brahma Kumaris in association with the WPA SRSP.

The 3rd Global Meeting in Spirituality and Mental Health, organized by the WPA SRSP, took the form of a specialized track during the 2017 WPA World Congress of Psychiatry in Berlin (October 8–12, 2017). It was of special significance, given that the World Congress of Psychiatry has been the most important scientific endeavor of the WPA. This Global Meeting was composed of 12 different scientific sessions in which SRSP members had contributed to, including sessions related to but not limited to S/R. For instance, Dr Avdesh Sharma chaired a symposium titled "Culture, Religion and Spirituality in the Promotion of Mental Health and Management of Mental Illnesses". The symposium was co-chaired by Dr Norman Sartorius, a former WPA President and former Director of the World Health Organization's (WHO) Division of Mental Health. In addition, to further develop collaborations between mental health professionals and faith leaders, Dr Alan Fung (SRSP EC member then) chaired the symposium "Interprofessional Collaborations and Education between Mental Health and Spiritual Care Professionals as a Pathway for Achieving High Quality, Person-centred Care"—co-chaired by Dr Avdesh Sharma.

Given the success of the first three Global Meetings, and significant supports from SRSP members based in Israel, especially Dr Haim Belmaker, the SRSP organized the 4th Global Meeting in Spirituality and Mental Health as the "2019 WPA International Congress in Spirituality and Psychiatry", held in Jerusalem, Israel on December 1–4, 2019. Dr Avdesh Sharma chaired the Congress International Organizing Committee, and Dr Alexander Moreira-Almeida chaired the Congress Scientific Committee. It was the first such Global Meeting that was organized as an independent conference, rather than as a specialized track of another conference. The Congress drew hundreds of participants from 35 countries and received rave reviews.

Building on the success of this conference, plans had been made to have further standalone global meetings in spirituality and mental health on a regular basis, with the following one to be held in India. Unfortunately, with the COVID-19 becoming a global pandemic in 2020, it was no longer feasible to have in-person conferences. In December 2020, Dr Avdesh Sharma, as Chair of the SRSP then, endeavored to overcome these issues by initiating the 2020 Virtual International Conference on Spirituality and Mental Health, which was also the 5th Global

Meeting in Spirituality and Mental Health, held on December 20th, 2020. The conference was organized by the WPA SRSP and in collaboration with the Indian Psychiatric Society (IPS), with Dr Avdesh Sharma chairing the Organizing Committee. The conference was titled "Interface of Religion, Spirituality and Meditation with Mental Health, especially in turbulent times". The conference received supports from the senior leaderships of both the WPA and the IPS, including Dr Afzal Javed (then WPA President) as the Chief Guest; Dr PK Dalal (then IPS President) and Dr Gautam Saha (then IPS President-Elect) as Guests of Honor; and Dr Dinesh Bhugra (former WPA President, 2014–2017) as an invited speaker. Recording of the conference was broadcast on TV in India to over 1 million people by estimation.

Educational Webinars Related to Spirituality/Religion and Psychiatry

Encouraged by the success of the 5th Global Meeting, and the rapid popularization of utilizing virtual technologies in professional educational endeavors since the COVID-19 pandemic, the WPA SRSP had also endeavored to increase its educational offerings to SRSP members and other professionals through webinars. The first such WPA SRSP webinar was held on November 12, 2021, with Dr Christopher Cook from the UK (SRSP EC member during 2020–2023 and Co-Chair during 2022–2023; recipient of the 2021 American Psychiatric Association (APA) Oskar Pfister Award for outstanding contributions in the field of psychiatry and religion) as the featured speaker. His presentation was titled "Spiritually Significant Voices". The second such SRSP webinar was held on June13, 2022, featuring Dr Alexander Moreira-Almeida from Brazil (Past Chair of the SRSP, 2014–2020), who presented on "Spirituality and Science of Life After Death: Evidences and Clinical Practice," followed by lively discussions from the attendees (over 80 registrants from 12 countries). Of note, this second webinar was held as part of a special online event to commemorate the life of Dr Avdesh Sharma (SRSP Chair, 2020–2022; Co-Chair, 2017–2020; EC Member since 2014), after his untimely passing in March 2022.

Subsequent to these first two educational webinars for SRSP members, several additional such webinars had been held. In February 2023, Dr Francis Lu, Kim Professor of Cultural Psychiatry, Emeritus at the University of California, Davis, USA, presented the third SRSP webinar, titled "Where do Religion and Spirituality Appear in DSM-5-TR?". He had discussed the Z-code Religious/Spiritual Problem, as well as the Cultural Formulation Interview.

In March 2024, in view of conflicts in different parts of the world, the SRSP held a special online interfaith panel presentation and discussion titled, "Responding to Trauma with the Resources of Major Religious Traditions". The presentation featured four USA-based psychiatrists from different faith traditions as panelists: Dr Farha Abbasi (Islam), Dr Shuchi Khosla (Hinduism), Dr Steve Moffic (Judaism), and Dr John Peteet (Christianity; recipient of the 2020 American Psychiatric Association Oskar Pfister Award). Dr Anahy Fonseca, SRSP EC Member, served as the discussant. The session focused on trauma as seen through the lens of four religious traditions—Christianity, Hinduism, Islam, and Judaism. The session aimed at helping participants identify varied religious scriptural references to trauma, compare the contributions of the major religions to trauma care, and utilize this understanding of resources to inform their responses as clinicians and community consultants.

In November 2024, the fifth SRSP webinar's featured speaker was Dr Peter Verhagen—Past Chair of the SRSP, 2009–2014; recipient of the 2024 American Psychiatric Association Oskar Pfister Award; Endowed Professor of the Department of Theology and Religious Studies at KU Leuven, Belgium. Dr Francis Lu served as the discussant. Titled "The religiousness gap: a developmental sequence", Dr Verhagen discussed the concept of the "religiosity gap" as a common thread in the recent history of psychiatry and religion; the conflicts and solutions surrounding the "religiosity gap" and how they came to be; as well as how to move forward.

Overall, such webinars have been welcomed by SRSP members, and have provided continuing learning opportunities related to S/R and psychiatry for SRSP members on a regular basis.

Key Educational Resource Related to Spirituality/Religion and Psychiatry for the World Psychiatric Association

In addition to serving the educational needs of its members, the SRSP would also like to address the general lack of educational resources related to S/R and psychiatry for psychiatrists worldwide. As such, SRSP EC members worked on designing a 2-hour webinar covering topics such as the roles of S/R in psychiatry; scientific evidence on the relevance of S/R to psychiatry; integrating S/R in psychiatric assessments and treatments, with case examples; spiritual experience and psychopathology; a South Asian perspective on spirituality, psychiatry, and wellness; educational/training issues regarding spiritual/religious competence in psychiatric residency; partnerships between mental health professionals and faith communities in enhancing mental health. On July 5, 2023, EC members delivered this 2-hour webinar, with introductory remarks from Dr Afzal Javed, then the WPA President. All SRSP EC members then were involved in this endeavor, including SRSP Chair Dr Alan Fung (Canada); Co-Chair Dr Christopher Cook (UK); Secretary Dr Bruno Paz Mosqueiro (Brazil); and other SRSP EC members including Dr Agatha Chong (HK SAR, China), Dr Sarah Eagger (UK), Dr Fabricio Oliveira (Brazil), Dr Kishan Porandla (India), and Dr Rajashree Ray (India). The webinar has subsequently been archived on the WPA Educational Portal, thus becoming a major educational resource in S/R and psychiatry for psychiatrists worldwide.

International Partnerships Related to Spirituality/Religion and Psychiatry

To enhance the reach and impact of its endeavors, the SRSP has been continuing to grow its collaborations with various international partners. For instance, the SRSP jointly organized a Webinar with the SAARC Psychiatric Federation on May 24, 2022, with Dr Christopher Cook from the SRSP presenting his research work on Hearing Voices. More than 170 delegates interacted with Dr Cook, who lucidly elaborated on the etiology, pathophysiology, and phenomenology of voices in the nonpsychotic states and the differences in the content and expression of voices in nonpsychotic and psychotic illnesses.

The SRSP has also been an associate organizing partner of the online International Day of Yoga Conference since June 2021. For instance, the 2022 Conference, held on

June 19, 2022 with the theme of "Integrating Yoga in Clinical Practice," had participants from more than 12 countries. This conference was hosted by the Yoga and Mental Health subcommittee of SAARC Psychiatric Federation, in association with the National Institute of Mental Health and Neurosciences (NIMHANS) (India) and American Academy of Yoga and Meditation. Dr Afzal Javed, then WPA President, served as the Chief Guest and delivered remarks. From the SRSP, Dr Alan Fung served on the Conference Board of Advisors and presented on the roles of spirituality and related interventions on mental health outcomes during the COVID-19 pandemic. Dr Bruno Paz Mosqueiro presented on spirituality and community resources to mental health. More than 300 delegates attended this event. In 2023, the Conference was held on June 18, 2023, and again chiefly organized by the SAARC Psychiatric Federation. The co-sponsors included the Asian Federation of Psychiatric Association, Indian Association of Private Psychiatry, Indian Association of Biological Psychiatry, and the WPA SRSP. Dr Afzal Javed, then WPA President, again served as the Chief Guest and delivered remarks. The SRSP EC Members, Dr Kishan Porandla and Dr Rajashree Ray, both served as Co-Chairpersons of the Conference. Dr Bruno Paz Mosqueiro presented on "Spiritually Integrated Care in Psychiatry," while SRSP EC members Dr Agatha Chong and Dr Fabrício Oliveira served as panelists on a panel titled "Evidence-based Integration of Yoga in Clinical Practise". In 2024, it was held in hybrid mode on June 22, 2024, and jointly organized by the IPS, the SAARC Psychiatric Federation, Asian Federation of Psychiatric Association, and the WPA SRSP. Among the featured speakers was Dr Anahy Fonseca, a SRSP EC Member, who presented on "C.J Jung's views on Kundalini Yoga".

Members of the SRSP also contributed to the International Conference on Spirituality in Mental Health and Wellness, organized by the IPS Spirituality Taskforce and held in Hyderabad, India on January 8, 2023, in the form of a webinar with a physical inaugural and valedictory functions. The conference focused on the role of spirituality in enhancing mental health and well-being, and explored various methods and practices for incorporating spirituality into mental health care. Dr Kishan Porandla, SRSP EC Member (2020–2023) and former Chairperson of the IPS Spirituality Taskforce, was the Organizing Secretary. Dr Alan Fung, Chair of the SRSP since 2022, was an Advisor as well as an Invited Speaker. Dr Peter J Verhagen, Founding Secretary and Past Chair of the SRSP (2009–2014), was a Guest of Honor. Dr Alexander Moreira-Almeida, Past Chair of the SRSP (2014–2020), was an Invited Speaker. Dr Agatha Chong, SRSP EC Member, served as a Session Chair.

Optimizing Collaborations between Mental Health Professionals and Faith Communities

In addition to aforementioned SRSP endeavors in optimizing collaborations between mental health professionals and faith communities, SRSP members have also been developing international partnerships to further this area of work. For instance, Dr Alan Fung has been an active steering committee member of the APA Mental Health and Faith Community Partnership, and has been acting as a liaison between the APA and the WPA SRSP in this regard. Also, Dr Peter Verhagen and Dr Alan Fung had collaborated with the World Council of Churches (WCC), and had presented at a special WCC webinar in October 2023 commemorating the 2023

World Mental Health Day. SRSP EC member Dr Farha Abbasi had founded the annual Muslim Mental Health Conference in the USA, and has been extensively collaborating with numerous Muslim faith communities. Other SRSP members have also been collaborating with faith communities and leaders in their countries/regions regarding mental health endeavors. In the book "Spirituality and Mental Health Across Cultures,"[9] co-edited by Dr Alexander Moreira-Almeida (SRSP Chair, 2014–2020), Dr Bruno Paz Mosqueiro (SRSP Co-Chair since 2023), and Dr Dinesh Bhugra (former WPA President, 2014–2017), there is a chapter titled "Fruitful Collaborations with Religious and Spiritual Communities to Foster Mental Health in General Society: An International Perspective,"[19] which was co-authored by several SRSP members (Dr Alan Fung, Dr Avdesh Sharma, and Dr Agatha Chong) and others. In the chapter, one will find further details on examples of such collaborations in different countries.

FUTURE DIRECTIONS

The *raison d'etre* for the WPA Section on Religion, Spirituality and Psychiatry is to be a major global voice and indeed, catalyst for growth, for the field of S/R and psychiatry. The continued recognition and adoption of the WPA Position Statement on Spirituality and Religion in Psychiatry in different countries/regions have significantly enhanced such endeavors. Moreover, new sections on S/R and psychiatry in national psychiatric associations are emerging. For instance, a special interest group on S/R has recently been approved by the Hong Kong College of Psychiatrists, with the effort spearheaded by Dr Agatha Chong, a SRSP EC member. This is the first formally-recognized S/R section in a professional psychiatric organization in East Asia. Furthermore, collaborations with international partners are instrumental for the growth of S/R and psychiatry endeavors worldwide. Indeed, for India and South Asia as a whole, such collaborations have been rapidly growing, especially with the IPS and the SAARC Psychiatric Federation, through leaders such as Dr Rajashree Ray, the incumbent SRSP Secretary who also currently serves as the Chairperson of the IPS Spirituality and Mental Health Specialty Section as well as the Chairperson of the SAARC Psychiatric Federation Spirituality, Yoga and Mental Health Sub-Committee. For instance, the WPA SRSP will be a co-sponsor of an upcoming webinar in December 2024 on "Consciousness: AI vs Epigenetics", organized by the IPS Spirituality and Mental Health Specialty Section. Additional joint events are in planning.

Last but not the least, the SRSP will continue to promote optimal collaborations between mental health professionals and spiritual/faith communities "in attaining quality, holistic, cost effective, culturally acceptable care which is also humane"—as the authors had delineated in the aforementioned chapter in the "Spirituality and Mental Health Across Cultures" book.[19]

REFERENCES

1. World Psychiatric Association—Homepage. [online] Available from https://www.wpanet.org/. [Last accessed December, 2024].
2. World Psychiatric Association. Section on Religion, Spirituality and Psychiatry. [online] Available from https://www.wpanet.org/religion-spirituality-and-psychiatry [Last accessed December, 2024].
3. Verhagen PJ, van Praag HM, López-Ibor JJ Jr, Cox JL, Moussaoui D (Eds). Religion and Psychiatry: Beyond Boundaries. UK: Wiley Blackwell; 2010.

4. Moreira-Almeida A, Sharma A, van Rensburg BJ, Verhagen PJ, Cook CC. WPA Position Statement on Spirituality and Religion in Psychiatry. World Psychiatry. 2016;15(1): 87-8.
5. Moreira-Almeida A, Fung WLA, Sharma A, van Rensburg BJ, Verhagen PJ, Cook CC. WPA Position Statement on Spirituality and Religion in Psychiatry – 2023 revision. World Psychiatric Association. 2023. [online] Available from https://www.wpanet.org/2023-position-statements [Last accessed December, 2024].
6. Cook CCH. Theology and Psychiatry. St Andrews Encyclopaedia of Theology. [online] Available from https://www.saet.ac.uk/Christianity/TheologyandPsychiatry [Last accessed December, 2024].
7. Pargament KI, Lomax JW. Understanding and addressing religion among people with mental illness. World Psychiatry. 2013; 12(1):26-32.
8. Moreira-Almeida A, Koenig HG, Lucchetti G. Clinical implications of spirituality to mental health: review of evidence and practical guidelines. Rev Bras Psiquiatr. 2014; 36(2):176-82.
9. Moreira-Almeida A, Mosqueiro BP, Bhugra D (Eds). Spirituality and Mental Health Across Cultures – Evidence-Based Implications for Clinical Practice. New York: Oxford University Press; 2021.
10. Koenig HG, VanderWeele T, Peteet JR. Handbook of Religion and Health, 3rd edition. New York: Oxford University Press; 2023.
11. Cook CCH, Powell A (Eds). Spirituality and Psychiatry, 2nd edition. United Kingdom: RCPsych Publications; 2022.
12. de Abreu Costa M, Moreira-Almeida A. Religion-Adapted Cognitive Behavioral Therapy: A Review and Description of Techniques. J Relig Health. 2022;61(1):443-66.
13. Captari LE, Hook JN, Hoyt W, Davis DE, McElroy-Heltzel SE, Worthington EL Jr. J Integrating clients' religion and spirituality within psychotherapy: A comprehensive meta-analysis. Clin Psychol. 2018;74(11): 1938-51.
14. VanderWeele TJ, Balboni TA, Koh HK. Invited Commentary: Religious Service Attendance and Implications for Clinical Care, Community Participation, and Public Health. Am J Epidemiol. 2022;191(1):31-5.
15. Cook CCH. Recommendations for Psychiatrists on Spirituality and Religion. Position Statement PS03/2011. London: Royal College of Psychiatrists; 2011.
16. Peteet J, Dell ML, Fung WLA (Eds.) Ethical Considerations at the Intersection of Psychiatry and Religion. New York: Oxford University Press; 2018.
17. Dike C, Briz L, Fadus M, Martinez R, May C, Milone R, et al. Resource document on the interface of religion, spirituality, and psychiatric practice. APA Official Actions, American Psychiatric Association; 2022.
18. Hathaway D, Oliveira e Oliveira FHA, Mirhom M, Moreira-Almeida A, Fung WLA, Peteet J. Teaching Spiritual and Religious Competencies to Psychiatry Residents: A Scoping and Systematic Review. Academic Medicine. 2022;97(2):300-10.
19. Fung WLA, Shepherd V, Chong KYA, Sharma SD, Sharma A. Fruitful collaborations with religious and spiritual communities to foster mental health on general society – an international perspective. In: Moreira-Almeida A, Paz Mosqueiro B, Bhugra D (Eds). Spirituality and Mental Health Across Cultures. Oxford: Oxford University Press; 2021.

Index

Page numbers followed *b* refer to box, *f* refer to figure, and *t* refer to table.

N

O

P

Q

R

S